LIBRARY OF HEBREW BIBLE/ OLD TESTAMENT STUDIES

473

Formerly Journal for the Study of the Old Testament Supplement Series

Editors
Claudia V. Camp, Texas Christian University
Andrew Mein, Westcott House, Cambridge

Founding Editors
David J. A. Clines, Philip R. Davies and David M. Gunn

Editorial Board
Richard J. Coggins, Alan Cooper, John Goldingay, Robert P. Gordon, Norman K. Gottwald, Gina Hens-Piazza, John Jarick, Andrew D. H. Mayes, Carol Meyers, Patrick D. Miller, Yvonne Sherwood

LAND OF OUR FATHERS

The Roles of Ancestor Veneration in Biblical Land Claims

Francesca Stavrakopoulou

BLOOMSBURY
NEW YORK · LONDON · NEW DELHI · SYDNEY

Bloomsbury T&T Clark
An imprint of Bloomsbury Publishing Plc

175 Fifth Avenue	50 Bedford Square
New York	London
NY 10010	WC1B 3DP
USA	UK

www.bloomsbury.com

First published by T&T Clark International 2010
Paperback edition first published 2012

© Francesca Stavrakopoulou, 2010

All rights reserved. No part of this publication may be reproduced or transmitted in any form or by any means, electronic or mechanical, including photocopying, recording, or any information storage or retrieval system, without prior permission in writing from the publishers.

No responsibility for loss caused to any individual or organization acting on or refraining from action as a result of the material in this publication can be accepted by Bloomsbury Academic or the author.

Library of Congress Cataloging-in-Publication Data
Stavrakopoulou, Francesca.
Land of our fathers : the roles of ancestor veneration in biblical land claims / Francesca Stavrakopoulou.
 p. cm. – (The library of Hebrew Bible/Old Testament studies ; #473)
Includes bibliographical references (p.) and indexes.
ISBN-13: 978-0-567-02881-5 (hardcover : alk. paper)
ISBN-10: 0-567-02881-X (hardcover : alk. paper) 1. Land tenure–Biblical teaching.
2. Ancestor worship–Biblical teaching. 3. Bible. O.T.–Criticism, interpretation, etc.
I. Title.
BS1199.L28S73 2010
221.8'20213–dc22   2010010320

ISBN: HB: 978-0-567-02881-5
PB: 978-0-567-41188-4

Typeset by Pindar NZ, Auckland, New Zealand
Printed and bound in the United States of America

For my mother and her Welsh father, with all my love

Contents

Preface	ix
Acknowledgements	x
Abbreviations	xii

Chapter 1
BONES, BURIALS AND BOUNDARIES — 1
- Placing the Dead — 8
- Venerating the Dead — 18
- Centralizing the Dead — 25

Chapter 2
ABRAHAM AT MACHPELAH — 29
- Marking Machpelah — 33
- (Ac)claiming Abraham — 39

Chapter 3
MOSES AT THE EDGE — 55
- Moses' Memorial — 56
- Torah Memorialized — 71

Chapter 4
CONTESTING BETHEL — 81
- Displacing the Dead — 81
- Ancestral Advocacy — 92

Chapter 5
CLAIMING JERUSALEM — 103
- City of the Dead — 104
- Entombing Temple — 120

Chapter 6
THE CREATION OF A NATION — 135
- Remapping the Land — 136
- Re-Placing the Dead — 142

Bibliography	149
Index of Ancient Sources	173
Index of Authors	179
Index of Subjects	183

Preface

I began thinking about the subject of this book in November 2004, when the Palestinian leader Yasser Arafat was dying. As was widely reported by the Western media at the time, his supporters called for his burial in Jerusalem, but their request was rejected by the Israeli government. Within the difficult context of the ongoing territorial struggle between Israel and Palestine, this response was perceived by many political commentators as a reassertion of Israel's control and possession of Jerusalem.[1] This view appeared to be encouraged by comments made at the time by the Israeli Justice Minister, Yosef Lapid, who announced that Arafat could not be buried in Jerusalem because it is 'a city where Jews bury their kings'.[2] Characterized in this way, government opposition to Arafat's Jerusalem burial was framed in terms of an appeal to the ancient heritage of the city as a Davidic burial site. This book is not about modern territorial assertions, and makes no claim at all to intervene in that complex and fraught debate. But modern ideas about Jerusalem as a 'city of tombs' take their inspiration from the Hebrew Bible, which presents an equally complex (if, necessarily, differently articulated) set of claims about the role of the dead in the delineation of land. The debate over Arafat's burial is a dramatic reminder of not only the power and persistence of these claims, but also their surprising adaptability to new and changing circumstances.

---

1. As Lara Sukhtian commented in the *Independent* newspaper (11 November 2004), the request to bury Arafat in Jerusalem was refused by Israel 'fearing a Jerusalem burial would strengthen Palestinians' claims to a city they envision as a capital of a future Palestinian state' (available online at http://www.independent.co.uk/news/world/middle-east/yasser-arafat-icon-of-palestinian-cause-is-dead-532846.html).

2. For examples of the ways in which this was reported in mainstream Western media, see the online CNN and BBC articles at http://edition.cnn.com/2004/WORLD/meast/11/05/arafat.health/index.html (accessed 8 November 2004); and http://news.bbc.co.uk/1/hi/world/middle_east/3983783.stm (accessed 11 November 2004).

Acknowledgements

The ideas presented in this book have kept me occupied for a few years now, but particular conversations with certain people have helped me work out how best to explore them and write about them. I am very grateful to Traci Ardren, John Barton, Joe Blenkinsopp, Mark Brett, Dexter Callender, David Chalcraft, Philip Davies, Philippe Guillaume, David Horrell, Anne Jeffers, Paul Joyce, Diana Lipton, Morwenna Ludlow and Mark Wynn, who have helped me think through many of the issues I deal with here. Alongside these colleagues and friends, I am also especially indebted to Kevin Cathcart, Diana Edelman, Louise Lawrence, Mark Leuchter, Stuart Macwilliam, Tim Whitmarsh and Nick Wyatt, who have all offered invaluable feedback on draft material at its various stages. In particular, Mark Leuchter and Tim Whitmarsh not only endured reams of writing, but also suffered a barrage of emails or text messages expressing my volatile relationship with this book – often couched in robust language.

Much of the research for this volume was funded by a generous grant from the British Academy, for which I am very grateful. Some of these funds were used to pay for invaluable periods of research at the École biblique et archéologique française de Jérusalem and at the universities of Oxford and Sheffield. The grant also paid for research assistance from Susannah Cornwall, who collated literature and helped prepare the manuscript and indexes for publication. I'm very grateful to her for this time-consuming work. I'd also like to thank the editors of the LHB/OTS series, Claudia Camp and Andrew Mein, for accepting this volume, and Dominic Mattos, Haaris Naqvi and Katie Gallof at Continuum, who have not only been great fun to work with, but incredibly helpful and patient too. A version of Chapter 2 was published by Gorgias Press as an essay in *A Palimpsest: Rhetoric, Ideology, Stylistics and Language Relating to Persian Israel* (E. Ben Zvi, D. V. Edelman and F. L. Polak, eds; Piscataway, NJ: Gorgias Press, 2009); sections of it are re-published here with permission. Other ideas in this book were presented initially as papers at various conferences, including the 2006 Summer Meeting of the Society for Old Testament Study, held in Durham, the annual meetings of the Society of Biblical Literature held in San Diego in 2007 and Boston in 2008, and the European Association of Biblical Studies meeting held in Lisbon in 2008.

After a very strange and difficult few years, I know how lucky I am to have been able to complete this particular book and (though it might seem a cliché) it really is because of the support from colleagues, friends and family that I've been able to do so. I owe a huge debt to good friends in the field who've done far more than I can say: James Crossley, Sue Gillingham, John Lyons, Adrian Thatcher, Catrin Williams and all my brilliant colleagues in the Department of Theology and Religion at the University of Exeter (yay!), including Mary Macneill, who's been especially supportive. And there are also my surrogate families and close friends who mean so much: Carrie, Dave, Em and Cate; Mildred and Geoffers; Lou and Dan; Kevin and Ann. Extra-special thanks also to the Professor, who's kept my heart safe (Song 5:1), Mr Blue Sky (even though it got cloudy), and the Other One (who's unlikely to bother reading this far . . .). But obviously, the most important and special thanks go to my mum. More than anyone else, she's taught me how to construct and maintain a sense and place of belonging. She really is the best mum in the world.

FS
Exeter, 2010

ABBREVIATIONS

AASOR	Annual of the American Schools of Oriental Research
AB	Anchor Bible
ABD	*The Anchor Bible Dictionary* (6 vols, edited by D. N. Freedman. New York: Doubleday, 1992).
ABRL	Anchor Bible Reference Library
ABS	Archaeology and Biblical Studies
ADAJ	Annual of the Department of Antiquities of Jordan
AfOB	Archiv für Orientforschung: Beiheft
AfR	*Archiv für Religionsgeschichte*
AHI	*Ancient Hebrew Inscriptions* (2 vols, edited by G. Davies. Cambridge: Cambridge University Press, 1991–2004.)
AJA	*American Journal of Archaeology*
AJBA	*Australian Journal of Biblical Archaeology*
AJSL	*American Journal of Semitic Languages and Literatures*
ALASP	Abhandlungen zur Literatur Alt – Syrien – Palästinas
ANEP	*The Ancient Near East in Pictures Relating to the Old Testament* (edited by J. B. Pritchard, 2nd edn. Princeton: Princeton University Press, 1969).
ANESS	Ancient Near Eastern Studies Supplement Series
ANET	*Ancient Near Eastern Texts Relating to the Old Testament* (edited by J. B. Pritchard, 3rd edn. Princeton: Princeton University Press, 1969).
AnOr	Analecta Orientalia
AOAT	Alter Orient und Altes Testament
AP	*Aramaic Papyri of the Fifth Century BC* (edited by A. E. Cowley. Oxford: Clarendon Press, 1923).
ASOR	American Schools of Oriental Research
ASORDS	American Schools of Oriental Research Dissertation Series
ASORMS	American Schools of Oriental Research Monograph Series
ASV	American Standard Version
AThANT	Abhandlungen zur Theologie des Alten und Neuen Testaments
AulOr	Aula Orientalis
BA	*Biblical Archaeologist*
BAIAS	*Bulletin of the Anglo-Israel Archaeological Society*
BAR	*Biblical Archaeology Review*

BASOR	*Bulletin of the American Schools of Oriental Research*
BBB	Bonner biblische Beiträge
BBS	*Bulletin of Biblical Studies*
BEAT	Beiträge zur Erforschung des Alten Testaments
BETL	Bibliotheca ephemeridum theologicarum lovaniensium
BFChTh	Beiträge zur Förderung christlicher Theologie
BHH	*Biblische-historisches Handwörterbuch: Landeskunde, Geschichte, Religion, Kultur* (4 vols, edited by B. Reicke and L. Rost. Göttingen: Vandenhoeck, 1962–66).
BHS	*Biblia Hebraica Stuttgartensia* (edited by K. Elliger and W. Rudolph. Stuttgart: Deutche Bibelstiftung, 1983).
Bib	*Biblica*
BibB	Biblische Beiträge
BibInt	*Biblical Interpretation*
BibOr	Biblica et orientalia
BIS	Biblical Interpretation Series
BJRL	*Bulletin of the John Rylands University Library of Manchester*
BJS	Brown Judaic Studies
BN	*Biblische Notizen*
BO	*Bibliotheca orientalis*
BR	*Bible Review*
BS	Biblical Seminar series
BWANT	Beiträge zur Wissenschaft vom Alten (und Neuen) Testament
BZ	*Biblische Zeitschrift*
BZAR	Beihefte zur Zeitschrift für altorientalische und biblische Rechtgeschichte
BZAW	Beihefte zur Zeitschrift für die alttestamentliche Wissenschaft
CAD	*The Assyrian Dictionary of the Oriental Institute of the University of Chicago* (21 vols, edited by M. T. Roth. Chicago: Oriental Institute of the University of Chicago, 1956–)
CANE	*Civilizations of the Ancient Near East* (4 vols, edited by J. M. Sasson. New York: Scribner, 1995)
CAT	Commentaire de l'Ancien Testament
CB	Century Bible
CBET	Contributions to Biblical Exegesis and Theology
CBQ	*Catholic Biblical Quarterly*
CBQMS	Catholic Biblical Quarterly Monograph Series
CHM	*Cahiers d'Histoire Mondiale*
CIS	Copenhagen International Seminar series
CIS	*Corpus inscriptionum semiticarum*
ConBOT	Coniectanea biblica: Old Testament series
COS	*The Context of Scripture* (3 vols, edited by W. W. Hallo. Leiden: Brill, 1997–2002).

CRAIBL	*Comptes rendus de l'Académie des inscriptions et belles-lettres*
CRRA	Compte rendu, Rencontre Assyriologique Internationale
CSA	Copenhagen Studies in Assyriology
CSF	Collezione di studi fenici
CTA	*Corpus des tablettes en cunéiformes alphabétiques découvertes à Ras Shamra-Ugarit de 1929 à 1939* (edited by A. Herdner. Mission de Ras Shamra 10. Paris: Imprimerie nationale, 1963).
DaF	Damaszener Forschungen
DDD	*Dictionary of Deities and Demons in the Bible* (edited by K. van der Toorn, B. Becking and P. W. van der Horst. 2nd extensively rev. edn. Leiden: Brill, 1999).
DISO	*Dictionnaire des inscriptions sémitiques de l'ouest* (edited by Ch. F. Jean and J. Hoftijzer. Leiden: Brill, 1965).
DJD	Discoveries in the Judaean Desert
DNWSI	*Dictionary of North-West Semitic Inscriptions* (2 vols, J. Hoftijzer and K. Jongeling. Leiden: Brill, 1995).
DULAT	*A Dictionary of the Ugaritic Language in the Alphabetic Tradition* (2 vols, edited by G. del Olmo Lete and J. Sanmartín. Translated by W. G. E Watson. HdO 67; Leiden: Brill, 2003).
EdF	Erträge der Forschung
EI	*Eretz Israel*
EPROER	Etudes preliminaries aux religions orientales dans l'empire romain
ESHM	European Seminar in Historical Methodology
ET	English Translation
ETL	*Ephemerides theologicae lovanienses*
ExpTim	*Expository Times*
FAT	Forschungen zum Alten Testament
FOTL	Forms of the Old Testament Literature
FRLANT	Forschungen zur Religion und Literatur des Alten und Neuen Testaments
FZPhTh	*Freiburger Zeitschrift für Philosophie und Theologie*
GUS	Gorgias Ugaritic Series
HAE	*Handbuch der althebräischen Epigraphik* (3 vols, J. Renz and W. Röllig. Darmstadt: Wissenschaftliche Buchgesellschaft, 1995 (vols I, II/1, III); Darmstadt: Wissenschaftliche Buchgesellschaft, 2003 (vol. II/2).
HALOT	*The Hebrew and Aramaic Lexicon of the Old Testament* (4 vols, L. Koehler, W. Baumgartner and J. J. Stamm. Translated and edited under the supervision of M. E. J. Richardson. Leiden: Brill, 1994–99).
HAR	*Hebrew Annual Review*
HAT	Handbuch zum Alten Testament

HdO	Handbuch der Orientalistik
HI	*Hebrew Inscriptions: Texts from the Biblical Period of the Monarchy with Concordance* (F. W. Dobbs-Allsopp, J. J. M. Roberts, C. L. Seow and R. E. Whitaker. New Haven: Yale University Press, 2005).
HS	*Hebrew Studies*
HSM	Harvard Semitic Monographs
HTR	*Harvard Theological Review*
HUCA	*Hebrew Union College Annual*
ICC	International Critical Commentary
IEJ	*Israel Exploration Journal*
IES	Israel Exploration Society
JA	*Journal Asiatique*
JAEI	*Journal of Ancient Egyptian Interconnections* (online)
JANER	*Journal of Ancient Near Eastern Religions*
JANESCU	*Journal of the Ancient Near Eastern Society of Columbia University*
JAOS	*Journal of the American Oriental Society*
JBL	*Journal of Biblical Literature*
JCS	*Journal of Cuneiform Studies*
JESHO	*Journal of the Economic and Social History of the Orient*
JETS	*Journal of the Evangelical Theological Society*
JHS	*Journal of Hebrew Scriptures*
JJS	*Journal of Jewish Studies*
JNES	*Journal of Near Eastern Studies*
JNSL	*Journal of Northwest Semitic Languages*
JPOS	*Journal of the Palestine Oriental Society*
JPS	Jewish Publication Society
JPSTCS	Jewish Publication Society Torah Commentary Series
JQR	*Jewish Quarterly Review*
JRS	*Journal of Ritual Studies*
JSJ	*Journal for the Study of Judaism in the Persian, Hellenistic and Roman Period*
JSNTS	Journal for the Study of the New Testament Supplement
JSOT	*Journal for the Study of the Old Testament*
JSOTS	Journal for the Study of the Old Testament Supplement Series
JSPS	Journal for the Study of the Pseudepigrapha Supplement Series
JSQ	*Jewish Studies Quarterly*
JSS	*Journal of Semitic Studies*
JTS	*Journal of Theological Studies*
K	Ketib
KAI	*Kanaänaische und aramäische Inscriften* (H. Donner and W. Röllig, 2nd edn. Wiesbaden: Harrassowitz, 1964–66).

KTU	*Die keilalphabetischen Texte Ugarit* (edited by M. Dietrich, O. Loretz and J. Sanmartin. AOAT 24/1. Neukirchen-Vluyn: Neukirchener Verlag, 1976).
LAI	Library of Ancient Israel
LHBOTS	Library of Hebrew Bible/Old Testament Studies
LSTS	Library of Second Temple Studies
LXX	Septuagint
MARI	*Mari: Annales des Recherches Interdisciplinaires*
MRS	Mission de Ras Shamra
MT	Masoretic Text
NCB	New Century Bible
NCBC	New Cambridge Bible Commentary
NEA	*Near Eastern Archaeology*
NEAEHL	*The New Encyclopaedia of Archaeological Excavations in the Holy Land* (4 vols, edited by E. Stern. Jerusalem: Magnes Press, 1993).
NEB	New English Bible
NICOT	New International Commentary on the Old Testament
NRSV	New Revised Standard Version
OBO	Orbis Biblicus et Orientalis
OEANE	*The Oxford Encyclopedia of Archaeology in the Near East* (edited by E. M. Meyers. New York: Oxford University Press, 1997).
OLA	Orientalia lovaniensia analecta
OrAnt	*Oriens antiquus*
OTE	*Old Testament Essays*
OTL	Old Testament Library
OTM	Oxford Theological Monographs
OTP	*The Old Testament Pseudepigrapha* (2 vols, edited by J. H. Charlesworth. New York: Doubleday, 1983).
OTS	Oudtestamentische Studiën
OTWSA	*Die Outestamentiese Werkgemeenschap in Suid-Afrika*
PEQ	*Palestine Exploration Quarterly*
POLO	Proche-Orient et littérature ougaritique
Q	Qere
QDAP	*Quarterly of the Department of Antiquities in Palestine*
RB	Revue biblique
RBS	Resources for Biblical Study
RdA	*Revue d'assyriologie et d'archéologie orientale*
RES	Répertoire d'épigraphie sémitique
RHR	Revue de l'histoire des religions
RivB	*Rivista biblica*
RlA	*Reallexikon der Assyriologie und vorderasiatischen Archäologie* (edited by E. Ebeling, *et al.* Berlin: de Gruyter, 1928–).

RPARA	*Rendiconti della Pontifica Accademia Romana di Archeologia*
RQum	*Revue de Qumrân*
RSO	Ras-Shamra – Ougarit
RSO	*Rivista degli studi orientali*
RSR	*Religious Studies Review*
RSV	Revised Standard Version
SAAB	*State Archives of Assyria Bulletin*
SAHL	Studies in the Archaeology and History of the Levant
SBAB	Stuttgarter biblische Aufsatzbände
SBLDS	Society of Biblical Literature Dissertation Series
SBLMS	Society of Biblical Literature Monograph Series
SBLSS	Society of Biblical Literature Semeia Series
SBLWAW	Society of Biblical Literature Writings from the Ancient World
SBS	Stuttgarter Bibelstudien
SEL	Studi epigrafici e linguistici sul Vicino Oriente Antico
SHAJ	*Studies in the History and Archaeology of Jordan*
SHANE	Studies in the History of the Ancient Near East
SHCANE	Studies in the History and Culture of the Ancient Near East
SHR	Studies in the History of Religions
SJOT	*Scandinavian Journal of the Old Testament*
SJSJ	Supplements to the *Journal for the Study of Judaism*
SOTS	Society for Old Testament Study
SP	Samaritan Pentateuch
SS	Studi semitici
SWBAS	Social World of Biblical Antiquity Series
TA	*Tel Aviv*
TAD	*Textbook of Aramaic Documents from Ancient Egypt: 1–4* (B. Porten and A. Yardeni. Hebrew University, Department of the History of the Jewish People, Texts and Studies for Students; Jerusalem: Hebrew University Press, 1986–99).
TBü	Theologische Bücherei
TDOT	*Theological Dictionary of the Old Testament* (15 vols, edited by G. J. Botterweck and H. Ringgren. Translated by J. T. Willis, G. W. Bromiley and D. E. Green. Grand Rapids, MI: Eerdmans, 1974–).
ThLZ	*Theologische Literaturzeitung*
ThQ	*Theologische Quartalschrift*
TRE	*Theologische Realenzyklopädie* (edited by G. Krause and G. Müller. Berlin: de Gruyter, 1977–).
TynBul	*Tyndale Bulletin*
TZ	*Theologische Zeitung*
UBL	Ugaritisch-biblische Literatur
UCOP	University of Cambridge Oriental Publications

UF	*Ugarit-Forschungen*
UUÅ	*Uppsala Universitets Årskrift*
VT	*Vetus Testamentum*
VTS	Vetus Testamentum Supplements
WBC	Word Biblical Commentary
WDSP	*Wadi Daliyeh II: The Samaria Papyri from Wadi Daliyeh* (D. M. Gropp) and *Qumran Cave 4: XXVIII Miscellanea, Part 2* (M. Bernstein, *et al.*) (DJD, 28; Oxford: Clarendon Press, 2001).
WUNT	Wissenschaftliche Untersuchungen zum Neuen Testament
WZKM	*Wiener Zeitschrift für die Kunde des Morgenlandes*
ZA	*Zeitschrift für Assyriologie*
ZABR	*Zeitschrift für altorientalische und biblische Rechtsgeschichte*
ZAW	*Zeitschrift für die alttestamentliche Wissenschaft*
ZDMG	*Zeitschrift der deutschen morgenländischen Gesellschaft*
ZDPV	*Zeitschrift des deutschen Palästina-Vereins*
ZNW	*Zeitschrift für die neutestamentliche Wissenschaft und die Kunde der älteren Kirche*
ZTK	*Zeitschrift fur Theologie and Kirche*

Chapter 1

BONES, BURIALS AND BOUNDARIES

Graves function as much for the living as for the dead. For the dead, a grave might be understood as an unchanging, perpetual and specialized place of dwelling, or a transformative space in which one might enter into a new form of existence.[1] For the living, it serves not merely to hold the remains of the deceased, and not only to memorialize the existence of an individual, but as a site of mortuary practices and their associated activities, a grave is also a socially structured space, shaped by and communicating something of the agency of those who render the space a burial place – the corpse included.[2] As such, a grave is a medium of social, cultural and ideological meaning communicated both among the living, and between the living and the dead.[3]

The role of the grave as a locus of meaning is essentially bound up with the living community's responses to the dead: the ways in which the living respond to and deal with a corpse is not simply a matter of disposing of a cadaver. Rather, the methods and means of dealing with a corpse constitute a process effecting

---

1. Among the vast literature on anthropological approaches to understanding death and burial, see in particular the now classic studies in S. C. Humphreys and H. King (eds), *Mortality and Immortality: The Anthropology and Archaeology of Death* (London: Academic Press, 1981); M. Bloch and J. Parry (eds), *Death and the Regeneration of Life* (Cambridge: Cambridge University Press, 1982) and P. Metcalf and R. Huntington, *Celebrations of Death: The Anthropology of Mortuary Ritual* (2nd edn; Cambridge: Cambridge University Press, 1991). Of particular importance among more recent contributions is E. Hallam, J. Hockey and G. Howarth, *Beyond the Body: Death and Social Identity* (London: Routledge, 1999).

2. See in particular E. Hallam and J. Hockey, *Death, Memory and Material Culture* (Oxford: Berg, 2001).

3. See especially M. Shanks and C. Tilley, 'Ideology, Symbolic Power and Ritual Communication: A Reinterpretation of Neolithic Mortuary Practices', in I. Hodder (ed.), *Symbolic and Structural Archaeology* (Cambridge: Cambridge University Press, 1982), 129–54; M. Parker Pearson, 'The Powerful Dead: Archaeological Relationships between the Living and the Dead', *Cambridge Archaeological Journal* 3.2 (1993), 203–99, and the essays collected in G. F. M. Rakita, J. E. Buikstra, L. A. Beck and S. R. Williams (eds), *Interacting with the Dead: Perspectives on Mortuary Archaeology for the New Millennium* (Gainesville, FL: University of Florida Press, 2005).

and maintaining the transformation of the deceased from a once-living person into a non-living entity, enabling the living community to negotiate and reframe their relationship with that individual.[4] In essence, two very broad types of corpse treatment function within this social context of death: the ideal or 'good' response to the corpse, by which the optimal social and cultural valuing of the dead is enacted through normative or 'proper' mortuary rituals, and the anti-ideal or 'bad' response to the corpse, by which the socially normative treatment of the dead is inverted or ignored.[5] For many social groups, burial (rather than cremation or exposure) in a marked, remembered and undisturbed place, functions as the ideal treatment of the corpse, coupled with the performance of other funerary and post-mortem practices.[6] It is in this sense, then, that graves – like corpses – absorb, negotiate and exhibit social meanings.[7] Whether expressed in terms of memory, community, tradition, kinship, status, identity or any other means of articulating a sense of social 'collectivity' or 'commonality', the grave

---

4. This is evident in the valuable findings of several socio-anthropological and ritual studies. The best known of these discussions are Metcalf and Huntington's *Celebrations of Death* and the collection of essays in Bloch and Parry, *Death and the Regeneration of Life*. Among more recent contributions, the most important include R. A. Joyce, 'Social Dimensions of Pre-Classic Burials', in D. C. Grove and R. A. Joyce (eds), *Social Patterns in Pre-Classic Mesoamerica* (Washington, DC: Dumbarton Oaks, 1999), 15–47; S. Gillespie, 'Mortuary Ritual, Agency, and Personhood: A Case Study from the Ancient Maya', *Journal of Anthropological Archaeology* 20.1 (2001), 73–112, and the essays collected in M. S. Chesson (ed.), *Social Memory, Identity, and Death: Anthropological Perspectives on Mortuary Rituals* (Archaeological Papers of the American Anthropological Association, 10; Arlington: American Anthropological Institute, 2001) and N. Laneri (ed.), *Performing Death: Social Analyses of Funerary Traditions in the Ancient Near East and Mediterranean* (University of Chicago Oriental Institute Seminars, 3; Chicago: Oriental Institute of the University of Chicago, 2007). See also Catherine Bell's account of the social dynamics of ritual in *Ritual: Perspectives and Dimensions* (Oxford: Oxford University Press, 1997), ch. 2. Though first published in the early twentieth century (1906–07), Robert Hertz's work on this subject continues to play an important role in present day discussions of the 'social life' of the corpse; his key essays were published in English as *Death and the Right Hand* (trans. R. Needham and C. Needham; Aberdeen: Cohen & West, 1960).

5. This is a familiar distinction, helpfully described, for example, in M. Bloch and J. Parry, 'Introduction', *Death and the Regeneration of Life*, 1–44, esp. 15–18; see also J.-P. Vernant, 'La belle mort et le cadaver outragé', in G. Gnoli and J.-P. Vernant (eds), *La mort, les morts dans les sociétés anciennes* (Paris: Maison des Sciences de l'Homme, 1982), 45–76. It is important to avoid over-systematizing constructions of 'ideal' and 'anti-ideal' responses to the corpse; within any one society or group, great variety and diversity in mortuary and other death rituals is likely to exist.

6. On the possible social dynamics of cremation (both 'positively' and 'negatively' construed), see D. J. Davies, *Death, Ritual and Belief: The Rhetoric of Funerary Rites* (2nd edn; London: Continuum, 2002), 25–35. See also Chapter 4 in the present volume.

7. Cf. Hallam, Hockey and Howarth, *Beyond the Body*, 125.

keeps alive the ongoing relationship between and among the living and the dead.[8] Thus a burial place 'does not only express, represent or materialize ideology – it is ideology'.[9]

This book is especially concerned with one particular ideological function of burial: its territoriality. It is now well recognized that burials can often signal proprietory or appropriative 'links to land' within many cultures, past and present.[10] Whether cast (for example) in the terms of competition between people for local or regional resources, or the marking of the places of descent groups, or the symbolic or material (re)integration of a community's dead into their local landscape, burials fix the dead in the land by rendering them permanently present at particular places.[11] As such, the dead can mark, and thus claim, land for the living.

Within what might usefully (though not unproblematically) be termed 'traditional' societies,[12] the agency and presence of the dead in the lives of the living is often richly reflected in the social casting of the dead as ancestors or 'spirits',

---

8. Adapting a similar view expressed by R. P. Harrison, *The Dominion of the Dead* (Chicago: University of Chicago Press, 2003), 22.

9. A. T. Smith, 'The Politics of Loss: Comments on a Powerful Death', in N. Laneri (ed.), *Performing Death: Social Analyses of Funerary Traditions in the Ancient Near East and Mediterranean* (University of Chicago Oriental Institute Seminars, 3; Chicago: Oriental Institute of the University of Chicago, 2007), 163–66, here 165.

10. Citing W. Ashmore and P. L. Geller, 'Social Dimensions of Mortuary Space', in G. F. M. Rakita, J. E. Buikstra, L. A. Beck and S. R. Williams (eds), *Interacting with the Dead: Perspectives on Mortuary Archaeology for the New Millennium* (Gainesville, FL: University of Florida Press, 2005), 81–92, here 84.

11. For an excellent and sophisticated overview (including a sharp critique of the well-known Saxe/Goldstein hypothesis), see M. Parker Pearson, *The Archaeology of Death and Burial* (Stroud: Sutton, 2003), 124–41. For more detailed studies on these interpretative themes, see particularly M. Bloch, *Placing the Dead: Tombs, Ancestral Villages, and Kinship Organisation in Madagascar* (London: Seminar Press, 1971); A. A. Saxe, 'Social Dimensions of Mortuary Practices in a Mesolithic Population from Wadi Halfa, Sudan', in J. Brown (ed.), *Approaches to the Social Dimensions of Mortuary Practices* (Washington, DC: Memoir of the Society for American Archaeology 25, 1971), 39–57; R. W. Chapman, 'Ten Years After – Megaliths, Mortuary Practices, and the Territorial Model', in L. Anderson Beck (ed.), *Regional Approaches to Mortuary Analysis* (New York: Plenum, 1995), 29–51; (in the same volume) D. K. Charles, 'Diachronic Regional Social Dynamics: Mortuary Sites in the Illinois Valley/American Bottom Region', (77–99); C. Toren, 'Seeing the Sites: Transformations in Fijian Notions of the Land', in E. Hirsch and M. O'Hanlon (eds), *The Anthropology of Landscape: Perspectives on Place and Space* (Oxford: Clarendon Press, 1995), 163–83.

12. The term is a difficult one, for it can carry with it derogatory associations of 'outdated' or 'pre-modern' practices. But it is preferable to other commonly used designations, including 'pre-industrial', which is wrongly to imply that 'traditional' societies do not exist within industrial cultures, and 'non-Western', which is to define a society in the imposed (and pseudo-colonial) terms of what it is not.

who are credited with a range of functions and requirements configured with the social, economic, religious, political, cultural and ideological concerns of the living community.[13] In these contexts, the control or appropriation of land is often correlated to notions of lineal descent, so that the territorial potency of burial places expresses the claims of the descendants of the dead to the land in which their ancestors are materially present, and on which they themselves live, work or depend. Accordingly, the appropriation and occupation of land is thus frequently marked by ancestral graves,[14] so that burial places themselves might function as or signal boundaries, coding the land of the living as a mortuary landscape.[15]

Within many ancient West Asian contexts, the territorial dead were the ancestors of the household cult – the once-living-now-dead members of the family group who continued to play important roles in the lives of their descendants. Simply put, the death of a family member did not irrevocably fracture the social

---

13. This is not to suggest that contemporary Western societies exhibit 'shallow' death cultures (cf. A. C. G. M. Robben, 'Death and Anthropology: An Introduction', in A. C. G. M. Robben [ed.], *Death, Mourning and Burial: A Cross-Cultural Reader* [Oxford: Blackwell, 2004], 1–16). Indeed, several studies indicate that death rituals and attitudes to the corpse continue to perform a richly profound and transformative function within seemingly 'secularized' societies; see, for example, D. Francis, L. Kellaher and G. Neophytou, 'The Cemetery: The Evidence of Continuing Bonds', in J. Hockey, J. Katz and N. Small (eds), *Grief, Mourning and Death Ritual* (Buckingham: Open University Press, 2001), 226–36; Davies, *Death, Ritual and Belief*; J. L. Foltyn, 'The Corpse in Contemporary Culture: Identifying, Transacting, and Recoding the Dead Body in the Twenty-First Century', *Mortality* 13.2 (2008), 99–104.

14. For a detailed study, see Maurice Bloch's important volume, *Placing the Dead* (1971); see also J. Goody, *Death, Property and the Ancestors: A Study of the Mortuary Customs of the LoDagaa of West Africa* (London: Tavistock, 1962); J. Glazier, 'Mbeere Ancestors and the Domestication of Death', *Man* (ns) 19.1 (1984), 133–47; K. Prag, 'The Dead Sea Dolmens: Death and the Landscape', in S. Campbell and A. Green (eds), *The Archaeology of Death in the Ancient Near East* (Oxbow Monograph 51; Oxford: Oxbow, 1995), 75–84; A. Porter, 'The Dynamics of Death: Ancestors, Pastoralism, and the Origins of a Third-Millennium City in Syria', *BASOR* 325 (2002), 1–36; H. Silverman and D. Small (eds), *The Space and Place of Death* (Archaeological Papers of the American Anthropological Association, 11; Arlington, VA: American Anthropological Association, 2002); D. Prendergast, *From Elder to Ancestor: Old Age, Death and Inheritance in Modern Korea* (Folkstone: Global Oriental, 2005); cf. I. Malkin, 'Land Ownership, Territorial Possession, Hero Cults, and Scholarly Theory', in R. M. Rosen and J. Farrell (eds), *Nomodeiktes: Greek Studies in Honor of Martin Ostwald* (Ann Arbor, MI: University of Michigan Press, 1993), 225–34; C. M. Antoniaccio, *An Archaeology of Ancestors: Tomb Cult and Hero Cult in Early Greece* (Lanham, MD: Rowman & Littlefield, 1995); S. J. Friesen (ed.), *Ancestors in Post-Contact Religion: Roots, Ruptures, and Modernity's Memory* (Cambridge, MA: Harvard University Press, 2001).

15. That is to say both that a burial might be appropriately sited on a boundary, and that a boundary might appropriately be evoked by the presence of a burial. On the fluid nature of boundaries and 'embodied' landscapes in small-scale societies, see C. Tilley, *A Phenomenology of Landscape: Places, Paths and Monuments* (Oxford: Berg, 1994).

dynamics of the group, it merely altered the nature of the family's interaction with the deceased individual.[16] Texts and inscriptions – including some from ancient Israel and Judah – suggest that the dead performed key functions for the living, including the giving of oracles and omens, and the bestowing of blessings and curses.[17] In particular, the ancestors played an important dual role within the lives of their descendants: they bore some responsibility for the fertility and perpetuation of the family line and household, and they acted as guardians and guarantors of inheritable property and places, including the plots of land upon which many ancient West Asian families depended, and upon which they themselves would likely be buried.[18]

Given the dominant imperial contexts of institutional land possession and management, this perception of the territorial ancestors was not incompatible with the urban-controlled economic infrastructures of ancient West Asian agriculture, nor with the ideological superstructures within which they were framed. While (primarily urban) perceptions of land possession rendered the god of the local city or the 'national' deity the landowner, and the king (whether domestic or imperial) the 'steward' or 'curator' of these divinely owned territories, fields, and plots, institutional 'stewardship' of agricultural land did not preclude a familial, ancestral dimension to its character. Mario Liverani argues that, under certain circumstances, land granted or 'loaned' from temples and palaces often became 'private' land in practice, so that, although initially only the *obligations* on the

---

16. On the nature and function of these household dynamics, see the literature cited in n. 18, below.

17. See the literature cited in T. J. Lewis, 'How Far Can Texts Take Us? Evaluating Textual Sources for Reconstructing Ancient Israelite Beliefs about the Dead', in B. M. Gittlen (ed.), *Sacred Time, Sacred Place: Archaeology and the Religion of Israel* (Winona Lake, IN: Eisenbrauns, 2002), 169–217.

18. On the role of the dead in household religions (sometimes described as or distinguished from 'family' religion), see most recently C. Meyers, 'Household Religion', in F. Stavrakopoulou and J. Barton (eds), *Religious Diversity in Ancient Israel and Judah* (London: T&T Clark, 2010), 118–34; K. van der Toorn, 'Family Religion in Second Millennium West Asia (Mesopotamia, Emar, Nuzi)', in J. Bodel and S. M. Olyan (eds), *Household and Family Religion in Antiquity* (Oxford: Blackwell, 2008), 20–36, esp. 25–28; (in the same volume) D. E. Fleming, 'The Integration of Household and Community Religion in Ancient Syria' (37–59, esp. 40–43); T. J. Lewis, 'Family, Household, and Local Religion at Late Bronze Age Ugarit' (60–88); S. M. Olyan, 'Family Religion in Israel and the Wider Levant of the First Millennium BCE' (113–26); P. Dutcher-Walls (ed.), *The Family in Life and Death: Sociological and Archaeological Perspectives* (LHBOTS, 504; New York: T&T Clark, 2009). See also R. Parker, *Polytheism and Society at Athens* (Oxford: Oxford University Press, 2005), 9–36. Less recent are the excellent volumes by K. van der Toorn, *Family Religion in Babylonia, Syria and Israel: Continuity and Change in the Forms of Religious Life* (SHCANE, 7; Leiden: Brill, 1996), esp. 42–65, 206–35, and G. Jonker, *The Topography of Remembrance: The Dead, Tradition and Collective Memory in Mesopotamia* (SHR, 68; Leiden: Brill, 1995), esp. 187–211.

land were heritable, the land itself soon was too.[19] Thus for families working or managing the land, the socio-religious dimensions of both their (agri)culture and territoriality (each essential components of identity) maintained household, local, and regional or even 'state' dimensions.[20] Even within the imperial context, therefore, claims to land might be plausibly framed within the context of appeals to the household or local ancestors held to be buried there.

One of the most significant functions of this workable (though perhaps tense) interface between imperial and ancestral landscapes was its maintenance of different perspectives on land, enabling two seemingly competing ideologies to be upheld: one institutional, the other ancestral, crucially rooting elites and non-elites to the land on which agrarian societies depended. And yet – and especially in times of forced migrations and territorial displacement – 'land' can become a particularly fractious field of changing perspectives on senses of place, belonging, ancestry, and identity, whether experienced from fixed or mobile, local or

---

19. M. Liverani, 'Land Tenure and Inheritance in the Ancient Near East: The Interaction between "Palace" and "Family"', in T. Khalidi (ed.), *Social Transformation in the Middle East* (Beirut: American University of Beirut, 1984), 33–44. A similar opinion is offered in G. H. Hamel, *Poverty and Charity in Roman Palestine, First Three Centuries C.E.* (Berkeley, CA: University of California Press, 1990); cf. M. Hudson and B. A. Levine (eds), *Urbanization and Land Ownership in the Ancient Near East* (Peabody Museum Bulletin, 7; Cambridge, MA: Peabody Museum of Archaeology and Ethnology, Harvard University, 1999). Note also J. N. Postgate, 'The Ownership and Exploitation of Land in Assyria in the First Millennium BC', in M. Lebeau and P. Talon (eds), *Reflets des deux fleuvres: volume de mélanges offerts à André Flint* (Akkadica, 6; Leuven: Peeters, 1989), 141–52. On the patrimonial state, manifested in the concept of the 'house of the father', see J. D. Schloen, *The House of the Father as Fact and Symbol: Patrimonialism in Ugarit and the Ancient Near East* (SAHL, 2; Winona Lake, IN: Eisenbrauns, 2001).

20. Cf. 2 Kgs 18:31-32. On the socio-religious and economic dimensions of various aspects of 'land' in ancient Israel and Judah, see, for example, J. Pastor, *Land and Economy in Ancient Palestine* (London: Routledge, 1997); C. E. Carter, *The Emergence of Yehud in the Persian Period: A Social and Demographic Study* (JSOTS, 294; Sheffield: Sheffield Academic Press, 1999); O. Lipschits, 'Achaemenid Imperial Policy, Settlement Processes in Palestine, and the Status of Jerusalem in the Middle of the Fifth Century BCE', in O. Lipschits and M. Oeming (eds), *Judah and the Judeans in the Persian Period* (Winona Lake, IN: Eisenbrauns, 2006), 19–52; B. A. Levine, 'The Clan-Based Economy of Biblical Israel', in W. G. Dever and S. Gitin (eds), *Symbiosis, Symbolism, and the Power of the Past: Canaan, Ancient Israel and Their Neighbors from the Late Bronze Age through Roman Palestine* (Winona Lake, IN: Eisenbrauns, 2003), 445–53; L. L. Grabbe, *A History of the Jews and Judaism in the Second Temple Period, Volume 1 Yehud: A History of the Persian Province of Judah* (LSTS, 47; London: T&T Clark, 2004), 189–208; J. Blenkinsopp, 'Did the Second Jerusalemite Temple Possess Land?', *Transeuphratène* 21 (2001), 61–68; J. Weinberg, *The Citizen-Temple Community* (trans. D. L. Smith-Christopher; JSOTS, 151; Sheffield: JSOT Press, 1992), 92–104.

global, individual or communal points of view.[21] Land is not simply land, but *landscape*: 'a cultural process'.[22] As Christopher Tilley comments:

> [L]andscapes are contested, worked and re-worked by people according to particular individual, social and political circumstances. As such they are always in process, rather than static, being and becoming.... [They are] palimpsests of past and present, outcomes of social practice, products of colonial and post-colonial identities... They get actively re-worked, interpreted and understood in relation to differing social and political agendas, forms of social memory, and biographically become sensuously embodied in a multitude of ways.[23]

This is an important backdrop to the present book, for this discussion is concerned with the ways in which perceptions of the territorial dead play a vital role in shaping the contours of certain biblical land claims – contours set against the ideologies of territorial flux during the Neo-Babylonian, Persian and Hellenistic periods in which the biblical portrayals of the past were likely composed and compiled.

As is well known, land is the dominant ideological referent in the Hebrew Bible for the mythic, social, ritual and political expressions of identity with which the biblical literature is so concerned. Whether real or imagined, and whether mytho-symbolic or geographic, 'land' thus functions in the Hebrew Bible as a narrated topography of cultural memory, shaped both selectively and meaningfully in order to map the biblical story of the past and its people onto the socio-religious and political agendas of the present.[24]

But although the ethno-territorial and religio-cultural dynamics of the Hebrew Bible are heavily shaped by its land ideologies,[25] relatively little attention has

---

21. See, for example, the excellent collection of essays in B. Bender and M. Winer (eds), *Contested Landscapes: Movement, Exile and Place* (Oxford: Berg, 2001).

22. E. Hirsch, 'Landscape: Between Place and Space', in E. Hirsch and M. O'Hanlon (eds), *The Anthropology of Landscape: Perspectives on Place and Space* (Oxford: Clarendon Press, 1995), 1–30 (here 22–23).

23. C. Tilley, 'Identity, Place, Landscape and Heritage', *Journal of Material Culture* 11 (2006), 7–32 (here 7–8), drawing on B. Bender, 'Place and Landscape', in C. Tilley, W. Keane, S. Kuechler, M. Rowlands and P. Spyer (eds), *Handbook of Material Culture* (London: Sage, 2006), 303–14. See also C. Holtorf and H. Williams, 'Landscapes and Memories', in D. Hicks and M. C. Beaudry (eds), *Cambridge Companion to Historical Archaeology* (Cambridge: Cambridge University Press, 2006), 235–54.

24. On the complexities of (understanding) social constructions of 'place', see M. C. Rodman, 'Empowering Place: Multilocality and Multivocality', *American Ethnologist* 94 (1992), 640–56. On 'narratives' of place, see (for example) S. M. Low and D. Lawrence-Zúñiga, 'Locating Culture', in S. M. Low and D. Lawrence-Zúñiga, *The Anthropology of Space and Place: Locating Culture* (Oxford: Blackwell, 2003), 1–47, esp 16–19.

25. E.g. G. Strecker (ed.), *Das Land Israel in biblischer Zeit* (Göttinger Theologische

been paid to the ways in which the dead mark or mar many of the territorial agendas set out or invoked in the biblical literature. And yet alongside (indeed, in spite of) a strong theological tendency in the Hebrew Bible towards the imaging of Yhwh as divine, imperial 'landlord',[26] certain biblical claims about land – including its appropriation, protection, loss and degradation – are directly related to a persistent and ideological appeal to the presence or absence of the dead.

Placing the Dead

Though the interrelation of ancestral tombs and territoriality in the Hebrew Bible has been noted in passing by some commentators,[27] the most detailed and clearly articulated study of this theme is the well-known assessment of the interrelation of kin, land and death by Herbert Brichto, published in 1973.[28] Though he makes little of the ways in which territoriality might be marked or signalled by the dead, Brichto draws particular attention to the biblical portrayal of the ancestral cult, arguing that the well-being of the living and their perpetuation on family land was dependent upon the continued well-being of the dead in the family tomb on that land:

> Property . . . was essentially a religious concept, particularly real property. The family was attached to the soil as the notion of the burial place as the ancestral home was extended to the surrounding fields. Laws of primogeniture, succession and inheritance rights, indivisibility and inalienability of real estate, the sacrilegious nature of the crime of moving a landmark all derive from this concept of the family and its real holdings as a unit in any given generation (. . . its horizontal modality) and as a unit extending from its first ancestors to all future progeny (its vertical modality).[29]

Arbeiten, 25; Göttingen: Vandenhoeck & Ruprecht, 1983); M. Weinfeld, *The Promise of the Land: The Inheritance of the Land of Canaan by the Israelites* (Berkeley, CA: University of California Press, 1993); N. C. Habel, *The Land Is Mine: Six Biblical Land Ideologies* (Minneapolis: Fortress Press, 1995); W. Brueggemann, *The Land: Place as Gift, Promise, and Challenge in Biblical Faith* (2nd edn; Minneapolis: Fortress Press, 2002); see also W. D. Davies, *The Territorial Dimension of Judaism* (2nd edn; Minneapolis: Fortress Press, 1991).

26. As discussed below.

27. E.g. L. E. Stager, 'The Archaeology of the Family in Ancient Israel', *BASOR* 260 (1985), 1–35 (here 23); followed by E. Bloch-Smith, *Judahite Burial Practices and Beliefs about the Dead* (JSOTS, 123; Sheffield: JSOT Press, 1992), 111, 115; see also R. S. Hallote, *Death, Burial, and Afterlife in the Biblical World: How the Israelites and Their Neighbors Treated the Dead* (Chicago: Ivan R. Dee, 2001), 34–35.

28. H. C. Brichto, 'Kin, Cult, Land and Afterlife – A Biblical Complex', *HUCA* 44 (1973), 1–54.

29. Ibid., 5.

Given the more socially-nuanced perspectives of contemporary biblical scholarship, some of the concepts and labels Brichto employs are now best considered somewhat unwieldy, outdated or uncritical – particularly his imaging of 'property'.[30] But his focus on the biblical construct of an ancestral tomb on ancestral land remains an important one. The biblical preference for interment in a marked, remembered and undisturbed place is frequently idealized in many texts as burial in the family tomb within or upon the bounds of ancestral land.[31] Though in many of these texts this particular type of mortuary practice is often presented theologically as a consequence of divine favour and blessing, it likely reflects a complex set of beliefs about the symbolism and effects of this type of burial: interment in the family tomb on ancestral land facilitated the transition of the dead into the underworld and manifested the integration of the individual into the realm of the ancestors;[32] it also transformed the corpse from its liminal state into a once-living-now-dead member of the social group, thereby reincorporating the individual into the community;[33] and – most significantly – interment in a family

---

30. For a more nuanced discussion of 'property', see M. Hudson, 'The New Economic Archaeology of Urbanization', in M. Hudson and B. A. Levine (eds), *Urbanization and Land Ownership in the Ancient Near East* (Peabody Museum Bulletin, 7; Cambridge, MA: Peabody Museum of Archaeology and Ethnology, Harvard University, 1999), 9–15. For biblical portrayals of 'property', see F. E. Deist, *The Material Culture of the Bible: An Introduction* (BS, 70; Sheffield: Sheffield Academic Press, 2002), 143–46.

31. For the biblical preference for interment, see (for example) 2 Sam. 3:31-36; 1 Kgs 13:28-30; 2 Chr. 16:14; Jer. 34:5; cf. Job 21:32-33; Jer. 16:5-8. For burial in the family tomb, see (for example) Judg. 8:32; 16:31; 2 Sam. 2:32; 21:12-14; 2 Kgs 9:28; 23:30; cf. Gen. 49:29-31; 50:13. See also the important study by S. M. Olyan, 'Some Neglected Aspects of Israelite Interment Ideology', *JBL* 124 (2005), 601–16.

32. The biblical imaging of burial in the ancestral tomb as an experience in which the deceased individual is 'gathered (to)' (אסף) or 'sleeps (with)' (שכב) the ancestors is frequently taken as indicative of a belief that the dead were united with deceased family members in the underworld (e.g. Gen. 25:8; 35:29; Num. 20:24; Judg. 2:10; 1 Kgs 2:10; 11:43; 14:20, 31; 15:8, 24). The 'house' imagery evident in some excavated Judahite tombs and in biblical portrayals of the grave (e.g. Job 17:13-14; 30:23) is similarly suggestive of a perceived household continuum between the living and the dead. As Mike Parker Pearson observes, mortuary practices cannot be interpreted in isolation, but 'as a set of activities which link with other social practices such as building, dwelling and subsistence' (*Archaeology of Death and Burial*, 5). An overview of the pertinent biblical and archaeological material can be found in Bloch-Smith, *Judahite Burial Practices*; see also G. Barkay, 'Burial Caves and Burial Practices in Judah in the Biblical Period', in I. Singer (ed.), *Graves and Burial Practices in the Land of Israel in Ancient Times* (Jerusalem: Yad Ben Zvi/Israel Exploration Society, 1994), 96–163 (Hebrew); cf. R. Gonen, *Burial Patterns and Cultural Diversity in Late Bronze Age Canaan* (ASORDS, 7; Winona Lake, IN: Eisenbrauns, 1992).

33. See the literature cited on p. 2 in nn. 4 and 5. Though cross-culturally mortuary practices and their functions are varied and diverse, to a certain degree anthropological studies remain indebted to the works of Arnold van Gennep (*The Rites of Passage* [trans. M. B. Vizedom and G. L. Caffee; Chicago: Chicago University Press, 1960 (1908)]) and Robert

tomb also embodied and reinforced the territorial claims of the deceased's living descendants and their socio-economic well-being, as the preceding discussion suggests.

Viewed thus through a social-scientific lens, this biblical idealization of the ancestral tomb makes good sense. But importantly, its idealization is also bound up with its biblical context, for the Hebrew Bible is a carefully crafted collection of texts, exhibiting complex (and at times conflicting) ideologies. As such, its imaging of the socio-religious past likely reflects in the main the idealized and specialized religious preferences of the scribal elites and their textual communities of the Persian and Hellenistic periods, whose representations of certain socio-religious groups and practices may be intentionally or unintentionally skewed.[34] After all, the Hebrew Bible can only offer 'versions of the past', not a reliable account of the past.[35] One of the difficulties presented by Brichto's study is thus the over-confidence with which he reads the biblical texts as a direct reflection of the historical realities of mortuary culture. A similar charge can also be levelled at some archaeological reconstructions of ancient Israelite and Judahite mortuary behaviours and their associated practices, which can often (though not consistently) use the biblical texts to over-interpret material data.[36] While this is not to dismiss the usefulness of the biblical texts altogether, it remains that they must be handled cautiously and carefully in historical reconstructions of the socio-religious past.[37] Thus the biblical imaging of the ancestral tomb as a marker of a landed, ancestral inheritance may be radically idealized – particularly given the spatial dynamics of the urban societies within which much of the biblical literature was produced.[38]

It is thus the contention of this book that the Hebrew Bible draws on powerful

---

Hertz (see above, n. 4) and their development of broadly socio-cultural and anthropological theories about mortuary rituals.

34. See F. Stavrakopoulou, '"Popular" Religion and "Official" Religion: Practice, Perception, Portrayal', in F. Stavrakopoulou and J. Barton (eds), *Religious Diversity in Ancient Israel and Judah* (London: T&T Clark, 2010), 37–58.

35. Here employing Paul Connerton's phrase in *How Societies Remember* (Cambridge: Cambridge University Press, 1989), 72.

36. E.g. Bloch-Smith, *Judahite Burial Practices*, 147–51; D. P. Wright, *The Disposal of Impurity: Elimination Rites in the Bible and in Hittite and Mesopotamian Literature* (SBLDS, 101; Atlanta, GA: Scholars Press, 1987), 115–28, esp. 128; cf. R. Tappy, 'Did the Dead Ever Die in Biblical Judah?' *BASOR* 298 (1995), 59–68.

37. On the potentials and pitfalls of both archaeological and textual material relating to mortuary culture in ancient Israel and Judah, see the excellent discussion in Lewis, 'How Far Can Texts Take Us?' 169–217.

38. Cf. E. Ben Zvi, 'The Urban Center of Jerusalem and the Development of the Literature of the Hebrew Bible', in W. E. Aufrecht, N. A. Mirau and S. W. Gauley (eds), *Urbanism in Antiquity: From Mesopotamia to Crete* (JSOTS, 244; Sheffield: Sheffield Academic Press, 1997), 194–209.

ideas about the territoriality of the dead and their graves to make certain claims about land – claims related to the wider biblical agenda concerned with the construction of identity, set against a landscape of the past. In many texts, this landscape is imaged as a rural idyll, parcelled into ancestral holdings, the ancient boundaries of which are carefully marked and honoured. Deuteronomy 19:14, for example, prohibits the removal of a neighbour's boundary marker set up by past generations, as though its ancient origins render it an inherently permanent fixture. Indeed, the sanctity of the ancestral boundary marker is also apparent in 27:17, in which the community threatens with a curse anyone who defies this prohibition.[39] Similar concerns are expressed in Prov. 23:10, in which the removal of ancient boundary markers is castigated and paralleled with territorial encroachment upon the fields of 'orphans' – perhaps those without living or dead kin to support familial claims to the plot.[40] This perspective is also evident in Prov. 22:27-28, in which the reader is warned not to remove the ancient landmarks set up by his ancestors in order to pay off his debts by selling his ancestral estate and its family tomb (here reading משכב as 'grave', rather than 'bed').[41] It is likely that this emphasis upon the inalienable nature of the ancestral landholding explains Naboth's refusal in 1 Kgs 21:1-4 to sell King Ahab his נחלה, his ancestral inheritance.[42]

---

39. The instruction in Deut. 19:14 exhibits an interesting tension between the land ideology of Deuteronomy and the socio-religious concerns of what is idealized in these texts as a traditionally 'ancestral' culture, for it implies that the allocation of even 'God-given' land must respect ancestral boundaries. These two perspectives ('God-given' land/ancestral land) also appear to be merged within the territorial ideology of the book of Joshua (see Habel, *The Land Is Mine*, 54–74). For a postcolonial response, see M. G. Brett, *Decolonizing God: The Bible in the Tides of Empire* (Sheffield: Sheffield Phoenix Press, 2008), 44–61. For the possible socio-political motivations of Deuteronom(ist)ic opposition to the ancestors and cults of the dead, see J. Blenkinsopp, 'Deuteronomy and the Politics of Post-Mortem Existence', *VT* 45 (1995), 1–16; see also Herbert Niehr's observations in 'The Changed Status of the Dead in Yehud', in R. Albertz and B. Becking (eds), *Yahwism After the Exile: Perspectives on Israelite Religion in the Persian Era* (Assen: Van Gorcum, 2003), 136–55; cf. B. Halpern, 'Jerusalem and the Lineages in the Seventh Century BCE: Kinship and the Rise of Individual Moral Liability', in B. Halpern and D. W. Hobson (eds), *Law and Ideology in Monarchic Israel* (JSOTS, 124; Sheffield: JSOT Press, 1991), 11–107.

40. The close correlation of older generations with the acquisition and maintenance of land is also attested in the Decalogue (Exod. 20:12; Deut. 5:16). For the view that these verses allude to the post-mortem honouring of the ancestors, see Brichto, 'Kin, Cult, Land and Afterlife', 30–35; a view rejected by C. J. H. Wright, *God's People in God's Land: Family, Land and Property in the Old Testament* (Grand Rapids, MI: Eerdmans, 1990), 152–55.

41. On the uses of משכב, see Chapter 5, n. 47.

42. On this expression, see particularly T. J. Lewis, 'The Ancestral Estate (*naḥălat ʾĕlōhîm*) in 2 Samuel 14:16', *JBL* 110 (1991), 597–612 and the discussion in Chapter 2, n. 21.

Though these texts do not explicitly characterize these landholdings as the sites of burials, they agree that this land is primarily and importantly ancestral in nature, and that the descendants have a religious responsibility to maintain the boundaries of these holdings not only in recognition of their ancestors' territoriality, but for the well-being of the living community. These texts and others like them (Isa. 5:8; Hos. 5:10; Mic. 2:2; Job 24:2) thus appear to imply that preserving the integrity of ancient landholdings is not only an ancestral ideal, but a matter of continued social integrity. For some, this is best considered a part of a broader 'ethical' or 'egalitarian' programme promoting the protection of the marginalized, economically down-trodden or 'poor'.[43] But this liberationist and socially sensitive interpretation of these texts perhaps takes too literally the somewhat caricatured tension between ruralism and urbanism exhibited in the biblical literature, in which the ancient agricultural land of the ancestors is often imaged as a target for the economic and commercial spread of an assertive urban power base.[44] Though this tension likely reflects in part the economic dependence of cities upon the agricultural lands of surrounding farms, it is perhaps better understood as a scribal, institutionalized and (perhaps) postcolonial discourse, which idealized the 'temple-garden' landscape of the constructed past as a utopia and cast the land-workers supporting the city-state as the divinely ordained farmers of the cosmos (cf. Gen. 2:4-25).[45] This tension between the urban contexts of biblical writing and the idealization of the ancestral, cultivated landscape in the literature (cf. 2 Kgs 18:31; Mic. 4:2-4; Zech. 3:10) has a notable impact on biblical ideologies of the territorial dead, as shall be seen in due course.

Other biblical texts image ancestral landholdings not so much as a rural idyll, but as parts of a mortuary landscape, the boundaries of which are marked by the graves of the dead. Thus Joshua is said to have been buried upon the boundary of

---

43. E.g. J. A. Dearman, *Property Rights in the Eighth-Century Prophets: The Conflict and Its Background* (SBLDS, 106; Atlanta, GA: Scholars Press, 1988); cf. J. A. Berman, *Created Equal: How the Bible Broke with Ancient Political Thought* (Oxford: Oxford University Press, 2008).

44. Drawing here on the biblical 'typology' of the town presented by B. A. Levine, 'The Biblical "Town" as Reality and Typology: Evaluating Biblical References to Towns and Their Functions', in M. Hudson and B. A. Levine (eds), *Urbanization and Land Ownership in the Ancient Near East* (Peabody Museum Bulletin, 7; Cambridge, MA: Peabody Museum of Archaeology and Ethnology, Harvard University, 1999), 421–53 (here 421–23).

45. On biblical mythologies and ideologies associated with land dispossession, ruralism and urbanism, see in particular Levine, 'The Biblical "Town"', 421–23; Brett, *Decolonizing God*, 94–112; P. R. Davies, 'Urban Religion and Rural Religion', in F. Stavrakopoulou and J. Barton (eds), *Religious Diversity in Ancient Israel and Judah* (London: T&T Clark, 2010), 104–17. For the biblical idealization of the temple-garden, see N. Wyatt, 'A Garden for the Living – Cultic and Ideological Aspects of Paradise' (forthcoming), and T. Stordalen, *Echoes of Eden: Genesis 2–3 and the Symbolism of the Eden Garden in Biblical Hebrew Literature* (CBET, 25; Leuven: Peeters, 2000).

his ancestral estate (Josh. 24:30; Judg. 2:9) and in 1 Sam. 10:2, the boundary of Benjamin is marked by the tomb of the 'local' ancestress, Rachel.[46] In Josh. 8:29, the grave of the Canaanite king of Ai is placed at the entrance of the city-gate and in the preceding chapter, Achan's corpse is buried in the Valley of Achor (Josh. 7:26), which elsewhere is situated on the boundary between Benjamin and Judah (Josh. 15:7).[47] These traditions are suggestive of a territoriality of burial familiar from social-scientific studies of communities in which the dead (usually imaged as ancestors) play an acknowledged social role.

It would appear that in these biblical traditions, the boundaries within the landscape are materialized and memorialized by the graves of the dead in a way significantly similar to the *monumental* materialization and memorialization of boundaries in other texts: in 1 Sam. 7:12, the boundary between Mizpah and Jeshanah is marked by a cultic stone (אבן) set up by Samuel and named 'Ebenezer'; in 2 Sam. 8:3, David asserts a claim to an imperial-sized territory by setting up a monument (יד) at the Euphrates river; in Josh. 15:6 and 18:17, the Stone of Bohan, also called 'Reuben's Descendant', is a prominent marker of one of Judah's boundaries (cf. 1 Sam. 20:19; 1 Kgs 1:9), and in the well-known oracle in Isa. 19:19 envisaging Yhwh's pseudo-colonial domination of Egypt, a cultic standing stone (מצבה) is placed on Egypt's border.[48]

The marking of boundaries in exhibited, monumentalized form coalesces in certain texts with their association with graves: Rachel's tomb is marked with a מצבה, a cultic standing stone (Gen. 35:20), while the burial places of assassinated elites or defeated enemies are memorialized with what appear to be stone

---

46. On the traditions concerning Rachel's tomb, see Chapter 4.

47. On the territorial burial of enemies, see F. Stavrakopoulou, 'Gog's Grave and the Use and Abuse of Corpses in Ezekiel 39:11-20', *JBL* 129 (2010), 67–84. On the Valley of Achor as a symbolic boundary of the promised land (cf. Isa. 65:9-10; Hos. 2:16-17), see R. Mosis, 'עבר', *TDOT*, 11.67–71. For the debate about biblical boundary lists, see the important essay by M. Noth, 'Studien zu den historisch-geographischen Dokumenten des Josua-Buches', *ZDPV* 58 (1935), 185–255, and the discussion of the term גבול by J. Rogerson, 'Frontiers and Borders in the Old Testament', in E. Ball (ed.), *In Search of True Wisdom: Essays in Old Testament Interpretation in Honour of Ronald E. Clements* (Sheffield: Sheffield Academic Press, 1999), 116–26.

48. Though these stone monuments might be likened to the Babylonian stelae commonly known as *kudurrus* or 'boundary' stones, the certainty surrounding these stones' function has been seriously challenged in recent years, most notably by Kathryn Slanski in her book *The Babylonian Entitlement narûs (kudurrus): A Study in their Form and Function* (Boston: ASOR, 2003). She argues that although *kudurrus* often bear inscriptions and iconography bound up with royal land grants and sales, they stood not in fields as boundary markers, but in temples as a type of royal monument, serving to commemorate and authorize the permanent acquisition or transference of sources of income. Cf. I. J. Gelb, P. Steinkeller and R. M. Whiting, *Earliest Land Tenure Systems in the Near East: Ancient Kudurrus* (2 vols. Chicago: Oriental Institute of the University of Chicago Press, 1991).

cairns (Josh. 7:26; 8:29; 10:27; 2 Sam. 18:17).[49] Elsewhere, the boundary wall of Jerusalem is defined with reference to the seemingly visible tombs of the Davidic dead (Neh. 3:16).[50]

The display of the dead in this way resonates with an ideological tone within the portrayed mortuary culture of the Hebrew Bible. Ideally, the dead are exhibited not by means of corpse-exposure, but through the constructed, ordered, 'built' environment: a tomb, a memorial, a boundary marker. There is thus a careful balance between display and non-display; between what is seen and what is unseen.[51] Though the corpses of the dead are concealed in their tombs from the eyes of the living, their presence is exhibited by means of their monumental memorialization. In this way, the essential materiality of the presence and placement of the dead localizes and imbues burial with a cultural and social agency bound up with the territoriality of the living that is not only 'remembered' or assumed, but experienced visually.[52] And yet this materialized territoriality is not solely bound to the visual exhibition of land tenure alone. More particularly, the material memorialization of the mortuary landscape goes some way to giving places socio-cultural 'genealogies',[53] rooting them to the past and structuring intergenerational social responses to the landscape – including its role, shared with the dead, in the mediation of cultural memory.[54]

---

49. Burial beneath or behind a cairn is presented in the Hebrew Bible as a form of interment associated with so-called dishonourable deaths (Achan in Josh. 7:26; the king of Ai in Josh. 8:29; five Amorite kings in Josh. 10:27; Absalom in 2 Sam. 18:17). Though not 'ideal', this form of corpse treatment nonetheless adheres to the apparent social preference for the burial of a corpse, and may reflect the belief that the 'spirits' of those suffering a violent death needed to be pinned down to prevent them rising up and causing trouble for the living (cf. Bloch-Smith, *Judahite Burial Practices*, 103) and/or to mark the burial site of the 'deviant' or 'dangerous' dead.

50. On this and associated texts, see Chapter 5.

51. On the biblical preference for interment, and the revulsion of exposed corpses, see the discussions in Olyan, 'Neglected Aspects', esp. 603–11; Stavrakopoulou, 'Gog's Grave', esp. 67–76.

52. On the role of the visual in memory-making and its mortuary contexts, see Hallam and Hockey, *Death, Memory and Material Culture*, 129–54.

53. Cf. P. A. McAnany, *Living with the Ancestors: Kinship and Kingship in Ancient Maya Society* (Austin, TX: University of Texas Press, 1995), 65; Hallam and Hockey, *Death, Memory and Material Culture*, 7.

54. See especially J. Assmann, *Das kulturelle Gedächtnis. Schrift, Erinnerung und politische Identität in frühen Hochkulturen* (München: Beck, 1992), who draws on Maurice Halbwachs' work on collective memory. An edited English translation of Halbwachs' discussion of the topography of memory can be found in M. Halbwachs, *On Collective Memory* (ed. and trans. L. A. Coser. Chicago: University of Chicago Press, 1992), 191–235. Halbwachs' study also informs the important work by Jonker, *Topography of Remembrance*, esp. 16–31. On the potential within mortuary culture to keep social memory 'in motion', see M. S. Chesson, 'Remembering and Forgetting in Early Bronze Age Mortuary Practices

Importantly, however, the monumentalized mortuary landscape need not be immovably and exclusively fixed in a particular past, but can acquire new and changing socio-cultural meanings as a part of its mediatory role in cultural memory. Thus within and beyond the Hebrew Bible, for example, Rachel's tomb functions both as a focus of 'household' mortuary practices and as a localized territorial marker (Gen. 35:16-20), but it also serves as a symbol of exile and restoration (Jer. 31:15-17), as a locus of reconstituted 'national' and 'messianic' identities (1 Sam. 10:2; Jer. 31:15-17; Jub. 32:34; cf. Ruth 4:11; Mic. 5:1; cf. Matt. 2:18), and even today as both a claimed socio-political stake in the ground and as a site of fertility petitions for many socio-religious groups.[55]

The monumentalized mortuary landscape is to be related in part to the use of standing stones within many death cultures throughout ancient West Asia and the eastern Mediterranean in the second and first millennia BCE. While standing stones are known to have served a variety of (not necessarily discrete) 'commemorative' functions, their frequent place in (perhaps higher status) mortuary and ancestral cults is now broadly accepted, particularly in view of Egyptian, Mesopotamian and Phoenicio-Punic inscribed monuments alluding to their cultic, mortuary associations, and the famous Ugaritic portrayal of the duties of the ideal son in the Tale of Aqhat, in which the setting up of a stela for a divine ancestor is most favourably presented (*KTU* 1.17.1.25-34; cf. 6.13; 6.14).[56]

The extent to which standing stones are seen to manifest, deify, or merely symbolize or represent the dead is uncertain – and likely dependent on the (changing) context-specific particularities of the stones themselves, including, perhaps, the perspective of the viewer before whom the stone is exhibited.[57] Also

---

on the Southeastern Dead Sea Plain, Jordan', in N. Laneri (ed.), *Performing Death: Social Analyses of Funerary Traditions in the Ancient Near East and Mediterranean* (University of Chicago Oriental Institute Seminars, 3; Chicago: Oriental Institute of the University of Chicago, 2007), 109–39.

55. See Chapter 4.

56. See especially J. C. de Moor, 'Standing Stones and Ancestor Worship', *UF* 27 (1995), 1–20; T. J. Lewis, *Cults of the Dead in Ancient Israel and Ugarit* (HSM, 39; Atlanta, GA: Scholars Press, 1989), 118–20; Bloch-Smith, *Judahite Burial Practices*, 113–14; van der Toorn, *Family Religion*, 206–35; M. S. Smith, *The Origins of Biblical Monotheism: Israel's Polytheistic Background and the Ugaritic Texts* (Oxford: Oxford University Press, 2001), 68–70; cf. C. F. Graesser, 'Standing Stones in Ancient Palestine', *BA* 35 (1972), 34–64; T. N. D. Mettinger, *No Graven Image? Israelite Aniconism in Its Ancient Near Eastern Context* (ConBOT, 42; Stockholm: Almqvist & Wiksell, 1995); Z. Zevit, *The Religions of Ancient Israel: A Synthesis of Parallactic Approaches* (London: Continuum, 2001), 256–62. There is some evidence to suggest that the cultic status of standing stones, and their close identification with the divine, led in some cases to their deification, see K. van der Toorn, 'Worshipping Stones: On the Deification of Cult Symbols', *JNSL* 23 (1997), 1–14.

57. Similar questions can be posed in discussing perceptions of the nature of cult statues. However, it may be that these questions are more problematic for some modern scholars than

uncertain is the degree to which a standing stone might function as a marker of a specific burial (whether there or elsewhere), or as a memorial indexing more broadly the presence of the dead (whether there or elsewhere). Indeed, there is some evidence to suggest that ancestral stelae were set up not at or near the tombs of the dead, but in a local sanctuary.[58] Despite these uncertainties, most are agreed that – among their various functions – standing stones are closely aligned with mortuary and ancestral practices.

There are several indications that similar perspectives inform some of the biblical portrayals of standing stones (often labelled מצבות). Though they are cult objects castigated in certain texts,[59] they are depicted more favourably or neutrally in others.[60] Significantly, these include texts in which they are associated with ancestor cults and mortuary practices. In 2 Sam. 18:18, it is claimed that the descendantless Absalom set up his own memorial monument (described as both a מצבה and a יד) to function after his death as a permanent invocation of his name – a sardonic variation on a theme already attested in the Ugaritic Tale of Aqhat.[61] A similar motif appears in Isa. 56:5, in which the functions of the ancestral cult – the perpetuation of the name, memory and existence of the dead – are mimicked in the promise that Yhwh will give the eunuch a monument (יד) and an eternally enduring name to outstrip the value of any descendants. And in Gen. 31:44-54, stone monuments are set up to mark a boundary agreement between Jacob and Laban in the names of their ancestral deities.[62]

This last text is one in a series of narratives in Genesis–Joshua argued by Alan Cooper and Bernard Goldstein to show that in certain biblical traditions, the setting up of stone monuments in Canaan signals the installation of Israel's deity by

for those more comfortable with the materiality of cult – ancient and modern. With this in mind, it is worth noting Karel van der Toorn's observations about the 'sophisticated theology of the cult image' according to which 'the god might inhabit his image, without ever being its prisoner' ('Worshipping Stones', 2). On this topic, see the collection of essays edited by van der Toorn, *The Image and the Book: Iconic Cults, Aniconism, and the Rise of Book Religion in Israel and the Ancient Near East* (CBET, 21; Leuven: Peeters, 1997).

58. See van der Toorn, *Family Religion*, 160–61; Lewis, 'Family, Household, and Local Religion', 69; Olyan, 'Family Religion', 115. Interestingly, this would render ancestral stelae more akin to Slanski's *kudurrus* than might be assumed (see n. 48). Temples are the locations of what appear to be memorial monuments in 1 Kgs 7:15-22 and Isa. 56:5 (see Chapter 5) and possibly also Gen. 28:18; 35:14 (see Chapter 4).

59. E.g. Exod. 23:24; 34:13; Lev. 26:1; Deut. 7:5; 12:3; 16:22; 1 Kgs 14:23; 2 Kgs 3:2; 10:26-27; 17:10; 18:4; 23:14; 2 Chr. 14:3; 31:1; Jer. 43:13; Mic. 5:13.

60. E.g. Gen. 28:18, 22; 31:13; 35:14, 20; Exod. 24:4; Hos. 3:4.

61. See B. G. Ockinga, 'A Note on 2 Samuel 18.18', *BN* 31 (1986), 31–34.

62. For a detailed discussion of Gen. 31:44-54, see Chapter 4. For Isa. 56:5, see Chapter 5. Other biblical examples of stone monuments set in a mortuary context include Gen. 35:19-20; 2 Kgs 23:15-18 and possibly Isa. 57:8.

imitating the ritual use of ancestral stelae to mark land occupation.⁶³ Though this important proposal might find some support in the present discussion, Cooper and Goldstein appear unaware of the ways in which some traditional societies mark land with the graves or mortuary symbols of the territorial dead, nor do they reflect upon biblical texts which appear to be more overt in engaging with this expression of territorialism. Rather, their theory is based on two explicit assumptions: first, that almost every מצבה in key texts represents a deified ancestor, and second, that because the term אלהים can in some biblical texts refer to the deified dead, it should be read wherever possible not as a reference to the God of Israel, nor to 'foreign' gods, but to the ancestors.⁶⁴ According to this position, the repeated insistence in several biblical narratives that Yhwh is Israel's אלהים is a polemical attempt to set Yhwh over and against the deified dead (אלהים) of local ancestor cults: 'There is only one ʾelohim, namely YHWH, and he is the sole owner of the land'.⁶⁵

Though their discussion is in many ways bold and illuminating, its detailed over-interpretation of complex traditions is further weakened by the somewhat heavy imposition of the aforementioned assumptions upon some ambiguous texts that contain no other allusions to ancestor worship and simply cannot bear the interpretative load placed upon them.⁶⁶ It also assumes a fixed form of cultural meaning for מצבות which is socio-culturally improbable, even within the crafted context of the biblical literature. By way of contrast, the present study will include a re-examination of some of these texts, offering what is intended to be a more nuanced, critical and developed evaluation of their territorial and ideological agendas.

In spite of its limitations, however, Cooper and Goldstein's emphasis on the territoriality of memorials usefully highlights the sharp, colonial tone sounded by many biblical polemics concerning space and place, which in other texts is imaged as dependent upon the kinship between the dead in their tombs and their living descendants. Without the dead already in place, the living have no claim to space, but instead will suffer only displacement and abandonment, as Isa. 22:16-18 threatens:

---

63. A. Cooper and B. R. Goldstein, 'The Cult of the Dead and the Theme of Entry into the Land', *BibInt* 1 (1993), 285–303. The texts they highlight are Gen. 12:1-9; 28:10-22; 31:1–32:3; 33:18-20; 35:1-20; Exod. 24:1-11; Deuteronomy 27; Joshua 24.

64. On the use of אלהים as a term for the deified dead, see below.

65. Cooper and Goldstein, 'The Cult of the Dead', 285–303, here 299, following Brichto, 'Kin, Cult, Land, and Afterlife', 11.

66. Key features of Cooper and Goldstein's interpretative scheme (including ritual meals and altar constructions) occur in many other biblical texts devoid of reference or allusion to practices pertaining to the dead. Note that Cooper and Goldstein's suggestion has been similarly criticized as 'maximalist' by Lewis, 'How Far Can Texts Take Us?', 187.

What right do you have here? Who do you have here, that you have cut out a tomb here for yourself, cutting a tomb on the height, and carving out a dwelling for yourself in the rock? Yhwh is about to hurl you away severely, fellow. He will seize firm hold of you, whirl you round and round and throw you like a ball into a wide land; there you shall die . . .

Venerating the Dead

The rooting of the dead and their descendants to place credits an ongoing and powerful social role to the deceased, congruent with the findings of many socio-anthropological and socio-archaeological studies of both territorialism and mortuary practice in so-called traditional societies. And yet, some might suppose that the dead are unlikely or even unable to have performed roles of this sort within ancient Israelite and Judahite cultures. Indeed, in spite of biblical and archaeological indications that the dead might be perceived as being socially powerful, some scholars assume or maintain that the social role of the dead in the lives of the living is improbable – not least given the emphatic insistence in certain biblical texts that corpses, bones and (by extension) graves are ritual and social pollutants,[67] a biblical view which is all too often held to account for the apparent tendency in Israelite and Judahite cultures to locate the dead beyond the settlements of the living.[68]

But as others have argued, biblical polemics against the dead are themselves suggestive of the dead being perceived (in certain circles at least) to perform powerful roles within the living community. Given the quality and quantity of studies devoted to this particular theme, there is no need here for a detailed rehearsal of this material;[69] collectively, however, these studies have made a

---

67. Lev. 21:1-15; 22:4; Num. 5:2; 6:1-12; 9:6-10; 19; 31:19-24; Deut. 26:13-15; Ezek. 39:11-15; Hagg. 2:12-14; cf. Deut. 21:23.

68. E.g. W. T. Pitard, 'Tombs and Offerings: Archaeological Data and Comparative Methodology in the Study of Death in Israel', in B. M. Gittlen (ed.), *Sacred Time, Sacred Place: Archaeology and the Religion of Israel* (Winona Lake, IN: Eisenbrauns, 2002), 145–67, here 150; see also Wright, *Disposal of Impurity*, 120; *contra* R. Wenning, 'Bestattungen im königszeitlichen Juda', *ThQ* 177 (1997), 82–93; see also S. R. Wolff, 'Mortuary Practices in the Persian Period', *NEA* 65 (2002), 131–37.

69. Among the most important contributions to the debate of the last twenty-five years are those by Lewis (1989, 1991, 2002, 2008), Bloch-Smith (1992), Cooper and Goldstein (1993 n. 63) and van der Toorn (1992, 2008), plus the following: K. Spronk, *Beatific Afterlife in Ancient Israel and in the Ancient Near East* (AOAT, 219; Neukirchen-Vluyn: Neukirchener Verlag, 1986); J. Tropper, *Nekromantie: Totenbefragung im Alten Orient und im Alten Testament* (AOAT, 223; Neukirchen-Vluyn: Neukirchener Verlag, 1989); S. Ackerman, *Under Every Green Tree: Popular Religion in Sixth-Century Judah* (HSM, 46; Atlanta, GA: Scholars Press, 1992); K. van der Toorn, 'Funerary Rituals and Beatific Afterlife in Ugaritic Texts and the Bible', *BiOr* 48 (1991), 40–66; idem, 'Ilib and the God

persuasive case for the continued and active social interrelation of the dead and the living, expressed in ritual form: interaction with the dead extended beyond funerary practices to include the invocation and perpetuation of their name (1 Sam. 28:15; 2 Sam. 18:18; cf. Prov. 10:7; Ps. 49:12; Ruth 4:10), the feeding of the dead (Deut. 26:14; Isa. 57:6; 65:1-4; Ps. 16:3-4; 106:28; Tob. 4:17; Sir. 30:18; cf. Gen. 15:2) and consulting the dead (1 Sam. 28:3-25; Isa. 8:19-20; 19:3; 29:4). As the designation אלהים in certain texts suggests (1 Sam. 28:13; Isa. 8:19; cf. 2 Sam. 14:16; Num. 25:2; Ps. 106:28), the dead were likely considered deified or divine, in the sense that they were active members of the divine worlds with which ancient Israelites and Judahites engaged, though in the seemingly tiered hierarchies of these worlds, they were unlikely to have been aligned with 'high gods' such as El, Baal and Yhwh.[70]

The powerful role of the dead in the lives of the living likely goes some way towards explaining the biblical condemnation of certain practices associated with the dead – most probably because within a context of what might be loosely described as emergent monotheisms, the dead posed considerable competition to the centralized, exclusive preferences of the biblical Yhwh.[71] And so it is interesting that for some scholars, too, the powerful dead of ancient Israel and Judah are also to be resisted: some have argued for a distinctly minimalist interpretation of

---

of the Father', *UF* 25 (1993), 379–87; H. Niehr, 'Ein unerkannter Text zur Nekromantie in Israel: Bemerkungen zum religionsgeschichtlichen Hintergrund von 2 Sam 12,16a', *UF* 23 (1991), 301–06; idem, 'Aspekte des Totengedenkeis im Juda der Königszeit' *ThQ* 178 (1998), 1–13; idem, 'Changed Status of the Dead in Yehud', 136–55; B. B. Schmidt, *Israel's Beneficent Dead: Ancestor Cult and Necromancy in Ancient Israelite Religion and Tradition* (FAT, 11; Tübingen: J. C. B. Mohr, 1994; repr. edn Winona Lake, IN: Eisenbrauns, 1996); idem, 'Memory as Immortality: Countering the Dreaded "Death After Death" in Ancient Israelite Society', in A. J. Peck and J. Neusner (eds), *Judaism in Late Antiquity* (Leiden: Brill, 2000), 87–100; J. Blenkinsopp, 'Deuteronomy and the Politics of Post-Mortem Existence', *VT* 45 (1995), 1–16; T. Podella, 'Nekromantie', *ThQ* 177 (1997), 121–33; M. Morisi, 'Il culto siro-palestinese dei morti e il culto greco degli eroi: l'intiquieta(nte) ricerca del sovrumano tra pietà privata e ufficialità', *Henoch* 20 (1998), 3–50; T. Veijola, '"Fluch des Totengeistes ist der Aufgehängte" (Deut 21, 23)', *UF* 32 (2000), 543–53; E. Bloch-Smith, 'Life in Judah from the Perspective of the Dead', *NEA* 65 (2002b), 120–30; C. Peri, *Il regno del nemico* (Studi Biblici, 140; Brescia: Paideia Editrice, 2003); J. N. Lightstone, *The Commerce of the Sacred: Mediation of the Divine among Jews in the Greco-Roman World* (2nd edn; New York: Columbia University Press, 2006), 41–62; H. Nutkowicz, *L'homme face à la mort au royaume de Juda: Rites, pratiques et représentations* (Paris: Cerf, 2006); Olyan, 'Family Religion in Israel and the Wider Levant', 113–26.

70. See Lewis, 'How Far Can Texts Take Us?', 198. Note, however, that the high status of the dead is suggested by certain theophoric names: K. van der Toorn, 'Ancestors and Anthroponyms: Kinship Terms as Theophoric Elements in Hebrew Names', *ZAW* 108 (1996), 1–11.

71. E.g. Lev. 19:28, 31; Deut. 14:1; 18:9-12; 26:14; Isa. 8:19-20; 57:3-13; 65:1-5; Ps. 106:28. On 'monotheism', see 143, n. 34.

material pertaining to death cult practices, asserting (for example) that the ancestors were of 'marginal importance' to the ancient Israelites and Judahites, who were 'more concerned with the living than the dead',[72] or claiming that within these societies, a belief in the beneficent and powerful dead was 'nonexistent', and that some ritual practices pertaining to the dead were simply 'foreign' imports from Mesopotamia, while ancestor cults themselves are the 'relics' of outdated anthropological models.[73] Others have dismissed the mortuary culture of ancient Israel and Judah as mere 'popular religion', opposed to or distinct from the 'official' religion of 'orthodox' Yahwism.[74]

As I have suggested elsewhere, these opinions may well be shaped to a degree by a cultural or intellectual difficulty in understanding the ritualized interrelation and interaction of ancestors and descendants – or even a discomfort with the perceived 'otherness' of certain beliefs and practices perhaps felt to be alien to contemporary (and ostensibly secularized) dominant Western responses to the dead.[75] Indeed, in most parts of Western Europe, the UK and the US today, the dead tend to be far more marginalized, isolated or separated from the living.[76] This distancing of the dead from the living is bound up with the modernist notion (notably perpetuated in Western academia)[77] which assumes that death

---

72. P. S. Johnston, *Shades of Sheol: Death and Afterlife in the Old Testament* (Leicester: Apollos, 2002), 195.

73. Schmidt, *Israel's Beneficent Dead*, 275, 292; followed by R. Schmitt, 'The Problem of Magic and Monotheism in the Book of Leviticus', *JHS* 8/11 (2008), 2–12. For a sharp critique of Schmidt's position, see Lewis, 'How Far Can Texts Take Us?', 189–202.

74. E.g. J. B. Segal, 'Popular Religion in Ancient Israel', *JJS* 27 (1976), 1–22; P. Xella, 'Il "culto dei morti" nell' Antico Testamento', in V. Lanternari, M. Massenzio and D. Sabbatucci (eds), *Scritti in memoria di Angelo Brelich* (Rome: Dedalo, 1982), 645–66; idem, 'Death and the Afterlife in Canaanite and Hebrew Thought', *CANE*, 4.2,059–70; Spronk, *Beatific Afterlife in Ancient Israel*, esp. 247–58, 281, 344–46; G. E. Mendenhall 'From Witchcraft to Justice: Death and Afterlife in the Old Testament', in H. Obayashi (ed.), *Death and Afterlife: Perspectives of World Religions* (London: Praeger, 1992), 67–81; J. Milgrom, *Leviticus 17–22: A New Translation with Introduction and Commentary* (AB, 3A; New York: Doubleday, 2000), 1,375–82; P. J. King and L. E. Stager, *Life in Biblical Israel* (LAI; Louisville, KY: Westminster John Knox Press, 2001), 376–80; cf. Zevit, *Religions of Ancient Israel*, 665.

75. Stavrakopoulou, '"Popular" Religion and "Official" Religion', esp. 44–47; cf. J. Hockey, 'The View from the West', in G. Howarth and P. C. Jupp (eds), *Contemporary Issues in the Sociology of Death, Dying and Disposal* (Basingstoke: Macmillan, 1996), 3–16.

76. N. Barley, *Dancing on the Grave: Encounters with Death* (London: John Murray, 1995); Parker Pearson, *Archaeology of Death and Burial*, 40–49.

77. C. Valentine, 'Academic Constructions of Bereavement', *Mortality* 11.1 (2006), 57–78; cf. D. Klass and R. Goss, 'Spiritual Bonds to the Dead in Cross-Cultural and Historical Perspective: Comparative Religion and Modern Grief', *Death Studies* 23 (1999), 547–67.

irrevocably breaks the active social relationship between the newly deceased and the living community of which they were a part, so that the living are unable to communicate with the dead, and the dead are unable to communicate with the living.[78] As Elizabeth Hallam, Jenny Hockey and Glennys Howarth comment:

> [The] empiricist, materialist models which lie at the core of Western thought and experience . . . relegate the dead to peripheral religious practices . . . Without muscles to flex, tongues to speak or fists to shake, the dead become nothing more than memories which are locked within the imaginations of others.[79]

As such, ancestor worship and other death cult practices have been heavily caricatured in Western intellectual discourse since the nineteenth century as 'primitive' or 'exotic' forms of religion,[80] and continue to be treated by many as inferior to the monotheisms dominating religious perspectives today.[81] However, it is also likely that a particular and persistent religio-cultural skepticism underlies an apparent preference within biblical scholarship towards diminishing the place or value of the dead within the cultures giving rise to the Hebrew Bible. This skepticism is probably shaped to a notable extent by the confessional heritage of biblical studies and its tendency (even today) towards the othering of non-Western attitudes to the dead. This may go some way towards explaining why some scholars are still careful to distance certain Israelite and Judahite practices dealing with the dead from contemporary Christian death rituals and their accompanying beliefs,[82] and why others attempt to minimize the religious role of the dead in Israel and Judah in favour of crediting Christianity with a unique and exclusive claim to agency beyond the grave.[83]

This tradition of a scholarly resistance in biblical studies to the powerful dead has contributed to the perpetuation of some of the more pejorative associations of descriptors frequently attested in discussions of this theme, including 'cult

---

78. D. Klass, P. Silverman and J. Nickman, *Continuing Bonds* (Philadelphia: Taylor and Francis, 1996); G. Bennett and K. M. Bennett, 'The Presence of the Dead: An Empirical Study', *Mortality* 5.2 (2000), 139–57; D. Francis, L. Kellaher and G. Neophytou, 'The Cemetery: The Evidence of Continuing Bonds', in J. Hockey, J. Katz and N. Small (eds), *Grief, Mourning and Death Ritual* (Buckingham: Open University Press, 2001), 226–36. Note also, however, the comments offered earlier in n. 13.

79. Hallam, Hockey and Howarth, *Beyond the Body*, 146.

80. E.g. L. B. Paton, *Spiritism and the Cult of the Dead in Antiquity* (London: Hodder & Stoughton, 1921); J. G. Frazer, *Folklore in the Old Testament: Studies in Comparative Religion, Legend and Law* (Abridged edn. London: Macmillan, 1923), N. J. Tromp, *Primitive Conceptions of Death and the Nether World in the Old Testament* (BO, 21; Rome: Pontifical Biblical Institute, 1969); Mendenhall, 'From Witchcraft to Justice', 67–81.

81. E.g. Milgrom, *Leviticus 17–22*, 1,783–84.

82. E.g. Schmidt, *Israel's Beneficent Dead*, 9–11.

83. E.g. Johnston, *Shades of Sheol*, 239.

of the dead', 'ancestor worship' and 'mortuary cult'. Earlier scholarship sought to remedy the ambiguity or confusion as to what these terms might or should signify, and the extent (if any) to which they ought to be distinguished.[84] But as discussions have moved during recent decades beyond the somewhat dry hyper-categorizing of rituals and practices pertaining to the dead, the label 'cult of the dead' has now become a widely used and broad designation for various ritual responses to the dead beyond the primary treatment of the corpse itself (whether buried, cremated, mutilated, lost or exposed).[85] Thus certain rituals – including the memorialization or invocation of the dead, the feasting with or alongside the dead, or prayers for or petitions to the dead – are now often discussed within the broad parameters of a 'death cult' or a 'cult of the dead'. But for some, this reflects a lack of clarity on the part of the interpreter, and risks mistaking or mislabelling what are merely commemorative acts for the dead as 'religious' behaviour – and indeed, as the worship of the dead.[86] This perspective is well illustrated in the work of Brian Schmidt, whose reductionist account of ancestor cult and necromancy is grounded on the supposition that within (what he terms) ancient Israelite religion, the dead 'do not appear to have the same degree or quality of divinity as the high god(s), nor can they act independently of the god(s)', and therefore 'they are not worthy of, and unlike the gods, they do not receive, worship'. Thus for Schmidt, the notion of an Israelite ancestor cult 'has persisted in biblical studies well beyond its allotted lifespan'.[87]

However, Schmidt roots his analysis in the influential works of Max Gluckman, Meyer Fortes and (especially) Ian Morris, who cumulatively impose what amounts to a sharp distinction between the social and antisocial aims of responses to the dead, whereby 'mortuary ritual' (both funerary and commemorative) consists of rite-of-passage practices to separate and keep the dead from the living, while 'death cult' (including ancestor cult and necromancy) employs rituals enabling the living to actively access (or 'manipulate') the dead.[88] But this distinction

---

84. E.g. W. O. E. Oesterley, *Immortality and the Unseen World – A Study in Old Testament Religion* (London: SPCK, 1921), 110–12; R. de Vaux, *Ancient Israel: Its Life and Institutions* (2nd edn; London: Darton, Longman & Todd, 1965), 56–61. See also the review of older scholarship on this topic in Spronk, *Beatific Afterlife*, 25–85.

85. For a convenient overview of the shifting emphases in this debate, see E. Bloch-Smith, 'Death in the Life of Israel', in B. M. Gittlen (ed.), *Sacred Time, Sacred Place: Archaeology and the Religion of Israel* (Winona Lake, IN: Eisenbrauns, 2002a), 139–43.

86. E.g. Y. Kaufmann, *The Religion of Israel: From Its Beginnings to the Babylonian Exile* (trans. M. Greenberg; New York: Schocken, 1972), 312–13; Schmidt, *Israel's Beneficent Dead*, esp. 4–13; note also the very cautious and somewhat conservative discussion in J. D. Levenson, *Resurrection and the Restoration of Israel: The Ultimate Victory of the God of Life* (New Haven: Yale University Press, 2006), 46–66, which draws heavily on Johnston's *Shades of Sheol*.

87. Schmidt, *Israel's Beneficent Dead*, 9, 292, see also 274–75.

88. M. Gluckman, 'Mortuary Customs and the Belief in Survival after Death among the

over-emphasizes the 'separation' processes employed to deal with the liminality of the corpse, at the cost of diminishing or ignoring the socially transformative, inclusive and constructive function of mortuary practices within the social group: in a majority of known societies, the biological death of the body 'articulates a boundary' that is not an 'end' but an 'event-horizon' – an aspect of a process in which 'the potential for death always resides in the living, and the living become the dead'.[89] Whether or not the dead are worshipped or merely commemorated, post-funerary practices articulate the ongoing social presence of the dead among the living, rather than their asocial absence.

As others have argued, it seems most likely that the ancient Israelite and Judahite dead were the recipients of cultic activities reaching beyond mere commemoration and instead placing them firmly within the sphere of household religion.[90] Indeed, the evidence available – though by nature only partial – is strongly suggestive of the veneration of the dead in cultic form. The extent to which this type of religious activity might be termed 'worship' is in many ways a question of the perspective of the interpreter, as much as a question of evidence. Given that the dead appear to have played a high-profile role in household cults in most ancient West Asian contexts (including royal and other elite households), there is good reason to accept the proposal that the dead might have been honoured not only in the more 'private' space of the home or tomb, but in both local and higher status cult places – including monumental temples used or sponsored by the ruling classes,[91] suggesting that the dead played a part at cult places inhabited by deities. And food and drink rituals and the invocation or addressing of the dead signal a response from the living less like commemoration and rather more like veneration, if not – sometimes – worship.

South-Eastern Bantu', *Bantu Studies* 11 (1937), 117–36; M. Fortes, 'Some Reflections on Ancestor Worship in West Africa', in M. Fortes and G. Dieterlin (eds), *African Systems of Thought* (Oxford: Oxford University Press, 1965), 122–24; I. Morris, 'Attitudes Toward Death in Archaic Greece', *Classical Antiquity* 8 (1989), 296–320; idem, 'The Archaeology of the Ancestors: The Saxe/Goldstein Hypothesis Revisited', *Cambridge Archaeological Journal* 1 (1991), 147–69; idem, *Death-Ritual and Social Structure in Classical Antiquity* (Cambridge: Cambridge Univesity Press, 1992): cf. Schmidt, *Israel's Beneficent Dead*, 4–13, 283–84, 289–91.

89. J. R. Sofaer, *The Body as Material Culture: A Theoretical Osteoarchaeology* (Cambridge: Cambridge University Press, 2006), 44, citing C. Battersby, 'Her Body/Her Boundaries: Gender and the Metaphysics of Containment', in A. Benjamin (ed.), *Journal of Philosophy and the Visual Arts: The Body* (London: Academic Group, 1993), 31–39, here 36.

90. See the literature cited in nn. 17 and 69. On the term 'household', see S. K. Stowers, 'Theorizing the Religion of Ancient Households and Families', in J. Bodel and S. M. Olyan (eds), *Household and Family Religion in Antiquity* (Oxford: Blackwell, 2008), 5–19.

91. Van der Toorn, *Family Religion*, 160–61; Lewis, 'Family, Household, and Local Religion', 69; Olyan, 'Family Religion', 115.

Thus in some settings, ritual practices concerning the dead might reflect a belief in the divine or deified nature of the deceased, while in others they may relate to a perception that the dead continue to play a social and influential role within the living community, whether or not the dead are considered 'divine'. Accordingly, the term 'veneration' is thus usefully and appropriately ambivalent for the purposes of the present discussion, which is both more interested in the territorial function of the dead than the degree to which they were considered divine, and keen to avoid the distortions produced by rigid over-distinctions between 'cult' and 'worship'.

But within these particular cultures, who are the dead? As social actors, the dead play a role in the lives of the living inextricably linked with forms of collective identity in the living community – of the family, of the household, of the local group. In many so-called traditional societies, this therefore renders the dead the ancestors, casting the living as their direct descendants and the inheritors of aspects or extensions of the personae of the dead, including land, wisdom, and even their very existence.[92] Inherent within this powerful notion of descent is thus 'the authority of the dead and the charisma of the ancestor'.[93] Importantly, much of this authority and charisma is exhibited not only by means of direct lineal descent within families, but across the living community too, manifested in the dynamics of 'nested' social groups, as Daniel Fleming suggests:

> Ancestors, real or imagined, bind people both into single households and into larger groups made up of multiple households . . . [the] veneration of ancestors should also contribute to the foundation for whole communities, not just for individual households.[94]

Indeed, in most ancient West Asian societies, a household's dead would tend to be cast as ancestors, although in a broader local context or in royal households, 'the dead' might also be presented as a communal and familiar but more generic collective (such as the Ugaritic *mtm*) within the divine domain.[95]

---

92. Among the Beng of West Africa, for example, babies are the reincarnations of ancestors; see A. Gottlieb, *The Afterlife Is Where We Come From: The Culture of Infancy in West Africa* (Chicago: University of Chicago Press, 2004). My thanks to Traci Ardren for bringing this book to my attention.

93. Harrison, *Dominion of the Dead*, 94

94. Fleming, 'Household and Community Religion', 53, drawing on McAnany, *Living with the Ancestors*, 159, 163–64.

95. Though this is not to diminish the status of some members of the (perhaps royal) dead at Ugarit as ancestors; indeed, on the 'household' and 'family' dynamics of the so-called pantheon of high gods at Ugarit, see Schloen, *The House of the Father*, esp. 349–57. In a recent essay, Karel van der Toorn suggests that 'the dead' might be the placed *remains* of deceased family members, while the family or ancestral 'gods' are the *images* used in the

It is thus the (enduring) active and social interrelation of the living and the dead which appears to characterize not only the mortuary cultures of these societies (including those of Israel and Judah), but their lived cultures as well. In casting the dead as ancestors venerated by the household and recognized (perhaps more generically) within the local community, the social group exhibits (or in its ritual setting, performs) what might be conveniently termed a 'mnemonics of belonging', by which the dead and the living collectively endorse and perpetuate their shared identity – an identity (as has been argued already) significantly rooted in place. Douglas Davies observes that 'it is in societies which believe that a beneficial relationship may exist between the living and the dead that kinship facts of descent are used to establish the ancestors as significant individuals'.[96] In the Hebrew Bible, this beneficial relationship is ideologically framed and territorially exploited.

Centralizing the Dead

Given the importance of the dead in marking territory, biblical land ideologies exhibit a clash between 'traditional' practice and the centralizing drive of the temple culture promoted by scribal elites primarily responsible for the composition and compilation of the Hebrew Bible. In its broadest terms, this clash is evident in the contrast between the persistent appeals to the presence of Israel's forefathers in the land, whose territories are presented as ancestral holdings, and the repeated imaging of Yhwh as an imperial landowner, sited in his temple-city, granting land to his people.

The centralizing, imperial imaging of Yhwh probably derives much (though not all) of its force from the Persian period contexts of Jerusalem's temple culture, a culture at the heart of the community claiming a 'return' from exile and legitimate ('rightful') occupation of the territories comprising Yehud.[97] Crucially,

---

ancestral cult ('Family Religion in Second Millennium West Asia', 27). For 'the dead' in the Hebrew Bible, see (for example) Isa. 26:14; Ps. 88:11.

96. Davies, *Death, Ritual and Belief*, 110.

97. The Persian empire's apparent preference for localized but carefully controlled governments, facilitated by forced migrations and 'repatriation' programmes, likely informs in part the biblical claim that the Persian monarchy endorsed the 'release' of captive communities and sponsored the rebuilding of the Jerusalem temple (Isa. 44:24-28; 45:1-4; Ezra 1:1-4; 6:3-5; 7:11-26; Neh. 2:7-8; 2 Chr. 36:22-23); see K. G. Hogland, *Achaemenid Imperial Administration in Syria-Palestine and the Missions of Ezra and Nehemiah* (SBLDS, 125; Atlanta, GA: Scholars Press, 1992), 237–39; M. Liverani, *Israel's History and the History of Israel* (trans. C. Peri and P. R. Davies; London: Equinox, 2005), 251–61; Lipschits, 'Achaemenid Imperial Policy'; J. Kessler, 'Persia's Loyal Yahwists: Power, Identity and Ethnicity in Achaemenid Yehud', in O. Lipschits and M. Oeming (eds), *Judah and the Judeans in the Persian Period* (Winona Lake, IN: Eisenbrauns, 2006), 91–121. It is important to note that the biblical imaging of Yhwh as an imperial landowner might also

this claim is in many texts pitched in the terms of a right to an inherited, ancestral land, symbolized or evoked either by the divine gift of land and lineage to the forefathers (for example, Gen. 12:7; 13:14-17; 15:7; 26:3-5; cf. Isa. 41:8-10; Jer. 30:10; 46:27; Ezek. 33:24), or as a return to inheritable ancestral landholdings akin to the allotted ancestral lands of the exodus/conquest generations (for example, Josh. 13:15, 24, 29; 15:1, 20; cf. Jer. 16:14-15; Ezra 2:1-70; Neh. 7:6-73).[98] In both traditions, of course, the indigenous populations are othered as 'Canaanites' or other 'foreign' peoples, to be out-bred, marginalized, displaced or eradicated from the landscape (so Gen. 19:30-38; Num. 33:51-53; Deut. 3:1-11; 7:1-6, 17-26; Josh. 24:11-13; Neh. 13:23-29).[99] The claim to an ancestral land is thus broadly centralized in its ideological focus on Yehud, imaging the God of Jerusalem as the imperial landowner granting land to the elites of the temple-city community who claim a 'return' from exile and direct and privileged descent from the former 'ancestral' occupiers of the land.

The dominant land ideologies of the Hebrew Bible are therefore both 'centralized' and 'ancestralized' – a preference credited paradigmatic expression in the patriarchal traditions of Genesis, in which the geneaological ancestors of the biblical Israel do not mark the land in a complex network of dead and buried kin, but are instead interred as just one household in just one tomb and in just one place: Machpelah. This centralization of the ancestors may well be shaped by an attempt to construct a shared identity for the incoming Yehudite community, while at the same time displacing the dead of local household cults and territories from their influential socio-religious position.[100] Thus at Machpelah, the past and

---

have been directed at diaspora groups living among 'foreigners'; however, the dominant ideologies of the Hebrew Bible nonetheless present the Jerusalem temple as the central and exclusive place of the cult of this 'imperial' god.

98. See K. W. Whitelam, 'Israel's Traditions of Origin: Reclaiming the Land', *JSOT* 44 (1989), 19–42; Liverani, *Israel's History*, 250–91.

99. The classic study remains that of N. P. Lemche, *The Canaanites and Their Land: The Tradition of the Canaanites* (JSOTS, 110; Sheffield: JSOT Press, 1991); cf. E. Ben Zvi, 'Inclusion in and Exclusion from "Israel" in Post-monarchic Biblical Texts', in S. W. Holloway and L. K. Handy (eds), *The Pitcher Is Broken: Memorial Essays for Gösta W. Ahlström* (JSOTS, 190; Sheffield: Sheffield Academic Press, 1995), 95–149; Brett, *Decolonizing God*, 79–93. For 'inclusive' readings of biblical attitudes to the 'foreign' inhabitants of the land, see the discussion in Chapter 2 and the literature cited there.

100. O. Loretz, 'Vom kanaanäischen Totenkult zur jüdischen Patriarchen – und Elternehung', *Jahrbuch des Anthropologie und Religionsgeschichte* 3 (1978), 149–201, esp. 178–89; T. Römer, 'Les récits patriarcaux contre la vénération des ancêtres: Une hypothèse concernant les "origins" d' "Israël"', in O. Abel and F. Smyth (eds), *Le Livre de Traverse: de l'exégèse biblique à l'anthropologie* (Paris: Cerf, 1992), 213–25. As Römer suggests, Yhwh's identification with the 'God(s) of the Father(s)' in the biblical traditions represents another aspect of this centralizing strategy to displace the local dead.

its tomb are modelled as an ideal for the territorial concerns of the present,[101] memorializing the patriarchal occupation of the land divinely promised, while rendering the 'traditional' mortuary culture of the ancestral dead mythologized in such a schematized manner that the past and its landscape are ostensibly centralized.[102]

It is beyond coincidence that the centralizing of the dead in the patriarchal traditions complements the strong biblical preference for centralization elsewhere (not least in the cultic centralization of the divine in the Jerusalem temple),[103] although this biblical emphasis on centralization (whether of the dead or of the god/s) likely has less to do with historical realism and more to do with an ideological resistance to plurality and diversity – and the competition between people and places that inevitably ensues. However, the central place of the patriarchs and their tomb in the biblical story of Israel also attests to the continued value of the territorial dead, despite the apparent dominance of the divine landowner in the Jerusalem temple.

Indeed, the homeland of the people 'Israel' in the Hebrew Bible is constructed as a mortuary landscape in many other biblical traditions, including the foundation myth dealing with exodus and conquest: in the book of Exodus, not only are the remains of the displaced ancestors brought 'home' to the land to support the occupation of the incoming Israelites (Gen. 47:30; 50:2-14, 25-26; Exod. 13:19; Josh. 24:32), but the exodus generation itself recognizes that belonging to a place requires the presence of graves, so that given their rootlessness and lack of belonging in Egypt, even the 'nowhere' of the wilderness becomes a potential 'somewhere' for death:[104]

> They said to Moses, 'Was it because there were no graves in Egypt that you have taken us away to die in the wilderness?' (Exod. 14:11)

In the biblical story of the past, the burial sites of the ancestors thus create a

---

101. Cf. Parker Pearson, *Archaeology of Death and Burial*, 207.

102. Note, however, that this centralization (and indeed patriarchalization) sits alongside indications in Genesis of competing and alternative constructs of lineage and descent: for traces of a system of matrilineal descent, see N. Jay, *Throughout Your Generations Forever: Sacrifice, Religion, and Paternity* (Chicago: University of Chicago Press, 1992), 94–111.

103. On this biblical preference, see D. Edelman, 'Cultic Sites and Complexes beyond the Jerusalem Temple', in F. Stavrakopoulou and J. Barton (eds), *Religious Diversity in Ancient Israel and Judah* (London: T&T Clark, 2010), 82–103.

104. On the construction of 'homeland' and 'death' for the wilderness generation, see also I. Pardes, *The Biography of Ancient Israel: National Narratives in the Bible* (Berkeley, CA: University of California Press, 2000), 122–26; A. B. Leveen, *Memory and Tradition in the Book of Numbers* (Cambridge: Cambridge University Press, 2008); and the discussion in Chapter 3.

genealogy of place, linking descendants by death to the landscape:[105] the ancestral dead are both literarily and literally 'the past personified'.[106] This is a story driven by the gain and loss of land: whether framed as emigration or immigration, exodus or exile, the perpetuation of the people of Israel is inextricably tied to their hold on the land predominantly constructed as 'home', and frequently and powerfully characterized in terms of the material, spatial, topographical and ideological dynamics of burial places and the dead they contain.

In the Hebrew Bible's portrayal of the past, there is thus displayed a tension between an ideological preference for centralization, which tends to be rendered dominant, and the often latent cultural practices and assumptions concerning the territorial dead, which are displaced and also simultaneously appropriated. The chapters that follow explore this tension by mapping out the place of the dead in the mortuary landscapes imaged in highly charged biblical traditions: from Abraham's tomb to Moses' unknown burial place, from Bethel's ancestral cult to the tombs encircling Jerusalem, the places of the dead are the sites at which biblical territorialism is set – to be exhibited, asserted and contested.

---

105. Cf. McAnany, *Living with the Ancestors*, 65.
106. Borrowing Joanna Sofaer's phrase in *Body as Material Culture*, 1.

Chapter 2

Abraham at Machpelah

From a biblical perspective, Abraham is the symbolic representative of the ancestral mediation of land and descendants. But importantly he is also the archetypal representative of the incomer: a migrant seeking a place to (make his) own. These twinned roles are quickly and programmatically established in the opening scenes of his biblical performance. Two texts illustrate this well. The first is Gen. 12:1-2, in which Yhwh says to Abra(ha)m: 'Go from your country and your kindred and your father's house to the land that I will show you; I will make of you a great nation'. Abra(ha)m's explicit dislocation from the place and people of his ancestral past smoothes his transformation into the founding father of the biblical Israel. It also renders him landless, thereby establishing his need for a new homeland, as the second text demonstrates: 'At that time the Canaanites were in the land. And Yhwh appeared to Abram and said, "To your seed I will give this land"' (Gen. 12:6-7). This is no shy acknowledgement that the land marked out for Abra(ha)m and his descendants is not empty. Rather, it is a sharp, pointed declaration that occupied land is available for the taking.

Yet in recent years it has become increasingly popular to read the Abraham narratives in the book of Genesis as a Persian-period manifesto designed to promote a peaceful, cooperative relationship between incoming (or 'returning') citizens of Yehud and indigenous communities. Framed within this context, and in contrast to the seemingly exclusivist ethnocentrism of the books of Ezra and Nehemiah,[1] Abraham is imaged not only as the founding father of the nation, but also as the paradigmatic immigrant, whose friendly relations with various 'Canaanite' groups model a tolerant and inclusive attitude to the non-Jewish groups living within and alongside the province of Yehud.[2] This reading of the Abraham narratives

---

1. See, for example, L. L. Grabbe, 'Triumph of the Pious or Failure of the Xenophobes? The Ezra-Nehemiah Reforms and Their Nachgeschichte', in S. Jones and S. Pearce (eds), *Jewish Local Patriotism and Self-Identification in the Graeco-Roman Period* (JSPS, 31; Sheffield: Sheffield Academic Press, 1998), 50–65; Ben Zvi, 'Inclusion in and Exclusion from "Israel"', 95–149; cf. D. L. Smith-Christopher, 'Between Ezra and Isaiah: Exclusion, Transformation, and Inclusion of the "Foreigner" in Post-Exilic Biblical Theology', in M. G. Brett (ed.), *Ethnicity and the Bible* (Leiden: Brill, 2002), 117–42.

2. E.g. J. L. Ska, 'Essai sur la nature et la signification du cycle d'Abraham (Gn. 11, 27–25,

is well illustrated in an essay by Albert de Pury, who argues that in the priestly traditions of Genesis, 'Abraham is placed from the beginning in an inter-tribal, inter-communitarian, "ecumenical" perspective'.[3] Accordingly, Abraham's biblical imaging as the father of a mixed multitude of tribal and ethnic groups renders him a symbol of an inclusive and foreigner-friendly nascent Judaism:

> The thoroughly positive view of Abraham as an ecumenical patriarch by the Priestly writer is remarkable. Especially if one remembers that this story was conceived and written down by a very pious and profound Jewish writer, and that the story was not originally intended to be broadcast to the world, but was meant to be read and mediated by the Jewish community in Jerusalem or wherever it lived in the diaspora . . . the Priestly writer's interpretation of Abraham is valuable not just as a testimony to a form of Jewish self-understanding in the beginning of the Persian period but as an attempt to conceive of a Jewish 'ecumenism' or monotheistic humanism in a differentiated but pacified world of (de-nationalized) nations.[4]

Others offer similarly inclusivist interpretations of the priestly perspective, some of which have been brought to bear upon debates concerning constructions of ethnicity, community, imperialism and scribal authority in Yehud.[5] Within these

---

11)', in A. Wénin (ed.), *Studies in the Book of Genesis: Literature, Redaction and History* (Leuven: Peeters, 2001), 153–77; Liverani, *Israel's History*, 258–67; cf. J. D. Levenson, 'The Universal Horizon of Biblical Particularism', in M. G. Brett (ed.), *Ethnicity and the Bible* (Leiden: Brill, 2002), 143–69. See also the nuanced discussion by J. Blenkinsopp, 'Abraham as Paradigm in the Priestly History in Genesis', *JBL* 128 (2009), 225–41.

3. A. de Pury, 'Abraham: The Priestly Writer's "Ecumenical" Ancestor', in S. L. McKenzie and T. Römer (eds), *Rethinking the Foundations: Historiography in the Ancient World and in the Bible: Essays in Honour of John Van Seters* (BZAW, 294; Berlin: de Gruyter, 2000), 163–81, here 167. Note also the description of 'ecumenical bonhomie' in R. W. L. Moberly, *The Old Testament of the Old Testament: Patriarchal Narratives and Mosaic Yahwism* (Minneapolis: Fortress Press, 1992), 104. Note too K. Schmid, 'Gibt es eine "abrahamitische Ökumene" im Alten Testament? Überlegungen zur religionspolitischen Theologie der Priesterschrift in Genesis 17', in A. C. Hagedorn and H. Pfeiffer (eds), *Die Erzväter in der biblischen Tradition* (BZAW, 400; Berlin: de Gruyter, 2009), 67–92. Regrettably, this important discussion came to my attention too late to take into account here.

4. De Pury, 'Abraham', 178; see also idem, 'Le choix de l'ancêtre', *TZ* 57 (2001), 105–14.

5. See, for example, the debates in E. T. Mullen, *Ethnic Myths and Pentateuchal Foundations: A New Approach to the Formation of the Pentateuch* (Atlanta, GA: Scholars Press, 1997); R. C. Heard, *Dynamics of Diselection: Ambiguity in Genesis 12–36 and Ethnic Boundaries in Post-Exilic Judah* (Atlanta, GA: Society of Biblical Literature, 2001); J. W. Watts (ed.), *Persia and Torah: The Theory of Imperial Authorization of the Pentateuch* (Atlanta, GA: Scholars Press, 2001); R. L. Cohn, 'Negotiating (with) the Natives: Ancestors and Identity in Genesis', *HTR* 96 (2003), 147–66; M. Douglas, *Jacob's Tears: The Priestly*

debates, perceptions of territoriality are particularly prominent. Set alongside Persian policies of forced migrations and 'repatriation' – which probably included land provision for settlers[6] – biblical portrayals of the 'post-exilic' period are frequently suggestive of conflict and competition between incoming groups and indigenous communities.[7] There is good reason to suspect that land tenure in Yehud was bound up with the socio-economic interests of the imperial overlords, and that these imperial interests were pointedly promoted in certain biblical texts (for example, Ezra 7:26; 10:8).[8] Against this background, then, the Abraham narratives continue to play an important role in assessing the shape and function of various – and likely competing – territorial ideologies of the Persian period.

Although several forms of land appropriation are imaged or implied in the Hebrew Bible,[9] the dominant dynamics of biblical territorialism are shaped by the 'national' foundation myths of patriarchs and conquest – both of which model the idea that land is allocated by divine deed[10] and that entitlement to that land is

Work of Reconciliation (Oxford: Oxford University Press, 2004); G. N. Knoppers and B. M. Levinson (eds), *The Pentateuch as Torah: New Models for Understanding its Promulgation and Acceptance* (Winona Lake, IN: Eisenbrauns, 2007).

6. P. Briant, *From Cyrus to Alexander: A History of the Persian Empire* (trans. P.T. Daniels; Winona Lake, IN: Eisenbrauns, 2002), 505–06; K. G. Hogland, *Achaemenid Imperial Administration in Syria-Palestine and the Missions of Ezra and Nehemiah* (SBLDS, 125; Atlanta, GA: Scholars Press, 1992), 237–39; D. V. Edelman, *The Origins of the 'Second' Temple: Persian Imperial Policy and the Rebuilding of Jerusalem* (London: Equinox, 2005), 342–43.

7. E.g. Ezra 4:1-4; 6:21; 9:1-2, 11-12, 14; 10; Neh. 2:10; 5:5, 12; 9:2; 10:29, 31-32.

8. See particularly P. Frei, 'Die persische Reichsautorisation: Ein Überblick', *ZABR* 1 (1996) 1–35, an English translation of which is included in the collection of essays in J. W. Watts (ed.), *Persia and Torah: The Theory of Imperial Authorization of the Pentateuch* (Atlanta, GA: Scholars Press, 2001), 1–35. The other essays in this significant volume offer responses to – and modifications of – Frei's theory; note in particular J. Blenkinsopp, 'Was the Pentateuch the Civic and Religious Constitution of the Jewish Ethnos in the Persian Period?' (41–62) and G. N. Knoppers, 'An Achaemenid Imperial Authorization of Torah in Yehud?' (115–34). Also important are the discussions in K. Schmid, 'The Persian Imperial Authorization as a Historical Problem and as a Biblical Construct: A Plea for Distinctions in the Current Debate', in G. N. Knoppers and B. M. Levinson (eds), *The Pentateuch as Torah: New Models for Understanding its Promulgation and Acceptance* (Winona Lake, IN: Eisenbrauns, 2007), 23–38, and (in the same volume) A. C. Hagedorn, 'Local Law in an Imperial Context: The Role of Torah in the (Imagined) Persian Period' (57–76).

9. These include ancestral inheritance, royal grant, divine deed, redemption, colonial seizure, strategies of debt recovery, legal transfer, environmental damage and the establishment of a cult site. For discussions of some of these, see J. Weinberg, *The Citizen-Temple Community* (trans. D. L. Smith-Christopher; JSOTS, 151; Sheffield: JSOT Press, 1992); Wright, *God's People in God's Land*; Habel, *The Land Is Mine*.

10. Perceptions of the 'divine deeding' of land are well known throughout ancient West Asia, and are particularly bound up with urban ideologies concerning the allotment and use of a city's agricultural hinterland. In the Hebrew Bible, this is particularly well illustrated

claimed, maintained and sustained by incomers, whether by means of peaceful immigration (the myth of the patriarchs) or military invasion (the conquest myth). But while the latter endorses the dispossession and annihilation of indigenous populations, the former appears to promote – and even rely upon – an ongoing coexistence with the inhabitants of the land, for individual plots are acquired by the incomer not through force, but through negotiation and purchase. Thus Abraham buys a plot of land from the Hittites ('sons of Heth') in Genesis 23,[11] Jacob purchases a portion of a field from the sons of Hamor at Shechem (Gen. 33:18-20; cf. Josh. 24:32) and in Egypt, Joseph buys the lands offered for sale by apparently willing Egyptians (Gen. 47:18-20).[12] If these narratives are read as Persian period propaganda, the patriarchal purchase of land presents territorial acquisition by incomers – whether 'returning' from or remaining within their diaspora contexts – as a process endorsed *both* by the imperial overlord (represented by Yhwh in Genesis 23; 33:18-20 and Pharaoh in Gen. 47:18-20; cf. vv. 4-6, 11-12) *and* by the inhabitants of the host country (represented by the Hittites, Shechemites and Egyptians), who are willing to give up their land to make room for the newcomers.[13] This seemingly cooperative and peaceful portrayal of land appropriation in Genesis has therefore particularly encouraged an inclusivist and postcolonial reframing of the portrait of Abraham as the archetypal immigrant.

And yet the biblical story of Abraham's land deal carries a loaded ideological charge: the piece of land he acquires is a burial ground – a potent symbol

---

in Leviticus 25–27, in which Yhwh is imaged as the divine patron and owner of land surrounding his sanctuary, which is allocated to his Israelite tenants. See R. P. Carroll, 'Textual Strategies and Ideology in the Second Temple Period', in P. R. Davies (ed.), *Second Temple Studies, Volume 1: Persian Period* (JSOTS, 117; Sheffield: JSOT Press, 1991), 108–24. On land tenure and the interrelation of urban and rural economies, see n. 25 and Chapter 1.

11. In Genesis 23, the local community are labelled בני־חת, 'the descendants of Heth', a designation complementing the claim in 10:15 (cf. 26:34; 36:2; 1 Chr. 1:13) that Heth is a son of Canaan. The majority of commentators agree that this designation is essentially synonymous with החתי(ם), the more usual biblical designation for the Hittites. Though some are convinced that these Hittites are the Anatolian-Syrian Hittites, they seem to be cast in the Hebrew Bible as an indigenous Canaanite group. See J. Van Seters, 'The terms "Amorite" and "Hittite"', *VT* 22 (1972), 64–81; G. McMahon, 'The Hittites and the Bible', *BA* (1989), 71–77; I. Singer, 'The Hittites and the Bible Revisited', in A. M. Maeir and P. de Miroschedji (eds), *'I Will Speak the Riddle of Ancient Times': Archaeological and Historical Studies in Honor of Amihai Mazar on the occasion of his Sixtieth Birthday* (Vol. 2; Winona Lake, IN: Eisenbrauns, 2006), 723–56.

12. However, Joseph's land deals are facilitated by his apparent enslavement of the indigenous vendors (47:13-26; cf. LXX 47:13). See further M. G. Brett, *Genesis: Procreation and the Politics of Identity* (London: Routledge, 2000), 128–31.

13. That Joseph's purchase of land leads to a familial 'land-holding' is made explicit in Gen. 47:4-6, 11-12, in which Pharaoh grants land to Jacob and to Joseph's brothers, land designated אחזה in v. 11. On the meaning and significance of this term, see the discussion in n. 21.

of indigenous, ancestral territorialism. And though the story of its purchase in Genesis 23 implicitly admits that incomers do not have a right to land, by the close of the book of Genesis, the burial ground is the model of an ancestral tomb, housing the remains of Abraham, Sarah, Isaac, Rebekah, Leah and Jacob (23:19; 25:9-10; 35:29; 49:29-32; cf. 47:29-30). Set within this frame, Abraham's appropriation of a plot of land is rendered more assertively territorial than inclusive or 'ecumenical'.

Marking Machpelah

The burial ground at Machpelah is the only piece of the promised land to come into Abraham's possession (Genesis 23). Its purchase is prompted by Sarah's death and the need for a tomb, requiring Abraham to enter into lengthy negotiations with the Hittites in order to secure a gravesite. Commentators tend to make much of Abraham's insistence on paying good money for the site, even though he is offered it for free (cf. 2 Sam. 24:22).[14] In particular, both Norman Habel and Mark Brett set this and other episodes in the Abraham narratives against biblical texts promoting more aggressive land-grab ideologies.[15] Habel describes Abraham as a 'welcome immigrant' who 'chooses to put down roots and buy land on the terms of the host country'.[16] He argues that although Abraham's descendants will one day control the land, they will empower – and not disempower

---

14. E.g. G. von Rad, *Genesis: A Commentary* (trans. J. H. Marks; 2nd edn. London: SCM Press, 1963), 248; C. Westermann, *Genesis 12–36* (trans. J. J. Scullion; Minneapolis: Ausburg, 1985), 375; G. J. Wenham, *Genesis 16–50* (WBC, 2; Waco, TX: Word, 1994), 128–29; V. P. Hamilton, *The Book of Genesis: Chapters 18–50* (NICOT; Grand Rapids, MI: Eerdmans, 1995), 135; L. A. Turner, *Genesis* (Readings; Sheffield: Sheffield Academic Press, 2000), 101; C. Hinnant, 'The Patriarchal Narratives of Genesis and the Ethos of Gift Exchange', in M. Osteen (ed.), *The Question of the Gift: Essays Across Disciplines* (London: Routledge, 2002), 105–17. Unfortunately, some analyses of Abraham's land deal (and particularly the role of the Hittites) deteriorate into the orientalism and racist caricature more familiar in the scholarship of generations past: note the unpleasant tones in N. M. Sarna, *Genesis* (JPS Torah Commentary; Philadelphia: Jewish Publication Society, 1989), 159; Wenham, *Genesis 16–50*, 126–29. Nathan MacDonald has also drawn attention to the orientalizing tendencies of commentators on Genesis 23 – and in particular offers a (somewhat cautious) critique of Wenham ('Driving a Hard Bargain? Genesis 23 and Models of Economic Exchange', in L. J. Lawrence and M. I. Aguilar (eds), *Anthropology and Biblical Studies: Avenues of Approach* (Leiden: Deo, 2004), 79–96, esp. 79–80); see also S. Schwartz, *Were the Jews a Mediterranean Society? Reciprocity and Solidarity in Ancient Judaism* (Princeton: Princeton University Press, 2009), 1–20 (esp. 12). For a recent discussion of orientalizing tendencies in biblical scholarship, see J. G. Crossley, *Jesus in an Age of Terror: Scholarly Projects for a New American Century* (Bibleworld; London: Equinox, 2009).

15. Habel, *The Land Is Mine*, 115–33; Brett, *Genesis*, 78–83, and idem, *Decolonizing God*, 112–31.

16. Habel, *The Land Is Mine*, 125, 119.

– the other nations of the host country (cf. Gen. 18:18). According to Habel, Machpelah is thus the setting for a lesson in the just treatment of the legal owners of land.[17] Similarly, Mark Brett reads Genesis 23 as an endorsement of peaceful land-sharing and tolerant coexistence with other peoples, undercutting the hostile exclusion or extinction of the inhabitants of the land promoted in texts such as Deut. 7:1 and 20:17.[18] Thus for both Brett and Habel, Genesis 23 is not about occupation but cooperation, an appeal directed at the biblical narrator's post-587 BCE audiences, for whom land was likely a live issue.[19]

But there are some problems with this view, not least of which is Abraham's refusal to accept the Hittites' initial offer of a free land transfer (23:10-13), which undermines Habel's suggestion that Abraham's compliance towards the Hittites is evident in his purchasing land on *their* terms; rather, he acquires the land in precisely the way *he* proposes (23:8-9).[20] More significantly, however, an inclusivist reading of this narrative overlooks the territorial significance of the burial ground Abraham acquires. This significance is revealed in the dynamics and language of the land deal itself. In approaching the Hittites, Abraham's initial request seems straightforward: 'I am a stranger and an alien among you; give me a burial property (אחזת־קבר) among you, so that I may bury my dead' (v. 4). But his language is loaded. And the Hittites know it. In employing the term אחזת־קבר, Abraham is asking for more than a grave (קבר); in using the term אחזה, he is asking for a land-holding, that is, '(landed) property' or a 'possession' that can be retained by his descendants and guarded by the generations buried there.[21] But the Hittites' response is similarly loaded: though they offer

---

17. Habel, *The Land Is Mine*, 120–22, 129.

18. Brett, *Genesis*, 78–79; Liverani, *Israel's History*, 261. For a more detailed discussion of Brett's views on Deuteronomy's portrayal of incomers and inhabitants, see his *Decolonizing God*, 79–93.

19. See, for example, S. Japhet, 'People and Land in the Restoration Period', in G. Strecker (ed.), *Das Land Israel in biblischer Zeit* (Göttinger Theologische Arbeiten, 25; Göttingen: Vandenhoeck & Ruprecht, 1983), 103–25; H. M. Barstad, *The Myth of the Empty Land: A Study in the History and Archaeology of Judah During the 'Exilic' Period* (Oslo: Scandinavian University Press, 1996); O. Lipschits, 'Demographic Changes in Judah between the Seventh and the Fifth Centuries BCE', in O. Lipschits and J. Blenkinsopp (eds), *Judah and the Judeans in the Neo-Babylonian Period* (Winona Lake, IN: Eisenbrauns, 2003), 323–77.

20. The inclusive ethic seemingly promoted in the patriarchal narratives is further cheapened by an ethnocentric bias against various indigenous communities – including the Hittites (26:34-35; 27:46). See Heard, *Dynamics of Diselection*; see also Brett's nuanced response to these aspects of the book of Genesis in *Decolonizing God*, 125–31.

21. G. Gerleman, 'Nutzrecht und Wohnrecht', *ZAW* 89 (1977), 313–25. Abraham's bid for land seems pointedly assertive given his use of the term אחזה. As several commentators observe, the term is employed in priestly texts to designate tenured land (e.g. Lev. 14:34; 25:13; 27:16, 22, 28), and is used in Gen. 17:8 and 48:4 to refer to the land divinely promised. Jacob Milgrom describes אחזה as 'a technical term denoting inalienable property received

him the pick of any grave (קבר), they neglect to use the expression אחזת־קבר, thereby ignoring his request for land (v. 6).[22]

The territorial concerns of both parties become increasingly transparent as the language of graves and burial places gives way to talk of fields and land: Abraham specifies that he wants the cave of Machpelah 'at the edge of the field (שדה)' owned by Ephron the Hittite (v. 9). The use of שדה here, sharing a context with אחזה, is suggestive of Abraham's request for an (untended) field for cultivation, a plot of land on which a living can be made.[23] Ephron's reply is a candid acknowledgement of Abraham's grounded interests, for he offers first the field and then the cave, though he pointedly avoids the phrase אחזת־קבר. The rhetorical dynamics of these detailed negotiations suggest that it is not the particulars of Sarah's burial that concern Abraham and Ephron, but the use of a burial site as a means to occupy and possess land. Indeed, without reference to the cave or the grave, Abraham's final petition is a direct and explicit appeal to buy the field – 'then', he says, 'I will bury my dead there' (v. 13). Similarly, Ephron's final words are choice and precise, his vocabulary exposing the valuable territorial function of the dead: he agrees to sell Abraham ארץ, both 'land' and 'underworld' – 'So now bury your dead' (v. 15).[24] The pun here does not cheapen the value of the land deal. Abraham has secured tenure of the adjoining

---

(or seized) from a sovereign', which is used to describe the land taken by incoming Israelites that becomes their inheritance (נחלה), thereby making sense of the conflated expression אחזת נחלה, 'inherited holding' (Num. 27:7; 32:35; cf. 35:2) (*Leviticus 1–16: A New Translation with Introduction and Commentary* [AB, 3; New York: Doubleday, 1991], 5–6, 866–67). Mario Liverani refines the ideological connotations of the priestly use of אחזה in suggesting that the term refers to landed property taken by returnees in the Persian period, so that the terminological shift from נחלה (employed particularly in Deuteronomistic texts to refer to hereditary land) to אחזה in the priestly literature 'apparently marks the transition from a judicial claim to an act of taking possession' (*Israel's History*, 258). On these key biblical terms and their cognates, see F. Horst, 'Zwei Begriffe für Eigentun (Besitz): *nahala* und *'ahuzza'*, in A. Kuschke (ed.), *Verbannung und Heimkehr: Beiträge zur Geschichte und Theologie Israels im 6. und 5. Jahrhundert v. Chr. Wilhelm Rudolph zum 70. Geburtstage* (Tübingen: J. C. B. Mohr, 1961), 135–56; Wright, *God's People in God's Land*, 19–20.

22. M. Sternberg, 'Double Cave, Double Talk: The Indirections of Biblical Dialogue', in J. P. Rosenblatt and J. C. Sitterson (eds), *'Not In Heaven': Coherence and Complexity in Biblical Narrative* (Bloomington, IN: Indiana University Press, 1991), 28–57, here 31; Hamilton, *Genesis 18–50*, 134 n. 14.

23. Gerleman argues that אחזה is often used in priestly texts (particularly Leviticus 25–27) to refer specifically to cultivated land ('Nutzrecht und Wohnrecht', 313–25). Similarly, the term שדה tends to be used in relation to a city or a settlement, suggesting a field cultivated to provide food (G. Wallis, 'שדה', *TDOT*, 14.37–45, here 39–40), though its topography might be more akin to a 'highland', see W. H. Propp, 'On Hebrew *śāde(h)*, "Highland"', *VT* 37 (1987), 230–36.

24. On ארץ as 'underworld', see, for example, *HALOT*, 1.91; M. Ottosson, 'ארץ', *TDOT*, 1.388–405, esp. 399–400.

field for cultivation. The presence of his dead in the tomb at the edge of the field thus marks his 'possession' of the land.

Throughout the narrative, the legality of the purchase is emphasized in the very public nature of the negotiations, the witnesses' characterization as those who go though the city-gate (vv. 10, 18), the careful reference to merchants' weights (v. 16), and the repetitive but detailed description of the plot sold (vv. 17-20).[25] The narrator is insistent that Abraham's claim to this site cannot be contested. The land deal is celebrated at the close of the chapter with a lengthy statement designed both to detail the precise location, borders and lie of the land purchased, and to underline the legitimacy of the transfer. The real focus of the story is revealed in the way in which the burial site is described in these closing verses, for repeatedly and explicitly, these verses demonstrate that Abraham's gain is a plot of land and everything within its boundaries – including, of course, its burial cave:

> So Ephron's field in Machpelah, which was to the east of Mamre, the field with the cave in it and all the trees that were in the field, within the confines of its whole boundary, passed to Abraham as a bought-possession (מקנה) in the presence of the Hittites, in the presence of all who went in at his city-gate. After this, Abraham buried Sarah his wife in the cave of the field of Machpelah facing Mamre (that is, Hebron) in the land of Canaan. The field and the cave in it passed from the Hittites to Abraham as a burial property (אחזת קבר) (Gen. 23:17-20).

In concluding the story in this way, the narrator cannot help but reveal that the primary concern of the story has not been Sarah's burial (whose death is merely the hook on which the land deal is hung),[26] nor the processes of negotiation, but

---

25. For various analyses of Abraham's land deal alongside ancient or contemporary purchase paradigms, see M. R. Lehmann, 'Abraham's Purchase of Machpelah and Hittite Law', *BASOR* 129 (1953), 15–18; H. Petschow, 'Zwiegesprächsurkunde und Genesis 23', *JCS* 19 (1965), 103–20; G. M. Tucker, 'The Legal Background of Genesis 23', *JBL* 85 (1966), 77–84; R. Westbrook, *Property and the Family in Biblical Law* (JSOTS, 113; Sheffield: JSOT Press, 1991); MacDonald, 'Driving a Hard Bargain?', 79–96.

26. The economic presentation of mortuary motifs in Genesis 23 has prompted James Bray to suggest that the narrative is a polemic against ancestor worship ('Genesis 23 – A Priestly Paradigm for Burial', *JSOT* 60 [1993], 69–73). In particular, Bray asserts that Abraham's wish to bury his dead מלפני, 'out of my sight' (vv. 4, 8) demonstrates the priestly writer's concern to depict burial as the removal of the unclean dead and to present death itself as 'an impenetrable frontier'. But if Genesis 23 is an attack on ancestor cult, it is a very stealthy one, for there is no direct injunction against interaction with the dead, and neither Sarah's corpse nor the mourning Abraham is imaged as unclean. Bray's forceful rendering of מלפני as 'out of my sight' may also be misleading. If מלפני is taken to mean 'from before me', it may function not spatially but temporally here, pointing to Abraham's

the possession of hereditary land, constructed around the territorial function of a tomb.

The territorial currency of Genesis 23 finds its value in a separatist ideology that distinguishes between Abraham, his kin and his land, on the one hand, and the Hittites and their land on the other. Although the Hittites locate Abraham 'in our midst' (בתוכנו) and offer him a choice of any one of their tombs (v. 6), Abraham specifically requests the cave of Machpelah 'at the edge' (בקצה) of Ephron's field (v. 9) – implying his resistance to incorporation among them. The sense, then, is that Abraham chooses not to be 'in the midst' of the Hittites, but separate from them.[27] As Meir Sternberg comments, 'The patriarch will not bury his wife, any more than in the next chapter he will marry his son, among the people of Canaan'.[28] But it seems likely that this separateness is constructed around the territorial function of a tomb as a boundary marker. It demarcates Abraham's dead from the Hittites' dead, his land from theirs. The territorial dynamics of the narrative thus endorse exclusiveness and separation, rather than an inclusive or 'ecumenical' attitude to indigenous communities.[29]

If Abraham is to be viewed as a paradigmatic incomer, the policy of land appropriation he models in Genesis 23 attempts to accommodate two concepts of territorial possession: one is the idea that land can be bought, and the other is the idea that land is ancestral. Each of these forms of territorial possession can play a crucial role in land claims (past and present), and they are often deemed to be ideologically opposed. Indeed, within the biblical context, the story of Naboth's vineyard would appear to illustrate this opposition, for he refuses to sell King Ahab his land because it is נחלת אבתי, 'my ancestral inheritance' (1 Kgs 21:3-4). But in Genesis 23, purchased land and ancestral land are held closely together within the same ideological frame.

Given his role as the paradigmatic incomer, Abraham's actions in buying Machpelah legitimize the purchase of property by immigrants in the host country. From this perspective, land becomes a commodity available to the incomer – and

---

expectation that he (and by implication, his descendants) will also be interred in that same tomb one day. More significantly, if the narrative is intended as an attack on ancestor cult, it appears not to have been very successful, for as is well known (and as Bray himself admits), the supposed location of the tomb at Machpelah became an important pilgrimage site.

27. Sternberg, 'Double Cave, Double Talk', 31–32.

28. Ibid., 31; cf. Mullen, *Ethnic Myths*, 145. Drawing on Sternberg's discussion, Robert Cohn ('Negotiating (with) the Natives', 160) similarly reads Abraham's request for a tomb at the edge of the field as a petition for ethnic separateness; *contra* Hamilton (*Genesis 18–50*, 131–32), who assumes Abraham's choice of a plot on the edge of Ephron's field is dictated 'by modesty' because his status 'restricts him to minimal privileges'; cf. Sarna, *Genesis*, 159.

29. This separateness is underscored further in the sharp contrast between Ephron's willingness to give away or sell his burial ground to an incomer and Abraham's determined acquisition of what amounts to an ancestral landholding.

so implicitly, it can be bought and sold time and time again. But conversely, Machpelah is also imaged as ancestral land, which within the Hebrew Bible is itself idealized as an exclusive and permanent possession of one descent group. Thus in the context of Abraham's purchase of Machpelah, the transformation of the land from commodity to ancestral holding ensures the perpetual possession of the incomer's plot, protecting it from resale in the future. There are therefore two models of land acquisition in this narrative, which may in certain circumstances conflict with each other. However, in Genesis 23, purchased land and ancestral land are mapped onto one another: the narrator turns a purchased plot into an ancestral landholding, transforming Abraham from a resident incomer into a perpetual landowner. In this way, Abraham is implicitly recast in the guise of an indigenous inhabitant, allowing his descendants to claim perpetual ownership of their 'ancestral' land.[30]

And so it is that at Machpelah, land occupation is marked by the dead on behalf of the living. But 'what does it suggest when those who go ahead into the land are the corpses, as if the front line of occupation is a cemetery? Is this then to be a land occupied by the dead?'[31] For those (ac)claiming Abraham at Machpelah, the answer to this last question is likely 'yes'.

---

30. The coalescence of purchased land and ancestral land as an effective means of territorial appropriation for incomers is also endorsed (though in a slightly different way) in Jeremiah 32, in which Jeremiah's purchase of his kinsman's field (32:6-14) triggers oracles promising the divine restoration of golah communities to the land by means of purchased plots (32:15-25, 42-44). In this narrative, Jeremiah himself functions as a paradigmatic exile, for he is imprisoned and cut off from his own community (32:2) – a captive who, in narrative terms, is soon to be exiled to Egypt, the very symbol and cipher of the landlessness of Israel's ancestors in this narrative (32:20-23). As Habel comments (*The Land is Mine*, 91), 'Jeremiah is introduced as the first Israelite to own land in the anticipated new order for Israel'. On the close similarities between Genesis 23 and Jeremiah 32 (cf. Ruth 4), see B. Perrin, *Trois textes bibliques sur les techniques d'acquisition immobilière (Genèse XXIII; Ruth IV; Jérémie XXXII, 8–15)* (Revue Historique de Droit Français et Étranger; Paris: Librairie Sirey, 1963). On land redemption, see Dearman, *Property Rights in the Eighth-Century Prophets*, ch. 2; J. Milgrom, 'The Land Redeemer and the Jubilee', in A. B. Beck, A. H. Bartelt, P. R. Raabe and C. A. Franke (eds), *Fortunate the Eyes That See: Essays in Honor of David Noel Freedman in Celebration of His Seventieth Birthday* (Grand Rapids, MI: Eerdmans: 1995), 66–69; J. A. Fayer, *Land Tenure and the Biblical Jubilee: Uncovering Hebrew Ethics through the Sociology of Knowledge* (JSOTS, 155; Sheffield: Sheffield Academic Press, 1993); J. Joosten, *People and Land in the Holiness Code: An Exegetical Study of the Ideational Framework of the Law in Leviticus 17–26* (VTS, 67; Leiden: Brill, 1996); J. S. Bergsma, 'The Jubilee: A Post-exilic Priestly Attempt to Reclaim Lands', *Bib* 81 (2000), 153–78.

31. Y. Sherwood, 'And Sarah Died', in Y. Sherwood (ed.), *Derrida's Bible (Reading a Page of Scripture with a Little Help from Derrida)* (New York: Palgrave Macmillan, 2004), 261–92, here 266, responding to Jacques Derrida's observation that it is by means of

(Ac)claiming Abraham

Appeals to the past are common features of claims to land. When those claims are contested, the past is often pitted against the present to the extent that the perceived legitimacy of one is measured against the perceived legitimacy of the other. In some biblical texts, Abraham represents the 'past' to which some groups refer in asserting their claims to territorial or dynastic inheritance. This is powerfully attested in Ezek. 33:23-24, in which Abraham's biblical function as paradigmatic landowner is clearly prominent. Set within the context of the aftermath of the Neo-Babylonian destruction of Judah, these verses are widely held to reflect the territorial conflicts between Judahite groups in the land and the exiled generations:[32]

> The word of Yhwh came to me: Son of Man, the inhabitants of these waste places upon the soil of Israel keep saying, 'Abraham was one, yet he possessed the land; we are many; surely the land is given as a possession to us'.

The appeal to Abraham as an archetypal possessor of land undercuts the better-known biblical emphasis upon the divine promise of land to Abraham's descendants, a promise fulfilled not in Abraham's time, but in the occupation of the land by the post-exodus generations. Indeed, the claimants do not identify themselves as the descendants of Abraham – though this is probably a distancing device on the part of the writer – but instead assert their right to possess land on the basis of their presence *in* the land (cf. 11:15-17). Contrary to Daniel Block, this is not a 'patently inaccurate, if not perverse' opinion that 'overestimates the patriarch's territorial rights'.[33] Rather, their territoriality is appropriately imaged on the model of Abraham as the landowning occupier – a motif that is elsewhere only drawn out in the tradition about the burial ground at Machpelah in Genesis. Though it would be hasty to assume that this tomb tradition directly informs the claimants' (imputed) assertion, the interrelation of grave and land notably forms the backdrop to the scathing attack they incur for their territorial claim; the oracle announcing their punishment indicates they are destined not only for death, but for the post-mortem neglect and destruction that in the Hebrew Bible accompany

---

Sarah's death that Abraham takes the land: J. Derrida, 'Hostipitality', *Acts of Religion* (ed. G. Anidjar; New York: Routledge, 2002), 356–420, here 414.

32. The extent to which these verses should be taken to reflect the likely historical realities of these territorial conflicts is uncertain. Note the summary discussion about the post-587 BCE dating of these verses in P. M. Joyce, *Ezekiel: A Commentary* (LHBOTS, 482; New York: T&T Clark, 2007), 193.

33. D. I. Block, *The Book of Ezekiel, Chapters 25–48* (NICOT; Grand Rapids, MI: Eerdmans, 1998), 260. Here, Block's sympathies clearly lie with Ezekiel's Babylonian community, rather than those left in the land, who for him exhibit a 'lack of spiritual sensitivity', 'smug self-interest' and (perhaps most amusingly of all) 'Darwinian materialism'.

the social abandonment of the dead in wartime.[34] In typical biblical fashion, the specifics of their crime are drawn on the lines of a type of religious malpractice that triggers expulsion from the land:

> Therefore say to them, 'Thus Lord Yhwh declares: You eat with the blood, you raise your eyes to your shitgods,[35] you shed blood – still you claim the land? You rely on the sword, you commit abominations, you defile each other's wives – still you claim the land?' This is what you shall say to them: 'Thus Lord Yhwh declares: As I live, whoever is in the waste places will fall by the sword; whoever is in the open field I will give to the wild animals as food; whoever is in the strongholds or in the caves will die of the plague. I will make the land a desolation and a waste. (Ezek. 33:27-28)

The land claims of the indigenous and occupying inhabitants are thus dismissed, and the land in which they live is to be emptied – in readiness, it would seem, for the return of the exiled group to whom it is claimed in 11:15-17 the land is to be given.[36]

Appeal to Abraham is similarly made in another text often held to reflect the concerns of a Persian period group. In Isa. 51:1-3a, an oracle of restoration is given to a community some argue to be in Babylon,[37] and others contend to have remained in Judah.[38] While adjudicating between these positions is problematic (the precise socio-historical circumstances of the oracles' composition are notoriously difficult to tease from their present literary contexts),[39] this text points to a Persian-period claim to Abraham and Sarah as the ancestors of a group to whom Zion's rejuvenation is promised:

---

34. Indeed, given their biblical context, in these verses death by the sword is suggestive of abandoned battlefield corpses; the threat of cadaver-devouring is indicative of corpse exposure; and the onset of plague implies the non-removal of corpses.

35. The term גלולים is a polemical designation, probably derived from גלל, 'be round', 'roll', and related to גללים, 'faeces'; its vocalization may reflect שקוץ, 'abhorrent' (*HALOT*, 1.192). As such, its rendering as 'shitgods' seems appropriate; see further D. Bodi, 'Les *gillûlîm* chez Ezéchiel et dans l'Ancien Testament, et les différentes practiques cultuelles associées à ce terme, *RB* 100 [1993], 481–510). The more polite expression 'dung-gods' might alternatively be employed, though this would soften the powerful impact of the Hebrew term.

36. Cf. D. Rom-Shiloni, 'Ezekiel as the Voice of the Exiles and Constructor of Exilic Ideology', *HUCA* 76 (2005), 1–45.

37. E.g. S. Japhet, 'People and Land in the Restoration Period', in G. Strecker (ed.), *Das Land Israel in biblischer Zeit* (Göttinger Theologische Arbeiten, 25; Göttingen: Vandenhoeck & Ruprecht, 1983), 106–9.

38. E.g. M. Goulder, 'Deutero-Isaiah of Jerusalem', *JSOT* 28 (2004), 351–62.

39. In her article entitled 'Abraham – A Judahite Prerogative' (*ZAW* 120 [2008], 49–66), Lena Tiemeyer argues that Ezek. 11:15; 33:23 and Isa. 51:1-2 are exilic Judahite texts reflecting the concerns of those left in the land after the deportations.

> ... Look to the rock from which you were hewn,
> and to the quarry-hole from which you were dug;
> look to Abraham your father,
> and to Sarah who bore you;
> for he was one when I called him,
> but I blessed him and made him many.
> Yhwh comforts Zion,
> he brings comfort to all her waste places ...

Imagery and language reminiscent of that in Ezek. 33:23-28 shows itself here: set against a wasteland (Isa. 51:3; Ezek. 33:24, 27), Abraham as 'one' is positioned in relation to the 'many' (Isa. 51:2; Ezek. 33:24). But in Isa. 51:2, the appeal to Abraham is not as a land-owning occupier, but as an ancestor, coupled with Sarah. Their pairing in this text is significant. In making her only biblical appearance beyond the book of Genesis, here Sarah is given a more prominent place in the biblical portrait of the ancestors than is usual. Rather than being overshadowed by the dominant emphasis upon the patrilineal group comprising Abraham, Isaac and Jacob (with occasional appearances by Joseph), in Isa. 51:2a, Sarah is paralleled with Abraham in their role as the ancestral couple: Abraham is father and Sarah is the birthing mother. However, as is evident in many ancestor-centred concepts of collective descent and identity,[40] these roles are not confined to the past.

Indeed, the language of Isa. 51:1-3a carries with it a sense that the fertility of the ancestral couple is of a perpetual and continuing significance to those claiming direct descent from them. The prophet instructs his audience to look to Abraham אביכם, 'your father', and to Sarah תחוללכם, '(who) has birthed you'. Some commentators take this as poetic language, encouraged by the assumption that the terms צור (rock) and מקבת בור (quarry-hole) function as metaphors either of Yhwh (to whom צור is frequently attributed as a title), or of the barrenness of Sarah from which fertility miraculously came forth (cf. Gen. 17:16-17; 18:10-12; cf. 11:30).[41] But these views have not been widely accepted, and most commentators are agreed that צור and מקבת בור refer respectively to Abraham and Sarah.[42] As such, this language is likely more than mere metaphor.

---

40. As discussed in Chapter 1, above.

41. E.g. B. J. van der Merwe, *Pentateuchtradisies in die Prediking van Deuterojesaja* (Groningen: Wolters, 1955), 104–15; cf. J. N. Oswalt, *The Book of Isaiah, Chapters 40–66* (NICOT; Grand Rapids, MI: Eerdmans, 1998), 334 (citing Calvin as his authority, who similarly reads this language as metaphor); T. C. Römer, 'Recherches actuelles sur le cycle d'Abraham', in A. Wénin (ed.), *Studies in the Book of Genesis: Literature, Redaction and History* (Leuven: Peeters, 2001), 179–211.

42. E.g. C. Westermann, *Isaiah 40–66* (trans. D. M. G. Stalker. OTL; London: SCM Press, 1969), 236; C. R. North, *Isaiah 40–55* (London: SCM Press, 1952), 209; R. N. Whybray, *Isaiah 40–66* (NCB; London: Oliphants, 1975), 155; J. Blenkinsopp, *Isaiah*

Rather, Isa. 51:1-2 echoes similar expressions occurring in cultic contexts in which deity and worshipper are bound together in familial terms. In Ps. 2:7, Yhwh designates the Davidic king בְּנִי, 'my son' and asserts he has 'birthed' or 'fathered' (יָלַד) him. The same verb is employed in Jer. 2:27, in which a group of worshippers is ridiculed for addressing a tree as 'father' (אָב) and a sacred stone (אֶבֶן) as the one that 'birthed' (יָלַד) them.[43] This imagery clearly resonates with that found in Isa. 51:2, in which Abraham appears to be portrayed as a fertile 'rock' (צוּר) and 'father' (אָב). But it is Deut. 32:18 that offers the closest parallel to the language of Isa. 51:1-2, for here, both צוּר and חוּל are employed in the castigation of worshippers who forget צוּר יְלָדְךָ, 'Rock who fathered you', paralleled with אֵל מְחֹלְלֶךָ, 'El who birthed you'.

This collection of texts demonstrates that the use of אָב and חוּל in Isa. 51:2 functions not as poetic metaphor, but as the language of a venerative cult. It also suggests that Abraham's designation צוּר, 'rock', functions here in its more usual sense: as a cultic title.[44] This title, paralleled with אָב, is suggestive of a tradition promoting Abraham as a venerated ancestor, while the stone-hewing (חצב) and digging (נקר) imagery employed in verse 1 to refer to the birth of the descendants of Abraham the 'Rock' and Sarah the 'quarry-hole' evokes a strong sense of an asserted genealogical relationship to the landscape itself.[45] Within this text, Abraham and Sarah are indeed the powerful, territorial dead.

Yet Abraham's powerful status is notably challenged in Isa. 63:16, in which formerly rebellious Yhwh worshippers petition their god for assistance and rehabilitation:

> For you are our Father,
> though Abraham does not know us,
> and Israel does not acknowledge us;
> You, O Yhwh, are our Father,
> From of old your name is 'Our Redeemer'.

56–66: A New Translation with Introduction and Commentary (AB, 19B; New York: Doubleday, 2003), 326.

43. On this text see Chapter 5, n. 44.

44. In the light of the parallel fertility function of אֶבֶן in Jer. 2:27, it is attractive (though speculative) to view צוּר in Isa. 51:2 as a standing stone in an ancestor cult.

45. For the suggestion that these verses reflect ancient myths about the birth of humankind from a rock or quarry, akin (perhaps) to Greek traditions about 'chthonic' origins, see P. Volz, *Jesaja II* (HAT, 9; Leipzig: Scholl, 1932), 110–11. It is not impossible that the language of stone-hewing and digging might also allude to a cult tradition associated with the ancestral burial place in the cave (מְעָרָה) at Machpelah; cf. N. A. van Uchelen, 'Abraham als Felsen (Jes 51,1)', *ZAW* 80 (1968), 183–91. The cave is a feature heavily emphasized in the biblical tradition: Gen. 23:9, 11, 17, 19; 25:9; 49:29, 30, 32; 50:13.

This verse has been taken as an indication of a cult of Abraham and Israel (Jacob). Duhm proposed that the text expresses worshippers' appeals to Yhwh for help, their necromantic petitions to their deified ancestors having failed (אברהם לא ידענו וישראל לא יכירנו).[46] As such, the verse represents a rejection of the cult of the ancestors in favour of the cult of Yhwh. This is an interesting idea, not least because the petitionary nature of the appeal for divine intervention in the surrounding verses (vv. 15, 17) complements the intercessory function of the deified dead known elsewhere.[47] In spite of Paul Hanson's well-known (but unsuccessful) attempt to persuade others that the names 'Abraham' and 'Israel' here are the designations of competing groups in post-exilic Jerusalem,[48] most commentators agree that the designations refer to the patriarchal figures, whose ancestral roles are contrasted with the perceived function of Yhwh as 'father' or 'ancestor' to his worshippers. Indeed, as others have observed, it is not common to find Yhwh addressed as אב in the Hebrew Bible, and most assume the scarcity of this epithet reflects a theological concern to distance Yhwh from the progenitive role other deities performed for their worshippers. 'Man is not God's child,' states Westermann, 'but his creature'.[49] However, other texts suggest that the term אב was appropriately employed by some Yhwh-worshippers[50] and its apparently

---

46. B. Duhm, *Das Buch Jesaia* (4th edn. HAT, 3.1; Göttingen: Vandenhoeck & Ruprecht, 1922), 469; see also I. Goldziher, *Der Mythos bei den Hebräern und seine geschichtliche Entwickelung* (Leipzig: Brockhaus, 1876), 229–30; K. van der Toorn, 'Echoes of Judaean Necromancy in Isaiah 28,7-22', *ZAW* 100 (1988), 199–217 (esp. 216). Fostered in a time of enthusiastic confidence in the theorizing and anatomizing of myth, and conjoined with the steady rise of a 'history of religions' approach to biblical traditions, scholarship of the late nineteenth and early twentieth centuries often identified the biblical patriarchs and matriarchs as deities or mythic symbols, later demythologized and recast as historical figures in Israel's ancestry. See, for example, E. Stucken, *Astralmythen der Hebraeer, babylonier und Aegypter* (Leipzig: Pfeiffer, 1896–1907); H. Gunkel, *The Legends of Genesis* (trans. W. H. Carruth; New York: Schocken, 1964); B. Luther, 'Die israelitischen Stämme', *ZAW* 21 (1901), 1–76; E. Meyer, *Die Israeliten und ihre Nachbarstämme* (Halle: Max Niemeyer, 1906), 263–70. For a discussion of some of these views, see H. Weidmann, *Die Patriarchen und ihre Religion im Licht der Forschung seit Julius Wellhausen* (Göttingen: Vandenhoeck & Ruprecht, 1968), 89–94.

47. It is perhaps worth considering that Abraham's role as an intercessor for Sodom in Gen. 18:22-33 owes something not only to a prophetic paradigm (cf. Exodus 32–34; 1 Sam. 12:23; Jer. 14:7-9, 13; 15:1; Amos 7:1-9), but also to a function of the ancestral dead.

48. P. D. Hanson, *The Dawn of Apocalyptic* (Philadelphia: Fortress Press, 1975), 92–100; for a response to this view, see H. G. M. Williamson, 'Isaiah 63,7–64,11: Exilic Lament or Post-Exilic Critique?', *ZAW* 102 (1990), 48–58.

49. Westermann, *Isaiah 40–66*, 393.

50. Isa. 64:7; Jer. 3:4, 19; Mal. 2:10; cf. Jer. 2:27; Deut. 32:6. Note also (with Blenkinsopp, *Isaiah 56–66*, 262) the attribution of fatherhood to Yhwh in theophoric personal names such as Abijah and Joab. Yhwh worshippers are imaged as his child or children in Exod. 4:22; Deut. 14:1; 32:6; Hos. 2:1; 11:1; Isa. 1:2; 45:10-12; Jer. 31:9; Mal. 1:6; 2:10. For the biblical

cultic usage in Isa. 51:1-2 and Jer. 2:27 (in addition to the parental language in Deut. 32:18; Ps. 2:7; cf. 2 Sam. 7:14) implies that the notion of divine parentage or deified ancestry is similarly in play here in Isa. 63:16.

And yet Duhm's proposal that Isa. 63:16 alludes to a venerative cult of the ancestors has not been widely adopted – ostensibly because most commentators (perhaps resistant to the possibility that the dead were understood to play an active social role in the lives of the living)[51] prefer to read the parental language here as mere epithet, guided by the more figurative function of the divine designation 'Father' in later literature and the assumption that Yhwh's role as begetter of the Davidic king in Ps. 2:7 (cf. 89:27-28; 2 Sam. 7:14; 1 Chr. 28:6) is simply symbolic.[52] From this perspective, then, if Yhwh is not a divine begetter in Isa. 63:16, neither are Abraham and Israel/Jacob.

But perhaps the strongest objection to Duhm's proposal is that Abraham's biblical appearances are neither frequent nor polemical enough to suggest the existence of a long-lived cult in which Abraham was hailed as a deified ancestor.[53] Indeed, there are few texts beyond the Torah in which Abraham is mentioned,[54] while references to Abraham in Exodus–Deuteronomy are somewhat formulaic in listing him along with Isaac and Jacob/Israel as the ancestors of the nation and

---

imaging of Yhwh as an ancestor, see Chapter 6. For Yhwh's involvement with conception and birth, see R. Albertz, 'Personal Piety', in F. Stavrakopoulou and J. Barton (eds), *Religious Diversity in Ancient Israel and Judah* (London: T&T Clark, 2010), 135–46.

51. See the discussion in Chapter 1.

52. E.g. J. Day, 'The Canaanite Inheritance in the Israelite Monarchy', in J. Day (ed.), *King and Messiah in Israel and the Ancient Near East* (JSOTS, 270; Sheffield: Sheffield Academic Press), 72–90, here 82. For a more persuasive perspective, see N. Wyatt, 'Royal Religion in Ancient Judah', in F. Stavrakopoulou and J. Barton (eds), *Religious Diversity in Ancient Israel and Judah* (London: T&T Clark, 2010), 61–81.

53. For an early advocate of the view that Abraham and company were originally localized deified dead, see L. B. Paton, 'The Hebrew Idea of the Future Life: IV. Yahweh's Relation to the Dead in the Earliest Hebrew Religion', *The Biblical World* 35 (1910), 246–58, esp. 251; idem, 'The Hebrew Idea of the Future Life: II. The Primitive Cult of the Dead', *The Biblical World* 35 (1910), 80–92, esp. 85–87.

54. Of those in which references to him do occur, the majority group him fleetingly and formulaically with Jacob/Israel and Isaac as the stereotypical ancestors (1 Kgs 18:36; 2 Kgs 13:23; 1 Chr. 16:16; 29:18; 2 Chr. 30:6; Ps. 105:9-10; Jer. 33:26); similarly, others pair or parallel Abraham with Jacob/Israel (Isa. 29:22; 63:16; Mic. 7:20; Ps. 105:6) or refer to him in genealogies (1 Chr. 1:27-28, 32, 34). The remaining occurrences of Abraham's name outside the texts of Torah image him explicitly as an ancestor (Josh. 24:2-3; Isa. 51:1-2; Ezek. 33:24; cf. Neh. 9:7; Isa. 41:8), a symbol of the covenant promise of land (Neh. 9:7), a servant of Yhwh (Ps. 105:42), a worshipper of God (אלהי אברהם in Ps. 47:9), and the 'lover' or 'friend' (אהב) of Yhwh (Isa. 41:8; 2 Chr. 20:7). On this last expression, see M. Goshen-Gottstein, 'Abraham – Lover or Beloved of God', in J. H. Marks and R. M. Good (eds), *Love and Death in the Ancient Near East: Essays in Honor of Marvin H. Pope* (Guildford; Four Quarters, 1987), 101–4.

the recipients of the covenant promises of land and descendants.[55] The relative scarcity of Abraham's biblical appearances beyond Genesis is either suggestive of a carefully managed portrayal, or an indication that the biblical traditions did not exhibit or ascribe a particularly prominent place to him.[56]

This stands in contrast to the collective 'ancestors' of the exodus and conquest traditions, who appear to enjoy a notably significant position in many texts. Indeed, in many of the biblical allusions to the origins of the people Israel, the 'ancestors' are not the patriarchs, but are more generally the exodus and wilderness generations.[57] Moreover, and as a number of commentators have observed, in several biblical recapitulations of the past, the patriarchal period is passed over altogether, giving way instead to the exodus, wilderness and conquest traditions as the origins of Israel's particular story.[58]

The absence of Abraham from large parts of the Hebrew Bible suggests that allusions to his veneration as an ancestor in Genesis, Isa. 51:1-2; 63:16 and Ezek. 33:23-24 are late features of the origin myths of the Hebrew Bible.[59] Indeed, the strongest evidence for the veneration of Abraham appears in texts of the Hellenistic and Roman periods – notably in explicit correlation with Hebron, the site at which in Genesis the tomb at Machpelah is located. In book four of his

---

55. Exod. 2:24; 6:3, 8; 32:13; 33:1; Lev. 26:42; Num. 32:11; Deut. 1:8; 6:10; 9:5, 27; 29:13; 30:20; 34:4.

56. In (perhaps intentional) contrast, many non-Tanakh texts reflect a greater interest in the character and career of Abraham. For the dismantling of the historicity of the patriarchs, see the now classic works of T. L. Thompson, *The Historicity of the Patriarchal Narratives: The Quest for the Historical Abraham* (BZAW, 133; Berlin: de Gruyter, 1974) and J. Van Seters, *Abraham in History and Tradition* (New Haven: Yale University Press, 1975). Though increasingly marginal, recent defenders of (the faith in) the patriarchs as historical figures include K. A. Kitchen, *On the Reliability of the Old Testament* (Grand Rapids, MI: Eerdmans, 2003), 313–72.

57. E.g. Deut. 10:22; 1 Kgs 8:53; 2 Kgs 21:15; Hos. 9:10; Ps. 106:6-33. See T. Römer, *Israels Väter. Untersuchungen zur Väterthematik imDeuteronomium und in der deuteronomistischen Tradition* (OBO, 99; Göttingen: Vandenhoeck & Ruprecht, 1990); J. Van Seters, 'Confessional Reformulation in the Exilic Period', *VT* 22 (1972), 448–59 and his *Prologue to History* (Louisville, KY: Westminster John Knox Press, 1992), 227–45. The clustering of land and fertility motifs associated elsewhere with the divine promise to Abraham is in Deut. 10:14-22 applied to the exodus generation, suggesting a disinterest in, or the eclipse of Abraham in favour of the exodus group. On this, see Chapter 3.

58. E.g. Deut. 4:32-38; Jer. 32:17-23; Ezek. 20:5; Pss. 95:3-11; 136:5-22; cf. Deut. 32:7-16. For the classic treatment of these two distinct 'election' traditions, see K. Galling, *Die Erwählungstraditionen Israels* (BZAW, 48; Giessen: Töpelmann, 1928). See more recently K. Schmid, 'The So-Called Yahwist and the Literary Gap between Genesis and Exodus', in T. B. Dozeman and K. Schmid (eds), *A Farewell to the Yahwist? The Composition of the Pentateuch in Recent European Interpretation* (SBLSS, 34; Atlanta, GA: Society of Biblical Literature, 2006), 29–50.

59. Cf. Römer, *Israels Väter*, 568–75.

Jewish War, Josephus portrays Hebron as a place of great ancestral significance, elevating it above the prestigious city of Memphis and impressing his Roman readers with its important and pivotal place in Jewish history:

> According to the statements of its inhabitants, Hebron is a town of greater antiquity not only than any other in the country, but even than Memphis in Egypt, being reckoned to be two thousand three hundred years old. They further relate that it was there that Abraham, the progenitor of the Jews (το ουδαιων προγόνου), took up his abode after his migration from Mesopotamia, and from here that his posterity went down into Egypt. (*War* 4.530-31)[60]

The ancestral credentials of Hebron are further emphasized in his description of the patriarchal tombs located there, focusing on the lavish, high-status quality of the monuments, before elevating Hebron and its tombs even further by associating the site with creation; for Josephus, this place is not important simply in terms of Jewish history, but in terms of universal history, too:

> Their tombs are shown in this little town to this day, of really fine marble and of exquisite workmanship. At a distance of six furlongs from the town there is also shown a huge terebinth (τερέβινθος)[61] which is said to have stood there ever since the creation. (*War* 4.532-33)

In referring here to the 'huge terebinth', two mythic motifs are combined: one is the association of Abraham and Hebron with sacred trees, reflected in several biblical texts (for example, Gen. 12:6; 13:18; 14:13; 18:1; 35:4); the second is the concept of the cosmic tree as the axis of the universe – hence its association here with creation. This mythic backdrop to Josephus' comments on the tombs of Hebron, and his emphasis upon the great ancestry and antiquity of the place, at the very least reflect perceptions of the high religio-historical status of the site. And while it would be incautious to accept Josephus' testimony at face value, his description of the tombs highlights notions of their prominent display and the wealth with which their exhibition is maintained. Given Josephus' account of the tombs, then, it would appear that the ancestors enjoyed a publicized and prestigious status among the living.

There is widespread agreement that the Haram el-Khalil, the present-day shrine of the patriarchs and matriarchs, comprises Herodian architecture, and was probably constructed over an older monument.[62] As Jack Lightstone observes, its

---

60. Translations here follow those of H. St. John Thackeray in the Loeb Classical Library series.
61. Cf. *Ant*. 1.186.
62. D. M. Jacobson, 'The plan of the ancient Haram El Khalil in Hebron', *PEQ* 113 (1981), 73–80; L. H. Vincent and J. E. Mackay, *Hebron, le Haram el-Khalîl: Sépulture des*

2. Abraham at Machpelah

large, enclosed courtyard is suggestive of a gathering place for sizeable groups, perhaps indicating that it was a place of pilgrimage, while the cultic function of the site is also indicated by the architectural similarities between the Herodian site at Hebron and Josephus' descriptions of Herod's temple in Jerusalem (*War* 5.18-19; *Ant.* 15.280-81),[63] suggesting that:

> ... one is a scaled-down version of the other – with of course one major difference; in place of the Sanctuary, which occupied the center of the Temple compound, one has in Hebron the six raised tombs of the Mausoleum. These facts invite the conclusion that the Mausoleum, and in particular the tombs therein, were considered by its pilgrims analogous in character and function to the Temple cult itself. Here, as at the altar, heaven and earth met. Here, as at the altar, goods and services between the two realms might efficaciously be exchanged.[64]

Though the textual and archaeological material pertaining to this site is by its nature fragmentary and ambiguous, it is not unreasonable to assume (with most scholars) that Hebron was home to a site identified as the tomb of Abraham at least as early as the latter half of the Second Temple period.[65] The extent to which a cult of Abraham existed (here or anywhere) before this period is uncertain, primarily given the limitations of the biblical material. But the available evidence

---

Patriarches (Paris: Leroux, 1923); O. Keel and M. Küchler, *Orte und Landshaften der Bibel. Ein Handbuch und Studien-Reiseführer zum Heiligen Land. Band II: Der Süden* (Göttingen: Vandenhoeck & Ruprecht, 1982), 670–713.

63. On Josephus' description of the Jerusalem temple, see L. H. Schiffman, 'Descriptions of the Jerusalem Temple in Josephus and the *Temple Scroll*', in D. Goodblatt, A. Pinnick and D. R. Schwartz (eds), *Historical Perspectives: From the Hasmoneans to Bar Kokhba in Light of the Dead Sea Scrolls* (Leiden: Brill, 2001), 69–82, and the literature cited there.

64. Lightstone, *Commerce of the Sacred*, 51. The possible nature of this 'exchange' might find some resonance in Jub. 22:1-6, a text of the late Second Temple period, which may be taken to reflect a tradition for the bestowing of family property upon an heir. Framed within the context of Abraham's imminent death (perhaps even set on the day of his death), these verses tell of a series of rituals performed at Hebron in honour of Abraham by Isaac, Ishmael, Jacob and Rebekah. These include a sacrifice offered by Isaac 'on his father's altar that he had made in Hebron' (v. 3), a thank-offering and ritual meal shared by Isaac and Ishmael (v. 4), a new-grain cake made by Rebekah and given by Jacob to Abraham to eat (v. 4), a thank-offering for Abraham, made by Jacob on behalf of Isaac, so that Abraham 'might eat and drink' (v. 5), and blessings given by Abraham to his descendants (vv. 4, 6). Though these rituals are set within the context of the first fruits festival (vv. 2-3), the emphasis on the dying Abraham as the focus and/or consumer (vv. 4, 6) of these sacrifices and offerings, coupled with the kinship and fertility contexts of the rituals, is strikingly reminiscent of activities associated elsewhere with the veneration of the dead. As such, it might be suggested that this text could hint at cultic activity at Hebron (cf. M. Dijkstra, 'Abraham', *DDD*, 3–5).

65. Keel and Küchler, *Orte und Landschaften der Bibel*, 670–96.

is suggestive of a move to promote Abraham as a communal ancestor – probably, as both Oswald Loretz and Thomas Römer argue, in an attempt to displace the dead of local household cults from their influential socio-religious position in favour of a constructed common ancestry.[66]

But a key consideration in assessing the status and religious profile of Hebron and its association with Abraham's tomb is the strong probability that during the Persian period (and continuing into the Hellenistic period), Hebron was not a part of Yehud, but a territory just beyond the border in what was formerly Edomite territory west of the Dead Sea, and later a part of Idumaea.[67] This suggests that the tomb cult might have been within the control of non-Yehudites during this period, a time when the book of Genesis – and its Abraham narratives – was likely compiled. Given the heavy emphasis in this text upon the role of Abraham as *the* national ancestor, and in particular the repeated insistence that he was the legitimate owner of the burial ground at Machpelah, Hebron's probable location beyond Yehud's thresholds raises interesting questions about the territorial associations of the ancestral tomb at this time. Whose land did this tomb mark? Whose ancestors did it house? Were claims to this place contested?

According to Albert de Pury's inclusivist and 'ecumenical' reading of the patriarchal narratives, Abraham has the potential to be claimed by diverse tribal, ethnic and religious groups as their forefather,[68] and the assumed venerative cult of Abraham in and around Hebron offered the so-called priestly writer of Genesis the opportunity to promote his belief that the communities immediately bordering Yehud's frontiers – including the Edomite, Arab and Jewish groups in the broad vicinity of the tomb site – were all the descendants of Abraham. In his vision of the biblical 'Israel', de Pury says, the Priestly Writer 'knew that some of the peoples around Israel, especially on the southern fringes of Palestine, but certainly elsewhere as well, were more closely related in their religious traditions to the Jews than others'.[69]

For de Pury, this inclusive perspective is indicated in Gen. 25:9, in which Abraham is buried in the cave of Machpelah by both Isaac and Ishmael (despite

---

66. Loretz, 'Vom kanaanäischen Totenkult zur jüdischen Patriarchen', 178–89; Römer, 'Les récits patriarcaux contre la vénération des ancêtres', 218–21.

67. Cf. Neh. 11:25-30; 1 Macc. 5:65. See A. Lemaire, 'Nabonidus in Arabia and Judah in the Neo-Babylonian Period', in O. Lipschits and J. Blenkinsopp (eds), *Judah and the Judeans in the Neo-Babylonian Period* (Winona Lake, IN: Eisenbrauns, 2003), 285–98, esp. 290; J. R. Bartlett, 'Edomites and Idumaeans', *PEQ* 131 (1999), 102–114; Grabbe, *History of the Jews and Judaism*, 43–53, 162–66; A. Lemaire, 'Populations et territoires de la Palestine à l'époque perse', *Transeuphratène* 3 (1990), 31–74.

68. De Pury, 'Abraham', 163–81; cf. F. Crüsemann, 'Human Solidarity and Ethnic Identity: Israel's Self-Definition in the Genealogical System of Genesis', in M. G. Brett (ed.), *Ethnicity and the Bible* (Leiden: Brill, 2002), 57–76.

69. De Pury, 'Abraham', 174.

Ishmael's apparent expulsion from the land earlier in the story) and in 35:29, in which Isaac is buried by both Jacob and Esau.[70] The 'ecumenical' nature of the tomb at Hebron is further reflected in the genealogical matrix set out in the book of Genesis, in which Abraham is the father of a variety of ethnic and religious groups, including Jews (identified as the descendants of Isaac), Arabs (identified as the descendants of Ishmael), Edomites (identified as the descendants of Esau), and perhaps also the inhabitants of the former northern kingdom of Israel and the Samaritans (groups whose territories are closely associated with Jacob). Thus the borderland location of the tomb of Abraham at Hebron offered, in de Pury's words, 'un lieu de ralliement partagé' ('a rallying-point') for all the descendants of Abraham.[71]

But this 'ecumenical' reading is perhaps too optimistic. It seems likely that the mix of Yehudite, Arab, 'Edomite' and non-Yehudite Jewish groups living in the Hebron highlands comprised 'an area of heterogeneous, interpermeable societies' typical of the 'frontiers' of traditional (as opposed to modern) states.[72] And so, given the territorial function of tombs as boundary markers, can it really be the case that Hebron was so unproblematic and inclusive a 'rallying-point' for these diverse groups?

While the politico-cultural ambiguities of Hebron's locality and some of the Genesis traditions may allow for an inclusive portrait of Abraham, the patriarchal tomb itself is nonetheless exclusive: in the Hebrew Bible, it is held to be the burial place of Abraham, Sarah, Isaac, Rebekah, Jacob and Leah (Gen. 23:19; 25:9-10; 35:29; 49:29-32; 50:13; cf. 47:29-30), but – significantly – it is not said to be the burial place of the 'rejects' Ishmael and Esau.[73] Indeed, their burial places go unmentioned.[74] Despite the extensive genealogical matrix detailed in Genesis, the

---

70. Ibid., 175.
71. A. de Pury, 'Le tombeau de Abrahamides d'Hébron et sa fonction au début de l'époque perse', *Transeuphratène* 30 (2005), 183–84, here 183.
72. J. W. Wright, 'Remapping Yehud: The Borders of Yehud and the Genealogies of Chronicles', in O. Lipschits and M. Oeming (eds), *Judah and the Judeans in the Persian Period* (Winona Lake, IN: Eisenbrauns, 2006), 67–89, here 72. Wright's important essay highlights the conceptual and ideological problems inherent within scholarly discussions of Yehud's 'borders'; cf. K. W. Whitelam, 'Lines of Power: Mapping Ancient Israel', in R. B. Coote and N. K. Gottwald (eds), *To Break Every Yoke: Essays in Honor of Marvin L. Chaney* (Sheffield: Sheffield Phoenix, 2007), 40–79.
73. Cf. Heard, *Dynamics of Diselection*, 174–78. Rachel is notably absent from the tomb, but buried instead at the place of her death, on the way to Ephrath (Gen. 35:16-20; 48:7; cf. 1 Sam. 10:2; Jer. 31:15); her corpse is not transferred to Machpelah (unlike that of Jacob: Gen. 47:29-30; 49:29-32; 50:5-14), nor is it disinterred for reburial (unlike the remains of Joseph: Gen. 50:25-26; Josh 24:32). See Chapter 4.
74. In Gen. 25:17, the reader is told simply that Ishmael was 'gathered to his people'. This death notice follows a list of Ishmael's descendants in their territories (vv. 12-15), implying, perhaps, that Ishmael's 'people' are these Arab groups. Esau's last appearance in

ancestral tomb – and the land it marks – memorializes just one line of Abrahamic descent. The burial ground is thus home to the ancestral tomb of Isaac's descendants, not Ishmael's; it is the ancestral tomb of Jacob's descendants, not Esau's. From this biblical perspective, the tomb cult at Persian-period Hebron appears more possessively territorial than 'ecumenical'.

This territorialism, closely focused on Machpelah, might also be evident in other ways. There are indications that other (perhaps rival) sanctuaries in different regions might have 'lost' their ancestors to Machpelah in the final, biblical cut of the patriarchal stories. In Gen. 50:7-11, Jacob appears to be buried in the borderlands of the Jordan[75] at the cult place (גרן, 'threshing floor') of Atad in 'Abel-mizraim', while a New Testament tradition claims he is buried at Shechem (Acts 7:15-16), the site at which Joseph's bones are buried in Josh. 24:32 (cf. Sir. 49:15).[76] Moreover, in what is likely a further (though possibly related) tradition in Gen. 50:5, the dying Jacob is said to have requested burial in the tomb he had 'purchased' or 'dug out' (כרה) for himself. This seems to be an allusion to the plot of land he purchases at Shechem, where according to Gen. 33:18-20, he simply sets up an altar, but where, according to Acts 7:15-16 (as noted above) his tomb is said to be located.[77] Though somewhat elusive, these

---

Genesis coincides with his voluntary disappearance from the promised land into Seir (36:6-8), where he and his descendants settle. A post-biblical Jewish tradition, however, states that Esau's head is buried in Machpelah, following his death at the site after a dispute over the patriarchal burial ground (*b.Sotah* 13a). Biblical anxieties about an Edomite claim to Machpelah might underlie the tradition in Gen. 26:34-35 that Esau married into the Hittites, the very group whose willing 'dispossession' of the burial ground is so emphatically asserted throughout Genesis.

75. B. Gemser, 'Beʿēber hajjardēn: In Jordan's Borderland', *VT* 2 (1952), 349–55.

76. The perpetual possession of land marked by the dead is asserted in Josh. 24:32: the site is portrayed as the ancestral land (נחלה) of those claiming descent from Joseph; its occupation and 'ownership' is demonstrated by the presence of the ancestor's bones and also legitimized by its purchase by an ancestor (here Jacob) from its former owners, who are pointedly named in the text. Given its present biblical context and position, this tradition is read in the light of Gen. 50:24-26 and Exod. 13:19, so that the burial of Joseph's bones is presented as a form of secondary interment, rendering his descendants' claim to the land as their נחלה a subsequent and later 'plot' development in the story of this site. This appears to complement Gen. 33:18-20, in which Jacob's purchase of the land is described without reference to any grave, or to bones, or to Joseph and his descendants. However, see the discussion in n. 77, below.

77. On these grave traditions, see S. E. Loewenstamm, 'The Death of the Patriarchs in the Book of Genesis', in *From Babylon to Canaan: Studies in the Bible and Its Oriental Background* (Jerusalem: Magnes, 1992), 78–108, esp. 87–93; see also G. R. H. Wright, 'Joseph's Grave under the Tree by the Omphalos at Shechem', *VT* 22 (1972), 476–86. On the possibility that Jacob buys land at Shechem for a burial ground, see E. Nielsen, *Shechem: A Traditio-Historical Investigation* (Copenhagen: Gad, 1955), 230, who observes: 'Jacob might have been seeking for a burial place, a place for his eternal tent . . . Josh. 24,32 has

fragmentary glimpses of alternative – or perhaps even competing – tomb traditions render the repeated biblical claim that Abraham, Isaac and Jacob are all buried together in Machpelah forcefully or even overly insistent. It is suggestive of a deliberate move to 'centralize' these ancestral figures within one tomb, in one place: Machpelah.

Ideologically, the biblical 'centralization' of the supposedly national ancestors at Machpelah may also betray a territorial interest. The story of Abraham's land purchase is markedly framed at its beginning and end by the close alignment of the tomb site with Hebron (Gen. 23:2, 13). Within the broader biblical context, the narrative framing of the tradition in this way is indicative of the tomb's 'Judahite' placement – and thus by strong implication, a 'Yehudite' claim to the site of Machpelah. It is significant, however, that although post-biblical texts are reasonably clear that the tomb of the patriarchs was located at Hebron, the biblical traditions are more confused about the precise identification and location of the burial ground. This confusion is evident in the ambiguous and changing designations of the tomb site in Genesis itself.

Though the patriarchal burial ground is primarily called 'Machpelah', the precise use of this designation is somewhat uncertain, for it is not always clear whether 'Machpelah' refers to the field, its burial cave, or the wider locality.[78] Contributing further to the confusion is the repeated aligning or identification of Machpelah with Mamre, Kiriath-arba and Hebron.[79] Throughout Genesis, all these toponyms crowd the ancestral burial site, jostling for recognition. Though it

---

preserved the memory of this motive, but connected with Joseph [sic]'. This is supported by the close parallels between Genesis 23 and 33:18-20, the key difference being that the grave at Machpelah is replaced with an altar at Shechem. Given the muted ritual tones of ch. 23, the cultic activity in 33:20 might suggest that the two land deals are distinct. And yet the explicit association in Josh. 24:32 of the land purchase at Shechem with the burial of Joseph's bones suggests that in another version of the tradition underlying Gen. 33:18-20, the land was purchased, like Machpelah, as a burial site. Traces of this aspect of the tradition might be detected in the use of נצב in 33:20, a verb employed in a cultic context in Genesis to refer to the setting up not of a מזבח (altar), but a מצבה (standing stone). On some of the ambiguities of the narrative concerning Jacob's burial, see J. Berman, 'Identity Politics and the Burial of Jacob (Genesis 50:1-14)', *CBQ* 68 (2006), 11–31.

78. Sarna, *Genesis*, 158. The term מכפלה is found in Gen. 23:9, 17, 19; 25:9; 49:30; 50:13. Given its occurrence with the definite article, it is generally thought unlikely to be a personal or divine name. Most translators and commentators (ancient and modern) relate it to כפל, '(to be) double', suggesting that the site's name refers to the 'double-cave' in which the patriarchal family is interred. For a critique of the tenuous view that Machpelah was a cult site of the goddess Cybele, see K. van der Toorn, 'Cybele', *DDD*, 214–15.

79. Machpelah is closely associated with Mamre in Gen. 23:17, 19; 25:9; 49:30; 50:13, which in its turn is identified with Hebron in Gen. 13:18; 23:19; 35:27. Kiriath-arba is identified with Hebron in Gen. 23:2; 35:27; Josh. 14:15; 15:13, 54; 20:7; 21:11; Judg. 1:10 and with Mamre in Gen. 35:27. The tomb site is identified with Hebron in Gen. 23:19 and aligned with Kiriath-arba and Hebron in 23:2.

is often assumed that these were all essentially the same place, the aligning, glossing or renaming of locations is frequently suggestive of changing or competing claims to ownership.[80] It is difficult to assess whether, or the extent to which, the toponymic competition over Abraham's burial ground reflects disputes between different groups, each claiming Abraham as their 'local' ancestor, or is more suggestive of rivalry between multiple sites, each competing for identification with Machpelah. Either way, this is likely something of the background to the different designations of the site in the book of Genesis.[81]

This possibility of competing claims is particularly attractive in considering the persistent association of Machpelah with Mamre (Gen. 23:17, 19; 25:9; 49:30; 50:13) and the insistent (if somewhat clumsy) assertion that these places are to be identified with Kiriath-arba and/or Hebron (13:18; 23:19; 35:27; cf. 23:2). It may be that, by the time the book of Genesis reached the form in which (broadly speaking) it is now found, the identification of all these sites was unproblematic, and that in particular, the 'double cave' was widely understood to be located in the region of Hebron. But the complexity of the means by which Hebron and Machpelah are aligned in the biblical texts is suggestive of a more determined and forceful assertion that the two designations ultimately refer to the same place. And the ideological potency of this assertion renders this suggestion more compelling. Within the context of the varied biblical traditions, Hebron carries great religious and political weight: in Num. 13:22, it is hailed as a city of great antiquity; in the books of Joshua and Judges, Hebron is the ancestral inheritance of Caleb, the conquering tribal hero of Judah (Josh. 14:13-15; 15:13; Judg. 1:20; cf. Josh. 21:11), and the 'locative center' of Judah's ancestral territory (1 Chr. 2:42-55),[82] while in Samuel and Kings, it is vividly portrayed as a ritual seat of Davidic kingship (2 Sam. 2:11; 5:1-5; 1 Kgs 2:1; cf. 2 Sam. 15:7-10). Within all these biblical traditions, Hebron is clearly a high-status *Judahite* location; its asserted function in Genesis as home to the Cave of Machpelah not only emphasizes this, but bolsters its credentials as a locus of cultic, ancestral and 'national' prestige.

In essence, then, the Persian period book of Genesis portrays the ancestral site of Machpelah as a place belonging to the citizens of Yehud, not those peoples beyond its borders. The biblical Cave of Machpelah therefore represents a

---

80. See O. Eissfeldt, 'Renaming in the Old Testament', in P. R. Ackroyd and B. Lindars (eds), *Words and Meanings: Essays Presented to David Winton Thomas* (Cambridge: Cambridge University Press, 1968), 70–83. As Hamilton points out (*Genesis 18–50*, 126), place names are often changed in biblical narratives when a change in ownership occurs, though the context is usually one of conflict or land seizure, e.g. Num. 32:42; Deut. 3:15; Josh. 19:47; cf. 2 Sam. 5:7-9.

81. *Pace* E. Lipiński, '*ʿAnaq – Kiryat ʾArbaʿ* – Hébron et ses sanctuaries tribaux', *VT* 24 (1974), 41–55.

82. Employing John Wright's phrase in 'Remapping Yehud', 79.

'centralized' ancestral tomb,[83] in which the similarly 'centralized' and paradigmatic ancestor Abraham is located, and by which the genealogical and territorial dimensions of an emergent, Persian period, biblical 'Judaism' are marked. In Genesis 23, the territorial potential of Machpelah is realized and exploited in two ways: on one level, it seeks to legitimize early 'Jewish' claims to the site of the tomb cult at Machpelah; on another, it serves as a paradigm of land-appropriation for incomers, whose acquisition and possession of land occupied by 'foreigners' is bolstered both by its commodification and ancestralization.

In the book of Genesis, Abraham may be presented as an inclusive ancestor, but his land deal is assertively territorial, and his tomb site is exclusively Judahite – and therefore pointedly 'Jewish'. An inclusive or 'ecumenical' reading of Abraham might be more palatable to modern readers, but in Genesis 23, it is counter to the essential territorialism of the biblical tradition. As such, Machpelah models more than an ancestral landmark on the biblical map of 'Israel'; it indexes – both within and beyond the Hebrew Bible – the ideological centrality of the past and the dead in the lives and the land of the living.

---

83. Cf. Römer, 'Les récits patriarcaux contre la vénération des ancêtres', 213–25, esp. 223. On the 'Judahite' claim to Abraham in the books of Isaiah and Ezekiel, see Tiemeyer, 'Abraham – A Judahite Prerogative', 49–66.

Chapter 3

Moses at the Edge

If Abraham is presented in the Hebrew Bible as the genealogical ancestor of the biblical Israel, Moses is cast as its 'vocational' ancestor.[1] Like Abraham, he is the recipient of a repeated divine promise of a homeland for future generations; like Abraham, he is dislocated from the foreign land of his past in order to secure this promised homeland; and as with Abraham, continued biblical claims to land are prominently marked with reference to him.[2] But unlike Abraham, Moses does not enter the land divinely promised. And unlike Abraham, he leaves no gravesite as a marker and memorial to the land claims of later generations. Instead, he leaves Torah:

> He said to them: 'Take to heart all the words I am giving in witness against you this day, with which you shall command your descendants, so that they may diligently observe all the words of this Torah. This is no trifling matter for you – it is your very life; through it you may live long in the land that you are crossing over the Jordan to possess.' (Deut. 32:46-47; cf. 31:12-13)

In the context of the territorial interests of the biblical traditions, it might thus be assumed that the Moses story offers an ideology of land possession opposed to overtly ancestral forms of territorial marking. Indeed, it is often recognized that two origins stories frame the identity ideologies of the Hebrew Bible. One traces the beginnings of the biblical Israel back to Abraham, while the other locates Israel's birth in the events of the exodus from Egypt under Moses. Though these foundation myths have been bound together as broadly consecutive episodes in the biblical story of Israel,[3] Moses' role as land-giver – symbolized not by an

---

1. De Pury, 'Abraham', 166; cf. M. Dijkstra, 'The Law of Moses: The Memory of Mosaic Religion in and after the Exile', in R. Albertz and B. Becking (eds), *Yahwism After the Exile: Perspectives on Israelite Religion in the Persian Era* (Assen: Van Gorcum, 2003), 70–98. For various nuances of Moses' biblical portrayal, see conveniently T. Römer (ed.), *La construction de la figure de Moïse* (Paris: Gabalda, 2007).

2. E.g. Josh. 1:3-4, 13-15; 9:24; 1 Sam. 12:8; Neh. 9:14-15; Bar. 1:20; cf. 2 Kgs 21:8; 2 Chr. 33:8; 2 Macc. 1:29.

3. See J. Van Seters, 'The Patriarchs and the Exodus: Bridging the Gap between Two

ancestral grave but scribal law – might be viewed as embodying an alternative and competing representation of land appropriation to that of Abraham.

Certain features of the story of Moses support this assumption about the land ideology with which he is associated, as shall be seen. And yet the contours of Moses' land legacy are also shaped by an adherence and appeal to beliefs and practices associated with the territoriality of the dead. In mapping Moses' land legacy, the discussion will begin at his lost tomb.

Moses' Memorial

In contrast to later Jewish and non-Jewish traditions, the Moses of the Hebrew Bible is not taken up to heaven upon or before his death,[4] but dies and is buried in Moabite territory, without setting foot in the promised land. Though his death is an explicit feature of four passages (Num. 27:12-14; Deut. 31:14-16; 32:48-52; 34:1-8), only the last of these, Deut. 34:1-8, describes Moses' burial and its location. Verses 5-6 of the Masoretic version read:

> Moses, the servant of Yhwh, died there in the land of Moab, at the decree of Yhwh. He [Yhwh][5] buried him in the valley in the land of Moab, near Beth Peor, and no one knows his burial place to this day.

Given the broad indication here of the location of Moses' grave, the claim that the precise whereabouts of his tomb is unknown is perhaps intended to be understood as a direct result of Moses' burial by Yhwh himself: this both ascribes an implicitly divine setting to the gravesite and explains why no mortal could possibly know its location.[6] But this burial story is not simply concerned with attributing an extraordinarily prestigious burial to such an elevated a figure; the lost tomb tradition also serves several related functions.

Origin Traditions', in R. Roukema (ed.), *The Interpretation of Exodus: Studies in Honour of Cornelis Houtman* (CBET, 44; Leuven: Peeters, 2006), 1–15; N. P. Lemche, *The Israelites in History and Tradition* (Louisville, KY: Westminster John Knox Press, 1998).

4. See particularly S. Loewenstamm, 'The Death of Moses', in G. W. E. Nickelsburg (ed.), *Studies on the Testament of Abraham* (Missoula, MT: Scholars Press, 1972), 185–217, and R. D. Aus, *The Death, Burial, and Resurrection of Jesus and the Death, Burial, and Translation of Moses in Judaic Tradition* (Lanham, MD: University Press of America, 2008).

5. Within the narrative context of these verses, Moses and Yhwh are the only two characters present, rendering Yhwh himself the subject of the verb in the phrase ויקבר אתו. A theological discomfort with this text is evident among some of the Versions, which instead assume ויקברו.

6. See also Loewenstamm, 'The Death of Moses', 195; R. D. Nelson, *Deuteronomy: A Commentary* (OTL; Louisville, KY: Westminster John Knox Press, 2002), 396; R. Lux, 'Der Tod des Moses, als "besprochene und erzählte Welt"', *ZTK* 84 (1987), 395–425, here 421.

3. *Moses at the Edge*

First, it renders Moses' burial a paradox: the lost tomb marks both the continual presence and continued absence of his corpse; the precise yet loose location of his burial hides the specific place of his grave; and the burial itself is performed by the very deity whose continued relationship with the living is supposedly marked by the necessity for the separation of the divine from the dead.[7] Thus in death – as in life – Moses traverses the socially sanctioned 'normative' and 'normalizing' boundaries both within and between the human and divine worlds. He is incomparably unique.

Second, the claimed existence of a lost tomb at once underlines the mortality of this 'divine man' (איש האלהים) whom Yhwh knew 'face to face',[8] and discourages (not altogether successfully) the belief that Moses was taken up to heaven. Possible motivations for this include Deuteronomy's intolerance of other divine beings and their cults, and a perceived theological need to distance the revelatory and mediatory roles of Moses from the magico-ritual divination of the divine man Elijah, who ascends to heaven (2 Kgs 2:11), and the divine man Elisha, whose tomb is a source and locus of resurrective power (2 Kgs 13:21).[9]

Third, the unknown location of the tomb theoretically robs localized groups of a territorial claim to Moses' grave. Indeed, the likelihood that there were conflicting – and perhaps competing – stories about the place of Moses' death might be indicated in Deut. 34:1. Here, the Moabite mountain from which Moses views the promised land and (implicitly, recalling 32:49-50) upon which he dies, is both Nebo and Pisgah, mountains which, in other texts, appear to be given separate locations.[10] While this double designation may echo mythic conceptions

---

7. As Ziony Zevit comments, 'In general, Yahwism as presented in extant biblical texts conceived of YHWH as lord of the living. Death was the ultimate contaminant of all that was particularly sacred to him' (*Religions of Ancient Israel*, 664). Note, however, the discussions in Chapters 1 and 6.

8. E.g. Exod. 33:11; Num. 12:8; Deut. 34:10-12; cf. Exod. 34:30-35. The designation איש האלהים is used of Moses in Deut. 33:1; Josh. 14:6. On the religio-historical implications of this title, see M. Dijkstra, 'Moses, the Man of God', in R. Roukema (ed.), *The Interpretation of Exodus: Studies in Honour of Cornelis Houtman* (CBET, 44; Leuven: Peeters, 2006), 17–36.

9. The title איש האלהים is used repeatedly of Elijah and Elisha: 1 Kgs 17:18, 24; 2 Kgs 1:9-13; 4:16, 21-22, 25, 27, 40; 5:8, 14-15, 20; 6:6, 9-15; 7:2, 17-19; 8:2-4, 7-8, 11. For the tradition concerning Elisha's grave, see most recently J. Shemesh, 'The Elisha Stories as Saint's Legends', *JHS* 8 (2008), article 5. The 'empty tomb' traditions associated with Jesus of Nazareth in New Testament texts also appear to function in similar ways; as well as claiming resurrection for the hero, they also assert his mortality while discouraging a corpse-cult; like Moses, Jesus is also believed to have ascended to the heavenly realm after his death (e.g. Mark 16:19; Acts 1:2, 11, 22). See Aus, *The Death, Burial, and Resurrection of Jesus and the Death, Burial, and Translation of Moses*, esp. 173–230.

10. E.g. Num. 33:47; Deut. 32:49; Jer. 48:1 (Nebo); Num. 21:20; 23:14; Deut. 3:17, 27; 4:49; Josh. 12:3; 13:20 (Pisgah); cf. *Sifre* Ha'azinu 338 and *Midrash Tannaim* on Deut. 32:49. Some commentators seek to smooth these traditions by conflating the precise

of the twin-peaked, cosmic mountain,[11] the indeterminacy concerning the place of Moses' death allows for an uncertainty concerning the precise place of his burial. The unknown location of Moses' tomb also discourages pilgrimage and other cultic activities which would undermine the idealized notion of centralized worship so highly prized in Deuteronomy.[12] A tomb cult of Moses would likely attract a particular sort of venerative attention given the tradition presenting the living Moses as the supreme mediator between the divine and human realms – how much more effective, then, would be Moses' post-mortem mediation?[13]

Finally, the lost tomb tradition might also reflect a concern that the scribal heart of Deuteronomic religion should not be overshadowed by a grave-cult of the figure from whom the archaic authority of Torah is derived. Indeed, citing an important work by Jean-Pierre Sonnet, Joachim Schaper comments:

> Deuteronomy tells us that the location of the grave of Moses is not known. This is in paradoxical contrast with the fact that his ספר is – or will be – known everywhere. Sonnet captures that when he writes: 'The actual removal of Moses' burial place from public knowledge (34:6, "and no one knows") is, analogically, the reverse of the actual publication of his Torah "book" throughout time and space [. . .]'. On the one hand, thus, death brings oblivion, but on the other hand, it makes room for a new, permanent life for Moses.[14]

The memorializing function of the written Torah is an important subject to which the discussion will presently return, for it plays a key role in the imaging of

---

locations of Moses' death scene; thus, for example, Moshe Weinfeld (*Deuteronomy and the Deuteronomic School* [Oxford: Clarendon Press, 1972], 177), identifies Pisgah as the name of the summit of Nebo, and Nebo as upon the heights of the Abarim (cf. *Sifre* 'Eqeb 37 on Deut. 7:12; 11:10).

11. See M. Dijkstra, 'The Weather-God on Two Mountains', *UF* 23 (1991), 127–40; N. Wyatt, *Space and Time in the Religious Life of the 'Ancient' Near East* (BS, 85; Sheffield: Sheffield Academic Press, 2001), 153–54. For Baal's burial on the cosmic mountain Zaphon, see below, 129.

12. Some post-biblical traditions attest to venerative cults of Moses at the site of his grave; see, for example, *Berakhah* 102; R. Raabe (ed. and trans.), *Petrus der Iberer: Ein Charakterbild zur Kirchen- und Sittengeschichte des 5. Jahrhunderts: Syrische Übersetzung einer um das Jahr 500 verfassten griechischen Biographie* (Leipzig: Hinrichs, 1895), 85, 88.

13. Cf. Lightstone, *Commerce of the Sacred*, 51.

14. J. Schaper, 'The Living Word Engraved in Stone: The Interrelationship of the Oral and the Written and the Culture of Memory in the Books of Deuteronomy and Joshua', in L. T. Stuckenbruck, S. C. Barton and B. G. Wold (eds), *Memory in the Bible and Antiquity: The Fifth Durham-Tübingen Research Symposium* (WUNT, 212; Tübingen: Mohr Siebeck, 2007), 9–23, here 17, citing J.-P. Sonnet, *The Book within the Book: Writing in Deuteronomy* (Biblical Interpretation Series, 14; Leiden: Brill, 1997), 230.

Moses' land legacy. But that legacy is also shaped by the *absence* of the biblical Moses – in life and in death – from the land promised to the people Israel.

The biblical Moses does not cross the Jordan and enter this promised land. Instead, he dies on its margins. The interrelation of Moses' death and his non-entry into the land is given a heavy emphasis in Deut. 32:48-52, which casts Moses' death within sight of the promised land as a divine punishment for his rebellion against Yhwh at Meribah, a story told in Num. 20:2-13. This particular tradition in Deuteronomy complements that attested in Num. 27:13-14, which similarly attributes Moses' death just beyond the land to his sin at Meribah. But in the story of the rebellion at Meribah itself, in Num. 20:2-13, Moses' punishment is not said to be death, but the divine decree that neither he nor Aaron will lead the assembled Israelites into the land (v. 12). Instead, it is Aaron alone who dies on a notably non-descript mountain at the edge of the promised land (vv. 23-26).[15] The other traditions in Deuteronomy concerning Moses' death do not present it as a punishment, but as the inevitable result of the divine decree that Moses simply would not cross into the land: in the lost tomb tradition, he is shown the land from a Moabite mountain top and informed by Yhwh that 'I have let you see it with your eyes, but you shall not cross over there' (Deut. 34:4); in 31:2-3, Moses' great age is related to his inability 'to go out and to come in' (לצאת ולבוא, in this context referring to invasion and warfare) and this in its turn is related to Yhwh's announcement that Moses will not cross over the Jordan. Notably, this brief passage does not even directly align Moses' absence from the promised land with his death, which is said several verses later to be drawing near (vv. 14, 16).

The interrelation of Moses' death and his non-entry into the land is thus neither a stable nor a coherent tradition in the Hebrew Bible. But neither is it necessarily a theologically negative tradition, contrary to its frequent scholarly portrayal.[16] In Deut. 31:3, for example, Yhwh is to function almost as Moses' substitute in leading the people across the Jordan and into warfare with the inhabitants of the land. There is, to be sure, bathos in the notion that Moses dies on the brink of fulfilling his divine duty. In this sense, as George Coats points out, he is a tragic but heroic figure, of a type familiar from other biblical and non-biblical

---

15. The mountain is here called הר ההר 'Mount Mountain', though it is significant that this place is given a borderland location at the edge of Edom (Num. 20:23).

16. See, for example, S. Schwertuer, 'Erwägungen zu Moses Tod und Grab in Dtn 34 5.6', *ZAW* 84 (1972), 25–46. Norman Habel comments: 'Joshua outshines Moses. Joshua, unlike Moses, has been totally faithful to YHWH and is the one privileged leader from the wilderness days to enter and enjoy the promised land' (*The Land is Mine*, 66, see also 47). In discussing Deut. 32:48-52, Richard Nelson refers to Moses' 'scandalous death outside the land' (*Deuteronomy*, 378). For a detailed discussion of Deut. 34:1-12 and its presentation(s) of the death of Moses, see C. Frevel, 'Ein vielsagender Abschied. Exegetische Blicke auf den Tod des Mose in Dtn 34,1-12', *BZ* 45 (2001), 209–34.

literatures.[17] But within the ideological frame of the Hebrew Bible, does Moses' death at the edge of the promised land relegate his land legacy to a catalogue of his lesser achievements, falling well behind liberation, Decalogue, covenant and Torah?

It is abundantly clear that Moses' absence from the land does not lessen the high ideological value of its promise, possession and inheritance in the texts of Torah and elsewhere in the Hebrew Bible. Indeed, in several passages, land claims are asserted and set within the explicit context of the binding commands of Moses (for example, Josh. 9:24; 2 Kgs 21:8); family and tribal territories are allotted by him (for example, Josh. 13:8, 15, 24, 29, 32); and the conquest itself, under the leadership of Joshua, is validated with Yhwh's explicit reference to the divine promise of land he made to Moses: 'Every place that the sole of your foot will tread upon I have given to you, as I promised to Moses' (Josh. 1:3). But though the Mosaic legitimation of the appropriation, allocation and possession of land is a recurring theme in the territorial ideologies of these texts, the theme is not grounded in the presence of Moses – dead or alive – in the land. It might thus be assumed that the placement of Moses' death and burial outside the land is a strong indication that land possession is not thought by the biblical tradents of the Moses traditions to be marked by the dead.

For the patriarchal family in Genesis (as the previous chapter has argued), burial on home ground is not simply an ideal, but an ideological necessity – hence Abraham's insistence on buying and owning the burial ground at Machpelah (Genesis 23); hence too the persistence of the tradition emphasizing Jacob's burial in the cave at Machpelah, despite his death in Egypt, and in spite of his association with other gravesites.[18] Even Joseph, a likely late-comer to the family group, is given a secondary burial in Canaan, following his interment in Egypt.[19] This ideological emphasis on the burial of the biblical ancestors *in* the land belonging to the biblical Israel clearly serves a territorial function, and equally clearly contrasts with Moses' burial *outside* the land. This contrast might be understood as an effort to endorse or encourage diaspora burials beyond the bounds of the homeland.[20] Or it might be perceived as a deliberate counter to

---

17. G. W. Coats, 'Legendary Motifs in the Moses Death Reports', *CBQ* 39 (1977), 34–44, reprinted in idem, *The Moses Tradition* (JSOTS, 161; Sheffield: JSOT Press, 1993), 76–87, here 82–83; see also H. Barzel, 'Moses: Tragedy and Sublimity', in K. R. R. Gros Louis, J. S. Ackerman and T. S. Warshaw (eds), *Literary Interpretations of Biblical Narratives* (Nashville, TN: Abingdon Press, 1974), 120–40.

18. See Gen. 47:29-30; 49:29-33; 50:5, 7-11; cf. Acts 7:15-16.

19. See Gen. 50:25-26; Exod. 13:19; Josh. 24:32 (cf. Gen. 48:21).

20. See T. Römer, 'Moses Outside the Torah and the Construction of a Diaspora Identity', *JHS* 8 (2008), article 15, who suggests that the tradition concerning Moses' burial outside the promised land functions as a discrete critique of diaspora Jews seeking ossuary burials in and around Jerusalem in order to avoid the 'curse' of burial in a foreign land. See also

the patriarchal tomb ideology of Genesis.[21] Indeed, the absence of any kin and descendants at Moses' gravesite, and the solitary nature of his 'unmarked' tomb, might similarly suggest an anti-familial, even an 'anti-patriarchal', perspective, undercutting the crucial, collective identity of the ancestors.[22] But as observed at this chapter's start, Moses is not presented as a genealogical ancestor of the biblical Israel; he is its vocational ancestor. Thus the place of his burial is not the site for a cult of kin. But neither is it anti-patriarchal in its placement outside the land. Rather, Moses' burial can be seen to perform a territorial function, for the location of his grave just beyond the Jordan in Moab is not only marginal, but liminal.

The liminality of Moses' burial is evident not only in its perpetually transitional character (a corpse that is present and absent; a gravesite that is at once placed and lost), but also in its location at the threshold of the promised land (Deut. 34:1-6), a border-location emphasized in the loaded reference to the prohibited 'crossing' (vv. 4-6), a point of transition between the wilderness and the land divinely promised:

> Yhwh said to him, 'This is the land of which I swore to Abraham, to Isaac, and to Jacob, saying, "I will give it to your descendants"; I have let you see it with your eyes, but you shall not cross over there'. Then Moses, the servant of Yhwh, died there in the land of Moab, at the decree of Yhwh. He [Yhwh] buried him in the valley in the land of Moab, near Beth Peor, and no one knows his burial place to this day. (Deut. 34:1-6)

This liminal location is also represented by the placing of Moses' tomb in neither the wilderness, in which the Israelite dead are left unmarked,[23] nor in the promised land, in which the Israelite dead are (to be) interred in their allocated land-holdings.[24] Moses' gravesite is placed in the space in between the landless and the landed; in between Israel's past and its future. But this should not be assumed to suggest that Moses' burial place is territorially impotent. On the

---

(for example), Jer. 20:6; Amos 7:17; cf. Gen. 47:29-30; Ezek. 37:12-14. On later diaspora attitudes to burial in and out of the land, see I. M. Gafni, *Land, Center and Diaspora: Jewish Constructs in Late Antiquity* (Sheffield: Sheffield Academic Press, 1997), 79–95.

21. Thus Sonnet, *Book within the Book*, 225–26.

22. For a redaction-critical perspective on the similarities and differences between the burials of the patriarchs, Aaron and Moses (but which assumes a territorial dimension only for the patriarchs), see D. Nocquet, 'La mort des patriarches, d'Aaron et de Moïse. L'apport de l'écriture sacerdotale à la constitution du Pentateuque à l'époque perse', *Transeuphratène* 29 (2005), 133–53. Moses' 'unknown' burial place contrasts with that of Aaron on the (ambiguously named) 'Mount Hor' (Num. 20:22, 28; cf. Deut. 10:6) and that of Miriam in Kadesh (Num. 20:1).

23. Leveen, *Memory and Tradition in the Book of Numbers*, 140–65.

24. E.g. Josh. 24:30, 33; Judg. 2:9.

contrary, as a boundary burial, Moses' gravesite functions as a territorial marker of particular mythic and symbolic significance.

An important indication of this is found in the description of the place of Moses' burial: '(Yhwh) buried him in the valley in the land of Moab, opposite Beth Peor' (Deut. 34:6). Certainly, the 'valley' is a most appropriate place for burial, marking the entrance to the underworld in the mytho-symbolic landscape. But Moses' grave is also specifically situated in relation to (מול) Beth Peor,[25] a biblical toponym around which are gathered a complex of territorial, mythic and cultic motifs particularly associated with the Transjordanian domain of the dead. Beth Peor (Deut. 3:29; 4:46; 34:6; Josh. 13:20) seems to be imagined as identical with the site named Peor in Num. 23:28, a Transjordanian cult place overlooking the wilderness.[26] Within its biblical context, this in its turn is probably best understood as the site of the cult of Baal of Peor (Num. 25:1-16; 31:16; Deut. 4:3; Josh. 22:17; Ps. 106:28; cf. Hos. 9:10).[27] Though many commentators dwell on the assumed role of ritual sex in the worship of Baal of Peor,[28] others emphasize the association of this sacred site with a cult of the dead in Ps. 106:28, a verse in which the Israelites' worship of Baal of Peor is framed alongside their eating sacrifices offered to (or for) the dead (ויאכלו זבחי מתים). The netherworld context implicit in this tradition merits serious consideration, for Peor is also a cult place associated with plague, itself personified and deified in biblical and non-biblical texts as one of the denizens of the underworld.[29] And as Klaas

---

25. The preposition מול might be rendered 'near', 'opposite', 'in front of', and can often refer to a boundary location (e.g. Josh 18:18; 19:46; 22:11; 1 Sam 14:5) or a liminal space in cultic matters, whether in spatial terms or with reference to apparatus or vestments (e.g. Exod 18:19; 26:9; 28:25, 37; 34:3; 39:18; Lev 8:9; Num 8:2, 3; Josh 8:33).

26. Cf. O. Henke, 'Zur Lage von Beth Peor', *ZDPV* 75 (1959), 155–63.

27. It is possible that the names פעור and בית פעור are contracted forms of the toponym *בית בעל פעור (see *HALOT*, 3.949–50).

28. In Numbers 25 (the most detailed version of the tradition concerning Baal of Peor), Israelite participation in this cult is directly related to and prompted by their 'whoring' with Moabite (and in some verses, Midianite) women. This has encouraged some commentators to assume that the cult of Baal of Peor is intended to be understood as a fertility cult comprising sexual rites (and thereby rendering the impaling of its male participants a suitably sardonic punishment for their phallic 'piercing' of the Moabite women). However, though this might go some way to explain the association of the worship of Baal of Peor with human infertility in Hos. 9:10-12 (cf. vv. 13-14), the assumption that ritual sex played a role in the worship of Baal of Peor is best handled carefully, given the common framing of religious malpractice as sexual malpractice in the Hebrew Bible. For a balanced overview of these issues, see B. A. Levine, *Numbers 21–36: A New Translation with Introduction and Commentary* (AB, 4A; New York: Doubleday, 2000), 294–97; see also S. L. Budin, *The Myth of Sacred Prostitution in Antiquity* (Cambridge: Cambridge University Press, 2008).

29. The term מגפה, 'plague' or 'pestilence', is used in the context of Peor in Num. 25:8, 9, 18; 31:16; Ps. 106:28, 29, 30 (cf. Josh. 22:17). Though מגפה itself does not appear to be attested as the name of a plague deity, it is directly related to the terminology employed to

Spronk observes, the name Peor itself points to a connection with the chthonic, for it is likely related to פער, 'open wide', a term employed of the swallowing mouth of Sheol in Isa. 5:14.[30] This imagery is drawn on the northwest Semitic portrayal of Mot (death) and/or the underworld as a voracious swallower of insatiable appetite, a notion with which several biblical writers appear to have been particularly familiar.[31] Indeed, the possibility that the toponym Peor alludes to the entrance to the netherworld finds contextual support in another Moses tradition which similarly images the wilderness as the swallowing underworld: the biblical story of Dathan and Abiram.

Though the lengthier version of this tradition occurs in Num. 16:12-34, references to it are also found in 26:9-10; Deut. 11:6 and Ps. 106:17. In the Numbers narrative (a complex composition interweaving several traditions, including that of Korah),[32] Dathan and Abiram are cast as rebellious Israelites, challenging the leadership and authority of Moses in the wilderness by doubting his vision of a land flowing with milk and honey and his promise of an ancestral landholding (נחלה). The response is striking:

> Dathan and Abiram came out and stood at the entrance of their tents, together with their wives, their sons, and their little ones. And Moses said, 'This is how you shall know that Yhwh has sent me to do all these works; it has not been of my own devising: If these men die as all men do, or if the common fate of men comes upon them, then Yhwh has not sent me. But if Yhwh creates something new, and the ground (אדמה) opens its mouth and swallows them up, with all that belongs to them, and they go down alive into Sheol, then you shall know that these men have spurned Yhwh'. As soon as he finished speaking all these words, the ground (אדמה) under them was split apart. The underworld (ארץ) opened its mouth and swallowed them up with their households, all Korah's people and all their property. So they with all that belonged to them went down alive into Sheol; the underworld (ארץ) closed over them, and they perished from the midst of the assembly. All Israel around them fled at their outcry, for they said, 'The underworld (ארץ) will swallow us too!' (Num. 16:27-34; cf. 13:22)

---

describe the activity of the Destroyer in Exod. 12:23, a biblical plague deity imaged in ways similar to the better-known plague deities of ancient West Asia; מגפה as a divine plague also appears to be personified in Num. 17:7-15 (ET 16:42-50); see S. A. Meier, 'Destroyer', *DDD*, 240–44, esp. 242–43.

30. K. Spronk, 'Baal of Peor', *DDD*, 147–48; see also idem, *Beatific Afterlife*, 231–32.

31. E.g. Prov. 1:12; 27:20; 30:15-16; Ps. 141:7; Hab. 2:5; cf. Isa. 25:8. For a recent (if cautious) examination of Mot in biblical and Ugaritic traditions, see S. U. Gulde, *Der Tod als Herrscher in Ugarit und Israel* (FAT, 22; Tübingen: Mohr Siebeck, 2007), esp. 129–57.

32. See M. Noth, *Numbers: A Commentary* (trans. J. D. Martin. OTL; London: SCM Press, 1968), 120–22; B. A. Levine, *Numbers 1–20: A New Translation with Introduction and Commentary* (AB, 4; New York: Doubleday, 1993), 423–32.

In its current context, this is presented as an extraordinary event (v. 30) designed to demonstrate Yhwh's endorsement of Moses, and seeking to implicate the rebellious Korah, who intrudes somewhat awkwardly into the tale of the fate of Dathan and Abiram. But motifs central to the veneration of the ancestral dead are also in view: descendants, property, and the household are all represented here (vv. 27, 32-33; cf. Deut. 11:6) and, along with Dathan and Abiram (and Korah), they are all swallowed by the underworld (vv. 32-33; Deut. 11:6) – their disappearance apparently unmarked, and their existence thereby lost. Even the names Abiram (אבירם) and Dathan (דתן), which appear infrequently in biblical texts, are indicative of a mythic backdrop to the biblical tradition, for the former means 'My Ancestor is Exalted', and the latter is the name of the most prominent among the deified royal ancestors at Ugarit, a netherworld figure most likely identified with 'Rapiu, King of the Hereafter' (*KTU* 1.108.1).[33]

Given this biblical story of the swallowing underworld, it is not unreasonable to credit the toponym Peor with a netherworld connotation. This is further rendered plausible in view of the chthonic associations of other biblical toponyms located in the same region as (Beth-) Peor, east of the Dead Sea: Oboth (Num. 21:10-11; 33:43-44) is also a cultic name associated with the dead in several biblical and non-biblical texts, while Raphon (1 Macc. 5:37) may well be related to the designation Rephaim, the mythic and collective name of the royal dead in biblical and Ugaritic literature.[34] But while these particular place names are mentioned only fleetingly in biblical texts dealing with this area of the Transjordan, the place called Abarim plays a more significant role. Like Oboth and Raphon, it too is given a location in the same Dead Sea region as (Beth-) Peor (cf. Num. 21:11; 33:44-48), and like (Beth-) Peor, it is a place closely associated with the death and burial of Moses.

In both Num. 27:12-13 and Deut. 32:49-50, Abarim (עברים) is the name of the mountain-range from which Moses views the promised land and upon which he dies.[35] This would appear to be a most appropriate location for death, for the designation עברים also alludes to the 'Oberim' (עברים), a collective name for

---

33. דתן and אבירם also occur in Num. 26:9; Deut. 11:6; Ps. 106:17 (cf. Sir. 45:18; 4 Macc. 2:17), all with reference to the tradition detailed in Numbers 16. The only other biblical occurrence of the name אבירם is in 1 Kgs 16:34, in which it is the name of the sacrificed firstborn of Hiel (on which see F. Stavrakopoulou, *King Manasseh and Child Sacrifice: Biblical Distortions of Historical Realities* [BZAW, 338; Berlin: de Gruyter, 2004], 187–88). For Dathan's appearances in Ugaritic and Akkadian texts, see K. Spronk, 'Dadan', *DDD*, 232–33 (with literature) and O. Loretz, *Götter – Ahnen – Könige als gerechte Richter: Der 'Rechtsfall' des Menschen vor Gott nach altorientalischen und biblischen Texten* (AOAT, 290; Münster: Ugarit-Verlag, 2003), 216–58. For Rapiu, see n. 50.

34. Spronk, *Beatific Afterlife*, 228–30. On the Rephaim, see below. For Oboth, see the literature cited in Chapter 6, n. 48.

35. In Deuteronomy's version of this tradition, the Abarim mountain top appears to be specified as Nebo (32:49; 34:1; cf. Num. 33:47). In Deut. 34:1, Pisgah, Abarim and Nebo are

the dead who 'cross over' (עבר) from the realm of the living into the underworld (cf. Job 33:18), and is cognate with the Ugaritic word ʿbrm, which denotes the deified dead (*KTU* 1.22 i 15). The term עברים thus designates the dead as 'the ones who cross over' to the netherworld, and occurs in precisely this context in the oracle against Gog in Ezek. 39:11-15.[36] In this text, the Valley of Oberim (גי העברים) is thus the 'valley of the dead'; it is the transition point into the underworld for the עברים and the fitting burial place of the defeated Gog and his army.[37] Located 'east of the sea' (Ezek. 39:11), this valley can be identified as lying at the roots of the Abarim mountain range, east of the Dead Sea, the place of Moses' death. The liminal nature of this location is thus a suitable setting for Moses' death and valley-burial, the point where he will 'cross over' from the land of the living into the realm of the dead.

But Abarim is also the liminal 'crossing' point into the land divinely promised, the place at which Moses is shown the land he will not enter: 'I have let you see it with your eyes, but you shall not cross over (עבר) there' (Deut. 34:4; cf. 3:27; 31:2). Moses' death and burial at this precise place of transition, at this 'crossing point' into the netherworld or into the promised land, is insistently, emphatically, marked in the biblical texts with the repeated presence of the word 'there' (שם) – 'there' is the land of promise but, in contrast, 'there', just beyond the border of the promised land, is the place where Moses dies: 'Yhwh said to him, "This is the land of which I swore to Abraham, to Isaac, and to Jacob ... but you shall not cross over *there*." Then Moses, the servant of Yhwh, died *there* in the land of Moab' (Deut. 34:4-5).[38] This profusion of deictics signals the interrelation of these different spaces, so that though his tomb is lost among the Abarim, the text sepulchres Moses 'there'.[39]

Moses' burial 'there' at the crossing point into the promised land, 'there' at Abarim, the valley of the dead, 'there' in front of Beth Peor, the cultic, open mouth of the swallowing underworld, is thus a boundary burial. In its narrative context, it marks both the entrance into the underworld and the entrance into the promised land, placed on the threshold between life in the land and death in the

---

all mentioned, suggesting an attempt to smooth a confusion of traditions about the mountain on which Moses died (as discussed above).

36. See S. Ribichini and P. Xella, 'La Valle dei Pasanti (Ezechiel 39.11)', *UF* 12 (1980), 434–37; Spronk, *Beatific Afterlife*, 229–30; M. H. Pope, 'Notes on the Rephaim Texts from Ugarit', in M. de Jong Ellis (ed.), *Ancient Near Eastern Studies in Memory of J. J. Finkelstein* (Hamden, CT: Archon, 1977), 163–82; B. P. Irwin, 'Molek Imagery and the Slaughter of Gog in Ezekiel 38 and 39', *JSOT* 65 (1995), 93–112.

37. On this text, see Stavrakopoulou, 'Gog's Grave', 67–84.

38. Emphasis added. See also Deut. 1:37-39; 32:49-50.

39. The 'sepulchring' function of words is drawn from a discussion of Abraham Lincoln's Gettysburg address in Robert Harrison's *Dominion of the Dead*, 28. It is noteworthy that in Num. 20:1, Miriam's death and burial is not marked with a tomb, but with the sepulchral use of שם (twice); see also Num. 20:28, referring to Aaron's death and (implied) burial.

wilderness. As a boundary burial, it also marks the territory given by Yhwh to the Israelites – hence it is a land explicitly mapped out before Moses' eyes, specifically on the point of his death and at the place of his burial, in Deut. 34:1-6.

In taking possession of the land Yhwh has promised them, the Israelites do not encounter a land empty of occupants. It is a land they must empty for themselves. But to do so, they must displace and replace those already occupying the land – living and dead. In reflecting on ways in which the dead mark place in contemporary Western constructions of the cultural past, Robert Harrison observes:

> To be human means to come after those who came before. Just as we are always preceded by our forebears, so too the ground in which we lay them to rest has always already received the bones of others – 'others' in the most radical sense of the term . . . .[40]

A comparable perspective is evident in the Hebrew Bible. In a particularly persistent biblical tradition, the territorial power of the dead is recognized to the extent that they are not only cast as the original occupants of the land, but they are 'othered' to the point of their re-mythologization as an extraordinary living race of giants: these are the Rephaim.

Though in other biblical texts the Rephaim (רפאים) are the perpetually-existent dead,[41] in the so-called historical books of the Hebrew Bible, they are the autochthonic inhabitants of the Transjordanian territories allotted to the tribes of Reuben and Gad and the half-tribe of Manasseh. Their gigantic stature is inferred from a loose collection of traditions associated with them: they are identified with obscure, pseudo-mythical peoples called the Emim, the Zamzummim, and the Anakim, the frightening giants related to the similarly statuesque Nephilim;[42] in

---

40. Harrison, *Dominion of the Dead*, 30.

41. E.g. Isa. 14:9-11 (cf. vv. 15-20); 26:14-19; Job 26:5; Ps. 88:11 (ET v.10); Prov. 2:18; 9:18; 21:16. For the Rephaim, see especially T. J. Lewis, 'Toward a Literary Translation of the Rapiuma Texts', in N. Wyatt, W. G. E. Watson and J. B. Lloyd (eds), *Ugarit, Religion and Culture: Proceedings of the International Colloquium on Ugarit, Religion and Culture Edinburgh July 1994* (UBL, 12; Münster: Ugarit-Verlag, 1996), 115–49; Smith, *Origins of Biblical Monotheism*, 68–69; B. A. Levine and J. -M. de Tarragon, 'Dead Kings and Rephaim: The Patrons of the Ugaritic Dynasty', *JAOS* 104 (1984), 649–59; H. Rouillard-Bonraisin, 'L'énigme des refā'îm bibliques résolue grace aux rapa'ūma d'Ougarit?', in J. M. Michaud (ed.), *La Bible et l'héritage d'Ougarit* (Sherbrooke, QC: Éditions GGC, 2005), 145–82; N. Wyatt, 'A la Recherche des Rephaïm Perdus', in J. -M. Michaud (ed.), *Actes du Congrès International Sherbrooke 2005 « Le royaume d'Ougarit de la Crète à l'Euphrate. Nouveaux axes de recherche »*, *Université de Sherbrooke du 5 au 8 juillet 2005* (POLO, 2; Sherbrooke, QC: Éditions GGC, 2007), 579–613.

42. According to *Gen. Rab.* 26:7; 31:12 and *Pirqe R. El.* 34, Rephaim is one of the names of the Nephilim. Their similarity to the Rephaim is suggested in Ezek. 32:27, in which the

2 Sam. 21:15-22 (cf. 1 Sam. 17:4-7; 1 Chr. 20:4-8), the supersized Philistine warriors defeated by David and his men are described as ילדי הרפה ('descendants of Rapha', or perhaps 'descendants of the Rephaim'),[43] a designation assumed by other tradents of the tradition to be related to the term רפאים and/or to refer to giants;[44] the dimensions given in Deut. 3:10-11 for the 'bed' (ערש) of King Og – who is described here and in Josh. 12:4; 13:12 as the last of the Rephaim – are vast.

In their biblical imaging as living giants, the Rephaim are artfully transformed: the owner-occupiers of the land promised to the Israelites are no longer the powerful and perpetually existent dead, but a formidable mortal foe to be defeated, destroyed and 'wiped out' altogether (cf. Gen. 15:19-21). It might be supposed, with Mario Liverani and others before him, that the biblical writers recast the Rephaim as giants because they believed that 'before being dead they must have been alive . . . They should thus have been a people, one that exists no more, but lived in Palestine before [the Israelites'] arrival'.[45] Ideologically, this is an effective territorial strategy, employed to uphold the biblical claim that the land divinely promised was indeed emptied by and for the Israelites. In selecting 'mythical' inhabitants of the land against whom the incoming Israelites must strive, the biblical writers ensure that the annihilation of the former inhabitants is 'attested' by their very non-existence: '[t]hose who do not exist are exterminated – and the fact that they do not exist demonstrates the fact that they have been exterminated!'[46] And so it is with the last of the Rephaim, King Og: 'they killed

---

Nephilim are listed among the denizens of the underworld. On the possible nature of the relationship between the Rephaim and the gigantic 'heroes of old', plus appeals to analogous Greek concepts and their accompanying myths, see J. C. de Moor, 'Rāpi'ūma – Rephaim', *ZAW* 88 (1976), 323–45; Spronk, *Beatific Afterlife*, 161–96, 227–29; E. C. Hostetter, *Nations Mightier and More Numerous: The Biblical View of Palestine's Pre-Israelite Peoples* (N. Richland Hills, TX: BIBAL Press, 1995), 109–11. The formidable size of the Anakim is portrayed in Num. 13:33; Deut. 1:28; 9:1-2 (cf. Josh. 14:12). For the Emim and the Zamzummim, see Deut. 2:10-11, 20 (cf. Gen. 14:5-6) and the discussions in Hostetter, *Nations Mightier and More Numerous*, 101–5, 109–11 and (with some caution) U. Hübner, *Die Ammoniter. Untersuchung zur Geschichte, Kultur und religion eines transjordanischen Volkes im 1. Jahrtausend v. Chr.* (Wisebaden: Harrassowitz, 1992).

43. See S. R. Driver, *Notes on the Hebrew Text and the Topography of the Books of Samuel* (2nd edn; Oxford: Clarendon Press, 1913), 353.

44. See C. E. L'Heureux, 'The Ugaritic and Biblical Rephaim', *HTR* 67 (1974), 265–74; cf. H. Rouillard, 'Rephaim', *DDD*, 692–700, here 698. A more conservative (and ultimately unpersuasive) view is offered by Schmidt, *Israel's Beneficent Dead*, 267–73.

45. Liverani, *Israel's History*, 276. See also Loretz, *Götter – Ahnen – Könige als gerechte Richter*, 259–66.

46. Liverani, *Israel's History*, 277. This strategy might also have served a religio-polemical purpose, denying the continued existence and potency of the underworld Rephaim.

him, his descendants, and all his people, until he had no survivor left; and they took possession of his land' (Num. 21:35; cf. Deut. 3:3).

But the mythic traditions embedded within these stories about the conquest of the living Rephaim bespeak the socio-religious perception that it is the dead of the land, and not simply the living, who must be disempowered and supplanted. This is perhaps the sense of Isa. 26:14-15, in which the Rephaim are not disguised as giants, but are the dead, annihilated for territorial gain:

> The dead will not live,
> the Rephaim will not rise –
> because you have punished and destroyed them,
> and wiped out all memory of them;
> you have increased the nation, O Yhwh,
> you have increased the nation – you are glorified!
> You have extended all the borders of the land!

To destroy the dead, as this text suggests, is to replace their continued 'life after death' with a permanent 'death after death' – to wipe out all memory of them.[47] In this way, their hold on their land is released. This appears to be a pervasive motif underlying some of the biblical conquest traditions, for further traces of the underworld context of the land's autochthonous inhabitants can be detected.

As well as being described as the last survivor of the Rephaim (Deut. 3:11; Josh. 12:4; 13:12), Og of Bashan is said to dwell בעשתרות ובאדרעי, 'in Ashtaroth and Edrei' (Deut. 1:4; Josh. 12:4; 13:12; cf. 9:10; 13:31).[48] These toponyms are identical to the Ugaritic name of the netherworld location ʿṯtrt-hdrʿy, the royal residence of 'Rapiu, King of the Hereafter' (rpʾu mlk ʿlm),[49] who is probably best understood as the eponymous figurehead of the rpʾum, the royal deified dead.[50] While this close paralleling of biblical and Ugaritic texts might suggest that Og is to be identified with Rapiu,[51] the underworld

---

47. The expression 'death after death' is borrowed from B. B. Schmidt, 'Memory as Immortality: Countering the Dreaded "Death After Death" in Ancient Israelite Society', in A. J. Peck and J. Neusner (eds), *Judaism in Late Antiquity* (Leiden: Brill, 2000), 87–100.

48. MT Deut. 1:4 is missing the conjunction between the toponyms.

49. *KTU* 1.108.1-3. For the title 'King of the Hereafter', see H. Niehr, 'Zur Semantik von nordwestsemitischen ʿlm als "Unterwelt" und "Grab"', in B. Pongratz-Leisten, H. Kühne and P. Xella (eds), *Ana Śadî Labnāni lū Allik: Festschrift für W. Röllig* (AOAT, 247; Neukirchen-Vluyn: Neukirchen Verlag, 1997), 295–305.

50. Rapiu can be identified with Milku, who is similarly said to dwell in ʿṯtrt (*KTU* 1.100.41; 1.107.17; RS 86.2235.17) and is the eponymous representative of the *mlkm*, a group equivalent to the *rpʾum*. See further Rouillard, 'Rephaim', 692–700. Note that Ugaritic Milku is not to be identified with the fictitious biblical character Molek (Stavrakopoulou, *King Manasseh and Child Sacrifice*, 211–15).

51. Wyatt, 'A la Recherche des Rephaïm Perdus', 579–613; K. van der Toorn, 'Funerary

character of Og's kingdom is also of particular relevance here. As Marvin Pope and Gregorio del Olmo Lete have argued, Ugaritic and biblical texts present the Transjordanian region called Bashan in the Hebrew Bible as an infernal divine abode, the netherworld dwelling place of dead kings and the location of the divine mountain (cf. Ps. 68:16).[52] The likely links between the name Bashan and Arabic *btn* ('soft, fertile ground') and Ugaritc *btn* ('serpent') are suggestive of a cosmic potency, a notion complemented by Bashan's biblical imaging as a place of mythic and cultic fertility:[53] its 'cows', 'bulls', 'fatlings', 'rams', 'lions' and 'oaks' (Amos 4:1; Mic. 7:14; Ezek. 39:18; Ps. 22:13; Deut. 32:14) form a powerful constellation of religio-symbolic motifs.[54] In mytho-geographic terms, then, Bashan is the netherworld, synonymous with 'the land of the Rephaim', as it is claimed in Deut. 3:13.

As a prominent denizen of this netherworld, Og and his biblical partner Sihon represent the dead occupants of the Transjordanian land marked out for Israelite occupation and possession. Though in their present biblical contexts Og and Sihon have become legendary but earthly rulers in the pre-Israelite Transjordan,[55] faint literary echoes of their netherworld domain reverberate in disparate details embedded in the narratives. As Scott Noegel observes, Sihon's city appears to be called the 'city of the dead' (עִיר־מְתֹם) in Deut. 3:6, and as the Israelites journey on their way to defeat Og and Sihon, they pass through Oboth and Iye-abarim (Num. 21:10-11; 33:43-44), toponyms with netherworld associations.[56] With this context in mind, Og's 'bed' (עֶרֶשׂ) in Deut. 3:11 is best understood as a grave, testifying on one level to the biblical boast of Og's earthly annihilation, and on another to his underworld domain within its mythic milieu.[57]

Rituals and Beatific Afterlife in Ugaritic Texts and in the Bible', *BibOr* 48 (1991), 40–66, esp. 57–59; *contra* D. Pardee, *Les textes paramythologiques* (RSO, 4; Paris: Éditions Recherche sur la Civilisations, 1988), 85–90.

52. M. Pope, 'The Cult of the Dead at Ugarit', in G. D. Young (ed.), *Ugarit in Retrospect: Fifty Years of Ugarit and Ugaritic* (Winona Lake, IN: Eisenbrauns, 1981), 159–79, here 171; G. del Olmo Lete, 'Bašan o el "infierno" cananeo', *SEL* 5 (1988), 51–60. Del Olmo Lete argues that the מַלְכִים of Ps. 68:13, 15 are to be identified as the dead deified kings of Bashan known from Ugaritic allusions to the same region.

53. See S. Noegel, 'The Aegean Ogygos of Boeotia and the Biblical Og of Bashan: Reflections of the Same Myth', *ZAW* 110 (1998), 411–26, esp. 420–22. As Noegel demonstrates, Bashan's serpentine mythological character is attested in its pervasive association with the cosmic, threatening ocean, a context shared with Og in biblical, ancient West Asian and eastern Mediterranean traditions.

54. See G. del Olmo Lete, 'Bashan', *DDD*, 161–63.

55. On the possible 'historical' contexts of the traditions concerning Og and Sihon, see J. Bartlett, 'Sihon and Og, Kings of the Amorites', *VT* 20 (1970), 257–77.

56. Noegel, 'The Aegean Ogygos', 416–17.

57. So T. Veijola, 'King Og's Iron Bed (Deut 3:11) – Once Again', in P. W. Flint, E. Tov and J. C. VanderKam (eds), *Studies in the Hebrew Bible, Qumran, and the Septuagint*

The biblical reimaging of the Rephaim – including Og – as a formidable and gigantic military foe marks the 'othering' of the dead owner-occupiers of the land destined for Israelite occupation. Accordingly (and specifically), Moses' defeat and destruction of Og and his cohort signifies the displacement of these underworld denizens from possession of the land – land that is, although east of the Jordan, portrayed as a part of Israel's divinely given territorial inheritance.[58]

The netherworld portrayal of this region not only bespeaks the contested place of these Transjordanian territories within the promised land, but also codes Moses' burial place with a powerful mytho-symbolism befitting the mortuary landscape in which his grave is set. Indeed, his burial at the edge of the promised land is neither insignificant nor unworthy. Rather, his grave is fixed at the crossing point between the earthly realm and the underworld, on the border between the wilderness and the land divinely promised. Its liminal location marks a boundary burial, which simultaneously displaces the indigenous dead and signals the Mosaic occupation of the land. In this way, Moses is cast as a territorial

---

Presented to Eugene Ulrich (VTS, 101; Leiden: Brill, 2006), 60–76. Though in the Hebrew Bible ערש usually means 'bed' or 'couch', it is paralleled with מטה in Ps. 6:7 and Amos 6:4, the term used to refer to Abner's funerary bier in 2 Sam. 3:31. And as Veijola points out, its Aramaic equivalent, ערסא, can similarly mean '(funerary) bier', and is the term used by the Targums of Og's 'bed' in Deut. 3:11. Indeed, the view that Og's bed is a tomb or sarcophagus has a long history: according to Josephus it is a 'grave' at which the bones of giants are displayed (*Ant.* 5.125; cf. *Hdt. Hist* 1.68, 181). The megalithic tombs known from the Transjordanian area were thought by Paul Karge to have given rise to the tradition about Og's visible and gigantic resting place (*Rephaim: Die vorgeschichtliche Kultur Palästinas und Phöniziens* [Paderborn: Schöningh, 1917], 638–40). Alan Millard advocates a more literal interpretation of Og's bed, arguing that Deut. 3:11 refers to an iron bedstead ('King Og's Iron Bed and Other Ancient Ironmongery', in L. Eslinger and G. Taylor [eds], *Ascribe to the Lord: Biblical and Other Studies in Memory of Peter C. Craigie* [JSOTS, 67; Sheffield: JSOT Press, 1988], 481–92). In 'Og von Baschan und sein Bett in Rabbat-Ammon (Deuteronomium 3,11)', *ZAW* 105 (1993), 86–92, Hübner similarly adopts a literal reading of the text, but argues that Og's vast bed is a polemical allusion to Ammonite cultic prostitution (cf. *Hdt. Hist* 1.181).

58. The traditions about Moses' defeat of Og and Sihon, and the allocation of their Transjordanian kingdoms to Israelite tribes, conflicts with the heavy biblical emphasis that it was Joshua who led the conquest of the promised land. This raises questions concerning the extent to which the land east of the Jordan was considered 'Israelite' and about the role of Moses in the conquest traditions – both within and beyond the Hebrew Bible. On these issues, see particularly K. A. D. Smelik, 'The Territory of Eretz Israel in the Hebrew Bible: The Case of the Transjordan Tribes', in M. Prudky (ed.), *Landgabe: Festschrift für Jan Heller zum 70. Geburtstag* (Kampen: Kok Pharos, 1995), 76–85; T. C. Römer, 'Mose in Äthiopien: Zur Herkunft der Num 12,1 zugrunde liegenden Tradition', in M. Beck and U. Schorn (eds), *Auf dem Weg zur Endgestalt von Genesis bis II Regum: Festschrift Hans-Christophe Schmitt zum 65. Geburstag* (Berlin: de Gruyter, 2006), 203–15; R. Havrelock, 'The Two Maps of Israel's Land', *JBL* 126 (2007), 649–67.

ancestor of Israel. Though his tomb is lost and hidden from the eyes of the living, its presence is pointedly and crucially 'revealed' in the words of Torah itself (Deut. 34:6). Here, tomb and Torah coalesce. But the textual memorialization of Moses and his land legacy moves beyond these few verses: it is also illustrated and manifested in other biblical traditions dealing with the Israelite colonization of the land, traditions in which this Mosaic form of ancestral territorialism is marked by or written in stone.

Torah Memorialized

At the outset of this discussion, Moses' ancestral role was explicitly tied to the characterization of Torah as a marker and memorial of Israel's land claims. This connection is made plain in Deut. 32:46-47 (a passage immediately preceding Yhwh's instruction to Moses to ascend the mountain on which he will die), in which the occupation of land and its perpetual possession is wholly bound up with adherence to Mosaic teaching:

> He said to them: 'Take to heart all the words I am giving in witness against you this day, with which you shall command your descendants, so that they may diligently observe all the words of this Torah. This is no trifling matter for you – it is your very life; through it you may live long in the land that you are crossing over the Jordan to possess.'[59]

The identification of land possession and adherence to Torah is given symbolic expression in Deut. 27:1-8, in which Moses relays the divine decree that the crossing of the Jordan into the promised land is to be marked with the setting up of stones and the inscribing of Torah upon them. This passage has attracted a great deal of scholarly attention, not least because it exhibits strong indications of a complex compositional history and is likely related to a number of other texts dealing with the setting up of stones and altars – including Deut. 27:17, which promotes the ritual endorsement of ancestral boundary markers (cf. Prov. 22:27-28).[60] But for the present purposes, it is the inscribing of Torah upon the stones that is of primary significance. In Deut. 27:1-8, key concerns converge: entry into the land, the installation of Torah in the land, the publication and promulgation of its words, and the imaging of Yhwh as the land-giving god of Israel's ancestors. Verses 2-3 read:

> On the day that you cross over the Jordan into the land that Yhwh your God is giving you, you are to set up large stones and coat them with plaster. You must write on them all the words of this Torah when you have crossed over, in order

---

59. Cf. Deut. 31:12-13.
60. See especially Exod. 24:4; Josh. 4:3-9, 20-24; 8:30-35; Josh. 24:1-33.

to go into the land that Yhwh your God is giving you, a land flowing with milk and honey, just as Yhwh the God of your ancestors promised you.

In these verses, the 'large stones' (אבנים גדלות) appear to have three interrelated functions. The first of these is liminal, for the stones are inextricably tied to the entry into the land. They are thus presented here as a 'gateway', facilitating and commemorating the transferral of the Israelites and Torah across the Jordan and into the land.[61] The perceived liminality of these 'crossing' stones is given further expression in Josh. 4:1-24. Here, the crossing of the Jordan (which is simply projected in Deut. 27:1-8) is enacted. In this convoluted narrative, twelve stones are taken from the river and set up to be 'a memorial (זכרון) to the Israelites forever' (Josh. 4:7). The Jordan's status as a mythic boundary, separating the promised land from the Transjordanian netherworld, is evident in its portrayal as the ים סוף (usually termed 'Sea of Reeds'), itself a cipher for the cosmic 'sea at the end of the world'.[62] The twelve stones thus manifest, actualize and memorialize the liminal nature of this crossing. And though they are uninscribed, the setting up of stones in Josh. 4:1-24 is a ritual action. With this text in mind, the inscribed stones of Deut. 27:1-8 are likely cultic in character, too. This is reflected not only in their liminal nature and their (likely secondary) identification with the cult site on Mount Ebal (vv. 4-8), but also in their plastering, which is suggestive of their imagined placement *inside* a cult room or building.[63]

Certainly, within their biblical context, the plastered stones inscribed with Torah are accorded great socio-religious prestige in their association with what has been assumed by many to be a covenant ceremony.[64] But in itself, the use and function of inscribed stones is well known as a powerful medium of display, magico-ritual witness and dominance throughout the ancient Mediterranean and West Asia, exhibiting and attesting to religio-political, legal, and other cultural assertions: the very existence of these stones was perceived to 'guarantee the continuing force' of the claims inscribed upon them.[65] Within societies in which

---

61. Sonnet, *Book within the Book*, 89–91.

62. Josh. 3:23; cf. 3:13-17; 4:19–5:1. See N. Wyatt, *Myths of Power: A Study of Royal Ideology in Ugaritic and Biblical Tradition* (UBL, 13; Münster: Ugarit-Verlag, 1996), 84–89; J. A. Montgomery, 'Hebraica. (2) *yam sup* ('the Red Sea') Ultimum Mare?', *JAOS* 58 (1938), 131–32.

63. Cf. Ezek. 13:10-15. The Deir 'Alla texts are well-known examples of exhibited writing on plaster; see J. Hoftijzer and G. van der Kooij (eds), *The Balaam Text from Deir ʿAllā Re-evaluated: Proceedings of the International Symposium held at Leiden 21–24 August 1989* (Leiden: Brill, 1991).

64. Though note the term ברית is not employed in this text. Cf. A. E. Hill, 'The Ebal Ceremony as Hebrew Land Grant?', *JETS* 31 (1988), 399–406.

65. R. Thomas, *Literacy and Orality in Ancient Greece* (Cambridge: Cambridge University Press, 1992), 85. See also B. S. Jackson, 'Ideas of Law and Legal Administration: A Semiotic Approach', in R. E. Clements (ed.), *The World of Ancient Israel: Sociological,*

3. *Moses at the Edge*

literacy, textuality and scribalism was often an elite or 'privileged' activity, an inscribed stone was thus not so much a tool of open textual address but a symbol or manifestation of power, testimony and remembrance.[66] The inscribed stones of Deut. 27:1-3 are thus at once a potent declaration and commemoration of the land-legacy of Torah. As Jean-Pierre Sonnet observes, 'By covering them with the "words of this Torah," the people publicize the terms of their entry into and their inheritance of the promised land'.[67]

As manifestations of declaration, set up by 'outsiders' entering the land, the stones are also symbols of an asserted dominance, and as such, they display an oppressive, colonial function. The large 'stones' (אבנים) stand in conspicuous contrast to the מצבות of the indigenous 'Canaanite' peoples, stones that are vociferously prohibited elsewhere in Deuteronomy, including 7:5 and 12:3 (cf. 16:22).[68] In these texts, the smashed standing stones represent the deities displaced – along with their worshippers – as the Israelites colonize the land. With this in mind, the language of land possession in 27:1-8 sounds a sharp colonial fanfare, and is reminiscent of the territorial tone of Isa. 19:19-20, in which Egypt is imaged as a land possessed by Yhwh:

> On that day there will be an altar to Yhwh in the centre of the land of Egypt, and a standing stone (מצבה) to Yhwh at its border. It will be a sign and a witness to Yhwh of Hosts in the land of Egypt.

The large inscribed stones of Deut. 27:1-8, intentionally and neutrally designated אבנים גדלות, might thus be identified as 'legitimized' Israelite מצבות, set up upon entry into the land to symbolize Yhwh's presence there.[69] And in this

---

Anthropological and Political Perspectives (Cambridge: Cambridge University Press, 1989), 185–202, esp. 189–92; D. C. Polaski, 'What Mean These Stones? Inscriptions, Textuality and Power in Persia and Yehud', in J. L. Berquist (ed.), *Approaching Yehud: New Approaches to the Study of the Persian Period* (Atlanta, GA: Society of Biblical Literature, 2007), 37–48.

66. See further J. Goody, *The Logic of Writing and the Organization of Society* (Cambridge: Cambridge University Press, 1986), esp. 22–44; J. Assmann, *Religion and Cultural Memory: Ten Studies* (trans. R. Livingstone; Stanford, CA: Stanford University Press, 2006), 85–87, and Paul Connerton's critique of social perceptions of inscription as the privileged transmission of cultural memory in *How Societies Remember*, 102.

67. Sonnet, *Book within the Book*, 90.

68. Cf. B. M. Levinson, *Deuteronomy and the Hermeneutics of Legal Innovation* (Oxford: Oxford University Press, 1998), 148. Note that in Exod. 24:4, the twelve stones set up by Moses (and imitated in Josh. 4:3-9, 20-24) are called מצבות.

69. *Contra* Nelson, *Deuteronomy*, 318; M. Fishbane, *Biblical Interpretation in Ancient Israel* (Oxford: Clarendon Press, 1985), 161–62. See E. T. Mullen, *Narrative History and Ethnic Boundaries: The Deuteronomistic Historian and the Creation of Israelite National Identity* (SBLSS; Atlanta, GA: Scholars Press, 1993), 107–19.

sense, they fulfil a territorial function – but crucially, this is a function served by the dead.

Alan Cooper and Bernard Goldstein seek to align these two interpretative positions by suggesting that the מצבות are best understood to represent or manifest the territorial ancestors. As was detailed in Chapter 1, they argue that several biblical passages (including Deut. 27:1-8 and Josh. 4:1-24) present Yhwh's occupation of the land in the symbolic terms of a stela ritual marking the territorial installation of the ancestors.[70] Given the territoriality of the dead, and the ways in which its related ideologies permeate biblical traditions concerning the acquisition of land, some of these narratives might well contain an allusion to ancestral methods of making and marking territorial claims. Though Cooper and Goldstein's proposal requires very careful handling, it is not altogether implausible in view of the repeated use of the standing stone motif in key narratives dealing with the colonization of the land – especially in Deut. 27:1-8 and Josh 4:1-24, in which the liminality of the stones is suggestive of a transition between the netherworld and the promised land, complementing the function of Moses' similarly liminal burial place. But the suggestion that the Israelites' standing stones symbolize Yhwh's presence in and ownership of the land does not go far enough.[71] Rather, it requires further nuancing in view of the territorial ideology constructed around the figure and influence of Moses in the biblical traditions, particularly in considering more closely the passages in Deuteronomy and Joshua to which Cooper and Goldstein have also drawn attention, namely Deut. 27:1-8; Josh. 4:1-24; 8:30-35 and 24:1-33.

In all of these texts (which are probably closely related), stones are set up and/or inscribed to mark entry into the land or the acquisition of land. But, despite the proposals of Cooper and Goldstein, these stones do not appear to symbolize or represent Yhwh; instead, and more specifically, they stand for Torah. This is clear in Deut. 27:1-8 and Josh. 8:30-35:

> ... set up large stones and coat them with plaster. You must write on them all the words of this Torah when you have crossed over, in order to go into the land that Yhwh your God is giving you, a land flowing with milk and honey, just as Yhwh the God of your ancestors promised you ... You shall write on the stones all the words of this Torah very clearly. (Deut. 27:2-3, 8)

> There, in the presence of the sons of Israel, [Joshua] wrote on the stones[72] a copy of the Torah of Moses, which he had written ... And afterwards he read all the

---

70. Cooper and Goldstein, 'The Cult of the Dead', 285–303.
71. Schaper ('Living Word Engraved in Stone', 19) also assumes the stones represent the presence of Yhwh, though he makes no mention of Cooper and Goldstein's discussion.
72. Most agree that the stones are not those of the Ebal altar, but standing stones, in direct fulfilment of Deut. 27:1-8.

words of the Torah, blessings and curses, according to all that is written in the book of Torah. There was not a word of all that Moses commanded that Joshua did not read before all the assembly of Israel, and the women, and the little ones, and the aliens, who resided among them. (Josh. 8:32, 34-35)

In Joshua 24, the words of Torah are not inscribed directly onto the large stone in the sanctuary at Shechem, but written in a book (ספר). However, the writing of Torah and the setting up of the stone are actions so closely aligned that the stone can be taken, as some have suggested, as a marker of Torah itself,[73] particularly if this text is read (as seems likely) as an explicit enactment of the instructions set out in Deut. 27:1-8, in which Torah is inscribed upon the large stones. Joshua 24:25-27 reads:

Joshua made a covenant with the people that day, and made statutes and ordinances for them at Shechem. Joshua wrote these words in the book of the Torah of God, and he took a large stone and set it up there under the oak tree in the sanctuary of Yhwh. Joshua said to all the people, 'See, this stone shall be a witness against us, for it has heard all the words of Yhwh that he spoke to us; therefore it shall be a witness against you if you deal falsely with your God'.

In presenting the stone as a 'witness' (עדה) to the words of Yhwh and against Israel's fated apostasy, it is credited with two roles. First, it fulfils the performative function of a cultic standing stone as 'living rock' – a stone which, in 'hearing' and 'witnessing' (Josh. 24:27) in the cult place, is not simply a material object poetically anthropomorphized, but an active manifestation of a divine or quasi-divine presence, much like the stones seemingly used to represent the ancestors of Jacob and Laban in Gen. 31:44-54.[74] But this is not to mistake this particular stone as a marker of Yhwh's presence, nor even that of an ancestral deity. Rather, as a 'witness', this particular stone's second role is to function as Torah, a role best perceived through the lens of the closely related Deuteronomy, which, in its explicit self-portrayal as written Torah (chs 31–32), characterizes itself as a 'witness' in the same way:

When Moses had finished writing down in a book the words of this Torah to the very end, Moses commanded the Levites who carry the ark of the covenant of Yhwh, saying: 'Take this book of Torah and put it beside the ark of the covenant

---

73. E.g. J. Gray, *Joshua, Judges, Ruth* (NCB; Grand Rapids, MI: Eerdmans, 1986), 182.

74. On this text, see the discussion in Chapter 4 and the bibliography cited there. On standing stones, see Chapter 1.

of Yhwh your God and let it be there as a witness (עד) against you.' (Deut. 31:24-26; cf. 32:46)[75]

It is not unreasonable, then, to take the stone of Josh. 24:25-27 as a symbol of the Torah book with which it is so closely aligned. The 'witnessing' function of the stone is complemented in other texts – including Exod. 31:18, in which the covenantal stone tablets (לֻחֹת אֶבֶן) written with God's finger are designated לֻחֹת הָעֵדֻת ('the tablets of testimony'),[76] but notably also in Joshua 4 (cf. Isa. 19:20). Though in this narrative the words of Torah are not inscribed (and the tradition about the standing stones has been combined with several others) the stones set up upon entry into the land are significantly designated a 'sign' (אוֹת) and 'memorial' (זִכָּרוֹן) for the Israelites and their descendants (vv. 6-7; cf. vv. 20-24), closely paralleling the role of Torah, which similarly functions as a fixed and enduring testimony to present and future generations. The assimilation of Torah and standing stone in these passages is further suggested by the very semantics of their biblical portrayals: just as the stone upon which the words of Torah are inscribed is 'set up' (*hiphil* קוּם) in Deut. 27:2, 4 (cf. Josh. 4:9, 20; 24:26), so too at the close of the narrative the people vow to 'uphold' (*hiphil* קוּם) the words of Torah (Deut. 27:26) – language which is employed of adherence to Torah, or to the covenant, or to the words of Yhwh, in several biblical texts.[77]

Of the four texts in Deuteronomy and Joshua identified by Cooper and Goldstein as reflecting the use of ancestral stelae to signal land possession, at least three explicitly identify or align Torah (rather than Yhwh, contrary to Cooper and Goldstein) with the standing stones (Deut. 27:1-8; Josh. 8:30-35; 24:25-27), while the fourth (Josh. 4:1-24) strongly alludes to the Torah-like function of the stelae. In these passages, then, Torah acts as a territorial marker: it both facilitates and marks the possession of land, just as Moses asserts in Deut. 32:46-47, which reads:

> Take to heart all the words I am giving in witness against you this day, with which you shall command your descendants, so that they may diligently observe all the words of this Torah. This is no trifling matter for you – it is your very life; through it you may live long in the land that you are crossing over the Jordan to possess.

And in being imaged as a standing stone, Torah performs and fulfils the role of the

---

75. On Deuteronomy's self-presentation, see Levinson, *Deuteronomy*, 151–52.
76. See D. J. McCarthy, *Treaty and Covenant: A Study in Form in the Ancient Oriental Documents and in the Old Testament* (2nd edn; Rome: Biblical Institute Press, 1981), 196–97; Sonnet, *Book within the Book*, 93.
77. E.g. 1 Sam. 15:11-13, in which Saul notably sets up (נצב) a standing stone (יד), and 2 Kgs 23:3, 24; Jer. 34:18; cf. 1 Kgs 6:12; 8:20; Ezek. 16:60, 62; Ps. 78:5.

ancestral dead in asserting and maintaining a territorial claim. The coalescence of the proprietary roles of Torah and the dead is further suggested in the immediate contexts of three of these particular texts: in Deuteronomy 27, the setting up of Torah as a standing stone is followed by a curse against those who dishonour their ancestors or move a neighbour's boundary marker (vv. 16-17; cf. Prov. 22:28); the writing of Torah upon the stones in Josh. 8:30-35 is immediately preceded by a description of the contrasting territorial stone cairn or circle marking the burial place (in the city-gate) of the executed king of Ai (v. 29); and the territorial efficacy of the standing stone ceremony in Joshua 24 is realized and emphasized as the people are sent to their assigned family plots (איש לנחלתו) at the close of the ritual (v. 28), before the narrator describes the burials of Joshua, Joseph and Eleazar, each on his ancestral land (vv. 29-33).[78]

In functioning as a standing stone, Torah not only mimics the territorial role of the dead, but assertively marks Moses' land legacy by memorializing his teaching in a territorial manner.[79] This has several significant and interrelated implications. In being embodied as an ancestral standing stone, Torah is a memorial and manifestation of the past in the present; as such, it at once materializes and realizes Moses' repeated command to actively, ritually 'remember'.[80] Moses' teaching is thus set in stone as a public act and symbol of cultic, cultural memory.[81] Indeed, in Deuteronomy in particular, the standing stone is one of a group of visible

---

78. In these verses, Joshua is buried 'on the boundary of his inheritance' at Timnath-serah; Joseph is buried in the tomb purchased by Jacob at Shechem, which thereby renders the land 'an inheritance of the descendants of Joseph', and Eleazar is buried on the land owned by his descendant Phinehas. Though the standing stones of Joshua 4 are not explicitly associated with ancestors or graves, they clearly function as boundary markers, and it is not impossible to interpret vv. 23-24 as a statement proclaiming the territorial potency of Yhwh's monument (יד) in the face of the netherworld, represented in these verses by the liminal Jordan – characterized as the mythic sea ים סוף – and the 'people of the underworld (ארץ)'.

79. Though theologically Moses is the mediator of Yhwh's teaching and Yhwh's promise of land, Torah is repeatedly and frequently portrayed as belonging to or being authored by Moses; note, for example, the labels 'Law of Moses' (Josh. 8:31, 32; 23:6; 1 Kgs 2:3; 14:6; 2 Kgs 23:25; 2 Chr. 23:18; 30:16; Ezra 3:2; 7:6; Neh. 8:1; Dan. 9:11, 13; cf. 2 Kgs 21:8) and 'Book of (the Law of) Moses' (Josh. 8:31; 23:6; 2 Kgs 14:6; 2 Chr. 25:4; 35:12; Neh. 13:1). Indeed, as Houtman points out ('Moses', *DDD*, 593–98), the heavy insistence in biblical traditions that Moses shared a close and unique relationship with Yhwh appears intended to emphasize that Moses' words are genuinely those of Yhwh himself.

80. On the command to remember, see particularly Y. H. Yerushalmi, *Zakhor: Jewish History and Jewish Memory* (Seattle and London: University of Washington Press, 1996 [1982]); B. M. Britt, 'Erasing Amalek: Remembering to Forget with Derrida and Biblical Tradition', in Y. Sherwood (ed.), *Derrida's Bible (Reading a Page of Scripture with a Litle Help from Derrida)*, (New York: Palgrave Macmillan, 2004), 61–77; and Chapter 6.

81. See Assmann, *Religion and Cultural Memory*, 16–21; cf. Schaper, 'Living Word Engraved in Stone', 9–23.

symbols employed to embody Mosaic teaching within the community – others in this group include symbols or excerpts of Torah worn on the head and hand (6:8; 11:18; cf. Prov. 3:3; 6:21) and inscriptions upon the doorposts of houses and gates (6:9; 11:20).[82] As Jan Assmann points out, all of these symbols, including the Torah-inscribed stones, can be understood as techniques employed in the formation and expression of cultural memory.[83] Other techniques are also evident in the book of Joshua's portrayal of the standing stones, for in 4:6-7, 20-24; 8:30-35; 24:1-27, the stones signal collective remembering in the form of oral recitation, copying, teaching and interpretation for generations past, present and pending.[84] Viewed from this perspective, the memorialization of Torah as a standing stone renders it a marker of the past in not only the present, but in the future, too.

In its biblical modelling as an inscribed standing stone, Torah is also transformed from an oral address to a written testimony, exhibiting its permanence, publication, commemoration, and fixity:

> Write on them all the words of this Torah . . . Write on the stones all the words of this Torah very clearly. (Deut. 27:3, 8)

> [Joshua] wrote on the stones a copy of the Torah of Moses, which he had written . . . he read all the words of Torah, blessings and curses, according to all that is written in the Book of Torah. There was not a word of all that Moses commanded that Joshua did not read . . . (Josh. 8:32, 34-35)

The 'fixing' of Torah in stone thereby renders those biblical texts that self-identify as Moses' teaching 'memorialized' too – and hence analogously fixed or 'canonized'. Though he mentions only in passing the standing stones discussed here, Brian Britt employs the metaphor of a stone monument to elucidate Deuteronomy's self-portrayal as Torah-as-witness, particularly in chs 31–32. Deuteronomy is, he argues, a 'textual memorial': 'Like a stone monument, the text ascribes itself didactic and memorial purposes for a community and its generations to come. As a textual memorial, the text [. . .] puts emphasis on the subject of writing and reciting, hence canonizing, הרות'.[85] Viewed from

---

82. Notice that in Deut. 11:18-21, these symbols are attributed territorial potency. For the 'embodiment' of Torah and its teaching as a bodily function, see J. L. Berquist, *Controlling Corporeality: The Body and the Household in Ancient Israel* (New Brunswick, NJ: Rutgers University Press, 2002), 168.

83. Assmann, *Religion and Cultural Memory*, 18–19.

84. For copying as a 'practice of power' in Yehud, see Polaski, 'What Mean These Stones?' 39–40.

85. B. Britt, *Rewriting Moses: The Narrative Eclipse of the Text* (JSOTS, 402/GCT, 14; New York: T&T Clark, 2004), 131. In a footnote (140 n. 28), Britt draws attention to James Young's perceptive observations about the interrelation of literary, monumental, and social

3. *Moses at the Edge*

this inner-biblical perspective, the alignment of written, scriptural Torah with Moses' own teaching and scribal activity simultaneously renders text (especially Deuteronomy), teacher, and interpreter (primarily Moses, secondarily Joshua and the Levites) legitimated, elevated, and celebrated.[86]

The petrifying, writing and reciting of Torah in the land thus 'immortalizes' Moses and his teaching, transferring both into the promised land and thereby transfiguring Moses and Torah into mediators of land. Jean-Pierre Sonnet comments:

> ... Moses will not enter the land. Yet he will reach it symbolically through the command he gives to erect 'large stones' upon the crossing and to write down on these stones 'all the words of this Torah'. The orality of Moses' Moab speech could have meant the vanishing of his words ... [but] Moses' command 'you shall write' is an ingenious way of transcending the limitations of time and space. Extending the range of his act of communication, he makes sure 'the words of this Torah' will be set up in the land as a gate to the land. Projecting his words beyond the Jordan, Moses projects them also beyond his death ... [87]

Inscribed in stone and liminal in nature, Torah becomes a *w*rite of passage for Moses and for Israel.[88] Thus memorialized, Torah physically, symbolically and scripturally marks and manifests Moses' land legacy.

And yet as a Mosaic memorial the very visibility and accessibility of Torah might appear to contrast too sharply with the invisibility of Moses' gravesite. Certainly, it is sometimes assumed that the writing and 'publication' of Torah

---

'witnesses' in *Writing and Rewriting the Holocaust* (Bloomington, IN: Indiana University Press, 1988).

86. Britt, *Rewriting Moses*, 165–71; Dijkstra, 'The Law of Moses', esp. 81–93; K. van der Toorn, *Scribal Culture and the Making of the Hebrew Bible* (Cambridge, MA: Harvard University Press, 2007), 166–70; see also R. Polzin, *Moses and the Deuteronomist: A Literary Study of the Deuteronomistic History* (New York: Seabury, 1980), 25–72; cf. J. Schaper, 'The Theology of Writing: The Oral and the Written, God as Scribe, and the Book of Deuteronomy', in L. J. Lawrence and M. I. Aguilar (eds), *Anthropology and Biblical Studies: Avenues of Approach* (Leiden: Deo, 2004), 97–119; D. M. Carr, *Writing on the Tablet of the Heart: Origins of Scripture and Literature* (Oxford: Oxford University Press, 2005).

87. Sonnet, *Book within the Book*, 95.

88. Cf. J. Assmann, 'Schrift, Tod und Identität: Das Grab als Vorschule der Literatur im alten Ägypten', in A. Assmann, J. Assmann and C. Hardmeier (eds), *Schrift und Gedächtnis: Beiträge zur Archäologie der literarischen Kommunikation* (München: Wilhelm Fink Verlag, 1983), 64–93. The expression 'write of passage' is adapted from T. Whitmarsh, 'The Writes of Passage: Cultural Initiation in Heliodorus' *Aethiopica*', in R. Miles (ed.), *Constructing Identities in Late Antiquity* (London: Routledge, 1999), 16–40.

necessarily and appropriately eclipses the religious need for a tomb for Moses. Duane Christensen, for example, asserts:

> Moses needs no grave or funerary monument to preserve his memory. His name is engraved in history by virtue of his work, which is far more enduring than any granite sarcophagus.[89]

But the publication of Torah in this material, proprietary way should not be assumed to cheapen the religious currency nor lessen the territorial value of his burial at the edge of the promised land – Moses' lost tomb is not a metaphor for the displacement of ancestral religion; rather, in its very liminality – indeed, its essential ambiguity – his gravesite remains crucial to the delimitation and appropriation of land, as the first part of this chapter has argued.[90]

Nor should it simply be assumed that Moses' missing tomb reflects a theological dismissal of the need for a corpse or a grave to measure the memory of so venerated a figure. His burial at the edge of the land and the memorialization of Torah amount to more than this. Moses' lost tomb and the memorialization of his teaching are in many ways religio-literary reflexes of the social processes of display and non-display employed in dealing with the dead. In his transformation from a social body to a non-living entity, Moses' death is to a certain extent 'displayed' and 'undisplayed' in the Hebrew Bible both by his absent grave and the 'reincarnation' of his teaching as a territorial, memorial monument.

These features – particularly memorialized Torah – are also a part of Moses' social transformation into a non-living entity as his legacy (or 'memory' of him) is distilled by and to the living community – generation after generation.[91] As Jon Levenson comments, Moses' legacy is 'Israel's dwelling in the promised land and living in deliberate obedience to the Torah book he bequeathed them . . . In Deuteronomy, all Israel has become, in a sense, the progeny of Moses'.[92] What is striking about Moses' legacy is that it is so thoroughly and pervasively territorial in character. Transferred into the realm of cultural memory and its reflected biblical ideology, Moses thus emerges as an 'ancestor' of Israel, whose death and burial facilitates the appropriation and perpetuation of land on a 'national' scale.

---

89. D. L. Christensen, *Deuteronomy 21:10–34:12* (WBC, 6B; London: Thomas Nelson, 2002), 874.
90. See also the discussion in Chapter 6.
91. Cf. Chesson, 'Remembering and Forgetting', 109.
92. Levenson, *Resurrection and the Restoration of Israel*, 77. In narrative terms, Moses' role as an ancestor is anticipated in Exod. 32:10, in which Yhwh asserts that he will raise up a great nation from Moses.

Chapter 4

CONTESTING BETHEL

The biblical Bethel has a particular association with the dead: it is the place from which the dead are displaced, for here bones are disinterred from tombs and burned at the sanctuary (2 Kgs 23:15-20); it is also the cult centre around which the dead are seemingly misplaced, for near here a servant is buried beneath a sacred tree (Gen. 35:8) and here too Rachel is buried at the roadside (35:16-20). As shall be seen, all these dead play a marked role in both the denigration and elevation of Bethel in biblical traditions, complementing and countering the ancestral pedigree credited to the cult site through the figure of Jacob, the founding father most closely associated with this place. Biblical traditions bound up with Bethel's dead, then, also betray territorial and ideological interests expressed as a more overt polemic against the religious value of the cult site in other biblical texts.[1] As recent studies have emphasized, Bethel is a place at which the identity of the biblical 'Israel' is configured – and reconfigured.[2] It thus plays a role no less significant than Machpelah, Jerusalem, or indeed the promised land itself in the biblical mapping of an ancestral land. The traditions about the placing, displacing and misplacing of the dead at Bethel are thus not merely localized tomb legends set within a loose narrative frame; they are also echoes of disputes about Bethel's religio-political potency as a cult centre of 'ancestral' pedigree.

Displacing the Dead

Though the movement of corpses or bones from their initial resting places might be perceived in some circumstances as a socially appropriate or permissible activity,[3] the disturbance or unauthorized removal of remains from a tomb is in

---

1. For a recent (if somewhat pedestrian) account of the biblical denunciation of Bethel, see V. H. Matthews, 'Back to Bethel: Geographical Reiteration in Biblical Narrative', *JBL* 128 (2009), 149–65. See also K. Koenen, *Bethel: Geschichte, Kult und Theologie* (OBO, 192; Göttingen: Vandenhoeck & Ruprecht, 2003).

2. See, for example, J. F. Gomes, *The Sanctuary of Bethel and the Configuration of Israelite Identity* (BZAW, 368; Berlin: de Gruyter, 2006); P. R. Davies, *The Origins of Biblical Israel* (LHBOTS, 485; New York: T&T Clark, 2007), esp. ch. 10.

3. Consider, for example, the re-storage of bones in a tomb niche, pit or ossuary, or the

many societies often perceived as an act of hostility towards both the dead and the living. Within an ancient West Asian context, to disinter the dead is to risk destabilizing their post-mortem existence and to fracture their relationship with the living community: the dead are displaced not only from their graves, but also from their secure place in the underworld and in the ancestral cult, so that they are deprived of their offerings, while the living are deprived of their ancestors' blessings and protection, which (particularly among the elites of a society) can often represent a strike against the political fabric of the living community. In this way, the displacement of the dead ruptures the carefully managed relationship between the dead and the living, upsetting the social dynamic between them. Disinterment thus functions as an act of aggression towards the living community, as well as the dead.

Accordingly, it is not uncommon to find burial inscriptions in tombs throughout ancient West Asia and the Mediterranean, warning potential intruders not to disturb the dead with threats of curses. In his description of his desecration of Elamite royal tombs, King Ashurbanipal boasts that he carried off the exhumed bones to Assyria in order to impose restlessness on their 'spirits' or 'ghosts' and to deprive them of offerings and libations.[4] In this inscription, the removal of bones is presented as a post-mortem punishment of previous generations of rulers,[5] a notion also attested in Jer. 8:1-2, a text in which it is decreed that the bones of Judah's kings, priests and other elites will be disinterred and – pointedly – not reburied.[6] The infliction of post-mortem punishment also appears to underlie the claim in 2 Kgs 23:15-18 that Josiah emptied tombs at Bethel:

---

transferral of bones from one tomb to another. See Bloch-Smith, *Judahite Burial Practices*, 36–37, 42–43 and E. M. Meyers, 'Secondary Burials in Palestine', *BA* 33 (1970), 2–29.

4. R. Borger, *Beiträge zum Inschriftenwerk Aššurbanipals* (Wiesbaden: Harrassowitz, 1996), 55, Prism A VI 70–76. On the risks of disturbing the dead, see J. Bottéro, 'La Mythologie de la mort en Mésopotamie ancienne', in B. Alster (ed.), *Death in Mesopotamia* (CRRA, 26/Mesopotamia, 8; Copenhagen: Akedemisk Forlag, 1980), 25–52; W. W. Hallo, 'Disturbing the Dead', in M. Brettler and M. Fishbane (eds), *Minhah le-Nahum: Biblical and Other Studies Presented to Nahum M. Sarna in Honour of his 70th Birthday* (JSOTS, 154; Sheffield: JSOT Press, 1993), 183–92; J. A. Scurlock, 'Death and the Afterlife in Ancient Mesopotamian Thought', *CANE*, 1,883–93; Lewis, 'How Far Can Texts Take Us?', 180 n. 36.

5. Ashurbanipal refers to the destruction of the tombs of the former and latter kings who had harassed his own ancestors (Prism A VI 70–76). For Merodach-Baladan II gathering the bones of his ancestors to take into exile, see M. Bayliss, 'The Cult of Dead Kin in Assyria and Babylonia', *Iraq* 35 (1973), 115–25.

6. See further the discussion in the following chapter and M. Cogan, 'A Note on Disinterment in Jeremiah', in I. D. Passow and S. T. Lachs (eds), *Gratz College Anniversary Volume* (Philadelphia: Gratz College, 1971), 29–34.

Moreover, the altar at Bethel, the cult place (במה) erected by Jeroboam ben Nebat, who caused Israel to sin – he pulled down that altar along with the cult place. He burned the cult place, crushing it to dust; he also burned (the) asherah. As Josiah turned, he saw the tombs there on the mount; and he sent and took the bones from the tombs, and burned them on the altar. So he defiled it, according to the word of Yhwh proclaimed by the Man of God[7] who told of these things. Then he said, 'What is that (memorial) marker I see?' And the people of the city told him, 'It is the tomb of the Man of God who came from Judah and proclaimed these things that you have done against the altar at Bethel'. He said, 'Let him rest; let no one disturb his bones'. So they left his bones together with the bones of the prophet who came out of Samaria.

This biblical attack on Bethel's temple and tombs forms the climax of a distinct anti-Northern polemic running throughout the books of Kings. In these texts, Bethel is a cult place disparaged and denigrated as an illegitimate and idolatrous sanctuary, most prominently in 1 Kings 12–13 and 2 Kings 23. Despite its more positive appraisal elsewhere in the Hebrew Bible as a legitimate cult place of prestigious pedigree, in Kings it is discredited as a place of politico-religious deviancy.[8] This intense hostility towards Bethel probably reflects the likely historical reality that Bethel was Jerusalem's greatest competitor and rival. Indeed, even in Kings it is depicted as a sanctuary much like Jerusalem: it is a high-profile cult place given a royal foundation (1 Kgs 12:28-33; 13:1-10), associated with authoritative prophetic activity (1 Kgs 13:11-32; 2 Kgs 2:1-3, 23-24) and even given a seemingly 'centralized' priestly law (2 Kgs 17:27-28).[9] But despite its acknowledged high-status calibre, Bethel remains a place of syncretism, idolatry and dubious religious authority for the pro-Jerusalem writer of Kings. The oracle against its altar (1 Kgs 13:1-3) and its apparent (though not quite precise) fulfilment in Josiah's attack on Bethel (2 Kgs 23:15-20) thus serve to discredit the cult at Bethel in favour of the distinctively Judahite religious authority with which Josiah's purges are aligned.

Accordingly, Josiah's desecration of the tombs at Bethel is set against the backdrop of his reform of Judahite cults, including that of the Jerusalem temple (2 Kgs 23:4-14). As is well known, the king is said to have rid the temple and the other sanctuaries (במות) of their supposedly idolatrous cults. The destruction of

---

7. The Septuagint appears to tie this verse more closely to the tradition reflected in 1 Kgs 13:1-2 by pinpointing the occasion of the Man of God's prophecy against Bethel's altar to the time 'when Jeroboam stood by the altar at the festival'.

8. For examples of Bethel's positive portrayal, see Gen. 28:11-12; 31:13; 35:1-16; Hos. 12:3-5 (cf. Gen. 12:8; 13:3-4); for Bethel's defamatory portrayal outside Kings, see (for example) Amos 4:4; 5:5-6; and the literature cited earlier in n. 1.

9. On this seemingly 'positive' but grudging acknowledgement in Kings of Bethel's religious calibre, see the discussion in Gomes, *The Sanctuary of Bethel*, 16–61.

these cults is heavily emphasized throughout the narrative: priests are deposed, sanctuaries and sacred buildings are broken down and altars are smashed. The destruction of sacred objects devoted to a variety of deities is similarly comprehensive: the narrator insists no fewer than three times that these cult objects have been removed from the temple and burned (vv. 4, 6, 11). As if to underscore further the eradication of these cults and their objects, it is also claimed that the burned remains of sacred vessels were scattered on graves (v. 6) and that the defiled sanctuaries in Jerusalem were filled with human bones (v. 14).[10] Mixing the contents of temple and tomb is here presented as a powerful act of aggression and destruction – a point to which the discussion will return.

Despite the seemingly complex compositional history of this text (suggested by its several peculiarities) the sequence of events appears to be deliberate and meaningful.[11] The narrator proceeds to state that Josiah's attention then turned to Bethel (v. 15), where he dismantled the altar and burned the sanctuary and its asherah. The most distinctive feature of the destruction of the cult at Bethel, however, is the emptying of nearby tombs and the burning of the bones they had housed. The purpose of this action would initially appear to be straightforward, for the narrator explains in v. 16 that Josiah 'took the bones from the tombs, and burned them on the altar. So he defiled it.' But it seems odd that Josiah should *burn* the bones on the altar in an effort to defile it. After all, simply bringing a sacred site into contact with human bones is presented in the same chapter (v. 14) as being a sufficient means of defiling the Jerusalem sanctuaries. Why, then, are the bones said to be *burned* on the altar?

The suggestion that the ashes would permeate the stone, rendering the altar irreversibly defiled,[12] has not been taken particularly seriously. Rather it is more plausible, in view of ancient West Asian anxieties about the disturbance or displacement of the dead (evident also, of course, in Judahite tomb inscriptions), that bone-burning in this biblical tradition is not intended simply to defile the altar, but to inflict post-mortem punishment upon the past inhabitants of Bethel who had participated in worship at a sanctuary depicted here and elsewhere in Kings

---

10. For a discussion of the possible implication that Josiah disinterred tombs in Jerusalem, see B. Halpern, 'Late Israelite Astronomies and the Early Greeks', in W. G. Dever and S. Gitin (eds), *Symbiosis, Symbolism, and the Power of the Past: Canaan, Ancient Israel, and Their Neighbors from the Late Bronze Age through Roman Palestinia* (Winona Lake, IN: Eisenbrauns, 2003), 323–52, esp. 335–45; see also n. 16.

11. For a range of views, see, for example, C. Hardmeier, 'King Josiah in the Climax of the Deuteronomistic History (2 Kings 22–23) and the Pre-Deuteronomistic Document of a Cult Reform at the Place of Residence (23.4-15): Criticism of Sources, Reconstruction of Literary Pre-Stages and the Theology of History in 2 Kings 22–23', in L. L. Grabbe (ed.), *Good Kings and Bad Kings: The Kingdom of Judah in the Seventh Century BCE* (LHBOTS, 393; London: T&T Clark, 2005), 123–63.

12. M. Haran, *Temples and Temple Service in Ancient Israel* (Oxford: Clarendon Press, 1978), 138.

as inherently and perpetually unlawful.[13] Burning the bones is perhaps intended to signal their unalterable displacement, preventing their reburial and the resultant reassimilation of the dead into the underworld and its cult.

That bone-burning is intended as a punishment is also suggested in the claim in 2 Kgs 23:19-20 that Josiah burned bones not only at Bethel, but also at all Samaria's supposedly idolatrous altars.[14] And yet, despite the narrator's assertion that Josiah destroyed the Samarian sanctuaries in just the same way he had the cult at Bethel (v. 19), the punishment appears to be directed not at *past generations* of worshippers, but at the current idolaters, for in a mocking caricature of a sacrifice, the bones burned on the altars would seem to be those of the sanctuaries' newly slaughtered priests (v. 20), rather than those of the long-since-dead. There is no mention here of disinterment.

Significantly, however, though Josiah's actions against the Samarian cult places do not appear precisely to parallel the measures he takes against Bethel, they do neatly complement the (notably Judahite) Man of God's prophecy against Bethel's altar in 1 Kgs 13:1-3, with which Josiah's actions are closely associated. Set within the context of Jeroboam ben Nebat's apparent inauguration of the royal sanctuary at Bethel (1 Kgs 12:26–13:10), this oracle forms the first part of the defamation of Bethel in Kings, itself a distinctive aspect of the pervading anti-Northern polemic of the book.[15]

But, strikingly, the Man of God's prophecy against Bethel makes no mention of disinterment. Instead, it suggests that the bones to be burned on the altar will be those belonging to the priests Josiah will seemingly sacrifice. Indeed, this also appears to be the way in which the Chronicler understood Josiah's actions. In his version of Josiah's reform, in which, interestingly, bone-burning takes place not in the North but in Jerusalem and Judah,[16] the bones of the high-place priests

---

13. W. B. Barrick, *The King and the Cemeteries: Toward a New Understanding of Josiah's Reform* (VTS, 88; Leiden: Brill, 2002), 173–81; see also W. G. Dever, 'The Silence of the Text: An Archaeological Commentary on 2 Kings 23', in M. D. Coogan, J. C. Exum and L. E. Stager (eds), *Scripture and Other Artifacts: Essays on the Bible and Archaeology in Honor of Philip J. King* (Louisville, KY: Westminster John Knox Press, 1994), 143–68, esp. 158.

14. These verses are widely regarded as an addition, perhaps specifically crafted to reflect anti-Samarian or anti-Samaritan tendencies. See M. Cogan, 'A Slip of the Pen? On Josiah's Actions in Samaria (2 Kings 23:15-20)', in C. Cohen, A. Hurvitz, and S. M. Paul (eds), *Sefer Moshe* (Winona Lake, IN: Eisenbrauns, 2004), 3–8.

15. On Kings' anti-Northern polemic, see Stavrakopoulou, *King Manasseh and Child Sacrifice*, 58–72.

16. Barrick (*King and the Cemeteries*, 61–63) argues that the Chronicler's version of events, set in Jerusalem, reflects the original (and historical) location of Josiah's bone-burning activities. His proposals essentially depend upon a disassembling and reassembling of the narratives in 1 Kings 12–13 and 2 Kings 23, which this reader finds too conjectural to be persuasive.

are burned on their own altars in punishment for their illegitimate worship, just as the ashes of destroyed cult statues appear to be scattered over the graves of those who had worshipped them (2 Chr. 34:4-5). Again, there is no mention of disinterment.

Thus, while bone-burning is a repeated motif in what appear to be closely related traditions about Josiah's destruction of illegitimate cults, bone-burning at Bethel is distinctive, for it deals not with the ritualized slaughter of priests and the immolation of their bones, but with the deliberate disinterment of the surrounding tombs and the burning of bones taken from them. While the broader context of this motif suggests it is to be taken as a form of post-mortem punishment, there is likely a further reason motivating this portrayal of bone-burning at Bethel. A clue lies in the way in which Josiah is said to have purged the cults in Jerusalem (2 Kgs 23:4-14).

Despite the narrator's disdain for these cults, their sacred status is underscored in the very nature of their destruction, for the cult objects devoted to foreign gods are burned to ashes in the Kidron Valley (vv. 4, 6; cf. vv. 11, 12). While their burning is to a degree familiar – it is reminiscent, for example, of descriptions of ritual destruction in biblical and Mesopotamian literature[17] – the location of the burning is also significant. The Kidron Valley is presented in several texts as a boundary of Jerusalem (e.g. 1 Kgs 2:37; Jer. 31:40) and so in this regard it is unsurprising that archaeological evidence attests to its important function as a burial site throughout the second and first millennia BCE.[18] Within the setting of the city's sacred geography, this valley was likely perceived in mythic-symbolic terms as a sacred boundary, a liminal space simultaneously marking three interrelated places: the transitional space between the ordered city and the uncultivated wilderness, the roots of the holy hill upon which the heavenly and earthly realms met, and the intersection of the earthly realm and the underworld.[19]

Accordingly, and contrary to some interpretations, the burning of cult objects in the Kidron Valley is not akin to the incineration of rubbish on the outskirts of a city, but rather, a ritual effecting the transformative 'decommissioning' of sacred vessels and their destructive transference across this boundary from one realm to another, thereby effecting their total annihilation. In the text, this is apparent in the claim that the ashes of the burnt cult objects are cast upon the graves in the Kidron Valley (2 Kgs 23:6, 12; cf. v. 4);[20] sacred sites are transformed into places for the dead by being covered with (or perhaps buried by) bones (vv. 12-13), and

---

17. Cf. Wright, *Disposal of Impurity*, esp. 288–90; Levine, *Numbers 1–20*, 471.
18. See further the following chapter and the literature cited there.
19. On these broad themes in mythic constructions of place, see Smith, *Origins of Biblical Monotheism*, 27–32.
20. Notice that the phrase בני העם in v. 6 need not be rendered 'common people', but may mean something like 'generations of people'; cf. Ug. plural *bnm* (here cstr. *bn*), 'family', 'clan', 'heirs' (*DULAT*, 1.224).

by strong implication, Bethel itself becomes a place of the dead in receiving the ashes of cult objects burned in the Kidron Valley (v. 4).[21]

While the ritual displacement of cult objects from Judahite temples thus seems intended to effect their cultic 'decommissioning', their material destruction is also suggestive of their irreversible disempowerment: in being transformed into ashes and dust, their essential material wholeness and potent identity is not only compromised but becomes a manifestation of destruction. In this way, their cultic efficacy is rendered permanently redundant. It is thus striking that the bones taken from the tombs in Bethel in v. 16 are subjected to a similar, though inverted process. They are taken from one sphere – their entombed place in the underworld – and ritually burned in another, suggesting that like the cult objects taken from the Jerusalem temple, they too were perceived to be sacred. Their burning not only prevents their reburial, but crucially suggests a perceived need to destroy their socio-religious valency. Indeed, it is the very *materiality* of the sacred dead that is of powerful significance here. Within a social frame, the cadaver or skeleton is both person and object,[22] so that as Joanna Sofaer comments, 'the social meanings attached to the body cannot be separated from its physical reality'.[23] Accordingly, the placing and presence of a corpse or its remains is critical to its symbolic efficacy and social significance.[24] As Howard Williams argues:

> [T]he physicality and materiality of the dead body and its associated artefacts, structures and places can be seen as extensions of the deceased's personhood, actively affecting the remembrance of the deceased by the living and structuring future social action.[25]

The 'social life' of a corpse or its remains is thus bound up with its materiality, by which the agency of the dead is directly constructed and effected. The perceived efficacy of the materiality of the dead thus seems to be reflected in the tradition claiming Josiah burned bones at Bethel: their burning marks their destructive

---

21. For methods of decommissioning temples, including their being buried or covered, see the discussion in D. Edelman, 'Hezekiah's Alleged Cultic Centralization', *JSOT* 32 (2008), 395–434.

22. Hallam and Hockey, *Death, Memory and Material Culture*, drawing on A. Gell, *Art and Agency: An Anthropological Theory* (Oxford: Oxford University Press, 1998).

23. Sofaer, *The Body as Material Culture*, 67.

24. See K. Verdery, 'Dead Bodies Animate the Study of Politics', in *The Political Lives of Dead Bodies: Reburial and Postsocialist Change* (New York: Columbia University Press, 1999), reprinted in A. C. G. M. Robben (ed.), *Death, Mourning, and Burial: A Cross-Cultural Reader* (Oxford: Blackwell, 2004), 303–10.

25. H. Williams, 'Death Warmed Up: The Agency of Bodies and Bones in Early Anglo-Saxon Cremation Rites', *Journal of Material Culture* 9 (2004), 263–91, here 266.

and irreversible transformation from recognizable and powerful human remains to a seemingly innocuous pile of calcinated ashes, rendering the dead socially unidentified and impotent.[26] This is reminiscent of some forms of Assyrian corpse abuse, which included the grinding of enemies' bones into powder,[27] an action strongly suggestive of the symbolic and social efficacy of the remains of the enemy dead – and hence the need to destroy them. Thus in emptying the tombs surrounding the sanctuary and burning the bones they had housed on the altar, Josiah is not simply defiling the cult place or preventing the bones' reburial, but he is also seeking to wholly destroy the bones and thereby render them socially impotent. The result is the irreversible destruction of the bones, the annihilation of the dead – and thus the elimination of Bethel's ancestral potency.[28]

Josiah's actions in ritually destroying sacred bones at Bethel are therefore best understood not simply as a post-mortem punishment inflicted upon idolatrous worshippers, but as the deliberate eradication of Bethel's dead, and hence as an attack on its ancestral cult. Indeed, the important role of Bethel in the Jacob traditions suggests that the sanctuary's ancestral credentials were (in certain circles at least) a crucial aspect of its religious profile. The tradition about burning bones at Bethel thus seems intended to undermine the ancestral potency of the cult place. And it is in considering further the ideological dynamics of this biblical attack on Bethel's dead that the socio-political and socio-religious implications of the displacing and destruction of the dead at Bethel are brought into sharper focus.

The prominent focus upon Bethel's tombs and bones in the biblical account of its desecration is particularly significant given that it is often presented in the Hebrew Bible as a boundary sanctuary, lying between the territories of Ephraim and Benjamin and in close proximity to the boundary between the northern and southern kingdoms (for example, Josh. 16:1-2; 18:13). Given the close interrelation of graves, boundaries and territorialism, it is possible that the biblical attack on Bethel's dead reflects competing and contested claims to control or 'ownership' of this crucial site by northern and southern territories at several points

---

26. Note also the comments about cremated remains made by Gordon Rakita and Jane Buikstra, who write: 'while the clean, dry skeleton of a corpse is easily recognized as the final remains of an individual, a pile of calcinated bone is not. Indeed, the identification of cremations archaeologically is often extremely difficult' (G. F. M. Rakita and J. E. Buikstra, 'Corrupting Flesh: Reexamining Hertz's Perspective on Mummification and Cremation', in G. F. M. Rakita, J. E. Buikstra, L. A. Beck and S. R. Williams [eds], *Interacting with the Dead: Perspectives on Mortuary Archaeology for the New Millennium* [Gainesville, FL: University Press of Florida, 2005], 97–106, here 104).

27. For grinding bones, see Borger, *Beiträge zum Inschriftenwerk Aššurbanipals*, 108, Prism B VI 97-VII 2; see also Scurlock, 'Death and the Afterlife in Ancient Mesopotamian Thought', 1,892.

28. Compare the impact of the 'mulching' of bones and corpses in the biblical oracle against Jerusalem's dead in Jer. 8:1-3, discussed in the following chapter. See also 2 Kgs 9:37; Ps. 83:11; Jer. 9:22; 16:4; 25:33.

throughout its history, as might be suggested by some of the inconsistencies in biblical boundary and town lists.[29]

Indeed, it is also notable that Josiah's portrayed excursion to Bethel has been taken by many as evidence of Judah's territorial expansion into the North,[30] whether during the reign of Josiah himself,[31] or perhaps at some point in the Neo-Babylonian period, when Bethel (and not Jerusalem) was probably the chief sanctuary and major political player in the region,[32] or more plausibly during the early Persian period, when Bethel was eventually eclipsed by Jerusalem as a cultic, economic and administrative centre of regional importance within the imperial context.[33] Thus, if the tradition in 2 Kgs 23:15-20 should allude to the annexing of Bethel, the bone-burning motif could well reflect the possibility that territorial gains were marked by the ritualized destruction of the ancestors who had guarded the boundaries and so occupied the land.

---

29. Cf. Josh. 18:22; Judg. 1:22. See Noth, 'Studien zu den historisch-geographischen Dokumenten des Josua-Buches', 185–255; Z. Kallai, *Historical Geography of the Bible: The Tribal Territories of Israel* (Leiden: Brill, 1986); Rogerson, 'Frontiers and Borders', 116–26; N. Na'aman and N. Lissovsky, 'A New Outlook on the Boundary System of the Twelve Tribes', *UF* 35 (2003), 291–332. See also R. Kletter, 'Pots and Polities: Material Remains of Late Iron Age Judah in Relation to the Political Borders', *BASOR* 314 (1999), 19–54; A. F. Rainey, 'Looking for Bethel: An Exercise in Historical Geography', in S. Gitin, J. E. Wright and J. P. Dessel (eds), *Confronting the Past: Archaeological and Historical Essays on Ancient Israel in Honor of William G. Dever* (Winona Lake, IN: Eisenbrauns, 2006), 269–73.

30. E.g. A. Alt, 'Judas Gaue unter Josia', *Palästinajahrbuch* 21 (1925), 100–116; M. Noth, *The History of Israel* (2nd edn; London: Black, 1960), 273; N. Na'aman, 'Josiah and the Kingdom of Judah', in L. L. Grabbe (ed.), *Good Kings and Bad Kings: The Kingdom of Judah in the Seventh Century BCE* (LHBOTS, 393; London: T&T Clark, 2005), 189–247.

31. See the discussion in F. M. Cross and G. E. Wright, 'The boundary and province lists of the Kingdom of Judah', *JBL* 75 (1956), 202–26; see also I. Finkelstein and N. A. Silberman, *The Bible Unearthed: Archaeology's New Vision of Ancient Israel and the Origin of Its Sacred Texts* (New York: Free Press, 2001), 345–53; M. Leuchter, *Josiah's Reform and Jeremiah's Scroll: Historical Calamity and Prophetic Response* (Sheffield: Sheffield Phoenix Press, 2006), 50–69. For the more plausible likelihood that Josiah's incursion into Bethel is an invented tradition, constructed during the post-exilic era, see H. Niehr, 'Die reform des Joschija: Methodische, historische und religionsgeschichtliche Aspekte', in W. Gross (ed.), *Jeremia und die 'deuteronomistische Bewegung'* (Weinheim: Beltz Athenäum, 1995), 33–54.

32. See the discussion in J. Blenkinsopp, 'Bethel in the Neo-Babylonian Period', in O. Lipschits and J. Blenkinsopp (eds), *Judah and the Judeans in the Neo-Babylonian Period* (Winona Lake, IN: Eisenbrauns, 2003), 93–107 and (in the same volume) that of E. A. Knauf, 'Bethel: The Israelite Impact on Judean Language and Literature' (291–350).

33. See, for example, P. R. Davies, 'Josiah and the Law Book', in L. L. Grabbe (ed.), *Good Kings and Bad Kings: The Kingdom of Judah in the Seventh Century BCE* (LHBOTS, 393; London: T&T Clark, 2005), 65–77, esp. 75–76; and idem, *The Origins of Biblical Israel*, 159–71, esp. 170–71.

Given the uncertainties clouding the relative waxing and waning of Bethel and Jerusalem, little can be assumed of the precise contexts giving rise to the tradition crediting Josiah with the desecration of Bethel. But the ideological contours of the tradition in 2 Kgs 23:15-20 itself are suggestive of an asserted claim to the socio-religious supremacy of Judah, crucially predicated on the territorial functions of the dead. Following the displacement and burning of Bethel's local dead, Josiah gives clear instructions to leave undisturbed the tomb housing the bones of the Judahite Man of God. The reader is told:

> He said, 'What is that (memorial) marker I see?' The people of the city told him, 'It is the tomb of the Man of God who came from Judah and proclaimed these things that you have done against the altar at Bethel'. He said, 'Let him rest; let no one disturb his bones'. (2 Kgs 23:17-18a)

Set alongside the displacement and destruction of the other dead at Bethel, this brief text further illuminates the social, territorial and ideological connotations of the tradition about Josiah's attack on Bethel. Unlike the indistinct, ashy dust of the displaced and annihilated dead, the emphatically marked tomb of the Man of God remains visibly, distinctively and ideologically placed. Though within its broader narrative context the burial of the Man of God at Bethel is constructed upon the premise of his own displacement (he is interred away from his ancestral tomb as a punishment for his disobedience to Yhwh in 1 Kgs 13:21-22),[34] his interment in what appears to be the family tomb of his northern[35] prophetic host (1 Kgs 13:30) ultimately endorses the displacement of Bethel's indigenous dead in 2 Kgs 23:17-18. Protected and left unharmed, the tomb of the notably nameless Judahite Man of God is thus pointedly exhibited, its grave marker prominently displayed, seemingly staking an ideological claim on the place by memorializing

---

34. Cf. 1 Kgs 13:8, 16.
35. There appears to be some confusion within 1 Kings 13 and 2 Kings 23 between Bethel and Samaria. In 1 Kgs 13:11, the old prophet buried in the tomb with the Judahite Man of God is said to come from Bethel, but in 2 Kgs 23:18b he is described as 'the prophet who came out of Samaria'. In view of the tradition in 1 Kings 13, most commentators detect a redactional or scribal error here, and assume the prophet from Bethel is the intended referent. A similar confusion is also evident in 1 Kgs 13:32 and 2 Kgs 23:19-20, in which the focused assault on Bethel slides into a general attack on Samaria and its sanctuaries. These problems are often blamed on a clumsy redactor, keen to extend the cult crimes and punishment of Bethel to a broader northern population, including, perhaps, the foreigners and 'Samarians' (שמרנים) said in 2 Kgs 17:24-41 to live in the territories of the former Northern Kingdom. It is possible that the sliding of designations in these texts is informed in some way by the tradition in 2 Kgs 17:27-28 that (a) priest(s) from Samaria relocated to Bethel to offer religious instruction to the local inhabitants. The apparent confusion of Bethel and Samaria seems likely to occupy redaction critics for some time yet, but also inhibits a more robust contextualization of the Bethel polemic in Kings.

the Judahite, prophetic word of judgement against the 'illegitimate' cult there.[36] Even the uncommon term used of the memorial marker (ציון) itself carries assertively territorial connotations (cf. Jer. 31:21; Ezek. 39:15),[37] so that it functions as a permanent sign of the displacement and destruction of Bethel's ancestral cult. The Judahite Man of God's tomb is thus imaged as a lone and exclusive symbol of social and cultic order amidst a landscape of devastation, rendering the cult at Bethel and its ancestral dead utterly and irreversibly impotent.[38]

The displacement of Bethel's dead in 2 Kings 23 thus manifests the disempowering of its ancestors, the disabling of its cult, and the destabilizing of its distinctively 'northern' territoriality. But this hostile tradition about the cult place and its dead contrasts sharply with the positive imaging of Bethel in other biblical traditions, in which the importance and legitimacy of the cult's ancestral credentials is reflected favourably in texts claiming Jacob as the sanctuary's founder.[39] Indeed, despite the scarcity of references to Jacob in the books of Kings (1 Kgs 18:31; 2 Kgs 13:23; 17:34), the attack on Bethel's dead in 2 Kings 23 is nonetheless strongly suggestive of the cult's high-profile ancestral pedigree.[40] While this contrast indicates that Bethel's religio-political status was for some a contested issue, it also raises questions about the particular ideological dynamics of the association of Jacob with Bethel in the Hebrew Bible, for it is Jacob, more than any other patriarchal character in the biblical literature, who plays a prominent role in the overtly 'ancestral' (re-)framing of practices associated with the dead.

---

36. The preservation of the bones of the 'prophet from Samaria' alongside those of the Judahite Man of God in 23:18b, whom most identify as the prophet of Bethel known from 1 Kings 13, does not eclipse this ideological claim on Bethel, for the apparent preservation of his bones appears to be incidental, rather than intentional. The implied supremacy of the Judahite prophetic word over that of Bethel is intimated in the northern prophet's apparent and humbling 'adoption' of the Judahite Man of God as his new (or perhaps replacement) kinsman (1 Kgs 13:30) and his wish to be interred with his prophetic 'brother' (13:31).

37. See further below, 95–96.

38. In this way, the prophetic memorial marker remains the only sign of the mythic intersection between the earthly realm and the underworld. This not only complements the interest in 2 Kgs 13:21 in the cultic efficacy of a prophet's tomb (here Elisha), but may also reflect an emerging interest in the tombs of prophets (rather than ancestors) as potent sites of cultic exchange. On the tombs of the prophets, see Niehr, 'The Changed Status of the Dead', 138–40, 154; Lightstone, *Commerce of the Sacred*, esp. 51–62. Traditions concerning the lives, deaths and burial places of the prophets are also reflected in the *Lives of the Prophets*; see D. R. A. Hare, 'The Lives of the Prophets', *OTP* 2.379-99.

39. E.g. Gen. 28:11-22; 31:13; 35:1-15; cf. Hos. 12:3-5. Note also Abraham's association with Bethel in Gen. 13:3-4 (cf. 12:8).

40. The scarcity of references to Jacob – and the other so-called patriarchs (1 Kgs 11:28; 18:36; 2 Kgs 13:23) – in the book of Kings might be explained as a reflection of its compositional context, in which, perhaps, the Jacob traditions and other patriarchal stories known from Genesis were either unknown, irrelevant, ignored or perhaps yet to emerge.

Ancestral Advocacy

'There are many different kinds of ancestors', Mary Douglas writes, 'Some ancestors do nothing at all, except to stand at the points of articulation of long and widely branching lineages, giving their name to the section of the tribe that descends from them'.[41] Jacob is an ancestor against whom no such charge could be brought. Though he fulfils a crucial role in standing at the pivotal point of the biblical Israel's ancestry, Jacob is far from being a passive patriarch. Rather, he plays an empowering role in the biblical imaging of the ancestors by modelling in Genesis what can be described as 'good practice' in relation to the territorial dead. While Abraham, Isaac and Joseph (and indeed the outcasts Ishmael and Esau) are granted a heavily tempered but idealized interest in the dead – interring and interment in the family tomb, with very little emphasis on mortuary cult – Jacob is presented as an ancestor actively and closely associated with practices pertaining to the dead. Of all the biblical ancestors, it is Jacob who cultivates both a landscape and culture of death.

This cultivation – or perhaps 'enculturation' – is particularly evident in Gen. 35:1-20, a narrative in which several traditions are closely and carefully aligned. Four scenes are presented, each in turn, and each of which exhibits a brief but focused cameo of ritual activity. The first two cameos present burial beneath what seems intended to be understood as a sacred tree: in vv. 1-4, Jacob buries 'foreign gods' beneath a tree near Shechem; in vv. 5-8, he buries Deborah, a wet-nurse, beneath a tree 'below' Bethel. Finally, the last two cameos show Jacob setting up a standing stone (מצבה): in vv. 9-15, it is in the cult place at Bethel; in vv. 16-20, it is at Rachel's grave. These latter texts will be treated here first.

The establishing or endorsing of cult places functions ideologically in Genesis not only as a means of identifying the patriarchal god with the non-Yhwistic, indigenous deities of sacred sites throughout the promised land, but also as a way of marking in exhibited, cultic form the ethnic occupation of that land. This ethno-territorialism is explicitly and repeatedly correlated to the overarching patriarchal themes of lineage and land, so it is to be expected to find it firmly embedded in Gen. 35:9-15, the third cameo of this particular narrative:

> Elohim said to him, 'I am El Shaddai. Be fruitful and multiply: a nation and an assembly of nations shall come from you, and kings shall issue from your loins. The land that I gave to Abraham and Isaac I will give to you, and I will give the land to your offspring after you'. (Gen. 35:11-12)

Much like its counterpart in 28:11-22, here in this text the cult place at Bethel is presented as a sanctuary at which are given oracles assuring territory and descendants; it is also presented as a cult place (or more likely, temple) endorsed

---

41. Douglas, *Jacob's Tears*, 181.

by means of the מצבה set up specifically by Jacob (35:14).[42] The material marking of the sanctuary, and the performance of cult at the place, ritualizes, mythologizes and authorizes the 'Jacobite', and hence 'Israelite', occupation of the land, an occupation made explicit by Jacob renaming the cult place (מקום) Bethel (35:15). Though it is possible – as Cooper and Goldstein have argued – that the ritual backdrop to this scene is the installation of deified ancestors at the site (manifested by the מצבה),[43] the dead make no explicit appearance in this cameo in its present form. But the significance of Jacob's actions at Bethel is underlined in the following cameo (vv. 16-20), in which the boundary-defining role of a tomb (particularly in relation to Bethel and its environs) is once again in evidence. Upon leaving Bethel, and immediately following the setting up of the מצבה there, Jacob's wife Rachel dies giving birth to Benjamin on the road to Ephrath (vv. 16-18). The narrator then states:

> So Rachel died, and she was buried on the way to Ephrath – that is, Bethlehem – and Jacob set up a standing stone (מצבה) at her tomb; it is the standing stone of Rachel's tomb, which is there to this day. (Gen. 35:19-20)

Within its broader narrative context, Jacob's decision to bury Rachel at the roadside (cf. 48:7) rather than transport her corpse to the patriarchal tomb at Machpelah (cf. 49:29; 50:7-14), has proved awkward for commentators.[44] But within the narrower frame of 35:1-20, the setting up of a standing stone at Rachel's tomb is strongly suggestive instead of an attempt to legitimize and endorse a tomb cult seemingly well known within the cultural heritage of the tradents of this tradition. Far from being a cursory and simple shallow grave,[45] Rachel's burial place is rendered a monumental cult site by means of the מצבה Jacob sets up there. Though standing stones are well known in ancient West

---

42. The setting up of standing stones seems to be the biblical Jacob's particular 'calling card' (Gen. 28:18, 22; 31:13, 45, 49, 51-52; 35:14, 20), for none of the other patriarchs in Genesis 'establish' cult places in this way. For the use of a standing stone in Jacob's land deal with Laban, see 99–101. For a discussion of the narrative parallel to that in 35:9-15, see J. Van Seters, 'Divine Encounter at Bethel (Gen 28,10-22) in Recent Literary-Critical Study of Genesis', *ZAW* 110 (1998), 503–13; cf. E. Blum, *Die Komposition der Vätergeschichte* (WMANT, 57; Neukirchen-Vluyn: Neukirchener Verlag, 1984), 7–65.

43. As discussed in Chapter 1.

44. For a recent overview of responses to this apparent problem, see B. D. Cox and S. Ackerman, 'Rachel's Tomb', *JBL* 128 (2009), 135–48. Cox and Ackerman suggest that Rachel's death in childbirth renders her perpetually and dangerously liminal, thereby necessitating her immediate isolation from the community, both living and dead – hence her hasty burial away from Machpelah. For biblical texts allowing for the transportation of corpses to or between burial places (alongside Gen. 49:29; 50:7-14), see Olyan 'Neglected Aspects', 612–15.

45. *Pace* Cox and Ackerman, 'Rachel's Tomb', 139.

Asian mortuary contexts,[46] within the imagined world created by the biblical writers – and particularly in Genesis – standing stones (מצבות) are primarily located at sanctuaries, rather than tombs.[47] (Even Absalom's standing stone in 2 Sam. 18:18 seems to be set apart from any gravesite.) Thus, following his ancestral advocacy of Bethel in Gen. 35:9-15 (cf. 28:11-22), Jacob's setting up of a מצבה at Rachel's tomb at once identifies and endorses the grave as a legitimate cult place, implicitly aligning it with that at Bethel. Indeed, and in keeping with the apparent function of his cultic activity elsewhere in Genesis, Jacob is here presented as the ancestral founder of the cult of Rachel's tomb: he creates the grave in which she is buried, and he marks it 'to this day' (עד־היום) as a sanctioned, sanctified cult site.

Though other biblical traditions about this cult site at Rachel's tomb can offer only partial glimpses of its perceived function, there are indications that the tomb cult is credited with attributes in line with those elsewhere associated with the deified dead: territorial marking and the giving of oracles. This is hinted at in 1 Sam. 10:1-2, in which Rachel's tomb is presented as an oracular cult place mediating ancestral territory (נחלה). But it is attested more strongly in Jer. 31:15-17, which reads:

> Thus says Yhwh:
> A voice is heard in Ramah,
> lamentation, bitter weeping:
> Rachel weeping for her children;
> she refuses to be comforted for her children,
> for they are no more.
> Thus says Yhwh:
> Keep your voice from weeping,
> and your eyes from tears,
> for there is reward for your labour –
> Oracle of Yhwh:
> They will return from the land of the enemy.
> And there is hope for your future –
> Oracle of Yhwh:
> Children shall come back to their boundary.

This poignant text engages in multivalent ways with perceptions of the deified dead. The voice at Ramah is that of the dead Rachel, uttering words from the

---

46. See the discussion in Chapter 1. For the deliberate coalescence of the mortuary and sanctuary contexts of standing stones, see the discussion of Isa. 56:5-6 in Chapter 5.

47. As Ziony Zevit comments, '[b]iblical texts report *massebot* at relatively few sites in Israel' (*Religions of Ancient Israel*, 259).

tomb, as might be expected at a cult place of the dead.[48] And yet the voice of the dead ancestor here is crying out from her grave in distress – perhaps a testimony, as Cox and Ackerman also suggest,[49] to a belief that the post-mortem existence of a woman killed by birthing her child would be restless and disquieted, rather than settled and sound. But Rachel's lament over her lost sons (בנים) also plays on the activities of the tomb cult, exchanging praxis for pathos, for rather than receiving the petitionary laments of generations of her children, it is the dead Rachel herself who here performs ritual mourning; she is a weeping progenitress, mourning her absent descendants.

Within its context, of course, the absent descendants of Rachel's lament are the exiles, lost in a metaphorical place of death (ארץ אויב, the land of the enemy),[50] from which Yhwh promises to return them.[51] This oracular promise is couched in emphatically territorial language in v. 17, complementing the territorial functions of the dead and their graves: children – or better, 'descendants' (בנים) – will come back to their 'boundary' (גבול), a term often used to refer to the boundaries of the homestead and its ancestral land or to the boundaries of tribal territory – indeed, Rachel's tomb is firmly located on the 'boundary' of Benjamin (גבול בנימן) in 1 Sam. 10:2.[52] The territoriality of Rachel's tomb seems to be paralleled a few verses later in the same collection of oracles, as Yhwh commands his returning people (imaged this time as 'Betulah Israel')[53] to set up 'monuments' (צינים) to mark their way to their homes (Jer. 31:21). The unusual term צינים is significant here, for it is only used elsewhere in the MT (and only in the singular) to refer to the territorially charged memorial monuments marking the remains of the dead in 2 Kgs 23:17 and

---

48. Texts suggestive of the oracular voice of the dead emanating from the underworld include 1 Sam. 28:15-19; Isa. 8:19-20; 29:4; cf. 14:1-10.

49. Cox and Ackerman, 'Rachel's Tomb', 147. The authors offer a range of examples from ancient West Asian (particularly Mesopotamian) texts and modern day traditional societies attesting to perceptions of the restlessness of the 'spirit' of a woman who dies in childbirth.

50. On the imaging of exile as death, see Chapter 5.

51. On the place of Rachel's lament within the overlaid literary-theological frames of barrenness and fertility, rescue from death and exile, and restoration, see Levenson, *Resurrection and the Restoration of Israel*, 142–55, esp. 147–48.

52. Examples include Deut. 19:14; 27:17; Prov. 15:25; 22:28; 23:10. גבול can also refer to a natural landscape boundary (such as a mountain ridge) and can thus be used to image larger territories on a 'national' scale (e.g. Num. 34:6) or of cosmic proportions (e.g. Ps. 104:9). See the literature cited in Chapter 1, n. 47.

53. On the label בתולה as the designation of a post-pubescent woman yet to give birth to her first child (not 'virgin'), see P. L. Day, 'From the Child is Born the Woman: The Story of Jephthah's Daughter', in P. L. Day (ed.), *Gender and Difference in Ancient Israel* (Minneapolis: Fortress Press, 1989), 58–74.

Ezek. 39:15.⁵⁴ In Jer. 31:15-17, then, Rachel's tomb is rendered a territorial marker of 'national' regeneration.

Given the territorial function of the dead, it is thus perhaps unsurprising to find the tomb imaged as a boundary burial in 1 Sam. 10:2. While the precise location and identification of the tomb's site appear to be contested in the biblical texts (and indeed in modern scholarship), most are agreed that this text and Jer. 31:15-17 locate the tomb on the border of Benjamin, before its subsequent aligning – probably in the Persian period – with Judahite Bethlehem/Ephrath (Gen. 35:19; 48:7; Jub. 32:34; cf. Ruth 4:11; Mic. 5:1), which fixed the 'northern' tomb firmly within the Judahite landscape of the new 'Israel'.⁵⁵ Though in the biblical tradition she was not re-placed at Machpelah – unlike, perhaps, Jacob – Rachel's tomb cult was thus nonetheless credited a more 'centralized' role in its Judahite relocation and related association with the place of Davidic ancestry, Bethlehem.⁵⁶

While the tomb's cameo appearance in Gen. 35:16-20 thus localizes and repatriates this 'national' ancestress within a Judahite context, it also represents the ancestral ethno-territorial marking of the promised land. Accordingly, Jacob's role in burying Rachel also renders him the tomb cult's founder, so that in constructing her burial place and memorializing her corpse with a מצבה, Jacob not only ritualizes the ancestral occupation of the land, but he also cultivates a mortuary landscape, marking its colonization. Indeed, this landscaping is already well established in the narrative, for in the first two cameos of the sequence (35:1-4, 5-8), two burials have already been performed and memorialized: one on the way to Bethel, and the other 'below' Bethel.⁵⁷

---

54. On ציון in 2 Kgs 23:17, see 90–91; on its use in Ezek. 39:15, see Stavrakopoulou, 'Gog's Grave', 79.

55. R. Schmitt, 'Cultural Memory and Family Religion'. Paper presented at the annual meeting of the European Association of Biblical Studies in Lisbon, Portugal, August 2008. See also Z. Kallai, 'Rachel's Tomb: A Historiographical Review', in J. A. Loader and H. V. Kieweler (eds), *Vielseitigkeit des Alten Testaments* (Frankfurt: Peter Lang, 1999), 215–23; cf. M. Tsevat, 'Studies in the Books of Samuel, II: Interpretation of I Sam 10:2, Saul at Rachel's Tomb', *HUCA* 33 (1962), 107–18; T. Knopf, 'Rahels Grab: Eine Tradition aus dem TNK', *Dielheimer Blätter zum Alten Testament und seiner Rezeption in der frühen Kirche* 27 (1991), 73–137.

56. Cf. P. K. McCarter, *I Samuel: A New Translation with Introduction, Notes and Commentary* (AB, 8; Garden City, NY: Doubleday, 1980), 181. On modern day socio-religious practices associated with Rachel's tomb, see S. S. Sered, 'Rachel's Tomb and the Milk Grotto of the Virgin Mary: Two Women's Shrines in Bethlehem', *Journal of Feminist Studies in Religion* 2 (1986), 7–22; idem, 'Rachel's Tomb: The Development of a Cult', *JSQ* 2 (1995), 103–48. On the socio-political ramifications of the tomb cult's recent history, see also Sered's 'Rachel's Tomb: Societal Liminality and the Revitalization of a Shrine', *Religion* 19 (1989), 27–40.

57. The repetition of the preposition תחת here and in v. 4 suggests a meaningful allusion to the cult figure of Deborah who sits *under* (תחת) the sacred tree in Judg. 4:5.

4. Contesting Bethel

In vv. 5-8, Jacob's founding of the cult at Bethel (building an altar and designating the site by invoking the name of the deity) is immediately followed by a death in his household:

> Then Deborah, Rebekah's wet-nurse, died, and she was buried below Bethel, under the oak tree (אלון). So it was called the Oak of Weeping (אלון בכות). (Gen. 35:8)

Assuming a lowly status for the Deborah named here, commentators often wonder why a grave tradition might be attached to so insignificant a figure and included in the Jacob cycle of ancestor stories. It has been suggested that an earlier form of the tradition might have located Rebekah's burial here; or it may be that Deborah has been confused with (or separated from) the judge, prophetess and matriarch (אם) also known by that name (Judg. 5:7), a woman whose cult place is identified in Judg. 4:5 as the oracular tree known as the 'Palm of Deborah' (תמר דבורה), located on the boundary between Ramah and Bethel, which is perhaps to be related to the 'Oak of Tabor' (אלון תבור) at Bethel (1 Sam. 10:3; cf. 1 Kgs 13:14).[58] At the very least, it seems likely that all these sacred trees claimed to be in the vicinity of Bethel are to be identified.[59] Accordingly, burial beneath a tree is thus neither a humble nor hurried mortuary act, but an interment of great significance (cf. 1 Sam. 31:13; 1 Chr. 10:12), for Deborah's burial here draws together the regenerative, protective and oracular association of both tomb cults and sacred trees.

Bethel's powerful potency as a place of the dead is heightened further by virtue of the life-giving nature of the two women buried here: Deborah is no mere servant, but Rebekah's wet-nurse (מינקת) – and perhaps by implication, Jacob's own nurturer – and thus a figure of fecundity and fruitfulness, on whom the perpetuation of the generations depends,[60] while from Rachel's death comes life, in the form of the son to whom she gives birth. Jacob's dead at Bethel are

---

58. Cf. von Rad, *Genesis*, 337–38.
59. For these possibilities, see N. Wyatt, 'Word of Tree and Whisper of Stone: El's Oracle to King Keret (Kirta), and the Problem of the Mechanics of Its Utterance', *VT* 57 (2007), 483–510; van der Toorn, *Family Religion*, 216; cf. Gomes, *Sanctuary of Bethel*, 135. For the cultic and mythic undertones of biblical traditions about (both) Deborah(s), see K. Spronk, 'Deborah, a Prophetess: The Meaning and Background of Judges 4:4-5', in J. C. de Moor (ed.), *The Elusive Prophet: The Prophet as a Historical Person, Literary Character and Anonymous Artist* (OTS, 45; Leiden: Brill, 2001), 232–42.
60. Cf. Gen. 24:59. Baruch Halpern similarly suggests that Deborah is nurse to Jacob in *The First Historians: The Hebrew Bible and History* (San Francisco: Harper & Row, 1988), 102, n. 27. See M. I. Gruber, 'Breast-feeding Practices in Biblical Israel and in Old Babylonian Mesopotamia', *JANES* 19 (1989), 61–83; M. Stol, *Birth in Babylonia and the Bible: Its Mediterranean Setting* (Groningen: Styx, 2000), 181–92; H. J. Marsman, *Women*

thus the powerfully *fertile* dead, memorialized in the sacred landscape as cultic testimonies to the fulfilment of the promise of lineage and land.[61]

But Jacob's active participation in practices dealing with the dead also extends beyond his role as the founder of gravesites, for in the tradition concerning Deborah's grave, the name given to the tree itself, אלון בכות ('Oak of Weeping'), signals Jacob's characterization here and elsewhere as a (perhaps paradigmatic) ritual mourner: in Gen. 37:34-35, Jacob refuses to cease his ritual weeping (בכה) for Joseph, and in Hos. 12:5, Jacob is cast as the ancestor who wept (בכה) to petition the deity. Both these verses employ the same terminology as that designating the sacred tree in Gen. 35:8, so it is perhaps unsurprising that Jacob is closely associated with the tree cult.[62] In other texts, Bethel itself is characterized as a place of weeping (Judg. 20:26; 21:2-4), so that, as Yarieh Amit and others have noted, its identification with (rather than distinction from) Bochim ('Weepers') (cf. LXX Judg. 2:1-5) marks it out as a cult place of weeping[63] – alluding, perhaps, to Bethel's particular association with practices pertaining to the dead.[64] Within the biblical traditions, both patriarch and place are notably associated with ritual mourning.

The deaths and burials of Rachel and Deborah signal in narrative terms a point of social and cultic transition for Jacob. Indeed, the birth of Benjamin and the interment of Rebekah's wet-nurse represent a socio-cultural crossing point for Jacob, marking the shifting of generations and his emerging role as *paterfamilias*. Moreover, Jacob's socio-cultural separation from Esau (Gen. 28:5-22; cf. 33:1-17) and Laban (Genesis 31) also illustrates this in stark terms

---

in Ugarit and Israel: Their Social and Religious Position in the Context of the Ancient Near East (OTS, 49; Leiden: Brill, 2003), 431.

61. Indeed, Hos. 10:1 offers a polemical reflection of the correlation of Jacob's fertility with his territorial, cultic colonization – including the setting up of מצבות.

62. Note also that Jacob also weeps in Gen. 29:11 and 33:4 (cf. Douglas, *Jacob's Tears*, 26–27). For other occurrences of בכה within a context of ritual mourning, see (for example) Gen. 23:2; 50:4; Deut. 34:8; 2 Sam. 1:24; 19:2; Isa. 15:2; 22:12; 30:19; Jer. 22:10; 31:15-16; Ezek. 8:14; 24:16, 23; 27:31; Joel 2:12; Mic. 1:10; Job 30:31; Ezra 10:1; Neh. 3:9; cf. 2 Kgs 18:12; Isa. 30:19; Lam. 1:2. On weeping as a ritual associated with incubation (and with direct reference to Jacob's dream at Bethel), see S. Ackerman, 'The Deception of Isaac, Jacob's Dream at Bethel, and Incubation on an Animal Skin', in G. A. Anderson and S. M. Olyan (eds), *Priesthood and Cult in Ancient Israel* (JSOTS, 125; Sheffield: JSOT Press, 1991), 92–120.

63. Y. Amit, 'Bochim, Bethel, and the Hidden Polemic (Judg 2,1-5)', in G. Galil and M. Weinfeld (eds), *Studies in Historical Geography and Biblical Historiography* (VTS, 81; Leiden: Brill, 2000), 121–31; C. F. Burney, *The Book of Judges* (New York: Ktav, 1970 [1918]), 37.

64. See K. Spronk, 'A Story to Weep About: Some Remarks on Judges 2:1-5 and its Context', in J. W. Dyk (ed.), *Unless Someone Guide Me: Festschrift for Karel A. Deurloo* (Maastricht: Shaker, 2000), 87–94, drawing on F. F. Hvidberg, *Weeping and Laughter in the Old Testament: A Study of Canaanite-Israelite Religion* (Leiden: Brill, 1962), 105–7.

within the Jacob cycle.[65] But significantly, Deborah's tree burial also marks and memorializes Jacob's territorial movement from place to place as a part of this transition. This is evident in the paralleling of this particular burial with that of the 'foreign gods' (אלהי הנכר) in the first of the narrative's cameos (35:1-4). In these verses, Jacob's occupation of Bethel is divinely ordained and authorized (v. 1) before being ritually marked not only by the building of an altar there (v. 3), but also by the separation of Jacob's household from the gods alien or non-indigenous to Bethel (vv. 2-4). Like broken cult objects, these deities (presumably figurines) are ritually decommissioned – if not disempowered – and left behind by being buried[66] beneath a tree at Shechem before Jacob sets out to 'settle' at Bethel.[67] As seems likely, these gods are probably best understood as the ancestral figurines (תרפים) belonging to Laban and stolen by Rachel (Gen. 31:19, 30, 34);[68] deified ancestors whose limited, restricted localization is attested in their ritual abandonment at Shechem, and sharply contrasted with the broader territorial potency of the god of Jacob, who is notably credited with having been with Jacob wherever he has travelled (35:3). Within this narrative context, Laban's ancestors are discredited as outlawed 'foreign gods' and left behind at Shechem – perhaps to be usurped by the installation of the bones of Joseph and also Torah itself (Josh. 24:26-27, 32), while Jacob's dead are firmly located at Bethel, staking a claim on the cult place there.

Throughout Genesis 35, Jacob's mortuary landscape thus bears the marks of a separatist ethno-territorialism that is in some ways reminiscent of Abraham's purchase of Machpelah (Genesis 23) – and yet thanks to its juxtaposed, complex cameos, it is composed of richer, sharper textures. This richness is also well illustrated in Gen. 31:44-54, in which Jacob's separation from Laban and his return to the land of his ancestors (31:3) is ritualized in the form of a boundary ceremony at Mizpah/Galeed. It is often assumed that this story is shaped by a

---

65. See Heard, *Dynamics of Diselection*, 97–137, 139–69.

66. That the burials of the wet-nurse and the 'foreign gods' are not to be identified but contrasted is suggested by the loaded use of the term טמן to describe the concealed burial of the 'foreign gods' (35: 4), as opposed to the more usual and neutral קבר, employed to refer to the burial of Deborah (35:8). On the likelihood that the burial of these deities is akin to the ritual burial of cult objects in favissae, see D. Edelman, 'Hidden Ancestral Polemics in the Book of Genesis?' (forthcoming), citing O. Keel, 'Das Vergraben der "fremden Götter" in Genesis XXXV 4b', *VT* 23 (1973), 305–33; cf. Wright, *Disposal of Impurity*, 288–90. On earrings as cultic symbols, see Exod. 32:2-4; Num. 31:50; cf. Judg. 8:24-26; Ezek. 16:12.

67. This sacred tree is perhaps intended to be identified with those featuring in the traditions told in Gen. 12:6; Josh. 24:23-27; Judg. 9:6, 37.

68. See K. van der Toorn, 'The Nature of the Biblical Teraphim in the Light of Cuneiform Evidence', *CBQ* 52 (1990), 203–22; K. van der Toorn and T. J. Lewis, 'תרפים', *TDOT*, 8.765-78; Brichto, 'Kin, Cult, Land and Afterlife', 46 n. 74; Cooper and Goldstein, 'Cult of the Dead', 295; Hamilton, *Genesis 18–50*, 375; Zevit, *Religions of Ancient Israel*, 275; Albertz, 'Family Religion', 98.

tradition concerning the relationship between Aramaeans and Israelites in the Transjordan, and the resolution of a dispute over the territory of Gilead.[69] Be this as it may, the biblical writer notably employs motifs related to traditional forms of land-marking, for Jacob and Laban's agreement not to encroach on each other's land is marked by the setting up of two memorial monuments: a מצבה and a גל (heap) of stones. Both vow not to pass beyond the monuments, which are claimed to act as 'witnesses' to the binding nature of the ritual (vv. 47, 52; cf. v. 44), much as materialized, memorialized Torah functions as a 'witness' in key biblical narratives associated with the possession of the land.[70] As Laban states (interrupted by a narrator):

> 'This heap is a witness, and the pillar is a witness, that I will not pass beyond this heap to you, and you will not pass beyond this heap and this pillar to me, for harm. May the Elohim of Nahor and the Elohim of Abraham' – the Elohim of their ancestor – 'judge between us'. (Gen. 31:52-53)

Given this context, and though the text is in some places problematic, some commentators suggest that rituals associated with ancestor veneration underlie the story, for alongside the setting up of stone monuments, Jacob and Laban offer vows by their ancestral deities (named in v. 53 as Elohim of Abraham and Elohim of Nahor) and Jacob partakes of a nocturnal, sacrificial meal with his kin-group.[71] Certainly, the setting up of stone memorials is closely associated with rituals central to mortuary cult practices, while their boundary location signals strongly the territorial presence of the memorialized ancestors to serve as guardians of the land and protectors of its boundaries.

However, certain features of the narrative suggest this is not so much an endorsement of the powerful dead or the rituals associated with them, but a caricature of traditional land-marking practices, intended to assert the efficacy of Jacob's god and crafted to belittle – or even disempower – Laban and the 'others' he represents. Indeed, this text seeks to claim Jacob's territorial dominance over Laban. Though it might be assumed that the standing stone (מצבה) and the pile of stones (גל) represent the deified ancestors of Jacob and Laban respectively, both these memorials are exclusively Jacob's, for they are set up by him and his household (vv. 45-46). Even when Laban tries to claim the pile of stones as his own by naming it in his own tongue (v. 47; cf. v. 51), Jacob assertively renames

---

69. See, conveniently, J. Loza Vera, 'La *bᵉrît* entre Laban et Jacob (Gn. 31.43-54)', in P. Daviau, P. M. Michèle, J. W. Wevers and M. Weigl (eds), *The World of the Aramaeans, I: Biblical Studies in Honour of Paul-Eugène Dion* (JSOTS, 324; Sheffield: Sheffield Academic Press, 2001), 57–69.

70. See the discussion in Chapter 3.

71. De Moor, 'Standing Stones', 1–20; Cooper and Goldstein, 'Cult of the Dead', 289–90, 295–96.

it in the language of his own household (v. 47) – a name Laban himself concedes and employs (v. 48), thereby acknowledging implicitly the cultural separation of his ritual world from that of Jacob, and the dominance of the latter over the former.[72] Viewed from this perspective, the pile of stones shares something in common with the cairns described elsewhere in the Hebrew Bible, which memorialize and publicize the broken corpses of the subjugated enemy.[73] The boundary markers in Gen. 31:44-54 are thus neither paired nor shared between the two men, but rather stake out the ethno-territorial interests of Jacob alone.

Jacob's dominance is also asserted in the ritual control he exhibits: it is Jacob and his kin who set up the stones (vv. 45-46); Jacob who offers a sacrifice (v. 54); Jacob who shares a ritual meal with his kin-group (vv. 46, 54). When Laban invokes the god(s) worshipped by their shared ancestors, Jacob swears only by what appears to be his exclusive ancestral deity – the 'Dread of Isaac' (v. 53; cf. v. 42).[74] This is Jacob's cult place, not Laban's. And as such, though it looks like a ritual in a venerative cult of the dead, it is a caricature of such a rite, for the deity apparently worshipped here is (as the narrator assiduously comments in v. 53) the single god Elohim, worshipped by Jacob in his various forms (including the so-called Dread of Isaac in v. 53). Laban's attempts to adhere to 'traditional', ancestral forms of land management are thus overturned and eclipsed by the cult of the god of Jacob. Here, this is the deity who apportions land; not the shared ancestors of an assumed 'family' religion invoked by the 'foreigner' Laban, from whom Jacob seeks to distinguish and separate himself.[75]

And yet in contrast to the apparent disempowering of ancestral religion in Gen. 31:44-54, the cameos of 35:1-20 exhibit the ways in which Jacob's *own* dead play a crucial role in marking his occupation of the land at Bethel. Indeed, these particular traditions suggest the indigenous land-giving deity of Bethel is not a deity intolerant of mortuary cult practices and their associated territorial functions. Throughout these verses, two forms of land-marking are thus combined in a twinned territorial strategy, signalling the appropriation of the memorial markers of the demonstrative dead by the ethno-colonial cult of Jacob's god. This is suggestive of a persistent and powerful role for the dead at Bethel within these

---

72. Cf. D. I. Block, 'The Role of Language in Ancient Israelite Perceptions of National Identity', *JBL* 103 (1984), 321–40.

73. See Josh. 7:26; 8:29; 2 Sam. 18:17 (in all of which the term גל is also employed). See Chapter 1, n. 49.

74. On the designation פחד אביו יצחק see M. Köckert, 'Fear of Isaac', *DDD*, 329–31. While at Gen. 31:53 the MT assumes the deities invoked by Laban are distinct (thereby reading a plural verb here: ישפטו), by contrast the LXX and SP suggest the deities are to be identified by assuming the singular form of the verb (ישפט).

75. On Gen. 31:44-54 as a biblical ('Elohistic') image of 'family' religion, see van der Toorn, *Family Religion*, 255–57.

traditions – despite the assertively dominant character of the cult of Jacob's god in the narratives themselves.

The close configuration of Jacob and Bethel in these traditions is mapped onto their shared association with the dead who are seemingly recognized and acknowledged by the patriarch at this place: here, Jacob constructs a mortuary landscape and models 'good practice' in dealing with the dead, thereby endorsing a particularly potent culture of the dead at Bethel. But in view of the more dominant version of the biblical story of the past, Jacob's association with Bethel's culture of the dead is eclipsed and ultimately subverted by his (dis)placement in death to Machpelah in Gen. 49:29-32 (cf. 47:29-30),[76] while Bethel's potency is lost in the elimination of its dead and the subjugation of the cult place to Jerusalem, as testified by the destruction of bones and the preservation of the memorialized tomb of the Judahite Man of God in 2 Kgs 23:15-20. And yet despite the disempowering of Bethel's territorial dead, and indeed the displacement of its territorial ancestor, Bethel's function as a cult place mediating land remains persistent: in Gen. 28:11-22 and 35:9-15 it is the explicit locus of the divine promise of land to the patriarchs, while in 1 Kgs 12:28-29 it is the sanctuary at which the territorial foundation myth communicated by the exodus tradition (and by implication, the ancestors associated with it) is celebrated. Though in the Hebrew Bible Bethel's dead may be devalued, displaced and destroyed, the territorial heritage of their place is nonetheless long-lived.

76. On Jacob's burial place, see the discussion in Chapter 2.

Chapter 5

CLAIMING JERUSALEM

The powerful interrelation of the dead, their tombs and the land might be thought incompatible with the dominant temple ideologies promoted in the Hebrew Bible. The biblical writers repeatedly portray Jerusalem as a place marked by its occupation by Yhwh, in the temple devoted to his seemingly exclusive worship. Indeed, unlike Bethel, Hebron and Shechem, Jerusalem appears to be a cult centre (*the* cult centre) unadorned and unendorsed by the dead. Rather, it is the dwelling place of the 'Living God', a designation which appears to distinguish and separate the God in Jerusalem from the deified ancestors of the so-called cult of the dead.[1] Neither Yhwh, nor Jerusalem, nor the people claiming these as theirs, would appear to have a territorial need of the dead. Ideologically, temple towers over tomb.

And yet, even in Ezra-Nehemiah – arguably the least socio-religiously tolerant of biblical books – the dead play a crucial role in the acquisition of Jerusalem. In petitioning the Persian king for a return to the land and the restoration of the city, Nehemiah stakes his claim to Jerusalem by appealing solely to the presence of the dead:

> The king said to me, 'Why is your face sad, since you are not sick? This can only be sadness of the heart'. I was very much afraid. I said to the king, 'May the king live forever! Why should my face not be sad, when the city, the place of my ancestors' graves, lies waste, its gates destroyed by fire?' Then the king said to me, 'What is it you request?', so I offered a prayer to the God of Heaven. Then I said to the king, 'If it pleases the king, and if your servant has found favour with you, send me to Judah, to the city of my ancestors' graves, and I will rebuild it'. (Neh. 2:2-5)

---

1. See Halpern, 'Late Israelite Astronomies', 343; cf. T. N. D. Mettinger, *The Riddle of Resurrection: 'Dying and Rising Gods' in the Ancient Near East* (ConBOT, 50; Stockholm: Almqvist & Wiksell, 2001), 41. For the divine title 'Living God', see (for example) Deut. 5:26; Jer. 10:10 (אלהים חיים); 2 Kgs 19:4, 16; Isa. 37:4, 17 (אלהים חי); Hos. 2:1 (ET 1:11) (אל חי); for the deified dead as 'gods' (אלהים), see 1 Sam. 28:13; Isa. 8:19; cf. 2 Sam. 14:16; Num. 25:2; Ps. 106:28.

Nehemiah's appeal to his ancestors' graves has been taken by some as an innocuous attempt to gain sympathy from his Persian overlord, and by others as a deliberate measure to present a return to the land as a personal rather than overtly political mission.[2] But its significance is greater than that. The book of Nehemiah frames the Persian period occupation of Judah and Jerusalem by incomers as a legitimate 'return' to an inherited land, endorsed not only by the Persian king and the God of Heaven, but also by means of the ancestral graves present in Jerusalem itself.[3] Within its immediate context, it is thus on behalf of the dead, rather than Yhwh, that the city will be repaired and restored; it is by means of the dead, rather than Yhwh, that Nehemiah and his followers will take Jerusalem.

Nehemiah's appeal to the graves of the dead is by no means anomalous in biblical traditions dealing with the acquisition and occupation of Jerusalem. Other texts concerned with the status of Jerusalem draw on a variety of ancestral and mortuary cult motifs in asserting or contesting possession of place. In exploring the ways in which these motifs are employed, it will be argued not only that the placing and spacing of the dead plays a powerful role in the territorialism of biblical portrayals of Jerusalem, but also that the territorial potency of the dead and their cults are employed even in those traditions which seem to be most hostile to the dead, precisely in order to furnish the biblical Yhwh and his temple in Jerusalem with a compelling proprietorial function akin to that of the dead. However, before turning to the 'entombing' of Yhwh's temple, the discussion will begin with Jerusalem's Davidic dead.

City of the Dead

The apparent absence of a tomb cult at Jerusalem marks the city out as a cult centre seemingly devoid of ancestral advocacy. Unlike other cult sites in the biblical story of Israel and Judah, the placing of the dead seems to play no role in legitimizing or endorsing Jerusalem's cultic status.[4] And yet, as is well

---

2. For the first of these opinions, see H. G. M. Williamson, *Ezra, Nehemiah* (WBC, 16; Waco, TX: Word, 1985), 179; for the second, see (for example) J. L. Wright, *Rebuilding Identity: The Nehemiah-Memoir and Its Earliest Readers* (BZAW, 348; Berlin: de Gruyter, 2004), 88; see also J. Blenkinsopp, *Ezra-Nehemiah: A Commentary* (OTL; Philadelphia: Westminster Press, 1988), 214. Gary Knoppers argues that Nehemiah's reference to ancestral graves reflects a particular construction of ethnic identity in 'Nehemiah and Sanballat: The Enemy Without or Within?' in O. Lipschits, G. N. Knoppers and R. Albertz (eds), *Judah and the Judeans in the Fourth Century B.C.E.* (Winona Lake, IN: Eisenbrauns, 2007), 305–31.

3. Nehemiah's petition exhibits notable similarities to Joseph's request to Pharaoh to return to the homeland in order to bury his father in his own tomb (Gen. 50:4-6).

4. Cf. Lightstone, *Commerce of the Sacred*, 49.

known, the dead surrounded the city.[5] The biblical mapping of Jerusalem's sacred landscape places the dead quite appropriately in the valleys at the roots of Mount Zion, themselves gateways to the underworld, forming religio-mythic boundaries around the city. But while some of these tombs and their dead feature in the biblical literature (for example, Isa. 22:15-19; Jer. 7:32-33), the tombs of the Davidic kings are less prominent than might be expected. Indeed, there is a biblical ambivalence about the placement of the royal dead, which raises several questions about perceptions of the nature and status of the dead kings and their tombs in the biblical 'memory' of the religious past.

The first of these questions concerns the placement of the Davidic dead and biblical appeals to the presence of their graves. The royal tombs are mentioned repeatedly throughout the book of Kings, though only apparently in passing as a fixed aspect of the formulaic death and burial notices, tying the reign of a dead king to the reign of a living king.[6] Their seemingly standardized form is familiar to readers: almost every Judahite king up to and including Ahaz is said to been buried 'with his ancestors in the City of David'.[7] The consistency with which the Davidic dead are located in the City of David functions as a narrative seam running through 1 Kings 2–2 Kings 16, emphasizing the perpetuation and duration of the Davidic dynasty as a continuous collective, each king joining his predecessors in the royal tomb.[8] But importantly, it also marks the City of David as the place of the Davidic dead. Like Bethel, Shechem and Hebron, Jerusalem too is a place occupied by the ancestral elite.

It is striking, then, that in the latter chapters of Kings, this topography of

---

5. See L. Y. Rahmani, 'Ancient Jerusalem's Funerary Customs and Tombs: Part One', *BA* 44 (1981), 171–77; idem, 'Ancient Jerusalem's Funerary Customs and Tombs: Part Two', *BA* 44 (1981), 229–35; idem, 'Ancient Jerusalem's Funerary Customs and Tombs: Part Three', *BA* 45 (1981), 43–53, 109–18; D. Ussishkin, *The Village of Silwan: The Necropolis from the Period of the Judean Kingdom* (trans. I. Pommerantz; Jerusalem: Israel Exploration Fund, 1993); A. Kloner, 'Iron Age Burial Caves in Jerusalem and its Vicinity', *BAIAS* 19–20 (2001–01), 95–118. For tombs and burials in Jerusalem's valleys in later periods, see R. Hachlili, *Jewish Funerary Customs, Practices and Rites in the Second Temple Period* (JSJS, 94; Leiden: Brill, 2006); A. Kloner and B. Zissu, *The Necropolis of Jerusalem in the Second Temple Period* (ISACR, 8; Leuven: Peeters, 2007).

6. Given that Kings is held by most as the earliest continuous narrative portrayal of the Davidic monarchy, the discussion here will focus on this text. It is possible, however, that Chronicles and perhaps some of the prophetic books draw independently on ancient traditions, rather than directly upon Kings.

7. David (1 Kgs 2:10), Solomon (11:43) and Abijam (15:8) are the notable exceptions, for their burial notices do not include the subclause '(buried) with his ancestors'. Opinions vary as to whether this reflects redactional or scribal variations or contextual considerations.

8. B. O. Long, *1 Kings with an Introduction to Historical Literature* (FOTL, 9; Grand Rapids, MI: Eerdmans, 1984), 22–28; see also K. -J. Illman, *Old Testament Formulas about Death* (Åbo: Åbo Akademi, 1979), 37–48.

dynastic death seems to be mapped differently – and consequently undermined. The burial notices for Ahaz's successors vary considerably, and significantly do not refer to the City of David: Manasseh and Amon are said to have been buried in the 'Garden of Uzza' (2 Kgs 21:18, 26); Josiah is buried 'in his tomb' (23:30); the burial places of Hezekiah and Jehoiakim go unmentioned (20:21; 24:6); Jehoahaz dies while captive in Egypt (23:34); and neither the deaths nor burials of Jehoiachin and Zedekiah are noted. These variations have been thought to reflect a change in royal burial practices during the reign of Hezekiah, whose concern for temple purity prompted him to relocate the royal tombs away from the City of David to a site beyond the city walls.[9] This interpretation, however, has its limitations, and the extent to which the changes in burial notices relate to religio-political realities is uncertain.[10] For the purposes of the present discussion, it is more helpful to consider the ideological implications of these changes in the royal burial notices, which point to an ambivalent attitude to the royal dead. As Jan Assmann observes, the past is formed solely by referring to it.[11] Thus, as references in the royal burial notices to the City of David give way to the non-mention of the City of David, it is the Davidic dead of the distant past who are held to occupy Jerusalem. The biblical displacement of the more recently dead kings from the City of David to seemingly discontinuous burial sites thus effectively distances these later monarchs from their ancestors – and each other.[12] This is a well-crafted way of imaging the City of David as the place occupied

---

9. E.g. R. Weill, *La cité de David: Compte rendu des fouilles executées à Jérusalem, sur le site de la ville primitive. Campagne de 1913–1914* (Paris: P. Geuthner, 1920), 35–40; N. Na'aman, 'Death Formulae and the Burial Place of the Kings of the House of David', *Bib* 85 (2004), 245–54; Schmidt, *Israel's Beneficent Dead*, 250–54; cf. K. Galling, 'Die Nekropole von Jerusalem', *Palästina-Jahrbuch* 32 (1936), 73–101; Wright, *Disposal of Impurity*, 122; Nutkowicz, *L'homme face à la mort*, 68–71. Others hold Manasseh responsible for the change in burial practices, e.g. Halpern, 'Late Israelite Astronomies', 344; J. R. Zorn, 'The Burials of the Judean Kings: Sociohistorical Considerations and Suggestions', in A. M. Maeir and P. de Miroschedji (eds), *'I Will Speak the Riddle of Ancient Times': Archaeological and Historical Studies in Honor of Amihai Mazar on the Occasion of his Sixtieth Birthday, Vol. 2* (Winona Lake, IN: Eisenbrauns, 2006), 810–20. For possibilities concerning the burial places of the kings of Israel, see N. Franklin, 'The Tombs of the Kings of Israel: Two Recently Identified 9th-Century Tombs from Omride Samaria', *ZDPV* 119 (2003), 1–11.

10. For a critique of the view that garden burials represent a marginalized or compromised royal burial practice in Judah, see F. Stavrakopoulou, 'Exploring the Garden of Uzza: Death, Burial and Ideologies of Kingship', *Bib* 87 (2006), 1–21.

11. J. Assmann, *Das kulturelle Gedächtnis. Schrift, Erinnerung und politische Identität in frühen Hochkulturen* (München: Beck, 1992), 31.

12. This is also mirrored in the dynastic dynamics of the later kings, whose line of succession is especially disrupted and/or confused by a series of coups, captures and killings: Amon (2 Kgs 21:23-24), Josiah (23:29-30), Jehoahaz (23:33-34), Jehoiachin (24:12-17); Zedekiah (25:6-7); cf. Gedaliah (25:25).

by the Davidic dead of the *distant* past, while at the same time displacing the more recent kings from their ancestral city and tomb, complementing the biblical writer's portrayal of an increasingly fractured and impotent kingship. In this way, the city maintains its territorial, ancestral heritage, while – in keeping with the tenor of Kings – the recent and potential efficacy of kingship and (by implication) its mortuary cult is cast into doubt.

Jerusalem is thus marked by the tombs of the Davidic dead of the distant past, much as Hebron and Shechem – and likely Bethel too – are places embodied by the distant past by means of ancestors long since dead. Though the selective references to the royal tombs in the book of Kings might reflect in part a shifting attitude to a Judahite royal cult of the dead (to which the discussion will shortly turn), it ought not to be assumed that they also attest to an increasing disinterest in the royal dead in post-monarchic literature.

Indeed, several texts exhibit a concern for the placement and displacement of dead Davidic kings. The Chronicler tailors his burial notices to suit his theological appraisal of each monarch, so that (for example) the favoured Hezekiah, whose burial place is not given in 2 Kgs 20:2, is accorded an honourable burial beside his royal ancestors in 2 Chr. 32:33, while reprobates and diseased kings (suffering on account of their sin), including Asa (16:13-14), Jehoram (21:18-20), Uzziah (26:23) and Ahaz (28:27), are excluded from the Davidic tombs.[13] In Jer. 22:19 and 36:30, Jehoiakim is divinely threatened with a dishonourable burial,[14] and many commentators take Ezek. 43:7-9 as a priestly appeal that the royal dead be disinterred and removed from their position of close proximity to the Jerusalem temple.[15] These texts hint at a persistent interest in the whereabouts of the dead kings, despite the cessation of the monarchy and the reinvention of the formerly royal Jerusalem temple cult in the Persian period.[16]

The territorial potency of the royal tombs is also suggested in biblical texts dealing with their presence – and contents. As was proposed above, Nehemiah's

---

13. Going beyond the carefully constructed presentation of the royal dead in Kings, the Chronicler's particular interest in the post-mortem placement of individual monarchs effectively distinguishes between kings, overshadowing the collective nature of the Davidic dead. Their collectivity is further breached in 2 Chr. 24:16, in which it is claimed that the priest Jehoiada was buried in the royal tombs in the City of David.

14. On Jehoiakim's burial in the 'Garden of Oza' in 4 Kgdms Lucianic 24:6, see S. Delamarter, 'The Vilification of Jehoiakim (a.k.a. Eliakim and Joiakim) in Early Judaism', in C. A. Evans and J. A. Sanders (eds), *The Function of Scripture in Early Jewish and Christian Tradition* (JSNTS, 154/SSEJC, 6; Sheffield: Sheffield Academic Press, 1998), 190–204, esp. 196–98; Stavrakopoulou, 'Exploring the Garden of Uzza', 3–4.

15. This important text is discussed in detail below.

16. This is also attested by the memorial plaque of King Uzziah of Judah, dated to the first century BCE and inscribed with the statement, 'The bones of Uzziah, king of Judah, were brought hither; not to be opened'; see E. L. Sukenik, 'The Funerary Tablet of Uzziah', *PEQ* 2 (1931), 217–21.

appeal to his ancestral tombs in Jerusalem credits the graves of the dead with a territorial function essential to the acquisition and restoration of the city (Neh. 2:2-5). While it is uncertain whether these graves are to be understood as the royal tombs (an identification that would render Nehemiah a claimed descendant of the Davidic line),[17] the graves of the Davidic dead (קברי דויד) reappear elsewhere in the book to define the reconstructed boundary wall of the restored city (3:16). This might appear to be merely a somewhat dry reference to a local landmark, but its likely underlying religio-mythic connotations are well illustrated in Jer. 31:38-40, in which the rebuilding of Jerusalem's boundaries is explicitly coupled with the divine protection of the sacred valleys of the dead.[18] Thus, although the fleeting reference in Neh. 3:16 is seemingly stripped of an explicit religio-mythic context in this passage (as is the accompanying בית הגברים, 'House of the Heroes'), it alludes nonetheless to the continuing function of the dead in Jerusalem's symbolic topography. Just as the genealogical lists in Neh. 7:5-73 and 12:1-26 illustrate the ancestral assertions of the new community in and around Jerusalem, so the city's ancestral graves are held to approve the incomers' occupation.

Indeed, it is the apparent displacement of the city's dead which is envisaged in other texts to manifest the dispossession of Jerusalem. In Jer. 7:32–8:3, the divine threat against Jerusalem and Judah of destruction and exile is illustrated in a series of mortuary abuses, beginning at Topheth in Jerusalem's Ben Hinnom Valley:

> Therefore behold: the days are coming – oracle of Yhwh – when it will no more be called Topheth, or the Valley of Ben Hinnom, but the Valley of Slaughter, for they will bury in Topheth until there is no more room. The corpses of this people will be food for the birds of the sky, and for the animals of the earth, with none

---

17. For this possibility, see U. Kellermann, *Nehemia: Quellen, Überlieferung und Geschichte* (BZAW, 102; Berlin: Töpelmann, 1967), 156–59; cf. Wright, *Rebuilding Identity*, 54 n. 43. Diana Edelman notes that Nehemiah's request to rebuild the city of his ancestors' graves would be wholly appropriate for a person of royal lineage, given that city-building is usually a prerogative of kingship (*The Origins of the 'Second' Temple: Persian Imperial Policy and the Rebuilding of Jerusalem* [Bibleworld; London: Equinox, 2005], 351 n. 8). For Nehemiah as a (royal) temple- and city-builder, and the possibility that he and Zerubbabel represent the same historical figure, see D. Edelman, 'Were Zerubbabel and Nehemiah the Same Person?' in D. Burns and J. W. Rogerson (eds), *In Search of Philip R. Davies: Whose Festschrift Is It Anyway?* (New York: T&T Clark, forthcoming).

18. For further examination of Jer. 31:38-40, see the discussion below. On the possible relationship between this oracle and traditions about Nehemiah's wall-building, see C. Levin, *Die Verheissung des neuen Bundes in ihrem theologiegeschichtlichen Zussamenhang ausgelegt* (FRLANT, 137; Göttingen: Vandenhoeck & Ruprecht 1985), 199; cited in W. McKane, *A Critical and Exegetical Commentary on Jeremiah, Volume 2: Commentary on Jeremiah XXVI-LII* (ICC; Edinburgh: T&T Clark, 1996), 833.

to frighten them off. And I will bring an end to the sound of mirth and gladness, the voice of the bride and bridegroom in the cities of Judah and the streets of Jerusalem; for the land shall become a waste. [8:1] At that time – oracle of Yhwh – the bones of the kings of Judah, the bones of its officials, the bones of the priests, the bones of the prophets, and the bones of the inhabitants of Jerusalem shall be brought out of their tombs; and they shall be spread before the Sun and the Moon and all the Host of Heaven, which they loved and served and followed, which they inquired of and worshipped. They shall not be gathered or buried; they shall be like mulch on the surface of the ground. Death shall be preferred to life by all the remnant that remains of this evil family in all the places where I have driven them – oracle of Yhwh of Hosts.

Here, two forms of corpse abuse illustrate the annihilation of the people of Jerusalem: non-burial (7:32-33) and disinterment (8:1-2).[19] As was discussed in the previous chapter, the disinterring of the dead is a powerful form of social destabilization within the cultural milieu of ancient West Asia. Displacing the dead from their secure place in the underworld and the ancestral cult fractures the carefully managed relationship between the dead and the living: the dead are unable to receive their descendants' offerings and libations, while the living are deprived of their ancestors' blessings and protection. The non-sanctioned disinterring of remains is thus an act of hostility against both the dead and the living community of which they are a part, bringing about social dysfunction.

Non-burial is also socially damaging for the dead and for the living. It marks the social abandonment of the dead, for whom mortuary and mourning rituals have not been performed,[20] leaving the corpse socially and culturally unplaced, so that the deceased individual's transition into post-mortem existence is neither wholly effected nor settled. The perpetual liminality of the abandoned corpse, and the resulting absence of the dead from the social group, renders the living and the deceased individual permanently estranged. The exposure of the corpse not only effects the social abandonment of the dead, but also invites the post-mortem annihilation of the individual, whose body becomes carrion. In destroying the

---

19. That disinterment is envisaged here, rather than a relic ritual (as Zevit suggests in *Religions of Ancient Israel*, 543), seems more likely, given the accompanying motif of non-burial in 7:32-34. Disinterment and non-burial (and its resultant post-mortem annihilation) are coupled together in texts including 2 Kgs 23:15-20 and Isa. 14:18-22. While relic rituals are a plausible aspect of Israelite and Judahite mortuary cults (cf. 2 Kgs 13:21) – and indeed, are likely to have played a part in the ossuary practices of the later Second Temple period – there is little evidence of an allusion to them in the present text. Rather, the threat of social disintegration and exile renders disinterment a more persuasive interpretation here. For Mesopotamian texts suggestive of skull and bone rituals, see Jonker, *Topography of Remembrance*, 206 n. 54.

20. Cf. Olyan, 'Neglected Aspects', 607.

very fabric of the corpse, the devouring of the dead by scavengers renders the dead ritually, socially, culturally and materially absent – and so wholly non-existent.[21]

The dynamics of corpse and mortuary abuse are thus graphically employed in Jer. 7:32–8:3 to image the destruction and displacement of the Jerusalemites. The Ben Hinnom Valley is filled with burials until it can contain no more. Topheth, the cult place of child sacrifice, is no longer a setting for rituals effecting the perpetuation of the generations,[22] but an overfull cemetery, clogged with corpses (7:32).[23] The destruction of any social context for regeneration is also portrayed in v. 34, in which the ritualized hope for conception and birth is brought to an end by the silencing of the bride and bridegroom, symbols and vehicles of social flourishing. This portrayal of social disintegration is also well illustrated by the absence of the living to care for the dead (cf. 2 Sam. 21:10) who, rather than being fed by their descendants, become food for scavenging birds and animals (Jer. 7:33).[24] In v. 32, the valley's renaming as the Valley of Slaughter (הֲרֵגָה), a designation used elsewhere of animals destined to be butchered (Zech. 11:4, 7), forewarns of the transformation of corpses into carcasses, carcasses into carrion. The displacement and destruction of the dead not only effects the collapse of society, but renders Judah and Jerusalem a rotting wasteland (Jer. 7:34).[25]

---

21. For the scavenging of unburied corpses, see, for example, Deut. 28:26; 2 Sam. 21:10; 1 Kgs 21:23-24; 2 Kgs 9:33-37; Jer. 7:33; 15:3; 16:4; 34:20; Ps. 79:2-3; cf. Isa. 18:6; Jer. 12:9. For further discussion, see Olyan, 'Neglected Aspects', 607, 611; Stavrakopoulou, 'Gog's Grave', esp. 74–75, 80–82. For the threat of non-burial as a formulaic curse in oaths and treaties, see D. J. Wiseman, *The Vassal Treaties of Esarhaddon* (London: British School of Archaeology, 1958), 60–80; D. R. Hillers, *Treaty Curses and the Old Testament Prophets* (BO 16; Rome: Pontifical Biblical Institute, 1964), 68–69; K. J. Cathcart, 'Treaty-Curses and the Book of Nahum', *CBQ* 34 (1973), 179–87, esp. 180–82.

22. On child sacrifice as a fertility ritual and its biblical portrayals, see Stavrakopoulou, *King Manasseh and Child Sacrifice*, 141–299.

23. It is often assumed that the corpses in the valley are intended to defile Topheth (e.g. L. C. Allen, *Jeremiah: A Commentary* [OTL; Louisville, KY: Westminster John Knox Press, 2008], 103), but this is neither stated not implied in the text. Only *some* biblical traditions claim that the dead are unclean; other traditions do not appear to share this perspective. See further Chapter 6.

24. The same interrelated themes of non-burial and social disintegration are presented in very similar terms in Jer. 16:1-13, which culminates in the exile of the people, who will be 'hurled' (טוּל) from the land (v. 13). Interestingly, this imagery (though not the precise language) is employed elsewhere to describe the abuse of corpses and their disinterment (e.g. Isa. 14:19; 22:17-18; Jer. 22:19). For the use of this motif and its relation to ritual terms for dishonouring the dead, see Saul Olyan's discussions in 'Neglected Aspects', 606–7, and 'Was the "King of Babylon" Buried Before His Corpse was Exposed? Some Thoughts on Isa 14,19', *ZAW* 118 (2006), 423–26.

25. Death imagery is also used of Jerusalem in Isa. 29:1-4, in which the besieged city is personified as a speaking (perhaps oracular) member of the dead in the underworld.

5. *Claiming Jerusalem* 111

The interrelation of the fate of the dead and the fate of the land is similarly and emphatically articulated in the continuation of this passage in 8:1-3. In these verses, the bones of Jerusalem's dead – including those of Judah's kings – are to be taken out of their tombs and spread out in view of Sun, Moon and the Host of Heaven – the deities to whom the dead had (by implication, formerly) offered cult.[26] Though this text has been taken as a reference to a relic ritual,[27] most commentators view it as a scene of post-mortem punishment, couched in the terms of treaty curses and thus inflicted on the religio-political elites of Judah.[28] Significantly, though, the displacement of the dead from their tombs marks the displacement of the living from the land. This evocation of exile is evident in v. 3, in which Yhwh refers to 'all the remnant that remains of this evil family in all the places where I have driven them', a dispersal that is perhaps to be inferred in v. 2 as the bones of the dead are 'spread out' or 'spread abroad' (שטח),[29]

---

26. The pointed use of the divine title יהוה צבאות, Yhwh of *Hosts* (v. 3), seems intended to eclipse the astral deities – collectively designated צבא השמים, the *Host* of Heaven (v. 2). On the biblical portrayal of Yhwh's competition with astral deities, see further Halpern, 'Late Israelite Astronomies', 323–52, and M. S. Smith, 'When the Heavens Darkened: Yahweh, El, and the Divine Astral Family in Iron Age II Judah', in W. G. Dever and S. Gitin (eds), *Symbiosis, Symbolism, and the Power of the Past: Canaan, Ancient Israel, and Their Neighbors from the Late Bronze Age through Roman Palestinia* (Winona Lake, IN: Eisenbrauns, 2003), 265–77. The aligning of the dead with these astral deities may reflect a belief that the ancestors were particularly associated with the heavenly host – hence (as Halpern suggests) the claim that the people Israel was to be as numerous as the stars (e.g. Gen. 15:5; 22:17; 26:4; Exod. 32:13; Deut. 1:10; 10:22; 28:62; 1 Chr. 27:23; Neh. 9:23; cf. Dan. 12:3). This might also find some support in Isa. 24:21-23, in which the Host of Heaven (here called צבא המרום) and 'the kings of the earth', or perhaps 'the (dead) kings of the netherworld' (מלכי האדמה) are to be jointly punished and imprisoned together in the underworld. However, while this view is plausible, in the particular context of Jer. 8:1-3 the disinterring of the bones of Judahite kings and other elites also recalls the oracle against the Babylonian king in Isa. 14:4-21, whose mythic enthronement and status in the divine assembly is described in astral terms (vv. 12-13), and whose corpse is cast out of its grave (vv. 18-20) following his descent into Sheol (vv. 12-15). The constellation of royal, astral, and disinterment motifs in this oracle of judgment thus complements the similar cluster of motifs exhibited in Jer. 8:1-3, which may go some way to explain why the disinterred dead are exposed specifically to the heavenly host. For a detailed discussion of Isa. 14:4-21, see R. M. Shipp, *Of Dead Kings and Dirges: Myth and Meaning in Isaiah 14:4b-21* (Leiden: Brill, 2002). On the broader contexts of the royal mythic motif of ascent and descent, see N. Wyatt, 'The Hollow Crown: Ambivalent Elements in West Semitic Royal Ideology', *UF* 18 (1986), 421–36; reprinted in idem, '*There's Such Divinity Doth Hedge a King': Selected Essays of Nicolas Wyatt on Royal Ideology in Ugaritic and Old Testament Literature* (SOTS; Aldershot: Ashgate, 2005), 31–48.

27. See n. 19.

28. See Cogan, 'A Note on Disinterment', 29–34.

29. Cf. J. A. Thompson, *The Book of Jeremiah* (NICOT; Grand Rapids, MI: Eerdmans, 1980), 295.

never to be 'gathered' (אסף). Indeed, the close interrelation of the living and the dead is emphasized by means of the kinship term משפחה (here translated 'family'), employed to refer to both the dead and the living who are displaced and dispersed by disinterment and exile (v. 3).[30] Emptying the tombs of the dead prefigures the emptying of the land of their descendants, so that the hold on the land on the part of the living is thus inextricably bound to the hold on the land on the part of the dead.[31]

The close alignment of the dead with the land is perhaps most graphically imaged in this text in the material transformation of the dead from bones to mulch. Throughout the passage, the materiality of the dead is emphasized: in 7:33, unburied corpses become the flesh of food; in 8:1-2, the bones of the dead are objects to be held and manipulated, exhibited and viewed, while in 8:2, the bones are to be left exposed, to become like דמן, 'mulch'. As Ziony Zevit points out, though this term is usually rendered 'excrement' or 'dung', its biblical usage is more suggestive of decomposing organic matter which is spread over the surface of the ground.[32] To become 'like דמן' is thus to decompose and rot away. Given the socio-mythic dynamics of beliefs about the dead, this translation makes good sense of the gravity of the threat in Jer. 8:2 and elsewhere that corpses and body parts left on the surface of the ground will inevitably putrefy – in other words, lose form, disintegrate and eventually disappear, rendering the dead non-existent. In an ironic subversion of the essential territorialism of the dead and their close identification with the land, the mulching of their bones results in the ancestors becoming indistinguishable from the land.

The disinterring of Jerusalem's high status tombs in Jer. 8:1-2 is just one of several biblical texts exhibiting a hostile attitude to the city's specifically *royal* dead. Others include a series of oracles in the book of Isaiah (28:14-22; 57:3-13; 65:1-5; cf. 24:21) and Ezek. 43:7-9; Jer. 22:18-19; 36:30. Collectively, these texts appear to represent an attack on the royal cult of the dead, the efficacy of which was likely called into question in some circles following the exile of the royal

---

30. Cf. R. P. Carroll, *Jeremiah: A Commentary* (OTL; London: SCM Press, 1986), 225.

31. Jer. 22:24-30 employs disinterment imagery to describe the exiling of Coniah (Jehoiachin) and his descendants, and the demise of the Davidic dynasty: 'I will hurl (טול) you and the mother who bore you into another country . . . he and his offspring (are) hurled out (טול) and cast away (שלך) in a land they do not know (vv. 26, 28; cf. v. 19; 22:15-18; Ezek. 32:4). It is no coincidence that the oracle is emphatically addressed to the (personified) land (v. 29), whose symbiotic relationship with the royal dynasty is now broken.

32. Zevit, *Religions of Ancient Israel*, 543 n. 97. A similar understanding of the term דמן is also evident in the translation of this passage by William McKane, who renders the term 'humus' in *A Critical and Exegetical Commentary on Jeremiah. Volume 1: Introduction and Commentary on Jeremiah I–XXV* (ICC; Edinburgh: T&T Clark, 1986), 181.

5. *Claiming Jerusalem*

household, the destruction of Jerusalem, and the failure to restore the Davidic dynasty to the throne in the Persian era.

As is now well known, the royal cult of the dead played a crucial role in Judahite kingship ideologies.[33] Comparative evidence suggests that, in keeping with their broader West Semitic cultural context and more particularly with their crucial ritual role during their lifetimes, upon their deaths Judahite kings were deified and joined the ranks of their divine ancestors, the Rephaim.[34] Contrary to the opinions of Brian Schmidt, the Rephaim were not impotent and ineffectual ghosts, but the powerful dead.[35] In cultic concert with their living descendants, they perpetuated and protected the dynastic house in ways similar to the functions of the ancestors of non-royal households. If the Judahite cult of the Rephaim was similar to that of Ugarit (as indeed the parallels between Isa. 14:4-21 and *KTU* 1.161 suggest),[36] the roles of the Rephaim probably included the bestowing of fertility upon the living king, imparting oracular information to him, performing healings, and conferring protective blessings upon the homestead. In cultic exchange, the royal dead were likely named and memorialized by their descendants, presented with offerings and libations, and perhaps also participated with the living in ritual meals, expressing their strength and solidarity as a social group.[37]

While during Judah's monarchic era the royal mortuary cult was a normative aspect of Jerusalem temple practice, the post-monarchic re-imaging of Yhwh and his divine household among some groups of elites gave rise to certain biblical traditions in which the royal cult of the dead was caricatured as deviant. Isaiah 65:1-5 offers a vivid illustration. Here, the cult's practitioners are presented as abandoning Yhwh, apparently in favour of their dead (cf. v. 5). Verses 3-4 describe them as sacrificing and burning incense,[38] sitting in tombs and spending

---

33. For a detailed overview of the religious dynamics of Judahite kingship, see N. Wyatt, 'Royal Religion in Ancient Judah', in F. Stavrakopoulou and J. Barton (eds), *Religious Diversity in Ancient Israel and Judah* (London: T&T Clark, 2010), 61–81. See also W. W. Hallo, 'Royal Ancestor Worship in the Biblical World', in M. Fishbane and E. Tov (eds), *Shar'arei Talmon: Studies in the Bible, Qumran, and the Ancient Near East Presented to Shemaryahu Talmon* (Winona Lake, IN: Eisenbrauns, 1992), 381–401; A. C. Cohen, *Death Rituals, Ideology, and the Development of Early Mesopotamian Kingship: Toward a New Understanding of Iraq's Royal Cemetery of Ur* (Leiden: Brill, 2005); H. Niehr, 'The Royal Funeral in Ancient Syria', *JNSL* 32 (2006), 1–24.

34. For the Rephaim, see the literature cited in Chapter 3, n. 41.

35. Schmidt, *Israel's Beneficent Dead*, 267–73. For a robust critique of Schmidt's position, see Lewis, 'How Far Can Texts Take Us?', 189–202.

36. Wyatt, 'Royal Religion in Ancient Judah', 73–74.

37. E.g. *KTU* 1.22 i 1–5; 1.124; 1.161. See in particular Rouillard, 'Rephaim', 692–700; G. del Olmo Lete, *Canaanite Religion according to the Liturgical Texts of Ugarit* (trans. W. G. E. Watson; Bethesda, MD: CDL Press, 1999), 193–207; Lewis, 'Household Religion', esp. 74–76; Wyatt, 'A la Recherche des Rephaïm Perdus', 579–613.

38. A marked variant is attested in 1QIsa[a], which refers not to burning incense on bricks,

the night in 'secluded places' (בנצורים) – probably an alternative designation for graves[39] – and eating the flesh of pigs and the broth of 'unclean things' (פגלים).[40] These foodstuffs are likely intended as a polemical representation of a ritual mortuary meal, imaged in exaggerated style by means of the loaded use of פגלים, which is used elsewhere to refer to unusable sacrificial meat (Lev. 7:18; 19:7; Ezek. 4:14), and the accusation of pork consumption, which not only epitomizes ritual disobedience and pollution, but may also reflect the netherworld associations of pigs.[41] The divinatory function of some of these activities is suggested by the contrast posed between the practitioners who spend the night in tombs (v. 4) – an allusion, perhaps, to incubation rituals (cf. LXX's δι' ἐνύπνια, 'through dreams') – and Yhwh, to whom the worshippers fail to turn for oracular consultation (vv. 1-2).[42]

The likelihood that this is a distorted depiction of a specifically *royal* cult of the dead is strongly suggested by the garden setting of these rituals (v. 3), indicative of a royal mortuary garden (cf. 2 Kgs 21:18, 26; Isa. 1:29-30; 66:17) – a sacred site used along with temple and tomb in many ancient West Asian cults of kingship. Drawing on the cosmic symbolism of temple gardens as manifestations of divinely cultivated and regenerative fertility, mortuary gardens were the sites of royal burials and cultic practices pertaining to the dead kings.[43] This setting

---

but claims the worshippers 'suck hands on the stones' (וינקו ידים על־האבנים). Its interpretation is uncertain, though some commentators take it as an allusion to ritualized sexual activity – encouraged, perhaps, by the garden setting of this ritual, which for some recalls the biblical association of trees with the language of whoring and adultery (cf. Isa. 57:3-5; Jer. 3:6). See Ackerman, *Under Every Green Tree*, 169–73; B. Schramm, *The Opponents of Third Isaiah: Reconstructing the Cultic History of the Restoration* (JSOTS, 193; Sheffield: Sheffield Academic Press, 1995), 156.

39. For Akkadian references to the grave as *ašar niṣirti*, 'the secluded place', see the discussion in Jonker, *Topography of Remembrance*, 194; Schmidt, *Israel's Beneficent Dead* 260, n. 544. For an alternative interpretation reading בין צורים for בנצורים, see M. Dahood, 'Textual Problems in Isaia', *CBQ* 22 (1960), 400–409.

40. Reading (with Versional support) Q ומרק (K ופרק).

41. Note also Isa. 66:3, in which burning memorial incense appears to be aligned with cultic swine. See W. Houston, *Purity and Monotheism: Clean and Unclean Animals in Biblical Law* (JSOTS, 140; Sheffield: JSOT Press, 1993), 161–68; cf. R. de Vaux, 'Le sacrifice des porcs', in J. Hempel and L. Rost (eds), *Von Ugarit nach Qumrân* (BZAW, 77; Berlin: Topelmann, 1958), 250–65; F. J. Stendebach, 'Das Schweineopfer im Alten Orient', *BZ* 18 (1974), 263–71; Ackerman, *Under Every Green Tree*, 209–12; J. L. Koole, *Isaiah Chapters 56–66* (HCOT; Leuven: Peeters, 2001), 416.

42. Cf. Nutkowicz, *L'homme face à la morte au royaume de Juda*, 276; Schmidt, *Israel's Beneficent Dead*, 260–62; Lewis, *Cults of the Dead*, 159–60; Ackerman, *Under Every Green Tree*, 194–202.

43. For further discussion, see Stavrakopoulou, 'Exploring the Garden of Uzza', 1–21; G. del Olmo Lete, 'GN, el cementerio regio de Ugarit', *SEL* 3 (1986), 62–64; S. Richardson, 'An Assyrian Garden of Ancestors: Room I, Northwest Palace, Kalḫu', *SAAB* 13 (1999–01),

of the royal ancestral cult complements both the mythic imaging of the king and his dynastic line as the cosmic tree (its roots plunging into the underworld, its branches reaching into the heavenly realm) and the close association of sacred trees with death, burial and the underworld.[44] If the likely Persian period context of Isa. 65:1-5 is taken seriously, this text appears to attest to a perception that the royal dead continued to play an important role in the lives of some elites despite (or because of) the political uncertainties of the Davidic dynasty in Yehud.

Isaiah 57:3-13 offers a similarly aggressive and polemical attack on the death-cult activities of a group of elites – though the extent to which it reflects actual practice is of course uncertain. In this complex and at times inscrutable poem, the setting is again Jerusalem, this time pictured in terms of the city's mythic landscape, in which the mountain described as גבה ונשא and קדש is the cosmic mountain Zion, imaged perhaps as Zaphon (vv. 7, 13; cf. Ps. 48:3), and encircled by the valleys (נחלים) that give access to the underworld (vv. 5, 6, 9; cf. Job 26:5-7). It is at these temple and valley locations that rituals suggestive of a cult of the dead are performed: grain, drink and flesh offerings (vv. 6-7), including child sacrifice (vv. 5, 10);[45] the setting up of a mortuary monument, variously

---

145–216; N. Wyatt, '"Supposing Him to be the Gardener" (John 20,15): A Study of the Paradise Motif in John', *ZNW* 81 (1990), 21–38.

44. Seth Richardson (ibid.) has highlighted the ancestral and mortuary connotations of the sacred tree within Neo-Assyrian kingship ideologies. Biblical allusions to this mythic complex include Judg. 9:6, in which Abimelech (whose name means 'My ancestor is king') is made a king in the presence of a sacred tree; the tradition concerning the burial of the bones of Saul and his sons beneath a sacred tree (1 Sam. 31:13; 1 Chr. 10:12; cf. Gen. 35:8) and Ezek. 31:14-18, in which kings imaged as trees – including those of the temple garden of Eden – are felled and consigned to Sheol (cf. Dan. 4:10-33). The portrayal of the Davidic dynasty as a fertile tree may also reflect this cultic context (Isa. 6:13; 11:1, 10; Ezek. 17:3-10; cf. 31:2-18), a context which appears to give rise to the designating of a future king as צמח, 'branch', נצר, 'sprout', or יונקת, 'offshoot' (e.g. Isa. 4:2; Jer. 23:5; 33:15; Ezek. 17:22-24; Zech. 3:8; 6:12; cf. 4:3). The ancestral associations of kings and trees might also offer a fresh interpretation of Jer. 2:26-27, in which the writer mocks those who address the tree as 'my father' (אבי) and credit the stone with giving birth to them. This verse is often regarded as a curiosity in view of the common assumption that a tree is a feminine symbol of fertility (e.g. Zevit, *Religions of Ancient Israel*, 537; S. M. Olyan, 'The Cultic Confessions of Jer 2,27a', *ZAW* 99 [1987], 254–59). However, 'masculine' and kingly figures are also the subject of tree imagery (including Yhwh in Hos. 14:8), while the motif of a fertile, birthing rock (צור) or stone (אבן) occurs in Gen. 49:24-26; Deut. 32:18; Isa. 51:2. The imaging of ancestors as trees may also underlie the prohibition of tree-felling in Deut. 20:19-20, which contains the explicit denial that trees are men.

45. The fictional deity 'Molek' is not in view in this verse; the term מלך likely refers to a royal offering; *pace.* J. Day, *Molech: A God of Human Sacrifice in the Old Testament* (UCOP, 41; Cambridge: Cambridge University Press, 1989). On this text, and on the nature of child sacrifice as a fertility ritual and its possible associations with cults of the dead, see Stavrakopoulou, *King Manasseh and Child Sacrifice*, esp. 252–57. For the biblical

described as a זכרון and a יד (v. 8; cf. v. 10);[46] and interaction with the dead at the burial site (משכב) in vv. 7-8.[47]

In this poem, the solidarity between the dead and the living is affirmed and the territorial functions of the dead are acknowledged by means of artful wordplay: 'With the dead of the valley (חלקי־נחל) is your portion (חלק); they, indeed they are your lot' (v. 6).[48] Though the territorial connotations of the cult's mortuary rituals are thus recognized here, the power of the dead to convey the land to their descendants is forcefully contested at the poem's close (v. 13), in which Yhwh claims:

> When you cry out, let your gathered ones (קבוציך)[49] rescue you;
> the wind will carry them all off,
> a breath will take them away.
> But whoever seeks refuge in me shall possess the land,
> and inherit my holy mountain.

---

association of child sacrifice with divination and death cult practices, see Deut. 18:9-12; 2 Kgs 21:6; 2 Chr. 33:6 (cf. Lev. 20:5-6).

46. Reading יד as 'memorial monument' (cf. 1 Sam. 15:12; 2 Sam. 18:18; 1 Chr. 18:3; Isa. 56:5), against some commentators who prefer to see here an allusion to a phallus or phallic symbol; e.g. Schramm, *Opponents*, 132, n. 1; Westermann, *Isaiah 40–66*, 323 n. c; Ackerman, *Under Every Green Tree*, 106 n. 14; M. Delcor, 'Two Special Meanings of the Word *yd* in Biblical Hebrew', *JSS* 12 (1967), 230–40. However, this interpretation is problematic. For further discussion, see the note below and pages 123–27.

47. Reading משכב here as 'grave' (cf. *DCH*, 5.526; *BDB*, 1012; Lewis, *Cults of the Dead*, 149–50). משכב, 'grave', is well attested in North-West Semitic inscriptions (*DNWSI*, 2.701). The more common rendering of משכב here as 'bed' reflects a somewhat misleading tendency among commentators to see in this poem images of ritual sex, a view likely prompted by the language of sexual deviancy in v. 3 (which ought not to be taken literally, but rather understood solely as a metaphor for religious malpractice) and further encouraged by some scholars' own assumptions about the nature of practices denigrated as 'foreign' in the Hebrew Bible. For further discussion, see Stavrakopoulou, *King Manasseh and Child Sacrifice*, 172–75, 254–60; S. Moughtin-Mumby, *Sexual and Marital Metaphors in Hosea, Jeremiah, Isaiah, and Ezekiel* (OTM; Oxford: Oxford University Press, 2008), 142–44.

48. MT חלקי is widely held to derive from the verb חלק, 'be smooth', and is thus usually translated 'smooth (stones)'. However, the paralleling of Ugaritic *ḫlq* and *mt* suggests that a further meaning of חלק is 'die', 'perish' (*DULAT*, 1.393–94; cf. Akkadian *ḫalāqu*; *CAD*, 6.36–40), rendering חלקי '(the) dead'; cf. W. H. Irwin, 'The Smooth Stones of the Wady? Isaiah 57:6', *CBQ* 29 (1967), 31–40; M. Dahood, 'Hebrew-Ugaritic Lexicography II', *Bib* 45 (1964), 393–412, esp. 408; Lewis, *Cults of the Dead*, 148; Ackerman, *Under Every Green Tree*, 103 n. 8, 146–48; Schmidt, *Israel's Beneficent Dead*, 255, 258; Blenkinsopp, *Isaiah 56–66*, 153, 158.

49. קבוצים is a *hapax legomenon*, probably equivalent to Ugaritic *qbṣm*, which itself occurs in parallel with *rpʾum* (*KTU* 1.161.9-10; cf. 1.15 iii 4, 15). See Lewis, *Cults of the Dead*, 151–52; *pace* Schmidt, *Israel's Beneficent Dead*, 257–58.

Collectively identified as קבוצים, the dead are here mockingly dismissed as transient, vaporous and territorially impotent. These are likely the royal dead of Judah's past, as suggested by the cult's setting in Zion, the allusions to the Jerusalem temple, and the strong implication that the cult's practitioners are petitioning their ancestors to secure Zion for themselves. But the thrust of the polemic is clear: the dead can no longer deliver the land to the living; it is Yhwh who, like an imperial landowner, guards and gifts the possession of Jerusalem.

Post-monarchic hostilities against the cult of the royal dead are perhaps best illustrated in Ezek. 43:7-9, a passage to which scholars often return in seeking to understand Jerusalem temple attitudes towards the dead during the period in which the city was rebuilt. This text is usually rendered along the following lines:

> Mortal, this is the place of my throne and the place for the soles of my feet, where I will dwell in the midst of the sons of Israel forever. The house of Israel shall no more defile my holy name, neither they nor their kings, by their whoring and the corpses of their kings at their deaths. When they placed their threshold by my threshold and their doorposts next to my doorposts, with a wall between me and them, and they defiled my holy name with the abominable practices they committed, I consumed them in my anger. But now let them put away from me their whoring and the corpses of their kings, and I will dwell among them forever.

According to this passage, dead kings pose a problem to Yhwh in his cult place. Several commentators suppose that the text alludes to the close proximity of the royal tombs to the temple, and understand Yhwh's objection to reflect a priestly concern that the presence of the dead might pollute the sanctuary.[50] Certainly, the language of defilement here (טמא) might well signal specialized anxieties about corpses as social and ritual pollutants. But the close aligning of the dead kings with the 'whoring' language of religious malpractice (זנה) is also indicative of the *cultic* presence of the dead in the temple. Indeed, מלכים in vv. 7 and 9 is likely employed as a cultic designation of the specifically dead, deified kings – cognate with Ugaritic *mlkm*, itself paralleled with *rpʾum*.[51] The phrase פגרי מלכיהם, which might thus be rendered 'the corpses of their (dead) kings',

---

50. On the possibility that this priestly complaint is related to the decommissioning or removal of royal tombs located too near the temple, see, for example, Spronk, *Beatific Afterlife*, 250; J. W. Wevers, *Ezekiel* (NCB; London: Thomas Nelson, 1969), 312; Schmidt, *Israel's Beneficent Dead*, 252; Na'aman, 'Death Formulae and the Burial Places of the Kings', 251–53; cf. S. Yeivin, 'The Sepulchers of the Kings of the House of David', *JNES* 7 (1948), 30–45; Bloch-Smith, *Judahite Burial Practices*, 116, 119.

51. Cf. Isa. 14:9; 24:21. See J. Healey, 'Mlkm/Rpʾum and the Kispum', *UF* 10 (1978), 89–91.

is perhaps better understood in this context to refer not to the presence of royal corpses in the temple, but rather to features of the royal cult of the dead, whether memorial monuments for the dead kings,[52] or more plausibly, mortuary offerings for the dead kings (cf. Lev. 26:30; *KTU* 6.13, 14),[53] perhaps performed not 'at their deaths' (as many commentators suggest), but at cultic platforms – here called במות – in or next to the temple itself.[54]

As Herbert Niehr suggests, this condemnation of Jerusalem's cult of dead kings likely represents a Persian period priestly move to separate the royal ancestral cult from its original context within the cult of the high god, Yhwh.[55] While this may represent to a degree an emergent discomfort with the veneration

---

52. E.g. D. Neiman, '*PGR*: A Canaanite Cult Object in the Old Testament', *JBL* 67 (1948), 55–60; W. F. Albright, 'The High Place in Ancient Palestine', in G. W. Anderson (ed.), *Congress Volume Strasbourg, 1956* (VTS, 4; Leiden: Brill, 1957), 242–58; see also W. Zimmerli, *Ezekiel 2 – A Commentary on the Book of the Prophet Ezekiel Chapters 25–48* (trans. J. D. Martin. Hermeneia; Philadelphia: Fortress Press, 1983), 409; L. C. Allen, *Ezekiel 20–48* (WBC, 29; Dallas, TX: Word, 1990), 257. On the possibility that the pillars in the Jerusalem temple known as 'Jachin' and 'Boaz' (1 Kgs 7:15-22) are memorial monuments in a royal ancestor cult, see the discussion in F. Stavrakopoulou, 'Ancestral advocacy and dynastic dynamics in the Books of Kings', in P. J. McCosker (ed.), *What is it that the Scripture Says? Essays in Biblical Interpretation, Translation and Reception* (London: T&T Clark, 2006), 10–24, and the literature cited there.

53. E.g. J. H. Ebach, '*PGR* = (Toten-)opfer? Ein Vorschlag zum Verständnis von Ez. 43,7.9', *UF* 3 (1971), 365–68; Niehr, 'Changed Status of the Dead', 138–40; Block, *Ezekiel 25–48*, 584–85; cf. I. J. Winter, 'Idols of the King: Royal Images as Recipients of Ritual Action in Mesopotamia', *JRS* 6 (1992), 14–42. A variation of this interpretation is offered by Margaret Odell, who argues that the offerings are sacrificed children, dedicated as *mlk* offerings to the deity: M. S. Odell, 'What was the Image of Jealousy in Ezekiel 8?', in L. L. Grabbe and A. O. Bellis (eds), *The Priests in the Prophets: The Portrayal of Priests, Prophets, and Other Religious Specialists in the Latter Prophets* (JSOTS, 408; New York: T&T Clark, 2004), 131–48.

54. Commentators often repoint MT בָּמוֹתָם in v. 7 as בְּמוֹתָם. See, for example, Lewis, *Cults of the Dead*, 141; Block, *Ezekiel 25–48*, 585. Albright ('The High Place', 242–58) is among those who read with MT. Gabriel Barkay argues that various tumuli located west of what would have been ancient Jerusalem were constructed as cultic settings for memorial fires made in honour of dead kings of Judah, as might be suggested by Jer. 34:5; 2 Chr. 16:14; 21:19; 32:33; cf. Jer. 51:25; see G. Barkay, 'Mounds of Mystery: Where the Kings of Judah were Lamented', *BAR* 29.3 (2003), 32–39, 66, 68. However, given the ambiguous nature of both the archaeological findings and the biblical references, the function of the tumuli and their relationship to royal funerary fires remains uncertain. Baruch Levine (*Numbers 1–20*, 475) suggests the biblical references to burnings reflect mortuary offerings for the royal dead, *contra* W. Zwickel, 'Über das angebliche Verbrennen von Räucherwerk bei der Bestattung des Königs', *ZAW* 101 (1989), 266–77, who argues the fires have an apotropaic function.

55. Niehr, 'Changed Status of the Dead', 139–40. The place of the royal ancestors in the cult of Yhwh might have reflected the perception that dead kings became a part of the ruling deity's household.

of the dead, it is also likely related to perceptions that the Davidic dynasty had ceased or failed to perform its religio-mythic function in promoting and guarding the well-being of Jerusalem and its citizens. Biblical traces of the anti-monarchic tendencies of some priestly circles are well recognized. But unlike texts such as Lev. 8:6-13 and Zech. 6:11-12 (cf. v. 13), in which the high priest or a priestly dynasty stands in the place of the former kings, Ezek. 43:7-9 replaces the royal dead not with a priestly figure, but with Yhwh himself, imaged as a divine king whose throne is to become fixed in the temple (v. 7)[56] – on condition that the royal dead are removed (v. 9).[57]

In Ezekiel 40–48, Yhwh's return to the city and land he had previously abandoned is thus directly and immediately related to the displacement of Jerusalem's royal dead. Once a site of the dynastic cult of dead kings, the temple is now exclusively the domain of the deity, its dynastic associations recast in the terms of the royal presence of Yhwh with the descendants (בנים) and lineage (בית) of Israel (43:7-8). Though the territorial function of the royal dead is not a theme directly addressed in this passage, the territorialism of Yhwh's return to Jerusalem and his temple are made explicit just a few verses beyond the call for the displacement of dead kings, for 'the whole territory on the top of the mountain all around shall be most holy' (v. 12), while in chapter 45, it is Yhwh, rather than the royal figures cast as נשיאם, 'princes' (vv. 8-9), who by means of divination apportions land-holdings (cf. Leviticus 25–27).[58]

Collectively, the biblical texts attest to an ambivalent attitude towards the dead (and particularly the royal dead) of Jerusalem. Some, including Jer. 31:8-9; Ezek.

---

56. Cf. J. T. Strong, 'God's *Kābôd*: The Presence of Yahweh in the Book of Ezekiel', in M. S. Odell and J. T. Strong (eds), *The Book of Ezekiel: Theological and Anthropological Perspectives* (SBLSS, 9; Atlanta, GA: Society of Biblical Literature, 2000), 69–95. On perceptions of human kingship in Ezekiel, see I. M. Duguia, *Ezekiel and the Leaders of Israel* (VTS, 56; Leiden: Brill, 1994).

57. A similarly intolerant attitude to the royal cult of the dead is presented in Isa. 28:14-22, in which the rulers of Jerusalem are mocked for making a 'covenant with Death/ Mot' and a 'pact with Sheol'. The oracle appears to allude to the rebuilding of the temple (v. 16), which will render the royal cult of the dead redundant (v. 18) and discomfort (or perhaps displace) the dead themselves (v. 20). On this text and its portrayal of mortuary cult practices, see B. Halpern, '"The Excremental Vision": The Doomed Priests of Doom in Isaiah 28', *HAR* 10 (1986), 109–21; K. van der Toorn, 'Echoes of Judaean Necromancy in Isaiah 28,7-22', *ZAW* 100 (1988), 199–217; J. Blenkinsopp, 'Judah's Covenant with Death (Isaiah XXVIII 14–22)', *VT* 50 (2000), 472–83. John Day (*Molech*, 58–64) proposes that the cult in view in this text is that of Molek, but the absence of explicit sacrificial imagery suggests this is unlikely.

58. Though note that the נשיא himself is given a landholding (vv. 7-8). On the casting of lots to apportion land-holdings, see Ezek. 47:22; 48:29. For the royal territorialism of Yhwh in chs 43–46, see S. S. Tuell, *The Law of the Temple in Ezekiel 40–48* (HSM, 49; Atlanta, GA: Scholars Press, 1992).

37:1-14; 39:11-20 and Neh. 2:2-5, credit the dead with a high religio-mythic value by casting the restoration and repopulation of Jerusalem in the terms of a post-mortem territorialism. By contrast – and though they recognize the potential religio-mythic value of the dead – others, among them Isa. 57:3-13; Jer. 8:1-3 and Ezek. 43:7-9, seek to counter the territorial efficacy of Jerusalem's dead by dispossessing them of their sacred spaces and cult places. It would thus appear that the placing or displacing of Jerusalem's dead was a live issue for those asserting or contesting a claim to post-monarchic Jerusalem. But despite the displacing of the city's dead in some traditions, their territorial function was not wholly disabled. Rather, the territorialism of the dead continued to play a role in the temple ideologies of the city throughout the Persian period, but was instead appropriated, embodied and epitomized by Yhwh in his sanctuary.

Entombing Temple

Despite the apparent move against Jerusalem's powerful dead in the post-monarchic era, the temple cult and its deity continued to be associated with the dead within certain traditions. In Jer. 31:38-40, the dead and their territories are incorporated into the sacred landscape of the new temple-city:

> Behold, the days are surely coming[59] – oracle of Yhwh – when the city shall be rebuilt for Yhwh from the Tower of Hananel to the Corner Gate. And the measuring line shall go out farther, straight from the hill Gareb, and shall then turn to Goah. The whole valley of the corpses (הפגרים) and the ashes, and all the terraces[60] as far as the Wadi Kidron, to the corner of the Horse Gate towards the east, shall be sacred to Yhwh. It shall never again be uprooted or overthrown.

In this text, the 'measuring line' envisaged to map the boundaries of the new city reaches beyond an idealized topography (cf. Zech. 14:10) into the realm of land-allotment ideologies and territorial expansion (cf. Isa. 34:17).[61] As observed earlier, the rebuilding of Jerusalem is here explicitly coupled with the sanctification of the territories of the dead, whose terraces and valleys are the liminal places to be made sacred to Yhwh (קדש ליהוה). In this sense, the dead

---

59. Inserting באים, with Versional support.
60. Reading שדמות for MT שרמות. The suggestion that שדמות ought to be rendered 'fields of death' or 'fields of Mot' has not been widely accepted. See M. R. Lehmann, 'A New Interpretation of the Term *šdmwt*', *VT* 3 (1953), 361–71; cf. N. Wyatt, 'A New Look at Ugaritic *šdmt*', *JSS* 37 (1992), 149–53.
61. For the territorial connotations of this imagery, see the discussion in G. L. Keown, P. J. Scalise and T. G. Smothers, *Jeremiah 26–52* (WBC, 27; Dallas, TX: Word, 1995), 138. On the possibility that this oracle sanctions a particular building project in the city, see the literature cited in n. 18.

remain the boundary keepers of the city, but they are also affirmed as *belonging* with the sacred city and to Yhwh, who claims the new Jerusalem for himself (ונבנתה העיר ליהוה) – a vivid contrast to their displacement, rejection and exclusion from the Jerusalem community in other texts, including Jer. 7:32-34, in which the corpse-filled valleys mark the city's rotting devastation. By strong implication, the sanctification of the city's burial grounds affords them the same divine and enduring protection the new city will have (Jer. 31:40), so that the sacred status of the dead will not be changed, whether by tomb desecration or corpse and bone abuse.[62]

In asserting the sacred status of the dead and their burial places (which are described as קדש ליהוה), the oracle in Jer. 31:38-40 conflicts with biblical reflections of ritual instructions which rendered the dead – and those who had come into contact with them – incompatible with Yhwh and his sacred space.[63] But though this primarily priestly teaching would become one of the more dominant forces shaping the attitudes of some later Jewish groups towards the presence of the dead, there likely existed throughout the Iron II, Persian and Hellenistic periods a constellation of views about the relationship between Yhwh and the dead, many of which allowed for a greater degree of interaction between mortuary practices and Yhwh worship than biblical legislation might suggest.[64] This is attested, for example, in Iron II tomb inscriptions and amulets invoking Yhwh's blessings upon – and perhaps protection of – the dead in their tombs (such as those from Khirbet Beit Lei, Khirbet el-Qom and Ketef Hinnom),[65] and is also widely evident in later periods, as (for example) ossuaries bearing

---

62. Cf. Carroll, *Jeremiah*, 617–18. For the suggestion that Josiah's defiling of the Kidron Valley and his profanation of Jerusalem's burial grounds (2 Kgs 23:4-14) are deliberately reversed in Jer. 31:40, see Halpern, 'Late Israelite Astronomies', 331.

63. E.g. Lev. 21:1-11; 22:4-8; Num. 5:2; 6; 9:6-12; 19; 31:19; Ezek. 44:25-27; Hagg. 2:13; cf. Deut. 21:22-23. For further discussion, see Levine, *Numbers 1–20*, 468–79, and Chapter 6. For Jerusalem as a sacred city, see M. L. Steiner, 'The Notion of Jerusalem as a Holy City', in R. Rezetko, T. H. Lim and W. B. Aucker (eds), *Reflection and Refraction: Studies in Biblical Historiography in Honour of A. Graeme Auld* (VTS, 113; Leiden: Brill, 2007), 447–58.

64. Cf. R. Wenning, 'Bestattungen im königszeitlichen Juda', *ThQ* 177 (1997), 82–93; idem, '"Medien" in der Bestattungskultur im eisenzeitlichen Juda?' in C. Frevel (ed.), *Medien im antiken Palästina* (Tübingen: Mohr Siebeck, 2005), 109–50; Niehr, 'Changed Status of the Dead', 137.

65. Note the comments of É. Puech, 'Palestinian Funerary Inscriptions', *ABD*, 5.126–35, esp. 128. For discussion of the tomb inscriptions from Khirbet Beit Lei and Khirbet el-Qom, see Zevit, *Religions of Ancient Israel*, 359–70, 405–37; for the inscribed silver amulets from Ketef Hinnom, see G. Barkay, 'The Priestly Benediction on Silver Plaques from Ketef Hinnom in Jerusalem', *TA* 19 (1992), 139–92; Nutkowicz, *L'homme face à la mort*, 166–73. For a post-monarchic dating of this amulet, see T. Renz, *Die althebräischen Inschriften, I* (Darmstadt: Wissenschaftliche Buchgesellschaft, 1995), 447–48.

schematic representations of temples and other temple-related motifs appear to demonstrate.[66]

These archaeological data indicate that the dead and their tombs were perhaps not as 'unclean' or as ritually hazardous as some biblical texts – particularly the priestly literature – assert.[67] Far from being excluded from any form of socio-religious exchange with both the living community and Yhwh, the dead appear to have been included within the dynamic relationship between the social group and the deity. Indeed, some biblical traditions point to this 'clean' view of the dead: Moses himself is portrayed as a bone-handler in carrying the remains of Joseph from Egypt into Canaan (Exod. 13:19; cf. Josh. 24:32); the grave and bones of Elisha are presented not as a locus of death-inducing defilement, but as a source of life-restoring, resurrective power (2 Kgs 13:21); the placing of Joseph's bones at the sanctuary at Shechem appears not to risk or damage the sacred status of the cult place (Josh. 24:32); Yhwh is imaged as walking among unburied bones and disinterring tombs (Ezek. 37:12-13); and the public performance of mortuary rituals secures his blessings upon the land (2 Sam. 21:9-14; cf. Deut. 21:23),[68] blessings which might also be transformed into curses through the ritual reversal of these practices, as indicated in Jer. 8:1-3.

Thus within this context, the sacred status accorded the dead and their tombs in Jer. 31:38-40 is neither curious nor anomalous. Instead, their inclusion within the newly built temple city accords well with the evidence highlighted here that suggests that the dead were not incompatible with the sanctity and sanctuary of Yhwh. Indeed, Yhwh and his temple had a place among the dead and their tombs. Jack Lightstone's proposal that the dead and their graves were perceived by some – particularly in the Persian and Hellenistic periods – to perform a mediatory function between the earthly and heavenly realms is particularly pertinent here. As he suggests, the close alignment of 'altar and tomb' in biblical and post-biblical traditions reflects their shared function as a 'gateway' to the divine realm, granting access to both the sacred dead and Yhwh.[69] For Lightstone, the intersection of altar and tomb gave rise to certain aspects of Jewish death cults in

---

66. Lightstone, *Commerce of the Sacred*, 60; following B. Goldman, *The Sacred Portal: A Primary Symbol in Ancient Judaic Art* (Detroit: Wayne State University Press, 1966); see also P. Figueras, *Decorated Jewish Ossuaries* (Leiden: Brill, 1983); E. M. Meyers, *Jewish Ossuaries: Reburial and Rebirth* (BO, 24; Rome: Biblical Institute Press, 1971); Hachlili, *Jewish Funerary Customs*, 127–62.

67. For the possibility that the dominant biblical traditions asserting the impurity of the dead are relatively late, see the important discussion in R. Achenbach, 'Verunreinigung durch die Berühung Toter. Zum Ursprung einer altisraelitischen Vorstellung', in A. Berlejung and B. Jankowski (eds), *Tod und Jenseits im Alten Israel und in seiner Umwelt: theologische, religionsgeschichtliche, archäologische und ikonograpische Aspekte* (FAT, 64; Tübingen: Mohr Siebeck, 2009), 347–69.

68. Cf. Lightstone, *Commerce of the Sacred*, 44–48.

69. Lightstone, *Commerce of the Sacred*, 50–51.

the Hellenistic era and later, such as the ease with which some of the dead began to be relocated from the netherworld to heaven (anticipated, perhaps in Dan. 12:2-3),[70] the emergence of tomb cults devoted to prophets and other religious specialists, and the use of temple symbolism in the funerary iconography of tombs and ossuaries.

But there is good reason to take this idea further and suggest that the cultic exchange effected by the close alignment of tomb and temple proceeded not just in the direction of tomb as temple, but in the other as well: temple as tomb. Key biblical images of the restored Jerusalem employ motifs associated with mortuary cults as a means of communicating particular ideas about the nature and function of Yhwh and his sanctuary. At first blush, these texts might appear merely to draw from a diverse range of religio-cultural themes and symbols derived from both the local and broader cultural milieu. But upon closer consideration, they are suggestive of the more deliberate 'entombing' of the temple – in part in an effort to displace the dead (among them the deceased Davidic kings) from the religious landscape of Jerusalem, but also in part to memorialize the temple and its new cult within the cultural memory of its worshippers.

The first of these texts is Isa. 56:1-8, in which worship in the new temple is imaged as a cult of regeneration, in which Yhwh bestows fertility blessings upon his worshippers. Verses 3-5 read:

3   The foreigner who has joined himself to Yhwh must not say,
    'Yhwh will surely cut me off from his people';
    and the eunuch must not say,
    'I am a dry tree'.
4   For thus says Yhwh:
    'The eunuchs who observe my sabbaths,
    who choose what I desire
    and hold fast to my covenant:
5   I shall give them, in my house and within my walls,
    a memorial and a name (יד ושם)
    better than sons and daughters;
    I shall give them[71] an everlasting name (שם עולם)
    which will not be cut off.

In this text, the poet draws heavily on mortuary cult imagery as a means of asserting the life-giving function of the cult of Yhwh in the Jerusalem temple.

---

70. Biblical and non-biblical traditions concerning the 'translation' of figures including Enoch, Moses, Elijah and Jesus also attest to this. For a discussion of Moses' relocation from the grave to heaven, see the literature cited in Chapter 3, n. 4.

71. Reading להם in place of לו, following 1QIsaª, with Versional support.

The combined 'memorial and name' (יד ושם) to which the writer refers (v. 5) is here most plausibly understood as aspects of ancestral cult: יד is the mortuary monument manifesting the ritualized remembering and cultic presence of the dead, while שם is the post-mortem memorialized 'name' of the dead, invoked in the cult to perpetuate (by remembering) their ongoing existence.[72] A concern for the perpetuation of the existence of the dead is also made explicit in the parallel promise of a שם עולם ('everlasting name'), an expression carrying – most appropriately for its mortuary cult context – connotations of divinity and deification, as is suggested by its application to Yhwh (Isa. 63:17; cf. Gen. 21:33; Exod. 3:15; 1 Kgs 9:3; 2 Kgs 21:7; Ps. 135:13) and the king in the cult (Ps. 72:17). As is widely accepted, this interpretation of יד ושם is closely supported by the tradition in 2 Sam. 18:18 in which Absalom sets up for himself a mortuary monument (described as both a יד and a מצבה) to memorialize his name (הזכיר שם) so as to secure his post-mortem existence, for he is without descendants to keep his cult.[73] The dynastic design of the ritual invoked in Isa. 56:3-5 is evident not only in the reference to descendants in v. 5 (בנים and בנות), but is also pointedly emphasized (v. 5; cf. v. 3) in the assurance that the post-mortem שם will not be 'cut off' (כרת) – a loaded and complex expression frequently used of the socio-cultic abandonment, displacement or annihilation of the dead, or of dynastic destruction, or of exclusion from the household and its cult, or of exile from the homeland.[74]

The territorial dynamics of the mortuary cult are also evident in this remarkable text, for as Sara Japhet observes, יד can also mean 'portion' or 'share', and is synonymous with חלק, which is often employed of an 'inheritance' or

---

72. See O. Loretz, 'Stelen und Sohnespflicht im Totenkult Kanaans und Israels: *skn* (*KTU* 1.17 I 26) und *jd* (Jes 56,5)', *UF* 21 (1989), 241–46; D. W. van Winkle, 'The Meaning of *yād wāšēm* in Isaiah LVI 5', *VT* 47 (1997), 378–85; cf. S. Talmon, '*Yād wāšēm*: An Idiomatic Phrase in Biblical Literature and Its Variations', *HS* 25 (1984), 8–17. The suggested presence of memorial monuments in the temple in this verse might reflect the possibility that stelae of the deified dead were set up in local sanctuaries or (in the case of the royal dead) in state-sponsored temples (see Chapter 1, n. 58). But if so, the practice is subverted ideologically in its Jerusalem context, as shall be seen presently.

73. Cf. 1 Sam. 15:12.

74. These varied usages are clearly interrelated (e.g. Isa. 14:18-22; 48:19; Jer. 9:21; Nah. 1:14; cf. Ruth 4:10). Note that in Jer. 11:19, a collection of motifs similar to those present in Isa. 56:3-5 (the symbol of the dynastic tree, cutting off the name, remembering the name) is employed to describe the intended annihilation of the prophet Jeremiah and his line (see also Isa. 55:13; Job 18:16-19). In Lev. 20:3-6, those participating in mortuary cults are to be cut off from their kin and the temple cult. On the 'blotting out' (מחה) of the name as an expression referring to the absence or wiping out of descendants, see, for example, Deut. 25:5-6; Judg. 21:17; Ps. 109:13. The term גזר (*niph.*) is used synonymously in similar contexts in Isa. 53:8-9; Ezek. 37:11; Ps. 88:6; Lam. 3:4. For further discussion of this term, see Olyan, '"We are Utterly Cut Off"', 43–51.

possession of a 'share' of land, and which in its own turn is also related within the same semantic field to the use of שׁם as a reference to a designated claim to or occupation of land, or an inheritable land holding (e.g. Num. 26:53-62; 27:3-4; Ruth 4:10).[75] But significantly, חלק is also the legacy of the territorial dead of the valley (חלקי־נחל) in Isa. 57:6, as observed earlier. Thus, while Japhet assumes that the expression יד ושׁם in 56:5 is simply a metaphorical reference to the 'enduring right' of the eunuch to a spiritual 'share' within the temple community (cf. Josh. 22:24-25), the vivid mortuary cult imagery of this verse, set within its broader context of dynastic regeneration, suggests that the poet is exploiting the ambivalence of language here (anticipating the attack on mortuary cults in the oracle following shortly after, in 57:3-13), so that the memorial and territorial connotations of יד ושׁם are intentionally aligned,[76] invoking the close interrelation of the ancestor cult and claims to place. Accordingly, the ritual stakes a designated and memorialized place for the worshipper not only in Yhwh's temple, but also in Yhwh's city (בחומתי, 'within my walls').

In couching this description of the new temple cult in the language of the mortuary cult, Yhwh himself is thus imaged in 56:3-5 as an active participant in his own version of a mortuary ritual, simultaneously playing the role of descendant and ancestor: he sets a memorial monument in the cult place and ensures the perpetual existence of the post-mortem name, and in doing so bestows fertility blessings upon his worshippers and secures them a holding within the place – here the temple city.[77] The ideological thrust of this oracle represents a polemical double-strike against the kinship contexts of ancestral cults. First, in asserting that the Yhwh temple can offer the community the regenerative and memorializing functions of the ancestral cult, the dead are rendered redundant, and the mortuary rituals associated with the household are appropriated and subsumed within the cultic control of the 'central' sanctuary.[78] Second, the foreigner and the eunuch to whom the divine promise of יד ושׁם is made represent those without a traditional claim to the area, neither past nor pending: the foreigner is without local ancestors to mark his place, and the eunuch is without descendants to maintain his place.[79]

---

75. S. Japhet, 'יד ושׁם (Isa 56:5) – A Different Proposal', *Maarav* 8 (1992), 69–80; building on the ideas presented in G. Robinson, 'The Meaning of יד in Isaiah 56:5', *ZAW* 88 (1976), 282–84.

76. Cf. van Winkle, 'Meaning of *yād wāšēm*', 381.

77. The divine performance of cultic actions is well known in many ancient cultures, including those of West Asia and the Mediterranean. On this, see K. C. Patton, *Religion of the Gods: Ritual, Paradox, and Reflexivity* (Oxford: Oxford University Press, 2009). Patton's discussion includes an assessment of rabbinic portrayals of the deity performing rituals.

78. On the dislocation of household practices to the 'central' sanctuary, see particularly Blenkinsopp, 'Deuteronomy and the Politics of Post-Mortem Existence', 1–16, and the discussion in Chapter 6.

79. On the (assumed) 'foreignness' of eunuchs, see the discussion in H. Tadmor, 'Was the Biblical *sarîs* a Eunuch?', in Z. Zevit, S. Gitin and M. Sokoloff (eds), *Solving Riddles and*

They are rootless and fruitless. This overturning of traditional kinship ties to Jerusalem is reinforced at the close of the oracle, in v. 8:

> Oracle of Lord Yhwh,
> who gathers the dispersed of Israel:
> 'I shall gather still others to him
> besides those already gathered.'

This is widely taken as a promise of restorative ingathering: those exiled and dispersed beyond the bounds of the land will be brought back to join those who have already returned (cf. Deut. 30:4; Mic. 4:6; Zeph. 3:19-20). In this particular context, however, the language of gathering (קבץ) also evokes images of the mortuary cult, in which the dead are united with their ancestors by means of the one who gathers their bones to those of their predecessors in the family tomb, here represented by the ancestor 'Israel'.[80] This reading is supported contextually not only by the ancestral cult motifs employed in vv. 3-5, but also in the repeated allusions to burial and death cults in the following chapter (57:1-13), including in 57:13 the designating of Jerusalem's ancestral dead as the 'gathered ones' (קבוצים). Thus in 56:8, Yhwh is imaged in mortuary-ritual terms as the bone-gatherer, collecting the dead – a metaphorical portrayal of the diaspora communities – to the ancestral grave, here represented by the temple on Zion (vv. 7-8).

This verse therefore employs mortuary imagery to depict Yehudite Jerusalem and its temple as a place embodied and memorialized by traditional manifestations of localized kinship networks and their corresponding death practices; the city and the sanctuary is a cult place at which the ongoing social and spatial relationship between the living and the dead is ritualized – and importantly, facilitated by Yhwh. But the more usual territorial and familial dynamics of this

---

Untying Knots: Biblical, Epigraphic, and Semitic Studies in Honor of Jonas C. Greenfield (Winona Lake, IN: Eisenbrauns, 1995), 317–25. Isaiah 56:3-5 is often assumed to be a deliberate counter to Deut. 23:2 (cf. Lev. 21:20), which excludes the man with crushed testicles or a cut-off penis from the Yhwh community. For a disability-studies perspective on biblical eunuchs, and with particular reference to Isa. 56:1-8, see S. M. Olyan, *Disability in the Hebrew Bible: Interpreting Mental and Physical Differences* (Cambridge: Cambridge University Press, 2008), 11–12, 84–85. Some scholars read a pun on יד in Isa. 56:5, so that the eunuch is promised a 'penis' that will not be 'cut off' (כרת). While this begs the question as to why and whether biblical eunuchs should be assumed to be 'dismembered', rather than having only their testicles removed, this sort of pun (if intended) may indeed serve to emphasize the fertility functions of ancestral cults.

80. In Ezek. 29:5, both קבץ and אסף are employed to describe the interment of the dead. As Lewis observes (*Cults of the Dead*, 151–52), Ugaritic *qbṣ* is similarly employed in a sense synonymous with *ʾasp*, 'gather', to refer to the dead in the underworld; cf. *KTU* 1.161.2-3.

imagery in v. 8 is also wholly subverted, for the 'dead' to be 'gathered' by Yhwh are not the indigenous and kindred inhabitants of Jerusalem, but newcomers (or rather, incomers) gathered from the diaspora – much like the 'dead' of the exile in Ezek. 37:11-14, who are disinterred by Yhwh and returned to their own ground (אדמה).[81] Indeed, the newcomers to be 'gathered' to Zion in Isa. 56:8 appear to be those Yhwh worshippers who will replace the localized 'gathered ones' (קבוציך) of 57:13, and who in this text (as argued above) are themselves to be 'carried off' and – by strong implication – disinherited from their land, rendering the sacred mountain a possession and inheritance instead for Yhwh's incoming worshippers, who are to be 'gathered' to a personified and ancestralized 'Israel' (56:8). Thus, while the seemingly universal perspectives of Isa. 56:1-8 may appear to offer an inclusive programme of community restoration in the eyes of today's modernist, globalized readers, within its ancient Yehudite context, this portrayal of the reconstituting of the temple-city's community seems designed to exclude the living descendants of the local dead, the dead through whom claim to that place can no longer be made.

The exclusionary contours of the new temple city are similarly depicted in a second key text, Neh. 2:20. This verse introduces the register of priests, ancestral households and selected local communities engaged by Nehemiah to reconstruct the city wall (3:1-32). While the perceived 'legitimacy' of some of these families' places among the Yehudite Jerusalem community is somewhat ambiguous elsewhere (cf. Ezra 2:59-63),[82] in Neh. 2:20, the groups represented by the 'foreigners' Sanballat the Horonite, Tobiah the Ammonite and Geshem the Arab are firmly excluded by Nehemiah with the words:

> The God of Heaven will give us success; we his servants shall arise and build; but you have no portion (חלק), or right (צדקה), or memorial (זכרון) in Jerusalem.

While this assertive dismissal of Nehemiah's opponents ostensibly denies them

---

81. For this motif see Stavrakopoulou, 'Gog's Grave', 83–84. On benevolent disinterment in this text, see also S. M. Olyan, 'Unnoticed Resonances of Tomb Opening and the Transportation of the Remains of the Dead in Ezekiel 37:12-14', *JBL* 128 (2009), 491–501.

82. On the asserted (and contested) genealogical claims to a legitimate place in the Yehudite community and its territories, see further Weinberg, *Citizen-Temple Community*, 49–61; J. Blenkinsopp, 'Temple and Society in Achaemenid Judah', in P. R. Davies (ed.), *Second Temple Studies, Volume I: Persian Period* (JSOTS, 117; Sheffield: JSOT Press, 1991), 22–53, esp. 47–48; cf. J. J. Collins, 'Marriage, Divorce and Family in Second Temple Judaism', in L. G. Perdue, J. Blenkinsopp, J. J. Collins and C. Meyers, *Families in Ancient Israel* (Louisville, KY: Westminster John Knox Press, 1997), 105–62.

a political stake in the new Jerusalem, its language also denies them a traditional and cultic claim to Jerusalem.[83] Within its narrative context, this claim is instead asserted on behalf of Nehemiah's allies: the wall-builders whose names are listed in the passage immediately following this verse in 3:1-32. As Jacob Wright observes, this register of names itself functions as a communal זכרון, resembling a building inscription commemorating the name of the donor or builder bringing the construction into being. In memorializing the wall-builders in this way, their portion (חלק) and right (צדקה) to the place is asserted, while the claims of their opponents are contested.[84]

The wall's function as a memorial to a place – and more specifically a חלק – within the new community thus mimics mortuary methods of claiming and marking place, for as has been seen, חלק and זכרון are terms carrying interlinked mortuary and territorial connotations. Moreover, both are associated with death rituals in Isa. 57:6, 8, and are synonymous with the terms יד and שם in Isa. 56:1-8,[85] terms themselves associated with mortuary practices, and here employed in a text similarly dealing with the constitution of the Jerusalem community – including, it would seem, claims to membership and land. By means of these loaded terms, the wall in Neh. 2:20 is portrayed not only as a physical and ideological boundary, but as a means of subverting claims to Jerusalem asserted by Nehemiah's opponents by memorializing their exclusion from the community within the very fabric of the bounded city itself. Here, then, the community's act of wall-building exhibits a similar ideological function to the divine giving of יד ושם in Isa. 56:5. Both texts adopt and adapt mortuary motifs to disinherit or discredit those asserting indigenous or traditional claims to Jerusalem in favour of incomers; within both texts, an inheritable claim to a place in Yehudite Jerusalem is marked by a memorial monument 'within the walls' of the new temple city.

Thus the biblical entombing of the temple and its cityscape draws on features familiar from traditional mortuary cults to make territorial and ideological claims about the place, status and function of the new temple city. Jerusalem's valleys of the dead become sacred markers of Yhwh's own land claims (Jer. 31:38-40), the city's new wall is rendered a memorial monument akin to the memorials of the dead (Neh. 2:20), and in the temple itself, Yhwh performs rituals appropriated from cults of the dead to promise the generation and perpetuation of the new community (Isa. 56:1-8). In this way, the innovations of the reconstituted temple city and its incoming community are presented in traditional, 'ancestralized' terms.

---

83. Cf. F. C. Fensham, *The Books of Ezra and Nehemiah* (NICOT; Grand Rapids, MI: Eerdmans, 1982), 169; Blenkinsopp, *Ezra-Nehemiah*, 226; cf. 2 Sam. 20:1; 1 Kgs 12:16, in which this language is used to speak of the rejection of the Davidic dynasty.

84. Wright, *Rebuilding Identity*, 111–12. Wright draws attention to the important promise made to Bagohi of a זכרון before Yahu if he agrees to the building of the temple (*TAD* A4.7.27).

85. Cf. Japhet, 'יד ושם', 78.

5. Claiming Jerusalem

The coalescence of temple and tomb in these biblical images might be thought incongruous. Jon Levenson, for example, has argued that 'death is as alien to the Temple, indeed, as repugnant to the Temple, as it is to Eden', and that '[h]oliness and death are at odds: there is something on the order of a magnetic repulsion between them'.[86] Certainly, the complementary biblical portrayals of Eden as a cosmic temple garden, and of the temple as the fertile, heavenly paradise projecting 'intimations of immortality',[87] promote the temple cult's life-giving and restorative functions, communicated in a mythologically rich symbol-system which includes the temple's cosmic streams, its sacred trees, and the portrayal of the king/priest as the heavenly gardener, cultivating ongoing regeneration.[88] And indeed, the temple cult's proclaimed potential to 'deliver' or 'return' the worshipping community from death (albeit cultic, social, cultural or 'spiritual') renders death itself as an ever-present threat with which to contend in the cult.[89] But in its very claim to perpetuate life in spite of death, the temple exhibits a function akin to that performed by the tomb: both represent and materialize the ongoing perpetuation of existence in the face of death – and the illustrations given in this discussion of a reciprocal appropriation of imagery and ideology between temple and tomb display this shared role. Both temple and tomb mark the *interconnectedness* of life and death, rather than their separateness.

Within West Semitic traditions, one of the most vivid illustrations of this occurs in *KTU* 1.6 i 15-18, in which Baal is buried atop the holy mountain of Zaphon (the site of his temple-palace) in a lofty grave, which is yet seemingly identified with the underworld 'hole' of the gods, while within the Hebrew Bible, the Edenic symbolism of the temple itself powerfully alludes to the mortuary gardens of royal myth and ritual, an association made explicit in later traditions depicting Eden as a burial ground.[90] With these examples in mind, the coalescence of temple and tomb is not as incongruent as might be assumed, and the

---

86. Levenson, *Resurrection and the Restoration of Israel*, 92.
87. Ibid., 95, employing Wordsworth's well-known phrase.
88. E.g. Gen. 2:8–3:24; 13:10; Isa. 51:3; 60:13; Ezek. 28:12-19; 36:35; 47:1-12; Joel 2:3; Zech. 14:8; Pss. 36:9-10; 92:13-15; 110:7. On the garden symbolism of the temple, see, for example, M. Dietrich, 'Das biblische Paradies und der babylonische Tempelgarten: Überlegungen zur Lage des Gartens Eden', in B. Ego and B. Janowski (eds), *Das biblische Weltbild und seine altorientalischen Kontexte* (Tübingen: Mohr Siebeck, 2001), 281–323; Stordalen, *Echoes of Eden*; S. R. Shimoff, 'Gardens: From Eden to Jerusalem', *JSJ* 26 (1995), 145–55; L. E. Stager, 'Jerusalem and the Garden of Eden', *EI* 26 (1999), 183–94. On the role of the king as the gardener of (the) god(s), see Wyatt, '"Supposing Him to be the Gardener"', 21–38; idem, 'When Adam Delved: The Meaning of Genesis III 23', *VT* 38 (1988), 117–22.
89. E.g. Isa. 66:6-13; Pss. 6:3-10 (ET vv. 2-9); 91; cf. Job 33:14-30.
90. E.g. *LAE* 48:6-7; cf. *T. Dan* 5:12. For the aligning of the temple and its Eden imagery with mortuary gardens, see especially Wyatt, '"Supposing Him to be the Gardener"', 21–38; cf. Stavrakopoulou, 'Exploring the Garden of Uzza', 1–21.

'magnetic repulsion' between holiness and death which Levenson emphasizes cannot be held to be fully representative of temple ideologies.

Viewed from this perspective, then, the entombing of the temple within certain Persian era biblical traditions claims an ongoing existence for the cultic community, despite the experience of 'death' in the form of both the temple's destruction and the diasporic origins of the incoming worshippers. Within this context of 'restoration', the entombing of the cult place also memorializes the deity within the temple – a deity whose occupation of Jerusalem is in other texts notably marked by the setting of his שם, 'name', in the cult place. Read within its narrative frame, biblical 'name theology' is often understood as a centralizing, deuteronomistic strategy to render Yhwh transcendent and/or aniconic, leaving his temple empty of an 'earthly' divine presence.[91] But juxtaposed with Isa. 56:1-8 and its imaging of the entombed temple, the setting of Yhwh's שם in the temple is rendered a bold assertion of the deity's perpetual occupation of the city, memorialized as an enduring post-mortem name, and marking the metaphorical emergence of the community's deity from the 'death' of cultic destruction and displacement.

While this is not to claim that within those circles giving rise to 'name theology' Yhwh was perceived as a 'dying-and-rising' god,[92] it is to take seriously the multivalent connotations of the term שם – particularly its territorial nuances, which can play an important role in its mortuary cult context. Indeed, this is directly related to the territorial ideology of the inscriptional associations of שם, which is argued to form the more dominant cultural frame of reference for biblical 'name theology'. Sandra Richter proposes that the biblical expression לשכן שמו שם (and its related forms) reflects a borrowed East Semitic idiom familiar from Mesopotamian texts and inscriptions, and derived from Akkadian

---

91. For detailed discussions of this view, see T. N. D. Mettinger, *The Dethronement of Sabaoth: Studies in the Shem and Kabod Theologies* (ConBOT, 18; Lund: Gleerup, 1982); M. Keller, *Untersuchungen zur deuteronomistischen Namenstheologie* (BBB, 105; Weinheim: Beltz Athenäum, 1996); cf. I. Wilson, *Out of the Midst of the Fire: Divine Presence in Deuteronomy* (SBLDS, 151; Atlanta, GA: Scholars Press, 1995), and the literature detailed in nn. 93, 94.

92. Though this is not to discount the possibility that the 'death' and 'burial' of the deity was a mythic aspect of some cults of Yhwh – a possibility I intend to explore in a separate publication. References to the burial of deities include *KTU* 1.6 i 15-18 (Baal) and *KAI* 277:8-9 (an unnamed deity). Certainly, there are considerable problems of definition and methodology with the 'dying-and-rising' paradigm (particularly in its Frazerian form), as also there are with some critiques of this model. But the claim that 'Yahweh does not die, even figuratively' (M. S. Smith, *The Early History of God: Yahweh and the Other Deities in Ancient Israel* [2nd edn; Grand Rapids, MI: Eerdmans, 2002], 204), is likely overstated. For a recent re-evaluation of the 'dying-and-rising' paradigm, including a detailed discussion of the 'deaths' of Osiris, Dumuzi/Tammuz, Melqart and Adonis, see Mettinger, *The Riddle of Resurrection*.

šuma šakānu, 'place the name', employed to describe the setting up of an inscribed monument proclaiming territorial occupation and ownership. Thus in setting his שם in Jerusalem, Yhwh claims the place as his own and establishes and exhibits his 'name' or 'reputation' upon it, just as an imperial conqueror sets up a monumental inscription, exhibiting his occupation of a newly acquired territory.[93]

Richter's proposal makes good sense of the land ideology of Deuteronomy and its related traditions. But the similarly territorialist connotations of land-staking, long-lived endurance and monumental memorialization conveyed by the term שם in its West Semitic mortuary settings are unlikely to have been lost on the scribes for whom 'name theology' was a key concern.[94] Thus, by asserting the presence of his שם in the temple, Yhwh's occupation of Jerusalem is powerfully displayed in a 'memorialized' form that evokes both imperial displays of land appropriation (setting up monumental inscriptions) and ancestral manifestations of territoriality (perpetuating the presence of the dead).[95] This is, of course, reminiscent of the role of memorialized Torah in the conquest traditions, as discussed in Chapter 3.[96]

Though the imperial trappings of the building and ideology of the new temple have long been recognized, the sanctuary's 'entombing' within certain traditions also plays a crucial mytho-symbolic part in its biblical imaging. The coalescence of temple and tomb grants the temple cult a territorial efficacy akin to that of the dead. Jerusalem is claimed as Yhwh's own and distanced from the dead of the city – including those of the royal ancestral cult, whom Yhwh displaces (and perhaps even replaces) in the newly centralized cult on Zion. The extent to which

---

93. S. L. Richter, *The Deuteronomistic History and the Name Theology: lešakken šemô šam in the Bible and the Ancient Near East* (BZAW, 318; Berlin: de Gruyter, 2001), esp. 36–40, 199–217. Going beyond Richter's interpretation, and in agreement with Victor Hurowitz in his review of Richter's book (*JHS* 5 [2004–05], available at http://www.arts.ualberta.ca/JHS/reviews/review157.htm), the notion of 'establishing a reputation', a secondary meaning of 'placing a name', also appears to be at play in the biblical texts, complementing the imaging of Yhwh as an imperial conqueror.

94. The West Semitic and East Semitic nuances of 'placing a name' are held together comfortably by Diana Edelman in 'God Rhetoric: Reconceptualizing YHWH Sebaot as YHWH Elohim in the Hebrew Bible', in E. Ben Zvi, D. Edelman and F. Polak (eds), *A Palimpsest: Rhetoric, Ideology, Stylistics and Language Relating to Persian Israel* (Piscataway, NJ: Gorgias Press, 2009), 89–108. She argues that 'name theology' is to be related to the tradition concerning the placement of the tablets of the law in the ark in the temple, which in its own turn is to be related to the writing and promotion of 'Torah theology' in the Persian era. Hurowitz ('Review') touches on similar ideas with reference to an unpublished paper by John Van Seters.

95. In this context, note also the interrelation of kings and standing stones in 1 Sam. 15:12; 2 Sam. 8:3; 18:18; cf. 2 Kgs 23:17.

96. On the role of the temple cult as 'landlord', see the discussion in Chapter 6.

this mythic-symbolic (re-)presentation of the temple, and its accompanying doing-away with the dead, reflect the likely historical realities and mechanics of Yehudite territorialism is uncertain. But some tentative conclusions about the likely context of this distinctively Jerusalemite, Yehudite ideology can be drawn here.

The intersecting of temple and tomb seems to mark a biblical move against certain practices of the household cult, including ancestor veneration and the care of the dead, in favour of a temple cult with a monopoly on the ritual exchange between the realms of the divine and the non-divine.[97] It also goes some way to explain in part why in the Hebrew Bible, Jerusalem appears not to house its own tomb cult: not because the dead were necessarily considered ritually incompatible with the temple, nor only that the royal dead were perceived to be religio-politically impotent, nor even simply that household cults of the dead risked compromising the emergent monotheism of the new Yhwh sanctuary, but because the idealized, innovative religion promoted for Jerusalem in the Hebrew Bible sought to present the new temple as the *only* localized, memorialized cult place for Yhwh worshippers, be they in Jerusalem or among the diaspora.[98] This spatial elasticity rendered the temple a cosmic landmark of local proportions, as well as a localized landmark of cosmic proportions. But the tomb symbolism of this innovative temple cult also re-presented the sacred localities of the familiar dead, competing with the memory-markers and memory-makers of family tombs and graves which played such a vital role in constructions of social identity and place. In doing so, the entombed temple likely risked destabilizing or even disabling the perceived potency of the local dead, particularly – if not primarily – in their territorial functions.[99]

It is thus in its very placement and symbolism in the land, and not simply in its

---

97. Cf. Bloch-Smith, *Judahite Burial Practices*, 131–32; Blenkinsopp, 'Politics of Post-Mortem Existence', 1–16; Halpern, 'Late Israelite Astronomies', 334–45; Brett, *Decolonizing God*, 47; *contra* Schmidt, *Israel's Beneficent Dead*, 291.

98. Like Abraham, David purchases a territorial plot from an indigenous inhabitant of the land, but the site is to become a cult place of Yhwh, not of the Davidic dead (2 Sam. 24:18-25).

99. As Jan Assmann observes: '[The] material world . . . is of social import, too: an object's value, its price, its significance as a status symbol, are social factors. Any kind of human association fosters such propensity for localization. Each of them, eager to consolidate themselves as a group, will strive to create for themselves specific places that are not merely arena of their interactions, but symbols of their identity and reference points for their recollections. Memory requires places, it tends towards localization . . . Group and space form a symbolical yet substantial communion. Even if separated from their original place, a group will adhere to it by symbolically reproducing the sacred localities' (J. Assmann, 'Cultural Memory: Script, Recollection, and Political Identity in Early Civilizations', Historiography East and West 1 [2003], 154–77, here 166; trans. of *Das kulturelle Gedächtnis*, 29–48, here 38–39.

solitary centrality, that the new temple of Yhwh attested to its efficacy – cultic, social, political and territorial – for the living. And it is for this reason that even in the biblical traditions, the territorialism of the dead was perpetuated in the appropriation and adaptation of symbols and aspects of their veneration, care and social function within the land claims of the accepted members of Yehudite Jerusalem. Just as the graves of the dead could mark an ongoing territorial occupation of place, so too the temple of Yhwh, entombed and memorialized in Jerusalem, sanctioned and safeguarded territorial acquisition for the new community.

Chapter 6

THE CREATION OF A NATION

In staking a claim to the nominated homeland, the biblical story of the past holds in dynamic tension two dominant territorial claims: the assertion that the land is taken over by Israel, and the assertion that the land is ancestral. According to the first of these claims, Israel is by nature a group of colonizing incomers, liberated from a foreign land; according to the second, Israel is in essence an indigenous people, whose ancestors settled to make the land their descendants' own. Within the biblical frame these seemingly conflicted territorial strategies are ostensibly smoothed and reconciled by the emphatic and centralizing claim that Yhwh is the ultimate agent of land.

In its broadest terms, this tension and its theological smoothing is evident in the sequential pairing of the patriarchal and exodus/conquest foundation myths in Genesis–Judges, so that the land taken by the incoming Israelites is indeed their ancestral heritage.[1] The ideological function of these twinned myths – fashioned into centrist shape by the overarching presence of Yhwh as landowner – is well illustrated in Ezra 2:59-63 (closely paralleled in Neh. 7:61-65), a narrative listing groups incoming from Babylonia to claim a place in Yehud. In this text, the status of particular families (including priestly groups) is under question: though they are accepted as 'returning' members of the golah community, their ancestral households and genealogical descent remain uncertain; can they really claim to 'belong' to Israel? As the ultimate mediator of land, it is Yhwh who decides – represented in this text by the centralizing role of the temple, the genealogical lists and rituals of which are employed to discern the legitimacy of (some of) these incomers (Ezra 2:63).[2]

However, despite the relatively cohesive biblical framing of Israel and the

---

1. Cf. Pardes, *Biography of Ancient Israel*, 106–7; see also Weinfeld, *Promise of Land*, 1–21.
2. The extensive use of genealogical and territorial lists in the books of Joshua, Ezra, Nehemiah and Chronicles to catalogue ancestral lands is of course suggestive of an inter-textual attempt to align the incomers of Yehud with their incoming 'ancestors' (cf. Blenkinsopp, *Ezra-Nehemiah*, 83–84). On the ideological dynamics of the portrayal of incomers in Ezra, see particularly B. Becking, 'Continuity and Community: The Belief System of the Book of Ezra', in B. Becking and M. C. A. Korpel (eds), *The Crisis of Israelite*

land, the key traditions explored in the present book nonetheless suggest that a 'harmonized' ideology of land appropriation – in which Yhwh is cast as agent – is not altogether sufficient in establishing or contesting territorial claims. Rather, dual appeal is repeatedly made to the notion that land might be acquired by incomers or descendants by employing, appropriating and/or supplanting 'traditional' land-claiming strategies bound up with the territorial dead. It is in this way that incomers (representing the interests of the biblical writers) are 'indigenized'. As Howard Morphy comments:

> People do not move in and take over a country by imposing new myths: rather they move in and act as if *they* are taken over by the new country. This makes the political struggle for land no less intense, but it preserves the illusion of continuity between people, place, and ancestral past.[3]

In the dominant traditions of the Hebrew Bible, these 'indigenizing' strategies of land-claiming ultimately have a transformative impact on the land envisaged, so that the 'traditional' mortuary landscape is remapped, and the dead who mark it are re-placed.

Remapping the Land

The biblical imaging of the tomb at Machpelah as a centralized ancestral burial site in one sense renders it the heartland of the remapped mortuary landscape. Strongly resisting the 'traditional' network of households, ancestors and land assumed in other traditions within and beyond the Hebrew Bible, Machpelah marks an exclusive, solitary and indigenous claim to the territories 'inherited' by the biblical Israel. Though other cult sites might assert as their ancestral endorsement the graves of the potent, territorial dead (e.g. Gen. 35:8, 19-20; 50:5, 7-11; Josh 24:32), their claims – and especially those of Bethel – are firmly contested in Torah by the prioritization of the patriarchal burial ground at Machpelah.[4]

The tomb is thus presented in Genesis as an uncontested manifestation of

---

Religion: Transformation of Religious Tradition in Exilic and Post-Exilic Times (OTS, 42; Leiden: Brill, 1999), 256–75.

3. H. Morphy, 'Landscape and the Reproduction of the Ancestral Past', in E. Hirsch and M. O'Hanlon (eds), *The Anthropology of Landscape: Perspectives on Place and Space* (Oxford: Clarendon Press, 1995), 184–209, here 186 (emphasis original).

4. For the possibility that the Jacob myths might have functioned as an autonomous foundation legend, see Albert de Pury's discussion (broadly in line with his 'inclusive' reading of the priestly agenda) in 'The Jacob Story and the Beginnings of the Formation of the Pentateuch', in T. B. Dozeman and K. Schmid (eds), *A Farewell to the Yahwist? The Composition of the Pentateuch in Recent European Interpretation* (SBLSS, 34; Atlanta, GA: Society of Biblical Literature, 2006), 51–65.

indigenization. James Cox describes the three components essential to constructs of an indigenous identity: identification with a locality that marks belonging to a place, an emphasis on lineage and kinship ties expressed through localized or regional societies, and a socio-religious focus on ancestors.[5] For those (ac)claiming Abraham as their ancestor, the homeland is duly marked at Machpelah by place, kin and the ancestral dead. In the Hebrew Bible, this indigenizing, centralized tomb renders all 'Israel' connected not only to its ancestral land, but to one another; the biblical community (whether real or imagined) is to assume a distinctive social solidarity and common cultural memory on the basis of a shared – but nonetheless exclusive – descent from the ancestors entombed in the land.[6] In this way and at this place, an Abrahamic claim to land is sited and cited in the world created in the Hebrew Bible.[7] This is, therefore, an idealized tomb in an idealized mortuary landscape, a 'legitimating memory center'[8] around which social memories about the past are created and social ideals about the future are mediated.[9]

This idealization of a territorial tomb is thus at the same time a mythologization of the past and its landscape – of a sort similar to that described by Christopher Tilley, who argues that:

> It is through making material reference to the past that identification with place occurs through the medium of 'traditional' material culture and representations of life-styles, urban and rural, that no longer exist.[10]

---

5. J. L. Cox, *From Primitive to Indigenous: The Academic Study of Indigenous Religions* (Aldershot: Ashgate, 2007), 158. Though Cox's study is focused on present-day indigenous religions, many of his findings bear upon biblical and scholarly constructions of socio-religious identities.

6. On the role of shared descent in 'remembering' the past, see particularly E. Zerubavel, *Time Maps: Collective Memory and the Social Shape of the Past* (Chicago: University of Chicago Press, 2003), esp. 55–81.

7. Adopting and adapting the phraseology of Douglas Charles and Jane Buikstra's essay, 'Siting, Sighting, and Citing the Dead', in H. Silverman and D. Small (eds), *The Space and Place of Death* (Archaeological Papers of the American Anthropological Association, 11; Arlington, VA: American Anthropological Association, 2002), 13–25.

8. A phrase borrowed from A. Orta, 'Burying the Past: Locality, Lived History and Death in an Aymara Ritual of Remembrance', *Cultural Anthropology* 17.4 (2002), 471–511, here 490.

9. Drawing on the description of mortuary culture offered by M. S. Chesson, 'Embodied Memories of Place and People: Death and Society in an Early Urban Community', in M. S. Chesson (ed.), *Social Memory, Identity, and Death: Anthropological Perspectives on Mortuary Rituals* (Archaeological Papers of the American Anthropological Association, 10; Arlington, VA: American Anthropological Institute, 2001) 100–113, here 110.

10. Tilley, 'Identity, Place, Landscape and Heritage', 14; cf. Bloch, *Placing the Dead*, 72; Parker Pearson, 'The Powerful Dead', 207.

Though the agrarian-urbanism of Yehudite society held a certain amount in common with the pre-Persian era societies of Israel and Judah, the biblical notion of a land worked by a network of interrelated ancestral households, each with its own field and tomb, is likely an idealized, politicized view of a contested landscape peopled by a variety of communities.[11] And so it is that at the biblical Machpelah, the 'traditional' mortuary culture of the ancestral dead is mythologized in such a schematized manner that the past and its landscape are ostensibly centralized.

This centralization, however, arguably has its limitations – despite assumptions to the contrary. Baruch Halpern suggests that the biblical promotion of a 'national' tomb site at Hebron would indeed 'centralize the elite ancestral cult' without (supposedly) compromising the temple cult of Yhwh in Jerusalem.[12] But while he here assumes the nature of this potential compromise would be a matter of ritual impurity – hence the distancing of the ancestral dead from the temple – it is also possible that the biblical centralization of the dead at Hebron would equally pitch the place as a cultic (and economic) competitor to Jerusalem (if a functioning 'ancestral' cult site at Hebron was perceived to exist during this period), compromising the asserted cultic exclusivity of Jerusalem.[13] Indeed, by the Greco-Roman era, the tomb of the patriarchs likely performed a role as a 'supplementary temple'.[14]

The project of centralization might also be further compromised by its limiting *localization*, potentially rendering the mortuary landscape of a biblical

---

11. For an overview of the socio-economic dynamics of Yehud, see Grabbe, *History of the Jews and Judaism I*, 189–208; see also Pastor, *Land and Economy*, 12–46. For biblical portrayals of an agrarian society, and their various regulations for the protection of the farmstead, see particularly E. W. Davies, 'Land: Its Rights and Privileges', in R. E. Clements (ed.), *The World of Ancient Israel: Sociological, Anthropological and Political Perspectives* (Cambridge: Cambridge University Press, 1989), 349–70, esp. 358–63; Habel, *The Land Is Mine*, 97–114; see also P. Guillaume, *Land and Calendar: The Priestly Document from Genesis 1 to Joshua 18* (LHBOTS, 391; New York: T&T Clark, 2009).

12. Halpern, 'Late Israelite Astronomies', 344.

13. For the literary-ideological tension between marginality and exclusivity inherent in Jerusalem's projected post-monarchic isolation in the biblical literature, see C. Mitchell, '"How Lonely Sits the City": Identity and the Creation of History', in J. L. Berquist (ed.), *Approaching Yehud: New Approaches to the Study of the Persian Period* (SBLSS, 50; Atlanta, GA: Society of Biblical Literature, 2007), 71–83.

14. Lightstone, *Commerce of the Sacred*, 61. For the possibility that the Jerusalem temple was already a pilgrimage site in the Persian era (though note this is a case constructed primarily on the basis of biblical texts), see M. D. Knowles, *Centrality Practiced: Jerusalem in the Religious Practice of Yehud and the Diaspora in the Persian Period* (Atlanta, GA: Society of Biblical Literature, 2006), 77–103. Hamilton (*Genesis 18–50*, 136) misses the point in his claim that 'God has no concern about burying the patriarchs privately in an unmarked grave as he did Moses . . . for there is no danger, as there was with Moses, that after the demise of the patriarchs a cult of the dead would flourish in their memory and honor. To none of the patriarchs did the people of Israel owe immediate debt as they did Moses'.

6. *The Creation of a Nation*

territorialism too parochial for some – particularly, perhaps, for diaspora communities.[15] Mario Liverani has raised similar objections to the overall efficacy of the patriarchal foundation myth as an overarching ideology of land occupation:

> The sagas of the 'patriarchs' offered an inadequate legitimation, because they were too remote and were localized only in a few symbolic places (tombs, sacred trees). A much more powerful prototype of the conquest of the land was created by the story of exodus [. . .] from Egypt, under the guidance of Moses, and of military conquest, under the leadership of Joshua.[16]

While the 'symbolic places' of the ancestors may combine to render the biblical portrayal of an unknown homeland and its sacred topography a more familiar landscape to diaspora groups,[17] the literary imaging of the wider spatio-territorial 'promised land' offers a construct of place (and 'home') familiar to those within and beyond its imagined delimitations – and the 'lost' grave of Moses at its edge marks its occupation for 'all Israel'. In this way, the potential limitations of too localized an ancestral tomb are countered and complemented by the mortuary marking of a broader landscape: if the patriarchal tomb centralizes the territorial focal point of the land, Moses' burial on the boundary of the promised land both 'nationalizes' the land beyond an ostensibly Yehudite frame and 'internationalizes' the mortuary landscape by rendering it a homeland in the world – and thus a land at the edges of which the diaspora dead are similarly buried.[18]

---

15. As was argued in Chapter 2, the 'homeland' image constructed by the portrayal of the tomb at Machpelah in Genesis is too exclusive and meaningful to render it a paradigm for burial easily accommodated by diaspora groups (unlike, perhaps, Moses' burial at the edge of the promised land). However, as inclusivist readers of the patriarchal stories have inferred, Abraham's negotiations with the Hittites may have been read as an encouragement to settle without conflict in a land of 'foreigners'.

16. Liverani, *Israel's History*, 277.

17. As James Snead and Robert Preucel observe: 'The organization of space through the imposition of a system of place names and corresponding references can be seen as a widespread cultural response to living within an otherwise uncontrollable world' (J. E. Snead and R. W. Preucel, 'The Ideology of Settlement: Ancestral Keres Landscapes in the Northern Rio Grande', in W. Ashmore and A. B. Knapp [eds], *Archaeologies of Landscape: Contemporary Perspectives* [Oxford: Blackwell, 1999], 169–97, here 172). Joe Cleary notes a similar strategy in Israeli Hebrew literature of the twentieth century, which initially was often 'largely involved in the project of taking imaginative possession of what was ideologically the ancient Biblical "homeland" but which was for settlers newly arrived from Europe a strange and alien landscape' (J. Cleary, *Literature, Partition and the Nation State: Culture and Conflict in Ireland, Israel and Palestine* [Cambridge: Cambridge University Press, 2002], here 81).

18. On being 'at home in the world', note Jonathan Z. Smith's observation: 'It is, perhaps, an irony that home is most frequently perceived as meaningful from the perspective of distance . . . Home is not, from such a point of view, best understood as the-place-where-

It is important to be clear, however, that the biblical myth of migration and conquest need not subvert the construct of an indigenous people asserted by the Hebrew Bible's mortuary landscaping. Indeed, as James Cox has shown, to claim to be indigenous is often also to prove adaptable to 'outside' – and particularly colonial – dynamics: within an indigenous society, claims to place can come to combine a migration or conquest myth with a tradition of an ancestral land, powerfully asserting that the ancestors first occupied the land before they came to possess it.[19] Thus, according to the biblical story of the past, just as the conquest generation took the land of their ancestors, so too the ancestors themselves had colonized that land before marking it with their tomb and making it their own.

The territorial function of Moses' burial place at the edge of the promised land thus appropriates methods of 'traditional' land-marking bound up with the ancestral dead. But along with its accompanying conquest myth, the appropriative strategy of the Mosaic burial tradition does not subvert the potency of the indigenous, territorial dead, but rather displaces the meanings associated with burial places to new locations.[20] One of these locations is of course the 'lost' tomb of Deut. 34:6, but the other is monumentalized, memorialized Torah, which in the books of Deuteronomy and Joshua takes on the function of the territorial dead by expressing and promulgating claims to land.[21] The setting up of copied Torah memorials (imitating the mortuary-territorial functions of standing stones) represents a centralized but replicated method of marking and colonizing the land, again broadening the territorial scope of the mortuary landscape beyond the fixed and more localized patriarchal tomb in Hebron. But beyond this too, the biblical imaging of memorialized Torah ultimately eclipses the territorial efficacy of both the dead and their tombs by indexing instead the Jerusalem temple and its teaching as the centre of the landscape.[22]

As Deut. 32:46-47 emphatically asserts, obedience to Torah is the means by

---

I-was-born or the-place-where-I-live. Home is the place where memories are "housed"' (J. Z. Smith, *To Take Place: Toward Theory in Ritual* [Chicago: University of Chicago Press, 1987], 29). It is significant, then, that according to the ideologies most dominant in the Hebrew Bible, that 'house' is the House of Yhwh in Jerusalem.

19. Cox, *From Primitive to Indigenous*, 137.

20. Drawing on the discussion of the colonial impact on 'traditional' landscapes in nineteenth-century Ghana in S. E. Greene, *Sacred Sites and the Colonial Encounter: A History of Meaning and Memory in Ghana* (Bloomington, IN: Indiana University Press, 2002), here 64.

21. As argued in Chapter 3.

22. Indeed, though in the Hebrew Bible the priests and Levites (with their special dynastic claim to Moses and Aaron) are 'landless', they nonetheless have Torah – and Yhwh (cf. Num. 18:20-24; Josh. 13:33; 14:4-5). On the question of why priestly descent is traced back to Aaron, rather than Moses, see S. D. Kunin, *We Think What We Eat: Neo-Structuralist Analysis of Israelite Food Rules and Other Cultural and Textual Practices* (JSOTS, 412; London: T&T Clark, 2004), 165–66; cf. F. M. Cross, 'The Priestly Houses

which Israel takes and keeps the land, generation after generation. The close biblical aligning of Torah with temple (primarily by means of a pervasive centralizing ideology) renders the Jerusalem temple the mediator of land through cultic exchange, socio-religious obedience and community membership. Indeed, several texts dealing with the allocation of land to incomers 'returning' to Yehud not only present land distribution as an activity controlled by temple and Torah, but also specifically present territorial plots as 'ancestral'.[23] To a certain extent, this can be understood as the legacy of widespread ideas about the territoriality of the patron deity of a temple city and its satellite villages and farmsteads (akin to the patrimonialism of Ugarit), coupled with the more topically politicized biblical portrayal of Yhwh as an imperial landowner.[24] But it is also likely shaped by an appropriation of functions and meanings closely and 'traditionally' associated with the burial places of the dead.

Psalm 16:2-6 is similarly suggestive of the appropriation of functions performed by the territorial dead by a more centralized, exclusive cult of Yhwh. In vv. 3-4 of this difficult text, the presence of the powerful dead appears to be acknowledged (קדושים אשר בארץ), but the poet vows he will not pour out 'blood' libations to them nor invoke their names.[25] Instead, and employing territorial language familiar from other texts, in vv. 5-6 he denotes Yhwh as his 'allotted share' (מנת חלקי) and land-giver:

> The boundary lines (חבלים) have fallen for me in pleasant places
> Yea, I have a beautiful inheritance (נחלה) (Ps. 16:6)

This brief text thus appears to attribute to Yhwh a 'traditional' territorialism elsewhere associated with the dead. Though seemingly present, the dead are nonetheless displaced. It is the agency of Yhwh, not the ancestors, which brings about land.[26] It is for this reason that the Jerusalem temple itself is 'entombed' in Isa. 56:3-5, rendering the centralized cult a place of territorial mediation, offering its adherents in Yehud and beyond a memorialized stake in the city itself.[27] But

---

of Early Israel', *Canaanite Myth and Hebrew Epic: Essays in the History of the Religion of Israel* (Cambridge, MA: Harvard University Press, 1973), 195–215.

23. E.g. Ezek. 47:13-23; cf. Josh. 19:51. On the issue of temple lands and their acquisition and distribution, see further Blenkinsopp, 'Did the Second Jerusalemite Temple Possess Land?', 61–68.

24. As described by Schloen, *House of the Father*. See also the discussion in Chapter 1.

25. On Ps. 16:4, see M. S. Smith, 'The Invocation of Deceased Ancestors in Psalm 49:12c', *JBL* 112 (1993), 105–7; see also Spronk, *Beatific Afterlife*, 249, 334–38.

26. See also van der Toorn, *Family Religion*, 210–11; cf. Lewis, *Cults of the Dead*, 166.

27. As proposed in Chapter 5.

in displacing the dead, the entombing of temple also forms a part of a broader biblical doing-away with the dead – and a recasting of Yhwh himself.

Re-Placing the Dead

The memorializing of Torah and the entombing of temple are not only acts of centralization, but manifestations of 'remembering' too: as was argued in earlier chapters, the ritual community collectively remembers Torah by means of the standing stones in Deut. 27:1-8; Josh. 4:6-7, 20-24; 8:30-35; 24:1-27, and is cultically memorialized in Jerusalem and its temple in Isa. 56:1-8 and Neh. 2:20. As Yosef Hayim Yerushalmi has famously demonstrated, 'remembering' is pivotal in the Hebrew Bible and post-biblical Judaisms.[28] This is exemplified by Torah's constant renewal as both 'teaching' and 'tradition',[29] which within a biblical frame (and particularly in Deuteronomy) is 'codified' as a transition from 'a tradition of living to one of learning'.[30] It is thus significant that the repeated biblical promotion of Yhwh's territorial agency is also central to this 'learning to remember':

> Remember (זכר) the word that Moses the servant of Yhwh commanded you, saying, 'Yhwh your God is providing you a place of rest, and will give you this land'. (Josh. 1:13)

'Remembering' Yhwh's role as land-giver is not simply to commemorate a tradition of land acquisition, but to perpetuate life in that land generation after generation by forming what Paul Connerton aptly terms 'a solidarity with the fathers' (cf. Deut. 4:9; 31:12-13; 32:12-13).[31] However, the act and exhibition of remembering is not exclusive to Israel, for Yhwh too is called to 'remember' his role as the agent of both land and lineage:

> Remember Abraham, Isaac, and Israel, your servants, how you swore to them by your own self, saying to them, 'I will multiply your descendants like the stars of heaven, and all this land that I have promised I will give to your descendants, and they shall inherit it forever.' (Exod. 32:13)

> I will remember my covenant with Jacob; I will remember also my covenant with Isaac and also my covenant with Abraham, and I will remember the land. (Lev. 26:42)

---

28. Yerushalmi, *Zakhor*, 5.
29. Ibid., 109.
30. Assmann, *Religion and Cultural Memory*, 16–21, here 19.
31. Connerton, *How Societies Remember*, 46.

In characterizing the relationship between Yhwh and Israel in this way,[32] the biblical portrayal of 'remembering' is pitched as 'remembering in common' – a collective activity essential to the social cohesion produced by and through the creation of cultural memory.[33] But more significantly, it is also sharply reminiscent of the social interrelation of the living and the dead, articulated through the memorializing – 'remembering' – practices performed to perpetuate their name. Consequently, the assertion of Yhwh's territoriality in these appropriative terms, combined with an emphasis on the exclusivity of the relationship of 'remembering' that binds Yhwh, Israel and the land, effectively subverts the relationship between the dead and the living – and thereby encourages the forgetting of the dead. Indeed, in Deut. 5:3, the ancestors are explicitly disinherited from the relationship between Yhwh and Israel:

> Not with our ancestors did Yhwh make this covenant, but with us, the living, all of us here today.

The connection between the exclusivity of cult and the disinheriting of the dead likely reflects in part the changes in Yhwh's own household in Jerusalem during the Persian period: along with so-called emergent monotheism[34] came the relegation and/or dismissal of the divine members of the household of which Yhwh was head (among whom were the Davidic dead),[35] and an increasing intolerance of the deities and the dead of other sanctuaries, including those of Bethel.[36] According to the biblical perspective, these changes within Yhwh's household required changes in the households of his worshippers, so that there too the dead were to

---

32. Cf. Yerushalmi, *Zakhor*, 5. Note that '*all* Israel' is in view here, for diaspora groups are also instructed to 'remember' (Jer. 51:50; cf. Ps. 137:1-6), just as Yhwh is called to 'remember' the exiles (Neh. 1:8-10).

33. Citing Connerton, *How Societies Remember*, 17.

34. On the problems of the term 'monotheism', see A. P. Hayman, 'Monotheism – A Misused Word in Jewish Studies?', *JJS* 42 (1991), 1–15. On this shift in Jerusalem temple ideology, see in particular the essays collected in D. V. Edelman (ed.), *The Triumph of Elohim: From Yahwisms to Judaisms* (CBET, 13; Kampen: Kok Pharos, 1995); see also W. Dietrich and M. A. Klopfenstein (eds), *Ein Gott allein? JHWH-Verehrung und biblischer Monotheismus im Kontext der israelitischen und altorientalischen Religionsgeschichte* (OBO, 139; Fribourg: Universitätsverlag; Göttingen: Vandenhoeck & Ruprecht, 1994); M. Krebernik and J. van Oorschot (eds), *Polytheismus und Monotheismus in den Religionen des Vorderen Orients* (AOAT, 298; Münster: Ugarit-Verlag, 2002); M. Oeming and K. Schmid (eds), *Der eine Gott und die Götter. Polytheismus und Monotheismus im antiken Israel* (AThANT, 82; Zürich: Theologischer Verlag, 2003).

35. On the divine household and its correspondence with the human household, see Schloen, *House of the Father*, 349–57; Smith, *Origins of Biblical Monotheism*, 54–60.

36. Note that the emphasis on the exclusivity of the Jerusalem temple cult sought to displace other Yhwhs, too – including Yhwh of Samaria and Yhwh of Bethel.

be 'retired' from active service and represented instead by the 'national' (and supposedly more innocuous) ancestors buried in Hebron.[37]

But to disempower the dead and appropriate their lands is necessarily also to recast Yhwh as a territorial ancestor. This is evident in certain texts in which the deity is portrayed as the ancestor of the people Israel:

> You are descendants (בנים) of Yhwh your God. You must not cut yourselves or shave the front of your heads for the dead. For you are a people holy to Yhwh your God . . . (Deut. 14:1-2a)[38]

That בנים here in this verse should be appropriately rendered 'descendants' (rather than 'sons') is evident in the clear contrast drawn between Yhwh and the dead; this is not the language of rhetoric or poetic metaphor,[39] nor even the familial construct of the relationship between deity and worshipper, or suzerain and vassal,[40] but a claim of sharp distinction. Yhwh is pitched here as the only ancestor for whom cult should be performed – a demand for exclusivity couched in the terms of 'fabricated descent' to render Israel Yhwh's firstborn son (cf. Exod. 4:22; Jer. 31:9; Hos. 11:1).[41]

The biblical imaging of Yhwh as Israel's ancestor has been taken by some as a vehicle to describe the ethical nature of this exclusive loyalty to Yhwh,[42] a position adopted by Christopher Wright in his suggestion that a landholder's responsibility to his field was 'a reflex of his primary responsibility to his God'.[43] But this is to misunderstand the significance of its territorial connotations. To

---

37. In the Hebrew Bible this is one of several ways in which the Jerusalem temple extends its reach into the culture of the household. Others include legislation for circumcision and Shabbat, the casting of certain festivals (including Passover) as 'centralized' activities, and the casting of Yhwh as a 'personal' deity. On these aspects of the household cult, see further Meyers, 'Household Religion', esp. 123–30; Albertz, 'Personal Piety', esp. 143–45. For perspectives on the biblical strategy to bring the household cult into line with temple policies, see Blenkinsopp, 'Deuteronomy and the Politics of Post-Mortem Existence', 1–16; Halpern, 'Jerusalem and the Lineages', 11–107.

38. Cf. Lev. 19:27-28; 21:5. On these forms of body modification as mourning rites (usually – though not appropriately – termed 'laceration and shaving' rites), see the discussions in Olyan, *Biblical Mourning*, 111–23, and S. Niditch, *'My Brother Esau is a Hairy Man': Hair and Identity in Ancient Israel* (Oxford: Oxford University Press, 2008), esp. 99–112.

39. *Contra* G. von Rad, *Deuteronomy: A Commentary* (trans. D. Barton; OTM; London: SCM Press, 1966), 101.

40. Cf. D. J. McCarthy, 'Notes on the Love of God in Deuteronomy and the Father-Son Relationship between Yahweh and Israel', *CBQ* 27 (1965), 144–47.

41. Borrowing Mary Douglas' phrase in *Jacob's Tears*, 190, to describe the adoption language employed of Israel's divine sonship.

42. Schmidt, *Israel's Beneficent Dead*, 291, following Brichto, 'Kin, Cult, Land and Afterlife', esp. 49–52.

43. Wright, *God's People in God's Land*, 158.

6. *The Creation of a Nation*

claim descent from the deity is to assert a claim to territory, as is suggested in Jer. 3:19 (cf. Deut. 32:8-9):[44]

> I thought how I would set you among my descendants (בנים)
> and give you a desirable land –
> the most beautiful inheritance (נחלה) of the host of nations;
> and I thought you would call me 'My Ancestor' (אבי)
> and would not turn from following me.

Within its biblical, 'covenantal' context, the divine gifting of land from a figure designated אב may well mimic the familial framing of West Asian suzerains' land grants,[45] but the language of an inherited plot (נחלה), so closely related in the Hebrew Bible to the ancestors, is in the context of Jer. 3:19 more indicative of the ancestralization of Yhwh, as is evident in Deut. 14:1.[46] Indeed, to render Yhwh the ancestor of Israel is to endorse the deity's enduring territoriality in the most persuasive of terms – those of the territorial dead.

But Yhwh's biblical role as an ancestor to Israel inevitably impacts on the dead, for Yhwh is a jealous god, intolerant of competitors (Exod. 20:3-5; 34:14; Deut. 5:9; 32:19), who will not share cult with the dead (Deut. 26:13-14). Thus as ancestor *par excellence*, the biblical Yhwh both subverts and surpasses the divine promise of lineage and land made to the patriarchs by claiming in Hos. 2:1 (ET 1:10):

> The number of the descendants of Israel shall be like the sand of the sea, which can be neither measured nor numbered; and in the place where it was said to them, 'You are not my kin (עמי)', it shall be said to them 'Descendants of the Living God' (בני אל־חי).[47]

The dead are thus replaced, displaced, disempowered. In further seeking to achieve this, one of the strategies employed in the more polemically charged texts renders the dead mute: their oracles are to be silenced, their mediators cut off, their wisdom unlearned (Lev. 19:31; 20:6, 27; Deut. 18:9-14; 1 Sam.

---

44. If Deut. 32:8-9 should image Elyon and the seventy sons of El (as is often suggested), it would offer a further mythic endorsement of the interrelation of divine descent and territorial gain.

45. Weinfeld, *Promise of Land*, 247–48.

46. In this way, the role of Yhwh of Jerusalem as *paterfamilias* is maintained, despite the dismantling of the divine household: he is bound now as ancestral father not to the living and dead kings, but to Israel, who will 'inherit' Yhwh's territorial portion (e.g. Exod. 15:17; Isa. 57:13; cf. Jer. 16:18).

47. Cf. Gen. 22:17; 32:12; 15:5; 16:10; 1 Kgs 3:8. For the designation 'Living God', see Chapter 5, n. 1.

28:3-25). Their muteness is pointedly contrasted with the oracular written oration of Yhwh's prophetic scribe, which is shared among the initiated:

> Bind up the testimony, seal the teaching among my disciples . . . Now if people should say to you, 'Consult the ghost-raisers and the knowers who chirp and mutter; should not a people consult their gods – the dead on behalf of the living, for teaching and for testimony?' Surely, those who speak like this will have no dawn! (Isa. 8:16, 18-20)[48]

The silencing of the dead, set against the articulation of Yhwh's teaching, recalls the publication of memorialized Torah in the books of Deuteronomy and Joshua – Mosaic memorials marking the land as mortuary monuments, standing in contrast to the 'mute' stones set up at Bethel by the ancestor Jacob.[49] This contrast points to an ideological emphasis on what Jan Assmann terms *Erinnerungskultur* ('memory-based culture'),[50] an emphasis which in this instance might be described as the prioritization of written and recited Torah over the material agency of the dead – anticipating and shaping in the West a dominant cultural privileging of the written word, rather than material practice, as a preferred vehicle of social communication and memory.[51]

According to the biblical traditions most hostile to the dead, it is the very materiality of the dead which demands they are to be set aside – rather than 'set apart' – by the living. The legislation detailed in Numbers 19 (and emphasized elsewhere) specifies that the corpse is the source of the most contagious of impurities, rendering unclean anyone who comes into contact with (or even within close or enclosed proximity to) a cadaver, bones, or a grave.[52] These texts primarily seek to distance the divine from the dead, imposing the forced

---

48. The designation 'ghost-raisers' for אובות is borrowed from S. Niditch, 'Experiencing the Divine: Heavenly Visits, Earthly Encounters and the Land of the Dead', in F. Stavrakopoulou and J. Barton (eds), *Religious Diversity in Ancient Israel and Judah* (London: T&T Clark, 2010), 11–22, here 21. For further discussion, see H. Rouillard and J. Tropper, 'Vom kanaanäischen Ahnenkult zur Zauberei. Eine Auslegungsgeschichte zu den hebräischen Begriffen ʾwb und ydʿny', *UF* 19 (1987), 235–54. The meaning of the term ידענים is uncertain, so is best rendered 'knowers' in this context (cf. Tropper, *Nekromantie*, 317–19), though it may refer to known ancestors (Nelson, *Deuteronomy*, 233). This term always occurs in parallelism with אוב in the Hebrew Bible (Lev. 19:31; 20:6, 26-27; Deut. 18:11; 1 Sam. 28:3, 9; 2 Kgs 23:24; Isa. 8:19-20; 19:3).

49. Cf. Sonnet, *Book within the Book*, 92. On tomb inscriptions as 'voices beyond the grave', see Lewis, 'How Far Can Texts Take Us?' 180–82.

50. Assmann, *Religion and Cultural Memory*, 87; see also idem, *Das kulturelle Gedächtnis*, 29–86.

51. Cf. Connerton, *How Societies Remember*, 102.

52. See also Lev. 21:1-15; 22:4; Num. 5:2; 6:1-12; 9:6-10; 31:19-24; Deut. 26:13-15; Ezek. 39:11-15; Hagg. 2:12-14; cf. Deut. 21:23.

distinction between the dead and Yhwh in his role as the 'Living God' of the Hebrew Bible, a god whose sacred status is often depicted as wholly incompatible with the dead.[53] Baruch Levine accurately captures the prevailing ideology embodied in these texts:

> The dead have no power, and they are no longer members of the ongoing community. Their exploits during their lifetimes are a source of inspiration and guidance to their descendants, but the community itself looks forward to the future and consigns ancestors to the realm of memory.[54]

A number of scholars endorse this belief that the living existed only in oppositional, dichotomous relation to the dead, and were thus to be kept categorically separate from them.[55] This widespread assumption among moderns demonstrates well the success of this particular biblical strategy to disinherit the dead. Dislocated from the living community and re-placed beyond the bounds of the social group, the dead were (it is claimed) marginalized and rendered harmful pollutants. This separation of the living from the dead is so pervasive in the Hebrew Bible – and arguably within modern scholarship too – that David Wright even opts to classify the corpse a 'non-human' bearer of impurity.[56] A human body is – strikingly, paradoxically – classed as inhuman. The dead are rendered the enemies of the living – as indeed they literally are in those traditions casting the Rephaim as the mythical territorial warriors who are to be displaced from the land.[57]

But biblical texts outlawing the dead offer only a partial and distorted portrait of the environment they claim to represent.[58] As Herbert Niehr comments: 'They form one stream of piety in Yehud which in our eyes seems to be the more dominant one but the reality seems to have been more complex by far'.[59]

---

53. See n. 47.

54. Levine, *Numbers 1–20*, 472–73.

55. E.g. Xella, 'Il "culto dei morti" nell' Antico Testamento', 645–66; Zevit, *Religions of Ancient Israel*, 664.

56. Wright, *Disposal of Impurity*, 115.

57. E.g. Gen. 15:17-21; Deut. 3:8-13. For further discussion, see above, Chapter 3. On the social function of enmity towards the dead in mortuary rituals, see particularly S. Oakdale, 'Forgetting the Dead, Remembering Enemies', in G. F. M. Rakita, J. E. Buikstra, L. A. Beck and S. R. Williams (eds), *Interacting with the Dead: Perspectives on Mortuary Archaeology for the New Millennium* (Gainesville, FL: University of Florida Press, 2005), 107–23.

58. See Chapter 5, 121–22.

59. Niehr, 'Changed Status of the Dead', 155; cf. Achenbach, 'Veruneinigung durch die Berührung Toter', 347–69. Niehr suggests a more negative view of the dead might have arisen among scribal and priestly groups exiled to Babylonia (ibid., 147), though it is important to note that the widespread assumption that within Mesopotamian mortuary culture the dead were perceived 'negatively' is to a large part dependent upon the magico-medical

Although some aspects of biblical legislation seek to disempower the dead, the success of that legislation in abnegating their impact is questionable. After all, to brand the dead as impure is nonetheless to assert their continued potency by casting them as a powerful threat – and so the ancestors are not rendered harmless, but harmful.

Indeed, the ongoing power of the dead is acknowledged in those regulations concerning corpse contamination that allow the burial places of the dead to remain undisturbed. Ancient West Asian tomb inscriptions threaten harm to those who would disturb the dead, and similarly biblical regulations about contact with corpse-contaminated graves protect not only the living from the dead, but also the dead from the living. Thus although the Hebrew Bible's distancing of the dead from the living might well play a part in Yhwh's appropriation of their roles and even their lands, it nonetheless also implicitly endorses the 'traditional' consignment of the deceased to their tombs, to dwell at the boundaries of the living community, within the mortuary landscape. There, the dead maintain their place.

---

and exorcism texts in which it is primarily the *disruptive* dead who are described. For these texts, see J. A. Scurlock, *Magico-Medical Means of Treating Ghost-Induced Illnesses in Mesopotamia* (Leiden: Brill/Styx, 2006). For a nuanced account of the social role of the Mesopotamian dead, see Jonker, *Topography of Remembrance*.

BIBLIOGRAPHY

Achenbach, R., 'Veruneinigung durch die Berührung Toter. Zum Ursprung einer altisraelitischen Vorstellung', in A. Berlejung and B. Jankowski (eds), *Tod und Jenseits im Alten Israel und in seiner Umwelt: theologische, religionsgeschichtliche, archäologische und ikonograpische Aspekte* (FAT, 64; Tübingen: Mohr Siebeck, 2009), 347–69.

Ackerman, S., 'The Deception of Isaac, Jacob's Dream at Bethel, and Incubation on an Animal Skin', in G. A. Anderson and S. M. Olyan (eds), *Priesthood and Cult in Ancient Israel* (JSOTS, 125; Sheffield: JSOT Press, 1991), 92–120.

——*Under Every Green Tree: Popular Religion in Sixth-Century Judah* (HSM, 46; Atlanta, GA: Scholars Press, 1992).

Albertz, R., 'Family Religion in Ancient Israel and its Surroundings', in J. Bodel and S. M. Olyan (eds), *Household and Family Religion in Antiquity* (Oxford: Blackwell, 2008), 89–112.

——'Personal Piety', in F. Stavrakopoulou and J. Barton (eds), *Religious Diversity in Ancient Israel and Judah* (London: T&T Clark, 2010), 135–46.

Albright, W. F., 'The High Place in Ancient Palestine', in G. W. Anderson (ed.), *Congress Volume Strasbourg, 1956* (VTS, 4; Leiden: Brill, 1957), 242–58.

Allen, L. C., *Ezekiel 20–48* (WBC, 29; Dallas, TX: Word, 1990).

——*Jeremiah: A Commentary* (OTL; Louisville, KY: Westminster John Knox Press, 2008).

Alt, A., 'Judas Gaue unter Josia', *Palästinajahrbuch* 21 (1925), 100–116.

Amit, Y., 'Bochim, Bethel, and the Hidden Polemic (Judg 2,1–5)', in G. Galil and M. Weinfeld (eds), *Studies in Historical Geography and Biblical Historiography* (VTS, 81; Leiden: Brill, 2000), 121–31.

Antoniaccio, C. M., *An Archaeology of Ancestors: Tomb Cult and Hero Cult in Early Greece* (Lanham, MD: Rowman & Littlefield, 1995).

Ashmore, W. and P. L. Geller, 'Social Dimensions of Mortuary Space', in G. F. M. Rakita, J. E. Buikstra, L. A. Beck and S. R. Williams (eds), *Interacting with the Dead: Perspectives on Mortuary Archaeology for the New Millennium* (Gainesville, FL: University of Florida Press, 2005), 81–92.

Assmann, J., 'Schrift, Tod und Identität: Das Grab als Vorschule der Literatur im alten Ägypten', in A. Assmann, J. Assmann and C. Hardmeier (eds), *Schrift und Gedächtnis: Beiträge zur Archäologie der literarischen Kommunikation* (München: Wilhelm Fink Verlag, 1983), 64–93.

——*Das kulturelle Gedächtnis. Schrift, Erinnerung und politische Identität in frühen Hochkulturen* (München: Beck, 1992).

——'Cultural Memory: Script, Recollection, and Political Identity in Early Civilizations', Historiography East and West 1 (2003), 154–77.

——*Religion and Cultural Memory: Ten Studies* (trans. R. Livingstone; Stanford, CA: Stanford University Press, 2006).

Aus, R. D., *The Death, Burial, and Resurrection of Jesus and the Death, Burial, and Translation of Moses in Judaic Tradition* (Lanham, MD: University Press of America, 2008).

Avigad, N., 'The Epitaph of a Royal Steward from Siloam Village', *IEJ* 3 (1953), 137–52.

Bahrani, Z., *Rituals of War: The Body and Violence in Mesopotamia* (New York: Zone, 2008).

Barkay, G., 'The Priestly Benediction on Silver Plaques from Ketef Hinnom in Jerusalem', *TA* 19 (1992), 139–92.

——'Burial Caves and Burial Practices in Judah in the Biblical Period', in I. Singer (ed.), *Graves and Burial Practices in the Land of Israel in Ancient Times* (Jerusalem: Yad Ben Zvi/Israel Exploration Society, 1994), 96–163 (Hebrew).
——'Mounds of Mystery: Where the Kings of Judah were Lamented', *BAR* 29.3 (2003), 32–39, 66, 68.
Barley, N., *Dancing on the Grave: Encounters with Death* (London: John Murray, 1995).
Barrick, W. B., *The King and the Cemeteries: Toward a New Understanding of Josiah's Reform* (VTS, 88; Leiden: Brill, 2002).
Barstad, H. M., *The Myth of the Empty Land: A Study in the History and Archaeology of Judah During the 'Exilic' Period* (Oslo: Scandinavian University Press, 1996).
Bartlett, J. R., 'Sihon and Og, Kings of the Amorites', *VT* 20 (1970), 257–77.
——'Edomites and Idumaeans', *PEQ* 131 (1999), 102–14.
Barzel, H., 'Moses: Tragedy and Sublimity', in K. R. R. Gros Louis, J. S. Ackerman and T. S. Warshaw (eds), *Literary Interpretations of Biblical Narratives* (Nashville, TN: Abingdon Press, 1974), 120–40.
Battersby, C., 'Her Body/Her Boundaries: Gender and the Metaphysics of Containment', in A. Benjamin (ed.), *Journal of Philosophy and the Visual Arts: The Body* (London: Academic Group, 1993), 31–39.
Bauman, Z., *Mortality, Immortality and Other Life Strategies* (Stanford, CA: Stanford University Press, 1992).
Bayliss, M., 'The Cult of Dead Kin in Assyria and Babylonia', *Iraq* 35 (1973), 115–25.
Becking, B., 'Continuity and Community: The Belief System of the Book of Ezra', in B. Becking and M. C. A. Korpel (eds), *The Crisis of Israelite Religion: Transformation of Religious Tradition in Exilic and Post-Exilic Times* (OTS, 42; Leiden: Brill, 1999), 256–75.
Bell, C., *Ritual: Perspectives and Dimensions* (Oxford: Oxford University Press, 1997).
Bender, B., 'Place and Landscape', in C. Tilley, W. Keane, S. Kuechler, M. Rowlands and P. Spyer (eds), *Handbook of Material Culture* (London: Sage, 2006), 303–14.
Bender, B. and M. Winer (eds), *Contested Landscapes: Movement, Exile and Place* (Oxford: Berg, 2001).
Bennett, G. and K. M. Bennett, 'The Presence of the Dead: An Empirical Study', *Mortality* 5.2 (2000), 139–57.
Ben Zvi, E., 'Inclusion in and Exclusion from "Israel" in Post-monarchic Biblical Texts', in S. W. Holloway and L. K. Handy (eds), *The Pitcher Is Broken: Memorial Essays for Gösta W. Ahlström* (JSOTS, 190; Sheffield: Sheffield Academic Press, 1995), 95–149.
——'The Urban Center of Jerusalem and the Development of the Literature of the Hebrew Bible', in W. E. Aufrecht, N. A. Mirau and S. W. Gauley (eds), *Urbanism in Antiquity: From Mesopotamia to Crete* (JSOTS, 244; Sheffield: Sheffield Academic Press, 1997), 194–209.
Bergsma, J. S., 'The Jubilee: A Post-exilic Priestly Attempt to Reclaim Lands', *Bib* 81 (2000), 153–78.
Berman, J. A., 'Identity Politics and the Burial of Jacob (Genesis 50:1–14)', *CBQ* 68 (2006), 11–31.
——*Created Equal: How the Bible Broke with Ancient Political Thought* (Oxford: Oxford University Press, 2008).
Berquist, J. L., *Controlling Corporeality: The Body and the Household in Ancient Israel* (New Brunswick, NJ: Rutgers University Press, 2002).
Blenkinsopp, J., *Ezra-Nehemiah: A Commentary* (OTL; Philadelphia: Westminster Press, 1988).
——*Ezekiel* (Interpretation; Louisville, KY: John Knox Press, 1990).
——'Temple and Society in Achaemenid Judah', in P. R. Davies (ed.), *Second Temple Studies, Volume I: Persian Period* (JSOTS, 117; Sheffield: JSOT Press, 1991), 22–53.
——'Deuteronomy and the Politics of Post-Mortem Existence', *VT* 45 (1995), 1–16.
——'Judah's Covenant with Death (Isaiah XXVIII 14–22)', *VT* 50 (2000), 472–83.
——'Did the Second Jerusalemite Temple Possess Land?', *Transeuphratène* 21 (2001), 61–68.

—'Was the Pentateuch the Civic and Religious Constitution of the Jewish Ethnos in the Persian Period?' in J. W. Watts (ed.), *Persia and Torah: The Theory of Imperial Authorization of the Pentateuch* (SBLSS, 17; Atlanta, GA: Scholars Press, 2001), 41–62.
—'Bethel in the Neo-Babylonian Period', in O. Lipschits and J. Blenkinsopp (eds), *Judah and the Judeans in the Neo-Babylonian Period* (Winona Lake, IN: Eisenbrauns, 2003), 93–107.
—*Isaiah 56–66: A New Translation with Introduction and Commentary* (AB 19B; New York: Doubleday, 2003).
—'Abraham as Paradigm in the Priestly History in Genesis', *JBL* 128 (2009), 225–41.
Bloch, M., *Placing the Dead: Tombs, Ancestral Villages, and Kinship Organisation in Madagascar* (London: Seminar Press, 1971).
Bloch, M. and J. Parry (eds), *Death and the Regeneration of Life* (Cambridge: Cambridge University Press, 1982).
Bloch-Smith, E., *Judahite Burial Practices and Beliefs about the Dead* (JSOTS, 123; Sheffield: JSOT Press, 1992).
—'Death in the Life of Israel', in B. M. Gittlen (ed.), *Sacred Time, Sacred Place: Archaeology and the Religion of Israel* (Winona Lake, IN: Eisenbrauns, 2002a), 139–43.
—'Life in Judah from the Perspective of the Dead', *NEA* 65.2 (2002b), 120–30.
Block, D. I., 'The Role of Language in Ancient Israelite Perceptions of National Identity', *JBL* 103 (1984), 321–40.
—*The Book of Ezekiel, Chapters 25–48* (NICOT; Grand Rapids, MI: Eerdmans, 1998).
Blum, E., *Die Komposition der Vätergeschichte* (WMANT, 57; Neukirchen-Vluyn: Neukirchener Verlag, 1984).
Bodi, D., 'Les *gillûlîm* chez Ezéchiel et dans l'Ancien Testament, et les différentes practiques cultuelles associées à ce terme, *RB* 100 (1993), 481–510.
Bøe, S., *Gog and Magog: Ezekiel 38–39 as Pre-Text for Revelation 19,17–21 and 20,7–10* (WUNT, 2.135; Tübingen: Mohr Siebeck, 2001).
Borger, R., *Beiträge zum Inschriftenwerk Aššurbanipals* (Wiesbaden: Harrassowitz, 1996).
Bottéro, J., 'La Mythologie de la mort en Mésopotamie ancienne', in B. Alster (ed.), *Death in Mesopotamia* (CRRA, 26/Mesopotamia 8; Copenhagen: Akedemisk Forlag, 1980), 25–52.
Bray, J. S., 'Genesis 23 – A Priestly Paradigm for Burial', *JSOT* 60 (1993), 69–73.
Brett, M. G., *Genesis: Procreation and the Politics of Identity* (London: Routledge, 2000).
—*Decolonizing God: The Bible in the Tides of Empire* (Sheffield: Sheffield Phoenix Press, 2008).
Briant, P., *From Cyrus to Alexander: A History of the Persian Empire* (trans. P. T. Daniels; Winona Lake, IN: Eisenbrauns, 2002).
Brichto, H. C., 'Kin, Cult, Land and Afterlife – A Biblical Complex', *HUCA* 44 (1973), 1–54.
Britt, B. M. 'Erasing Amalek: Remembering to Forget with Derrida and Biblical Tradition', in Y. Sherwood (ed.), *Derrida's Bible (Reading a Page of Scripture with a Little Help from Derrida)* (New York: Palgrave Macmillan, 2004), 61–77.
—*Rewriting Moses: The Narrative Eclipse of the Text* (JSOTS, 402/GCT, 14; New York: T&T Clark, 2004).
Brueggemann, W., *Genesis* (Interpretation; Louisville, KY: Westminster John Knox Press, 1982).
—*The Land: Place as Gift, Promise, and Challenge in Biblical Faith* (2nd edn; Minneapolis: Fortress Press, 2002).
Budin, S. L., *The Myth of Sacred Prostitution in Antiquity* (Cambridge: Cambridge University Press, 2008).
Burney, C. F., *The Book of Judges* (New York: Ktav, 1970 [1918]).
Carr, D. M., *Writing on the Tablet of the Heart: Origins of Scripture and Literature* (Oxford: Oxford University Press, 2005).
Carroll, R. P., *Jeremiah: A Commentary* (OTL; London: SCM Press, 1986).
—'Textual Strategies and Ideologies in the Second Temple Period', in P. R. Davies (ed.), *Second Temple Studies, Volume 1: Persian Period* (JSOTS, 117; Sheffield: JSOT Press, 1991), 108–24.

Carter, C. E., *The Emergence of Yehud in the Persian Period: A Social and Demographic Study* (JSOTS, 294; Sheffield: Sheffield Academic Press, 1999).

Cathcart, K. J., 'Treaty-Curses and the Book of Nahum', *CBQ* 34 (1973), 179–87.

Chapman, R. W., 'Ten Years After – Megaliths, Mortuary Practices, and the Territorial Model', in L. Anderson Beck (ed.), *Regional Approaches to Mortuary Analysis* (New York: Plenum, 1995), 29–51.

Charles, D. K., 'Diachronic Regional Social Dynamics: Mortuary Sites in the Illinois Valley/American Bottom Region', in L. Anderson Beck (ed.), *Regional Approaches to Mortuary Analysis* (New York: Plenum, 1995), 77–99.

Charles, D. K. and J. E. Buikstra, 'Siting, Sighting, and Citing the Dead', in H. Silverman and D. Small (eds), *The Space and Place of Death* (Archaeological Papers of the American Anthropological Association, 11; Arlington, VA: American Anthropological Association, 2002), 13–25.

Chesson, M. S., 'Embodied Memories of Place and People: Death and Society in an Early Urban Community', in M. S. Chesson (ed.), *Social Memory, Identity, and Death: Anthropological Perspectives on Mortuary Rituals* (Archaeological Papers of the American Anthropological Association, 10; Arlington, VA: American Anthropological Institute, 2001), 100–13.

——(ed.) *Social Memory, Identity, and Death: Anthropological Perspectives on Mortuary Rituals* (Archaeological Papers of the American Anthropological Association, 10; Arlington, VA: American Anthropological Institute, 2001).

——'Remembering and Forgetting in Early Bronze Age Mortuary Practices on the Southeastern Dead Sea Plain, Jordan', in N. Laneri (ed.), *Performing Death: Social Analyses of Funerary Traditions in the Ancient Near East and Mediterranean* (University of Chicago Oriental Institute Seminars, 3; Chicago: Oriental Institute of the University of Chicago, 2007), 109–39.

Christensen, D. L., *Deuteronomy 21:10–34:12* (WBC, 6B; Nashville, TN: Thomas Nelson, 2002).

Cleary, J., *Literature, Partition and the Nation State: Culture and Conflict in Ireland, Israel and Palestine* (Cambridge: Cambridge University Press, 2002).

Coats, G. W., 'Legendary Motifs in the Moses Death Reports', *CBQ* 39 (1977), 34–44.

——*The Moses Tradition* (JSOTS, 161; Sheffield: JSOT Press, 1993).

Cogan, M., 'A Note on Disinterment in Jeremiah', in I. D. Passow and S. T. Lachs (eds), *Gratz College Anniversary Volume* (Philadelphia: Gratz College, 1971), 29–34.

——'A Slip of the Pen? On Josiah's Actions in Samaria (2 Kings 23:15–20)', in C. Cohen, A. Hurvitz and S. M. Paul (eds), *Sefer Moshe* (Winona Lake, IN: Eisenbrauns, 2004), 3–8.

Cohen, A. C., *Death Rituals, Ideology, and the Development of Early Mesopotamian Kingship: Toward a New Understanding of Iraq's Royal Cemetery of Ur* (Leiden: Brill, 2005).

Cohn, R. L., 'Negotiating (with) the Natives: Ancestors and Identity in Genesis', *HTR* 96 (2003), 147–66.

Collins, J. J., 'Marriage, Divorce and Family in Second Temple Judaism', in L. G. Perdue, J. Blenkinsopp, J. J. Collins and C. Meyers, *Families in Ancient Israel* (Louisville, KY: Westminster John Knox Press, 1997), 105–62.

Connerton, P., *How Societies Remember* (Cambridge: Cambridge University Press, 1989).

Cooper, A. and B. R. Goldstein, 'The Cult of the Dead and the Theme of Entry into the Land', *Bib Int* 1 (1993), 285–303.

Cox, B. D. and S. Ackerman, 'Rachel's Tomb', *JBL* 128 (2009), 135–48.

Cox, J. L., *From Primitive to Indigenous: The Academic Study of Indigenous Religions* (Aldershot: Ashgate, 2007).

Cross, F. M. 'The Priestly Houses of Early Israel', *Canaanite Myth and Hebrew Epic: Essays in the History of the Religion of Israel* (Cambridge, MA: Harvard University Press, 1973), 195–215.

Cross, F. M. and G. E. Wright, 'The Boundary and Province Lists of the Kingdom of Judah', *JBL* 75 (1956), 202–26.

Crossley, J. G., *Jesus in an Age of Terror: Scholarly Projects for a New American Century* (Bibleworld; London: Equinox, 2009).
Crüsemann, F., 'Human Solidarity and Ethnic Identity: Israel's Self-Definition in the Genealogical System of Genesis', in M. G. Brett (ed.), *Ethnicity and the Bible* (Leiden: Brill, 2002), 57–76.
Dahood, M., 'Textual Problems in Isaia', *CBQ* 22 (1960), 400–409.
——'Hebrew-Ugaritic Lexicography II', *Bib* 45 (1964), 393–412.
Davies, D. J., *Death, Ritual and Belief: The Rhetoric of Funerary Rites* (2nd edn; London: Continuum, 2002).
Davies, E. W., 'Land: Its Rights and Privileges', in R. E. Clements (ed.), *The World of Ancient Israel: Sociological, Anthropological and Political Perspectives* (Cambridge: Cambridge University Press, 1989), 349–70.
Davies, P. R., 'Josiah and the Law Book', in L. L. Grabbe (ed.), *Good Kings and Bad Kings: The Kingdom of Judah in the Seventh Century BCE* (LHBOTS, 393; London: T&T Clark, 2005), 65–77.
——*The Origins of Biblical Israel* (LHBOTS, 485; New York: T&T Clark, 2007).
——'Urban Religion and Rural Religion', in F. Stavrakopoulou and J. Barton (eds), *Religious Diversity in Ancient Israel and Judah* (London: T&T Clark, 2010), 104–17.
Davies, W. D., *The Territorial Dimension of Judaism* (2nd edn; Minneapolis: Fortress Press, 1991).
Day, J., *Molech: A God of Human Sacrifice in the Old Testament* (UCOP, 41; Cambridge: Cambridge University Press, 1989).
Day, P. L., 'From the Child is Born the Woman: The Story of Jephthah's Daughter', in P. L. Day (ed.), *Gender and Difference in Ancient Israel* (Minneapolis: Fortress Press, 1989), 58–74.
Dearman, J. A., *Property Rights in the Eighth-Century Prophets: The Conflict and Its Background* (SBLDS, 106; Atlanta, GA: Scholars Press, 1988).
Deist, F. E., *The Material Culture of the Bible: An Introduction* (BS, 70; Sheffield: Sheffield Academic Press, 2002).
Delamarter, S., 'The Vilification of Jehoiakim (a.k.a. Eliakim and Joiakim) in Early Judaism', in C. A. Evans and J. A. Sanders (eds), *The Function of Scripture in Early Jewish and Christian Tradition* (JSNTS, 154/SSEJC, 6; Sheffield: Sheffield Academic Press, 1998), 190–204.
Delcor, M., 'Two Special Meanings of the Word *yd* in Biblical Hebrew', *JSS* 12 (1967), 230–40.
Derrida, J., 'Hostipitality', *Acts of Religion* (ed. G. Anidjar; New York: Routledge, 2002), 356–420.
Dever, W. G., 'The Silence of the Text: An Archaeological Commentary on 2 Kings 23', in M. D. Coogan, J. C. Exum and L. E. Stager (eds), *Scripture and Other Artifacts: Essays on the Bible and Archaeology in Honor of Philip J. King* (Louisville, KY: Westminster John Knox Press, 1994), 143–68.
Dietrich, M., 'Das biblische Paradies und der babylonische Tempelgarten: Überlegungen zur Lage des Gartens Eden', in B. Ego and B. Janowski (eds), *Das biblische Weltbild und seine altorientalischen Kontexte* (Tübingen: Mohr Siebeck, 2001), 281–323.
Dietrich, W. and M. A. Klopfenstein (eds), *Ein Gott allein? JHWH-Verehrung und biblischer Monotheismus im Kontext der israelitischen und altorientalischen Religionsgeschichte* (OBO, 139; Fribourg: Universitätsverlag; Göttingen: Vandenhoeck & Ruprecht, 1994).
Dijkstra, M., 'The Weather-God on Two Mountains', *UF* 23 (1991), 127–40.
——'Abraham', *DDD*, 3–5.
——'The Law of Moses: The Memory of Mosaic Religion in and after the Exile', in R. Albertz and B. Becking (eds), *Yahwism After the Exile: Perspectives on Israelite Religion in the Persian Era* (Assen: Van Gorcum, 2003), 70–98.
——'Moses, the Man of God', in R. Roukema (ed.), *The Interpretation of Exodus: Studies in Honour of Cornelis Houtman* (CBET, 44; Leuven: Peeters, 2006), 17–36.
Douglas, M., *Jacob's Tears: The Priestly Work of Reconciliation* (Oxford: Oxford University Press, 2004).

Driver, S. R., *Notes on the Hebrew Text and the Topography of the Books of Samuel* (2nd edn; Oxford: Clarendon Press, 1913).
Duguia, I. M., *Ezekiel and the Leaders of Israel* (VTS, 56; Leiden: Brill, 1994).
Duhm, B., *Das Buch Jesaia* (4th edn. HAT, 3.1; Göttingen: Vandenhoeck & Ruprecht, 1922).
Dutcher-Walls, P. (ed.), *The Family in Life and Death: Sociological and Archaeological Perspectives* (LHBOTS, 504; New York: T&T Clark, 2009).
Ebach, J. H., '*PGR* = (Toten-)opfer? Ein Vorschlag zum Verständnis von Ez. 43,7.9', *UF* 3 (1971), 365–68.
Edelman, D., (ed.), *The Triumph of Elohim: From Yahwisms to Judaisms* (CBET, 13; Kampen: Kok Pharos, 1995).
——*The Origins of the 'Second' Temple: Persian Imperial Policy and the Rebuilding of Jerusalem* (BibleWorld; London: Equinox, 2005).
——'Hezekiah's Alleged Cultic Centralization', *JSOT* 32 (2008), 395–434.
——'God Rhetoric: Reconceptualizing YHWH Sebaot as YHWH Elohim in the Hebrew Bible', in E. Ben Zvi, D. Edelman and F. Polak (eds), *A Palimpsest: Rhetoric, Ideology, Stylistics and Language Relating to Persian Israel* (Piscataway, NJ: Gorgias Press, 2009), 89–108.
——'Cultic Sites and Complexes beyond the Jerusalem Temple', in F. Stavrakopoulou and J. Barton (eds), *Religious Diversity in Ancient Israel and Judah* (London: T&T Clark, 2010), 82–103.
——'Hidden Ancestral Polemics in the Book of Genesis?' (forthcoming).
——'Were Zerubbabel and Nehemiah the Same Person?' in D. Burns and J. W. Rogerson (eds), *In Search of Philip R. Davies: Whose Festschrift Is It Anyway?* (New York: T&T Clark, forthcoming).
Eissfeldt, O., 'Renaming in the Old Testament', in P. R. Ackroyd and B. Lindars (eds), *Words and Meanings: Essays Presented to David Winton Thomas* (Cambridge: Cambridge University Press, 1968), 70–83.
Fayer, J. A., *Land Tenure and the Biblical Jubilee: Uncovering Hebrew Ethics through the Sociology of Knowledge* (JSOTS, 155; Sheffield: Sheffield Academic Press, 1993).
Fensham, F. C., *The Books of Ezra and Nehemiah* (NICOT; Grand Rapids, MI: Eerdmans, 1982).
Figueras, P., *Decorated Jewish Ossuaries* (Leiden: Brill, 1983).
Finkelstein, I. and N. A. Silberman, *The Bible Unearthed: Archaeology's New Vision of Ancient Israel and the Origin of Its Sacred Texts* (New York: Free Press, 2001).
Fishbane, M., *Biblical Interpretation in Ancient Israel* (Oxford: Clarendon Press, 1985).
Fleming, D. E., 'The Integration of Household and Community Religion in Ancient Syria', in J. Bodel and S. M. Olyan (eds), *Household and Family Religion in Antiquity* (Oxford: Blackwell, 2008), 37–59.
Foltyn, J. L., 'The Corpse in Contemporary Culture: Identifying, Transacting, and Recoding the Dead Body in the Twenty-First Century', *Mortality* 13.2 (2008), 99–104.
Fortes, M., 'Some Reflections on Ancestor Worship in West Africa', in M. Fortes and G. Dieterlin (eds), *African Systems of Thought* (Oxford: Oxford University Press, 1965), 122–24.
Francis, D., L. Kellaher and G. Neophytou, 'The Cemetery: The Evidence of Continuing Bonds', in J. Hockey, J. Katz and N. Small (eds), *Grief, Mourning and Death Ritual* (Buckingham: Open University Press, 2001), 226–36.
Franklin, N., 'The Tombs of the Kings of Israel: Two Recently Identified 9th-Century Tombs from Omride Samaria', *ZDPV* 119 (2003), 1–11.
Frazer, J. G., *Folklore in the Old Testament: Studies in Comparative Religion, Legend and Law* (Abridged edn. London: Macmillan, 1923).
Frei, P., 'Die persische Reichsautorisation: Ein Überblick', *ZABR* 1 (1996) 1–35 (ET 'Persian Imperial Authorization: A Summary', in J. W. Watts (ed.), *Persia and Torah: The Theory of Imperial Authorization of the Pentateuch* (SBLSS, 17; Atlanta, GA: Scholars Press, 2001), 1–35.

Bibliography

Frevel, C., 'Ein vielsagender Abschied. Exegetische Blicke auf den Tod des Mose in Dtn 34,1–12', *BZ* 45 (2001), 209–34.
Friesen, S. J., (ed.), *Ancestors in Post-Contact Religion: Roots, Ruptures, and Modernity's Memory* (Cambridge, MA: Harvard University Press, 2001).
Gafni, I. M., *Land, Center and Diaspora: Jewish Constructs in Late Antiquity* (Sheffield: Sheffield Academic Press, 1997).
Galling, K., *Die Erwählungstraditionen Israels* (BZAW, 48; Giessen: A. Töpelmann, 1928).
——'Die Nekropole von Jerusalem', *Palästina-Jahrbuch* 32 (1936), 73–101.
Gelb, I. J., P. Steinkeller and R. M. Whiting, *Earliest Land Tenure Systems in the Near East: Ancient Kudurrus* (2 vols. Chicago: Oriental Institute of the University of Chicago Press, 1991).
Gell, A., *Art and Agency: An Anthropological Theory* (Oxford: Oxford University Press, 1998).
Gemser, B., '*Beʿēber hajjardēn*: In Jordan's Borderland', *VT* 2 (1952), 349–55.
Gerleman, G., 'Nutzrecht und Wohnrecht', ZAW 89 (1977), 313–25.
Gillespie, S., 'Mortuary Ritual, Agency, and Personhood: A Case Study from the Ancient Maya', *Journal of Anthropological Archaeology* 20.1 (2001), 73–112.
Glazier, J., 'Mbeere ancestors and the domestication of death', *Man* (ns) 19.1 (1984), 133–47.
Gluckman, M., 'Mortuary Customs and the Belief in Survival after Death among the South-Eastern Bantu', *Bantu Studies* 11 (1937), 117–36.
Goldman, B., *The Sacred Portal: A Primary Symbol in Ancient Judaic Art* (Detroit: Wayne State University Press, 1966).
Goldziher, I., *Der Mythos bei den Hebräern und seine geschichtliche Entwickelung* (Leipzig: Brockhaus, 1876).
Gomes, J. F., *The Sanctuary of Bethel and the Configuration of Israelite Identity* (BZAW, 368; Berlin: de Gruyter, 2006).
Gonen, R., *Burial Patterns and Cultural Diversity in Late Bronze Age Canaan* (ASORDS, 7; Winona Lake, IN: Eisenbrauns, 1992).
Goody, J., *Death, Property and the Ancestors: A Study of the Mortuary Customs of the LoDagaa of West Africa* (London: Tavistock, 1962).
——*The Logic of Writing and the Organization of Society* (Cambridge: Cambridge University Press, 1986).
Goshen-Gottstein, M., 'Abraham – Lover of Beloved of God', in J. H. Marks and R. M. Good (eds), *Love and Death in the Ancient Near East: Essays in Honor of Marvin H. Pope* (Guildford; Four Quarters, 1987), 101–4.
Gottlieb, A., *The Afterlife Is Where We Come From: The Culture of Infancy in West Africa* (Chicago: University of Chicago Press, 2004).
Goulder, M., 'Deutero-Isaiah of Jerusalem', *JSOT* 28 (2004), 351–62.
Grabbe, L. L., 'Triumph of the Pious or Failure of the Xenophobes? The Ezra-Nehemiah Reforms and Their Nachgeschichte', in S. Jones and S. Pearce (eds.), *Jewish Local Patriotism and Self-Identification in the Graeco-Roman Period* (JSPS, 31; Sheffield: Sheffield Academic Press, 1998), 50–65.
——*A History of the Jews and Judaism in the Second Temple Period, Volume 1 Yehud: A History of the Persian Province of Judah* (LSTS, 47; London: T&T Clark, 2004).
Graesser, C. F., 'Standing Stones in Ancient Palestine', *BA* 35 (1972), 34–64.
Gray, J., *Joshua, Judges, Ruth* (NCB; Grand Rapids, MI: Eerdmans, 1986).
Greene, S. E., *Sacred Sites and the Colonial Encounter: A History of Meaning and Memory in Ghana* (Bloomington, IN: Indiana University Press, 2002).
Gruber, M. I., 'Breast-feeding Practices in Biblical Israel and in Old Babylonian Mesopotamia', *JANES* 19 (1989), 61–83.
Guillaume, P., *Land and Calendar: The Priestly Document from Genesis 1 to Joshua 18* (LHBOTS, 391; New York: T&T Clark, 2009).
Gulde, S. U., *Der Tod als Herrscher in Ugarit und Israel* (FAT, 22; Tübingen: Mohr Siebeck, 2007).
Gunkel, H., *The Legends of Genesis* (trans. W. H. Carruth; New York: Schocken, 1964).

Habel, N. C., *The Land Is Mine: Six Biblical Land Ideologies* (Minneapolis: Fortress Press, 1995).

Hachlili, R., *Jewish Funerary Customs, Practices and Rites in the Second Temple Period* (JSJS, 94; Leiden: Brill, 2006).

Hagedorn, A. C., 'Local Law in an Imperial Context: The Role of Torah in the (Imagined) Persian Period', in G. N. Knoppers and B. M. Levinson (eds), *The Pentateuch as Torah: New Models for Understanding its Promulgation and Acceptance* (Winona Lake, IN: Eisenbrauns, 2007), 57–76.

Halbwachs, M., *On Collective Memory* (ed. and trans. L. A. Coser; Chicago: University of Chicago Press, 1992).

Hallam, E. and J. Hockey, *Death, Memory and Material Culture* (Oxford: Berg, 2001).

Hallam, E., J. Hockey and G. Howarth, *Beyond the Body: Death and Social Identity* (London: Routledge, 1999).

Hallo, W. W., 'Royal Ancestor Worship in the Biblical World', in M. Fishbane and E. Tov (eds), *Shar'arei Talmon: Studies in the Bible, Qumran, and the Ancient Near East Presented to Shemaryahu Talmon* (Winona Lake, IN: Eisenbrauns, 1992), 381–401.

——'Disturbing the Dead', in M. Brettler and M. Fishbane (eds), *Minhah le-Nahum: Biblical and Other Studies Presented to Nahum M. Sarna in Honour of his 70th Birthday* (JSOTS, 154; Sheffield: JSOT Press, 1993), 183–92.

Hallote, R. S., *Death, Burial, and Afterlife in the Biblical World: How the Israelites and Their Neighbors Treated the Dead* (Chicago: Ivan R. Dee, 2001).

Halpern, B., 'The Excremental Vision": The Doomed Priests of Doom in Isaiah 28', *HAR* 10 (1986), 109–21.

——*The First Historians: The Hebrew Bible and History* (San Francisco: Harper & Row, 1988).

——'Jerusalem and the Lineages in the Seventh Century BCE: Kinship and the Rise of Individual Moral Liability', in B. Halpern and D. W. Hobson (eds), *Law and Ideology in Monarchic Israel* (JSOTS, 124; Sheffield: JOST Press, 1991), 11–107.

——'Late Israelite Astronomies and the Early Greeks', in W. G. Dever and S. Gitin (eds), *Symbiosis, Symbolism, and the Power of the Past: Canaan, Ancient Israel, and Their Neighbors from the Late Bronze Age through Roman Palestinia* (Winona Lake, IN: Eisenbrauns, 2003), 323–52.

Hamel, G. H., *Poverty and Charity in Roman Palestine, First Three Centuries C.E.* (Berkeley, CA: University of California Press, 1990).

Hamilton, V. P., *The Book of Genesis: Chapters 18–50* (NICOT; Grand Rapids, MI: Eerdmans, 1995).

Hanson, P. D., *The Dawn of Apocalyptic* (Philadelphia: Fortress Press, 1975).

Haran, M., *Temples and Temple Service in Ancient Israel* (Oxford: Clarendon Press, 1978).

Hardmeier, C., 'King Josiah in the Climax of the Deuteronomistic History (2 Kings 22–23) and the Pre-Deuteronomistic Document of a Cult Reform at the Place of Residence (23.4–15): Criticism of Sources, Reconstruction of Literary Pre-Stages and the Theology of History in 2 Kings 22–23', in L. L. Grabbe (ed.), *Good Kings and Bad Kings: The Kingdom of Judah in the Seventh Century BCE* (LHBOTS, 393; London: T&T Clark, 2005), 123–63.

Hare, D. R. A., 'The Lives of the Prophets', *OTP* 2.379–99.

Harrison, R. P., *The Dominion of the Dead* (Chicago: University of Chicago Press, 2003).

Havrelock, R., 'The Two Maps of Israel's Land', *JBL* 126 (2007), 649–67.

Hayman, A. P., 'Monotheism – A Misused Word in Jewish Studies?', *JJS* 42 (1991), 1–15.

Healey, J., 'Mlkm/Rpʾum and the Kispum', *UF* 10 (1978), 89–91.

Heard, R. C., *Dynamics of Diselection: Ambiguity in Genesis 12–36 and Ethnic Boundaries in Post-Exilic Judah* (SBLSS, 39; Atlanta, GA: Society of Biblical Literature, 2001).

Heider, G. C., *The Cult of Molek: A Reassessment* (JSOTS, 43; Sheffield: JSOT Press, 1985).

Henke, O., 'Zur Lage von Beth Peor', *ZDPV* 75 (1959), 155–63.

Hertz, R., *Death and the Right Hand* (trans. R. Needham and C. Needham; Aberdeen: Cohen & West, 1960).

Hill, A. E., 'The Ebal Ceremony as Hebrew Land Grant?', *JETS* 31(1988), 399–406.

Hillers, D. R., *Treaty Curses and the Old Testament Prophets* (BO, 16; Rome: Pontifical Biblical Institute, 1964).
Hinnant, C., 'The Patriarchal Narratives of Genesis and the Ethos of Gift Exchange', in M. Osteen (ed.), *The Question of the Gift: Essays Across Disciplines* (London: Routledge, 2002), 105–17.
Hirsch, E., 'Landscape: Between Place and Space', in E. Hirsch and M. O'Hanlon (eds), *The Anthropology of Landscape: Perspectives on Place and Space* (Oxford: Clarendon Press, 1995), 1–30.
——'Landscape, Myth and Time', *Journal of Material Culture* 11 (2006), 151–65.
Hockey, J., 'The View from the West', in G. Howarth and P. C. Jupp (eds), *Contemporary Issues in the Sociology of Death, Dying and Disposal* (Basingstoke: Macmillan, 1996), 3–16.
Hoftijzer, J. and G. van der Kooij (eds), *The Balaam Text from Deir ʿAllā Re-evaluated: Proceedings of the International Symposium held at Leiden 21–24 August 1989* (Leiden: Brill, 1991).
Hogland, K. G., *Achaemenid Imperial Administration in Syria-Palestine and the Missions of Ezra and Nehemiah* (SBLDS, 125; Atlanta, GA: Scholars Press, 1992).
Holtorf, C. and H. Williams, 'Landscapes and Memories', in D. Hicks and M. C. Beaudry (eds), *Cambridge Companion to Historical Archaeology* (Cambridge: Cambridge University Press, 2006), 235–54.
Horst, F., 'Zwei Begriffe für Eigentun (Besitz): *naḥala* und *ʾahuzza*', in A. Kuschke (ed.), *Verbannung und Heimkehr: Beiträge zur Geschichte und Theologie Israels im 6. und 5. Jahrhundert v. Chr. Wilhelm Rudolph zum 70. Geburtstage* (Tübingen: J. C. B. Mohr, 1961), 135–56.
Hostetter, E. C., *Nations Mightier and More Numerous: The Biblical View of Palestine's Pre-Israelite Peoples* (N. Richland Hills, TX: BIBAL Press, 1995).
Houston, W., *Purity and Monotheism: Clean and Unclean Animals in Biblical Law* (JSOTS, 140; Sheffield: JSOT Press, 1993).
Houtman, C., 'Moses', *DDD*, 593–98.
Hübner, U., *Die Ammoniter. Untersuchung zur Geschichte, Kultur und religion eines transjordanischen Volkes im 1. Jahrtausend v. Chr.* (Wisebaden: Harrassowitz, 1992).
——'Og von Baschan und sein Bett in Rabbat-Ammon (Deuteronomium 3,11)', *ZAW* 105 (1993), 86–92.
Hudson, M., 'The New Economic Archaeology of Urbanization', in M. Hudson and B. A. Levine (eds), *Urbanization and Land Ownership in the Ancient Near East* (Peabody Museum Bulletin, 7; Cambridge, MA: Peabody Museum of Archaeology and Ethnology, Harvard University, 1999), 9–15.
Hudson, M. and B. A. Levine (eds), *Urbanization and Land Ownership in the Ancient Near East* (Peabody Museum Bulletin, 7; Cambridge, MA: Peabody Museum of Archaeology and Ethnology, Harvard University, 1999).
Humphreys, S.C. and H. King (eds), *Mortality and Immortality: The Anthropology and Archaeology of Death* (London: Academic Press, 1981).
Hurowitz, V., 'Review of S. L. Richter, *The Deuteronomistic History and the Name Theology*', *JHS* 5 (2004–2005). Available online at http://www.arts.ualberta.ca/JHS/reviews/review157.htm (accessed 22 July 2009).
Hvidberg, F. F., *Weeping and Laughter in the Old Testament: A Study of Canaanite-Israelite Religion* (Leiden: Brill, 1962).
Illman, K. -J., *Old Testament Formulas about Death* (Åbo: Åbo Akademi, 1979).
Irwin, B. P., 'Molek Imagery and the Slaughter of Gog in Ezekiel 38 and 39', *JSOT* 65 (1995), 93–112.
Irwin, W. H., 'The Smooth Stones of the Wady? Isaiah 57:6', *CBQ* 29 (1967), 31–40.
Jacobson, D. M., 'The plan of the ancient Haram El Khalil in Hebron', *PEQ* 113 (1981), 73–80.
Jackson, B. S., 'Ideas of Law and Legal Administration: A Semiotic Approach', in R. E. Clements (ed.), *The World of Ancient Israel: Sociological, Anthropological and Political Perspectives* (Cambridge: Cambridge University Press, 1989), 185–202.

Japhet, S., 'People and Land in the Restoration Period', in G. Strecker (ed.), *Das Land Israel in biblischer Zeit* (Göttinger Theologische Arbeiten, 25; Göttingen: Vandenhoeck & Ruprecht, 1983), 103–25.

——'יד ושם (ISA 56:5) – A Different Proposal', *Maarav* 8 (1992), 69–80.

Jay, N., *Throughout Your Generations Forever: Sacrifice, Religion, and Paternity* (Chicago: University of Chicago Press, 1992).

Johnston, P. S., *Shades of Sheol: Death and Afterlife in the Old Testament* (Leicester: Apollos, 2002).

Jonker, G., *The Topography of Remembrance: The Dead, Tradition and Collective Memory in Mesopotamia* (SHR, 68; Leiden: Brill, 1995).

Joosten, J., *People and Land in the Holiness Code: An Exegetical Study of the Ideational Framework of the Law in Leviticus 17–26* (VTS, 67; Leiden: Brill, 1996).

Joyce, P. M., *Ezekiel: A Commentary* (LHBOTS, 482; New York: T&T Clark, 2007).

Joyce, R. A., 'Social Dimensions of Pre-Classic Burials', in D. C. Grove and R. A. Joyce (eds), *Social Patterns in Pre-Classic Mesoamerica* (Washington, DC: Dumbarton Oaks, 1999), 15–47.

Kallai, Z., *Historical Geography of the Bible: The Tribal Territories of Israel* (Leiden: Brill, 1986).

——'Rachel's Tomb: A Historiographical Review', in J. A. Loader and H. V. Kieweler (eds), *Vielseitigkeit des Alten Testaments* (Frankfurt: Peter Lang, 1999), 215–23.

Karge, P., *Rephaim: Die vorgeschichtliche Kultur Palästinas und Phöniziens* (Paderborn: Schöningh, 1917).

Kaufmann, Y., *The Religion of Israel: From Its Beginnings to the Babylonian Exile* (trans. M Greenberg; New York: Schocken, 1972).

Keel, O., 'Das Vergraben der "fremden Götter" in Genesis XXXV 4b', *VT* 23 (1973), 305–33.

Keel, O. and M. Küchler, *Orte und Landshaften der Bibel. Ein Handbuch und Studien-Reiseführer zum Heiligen Land. Band II: Der Süden* (Göttingen: Vandenhoeck & Ruprecht, 1982).

Keller, M., *Untersuchungen zur deuteronomistischen Namenstheologie* (BBB, 105; Weinheim: Beltz Athanäum, 1996).

Kellermann, U., *Nehemia: Quellen, Überlieferung und Geschichte* (BZAW, 102; Berlin: Töpelmann, 1967).

Keown, G. L., P. J. Scalise and T. G. Smothers, *Jeremiah 26–52* (WBC, 27; Dallas, TX: Word, 1995).

Kessler, J. 'Persia's Loyal Yahwists: Power, Identity and Ethnicity in Achaemenid Yehud', in O. Lipschits and M. Oeming (eds), *Judah and the Judeans in the Persian Period* (Winona Lake, IN: Eisenbrauns, 2006), 91–121.

King, P. J. and L. E. Stager, *Life in Biblical Israel* (LAI; Louisville, KY: Westminster John Knox Press, 2001).

Kitchen, K. A., *On the Reliability of the Old Testament* (Grand Rapids, MI: Eerdmans, 2003).

Klass, D. and R. Goss, 'Spiritual Bonds to the Dead in Cross-Cultural and Historical Perspective: Comparative Religion and Modern Grief', *Death Studies* 23 (1999), 547–67.

Klass, D., P. Silverman and J. Nickman, *Continuing Bonds* (Philadelphia: Taylor and Francis, 1996).

Kletter, R., 'Pots and Polities: Material Remains of Late Iron Age Judah in Relation to the Political Borders', *BASOR* 314 (1999), 19–54.

Kloner, A., 'Iron Age Burial Caves in Jerusalem and Its Vicinity', *BAIAS* 19–20 (2001–2002), 95–118.

Kloner, A. and B. Zissu, *The Necropolis of Jerusalem in the Second Temple Period* (ISACR, 8; Leuven: Peeters, 2007).

Knauf, E. A., 'Bethel: The Israelite Impact on Judean Language and Literature', in O. Lipschits and J. Blenkinsopp (eds), *Judah and the Judeans in the Neo-Babylonian Period* (Winona Lake, IN: Eisenbrauns, 2003), 291–350.

Knopf, T., 'Rahels Grab: Eine Tradition aus dem TNK', *Dielheimer Blätter zum Alten Testament und seiner Rezeption in der frühen Kirche* 27 (1991), 73–137.

Knoppers, G. N., 'An Achaemenid Imperial Authorization of Torah in Yehud?' in J. W. Watts (ed.), *Persia and Torah: The Theory of Imperial Authorization of the Pentateuch* (SBLSS, 17; Atlanta, GA: Scholars Press, 2001), 115–34.

——'Nehemiah and Sanballat: The Enemy Without or Within?' in O. Lipschits, G. N. Knoppers and R. Albertz (eds), *Judah and the Judeans in the Fourth Century B.C.E.* (Winona Lake, IN: Eisenbrauns, 2007), 305–31.

Knoppers, G. N. and B. M. Levinson (eds.), *The Pentateuch as Torah: New Models for Understanding its Promulgation and Acceptance* (Winona Lake, IN: Eisenbrauns, 2007).

Knowles, M. D., *Centrality Practiced: Jerusalem in the Religious Practice of Yehud and the Diaspora in the Persian Period* (Atlanta, GA: Society of Biblical Literature, 2006).

Köckert, M., 'Fear of Isaac', *DDD*, 329–31.

Koenen, K., *Bethel: Geschichte, Kult und Theologie* (OBO 192; Göttingen: Vandenhoeck & Ruprecht, 2003).

Krebernik, M. and J. van Oorschot (eds), *Polytheismus und Monotheismus in den Religionen des Vorderen Orients* (AOAT 298; Münster: Ugarit-Verlag, 2002).

Kunin, S. D., *We Think What We Eat: Neo-Structuralist Analysis of Israelite Food Rules and Other Cultural and Textual Practices* (JSOTS, 412; London: T&T Clark, 2004).

Laneri, N. (ed.), *Performing Death: Social Analyses of Funerary Traditions in the Ancient Near East and Mediterranean* (University of Chicago Oriental Institute Seminars, 3; Chicago: Oriental Institute of the University of Chicago, 2007).

Lehmann, M. R., 'Abraham's Purchase of Machpelah and Hittite Law', *BASOR* 129 (1953), 15–18.

——'A New Interpretation of the Term *šdmwt*', *VT* 3 (1953), 361–71.

Lemaire, A., 'Populations et territoires de la Palestine à l'époque perse', *Transeuphratène* 3 (1990), 31–74.

——'Nabonidus in Arabia and Judah in the Neo-Babylonian Period', in O. Lipschits and J. Blenkinsopp (eds), *Judah and the Judeans in the Neo-Babylonian Period* (Winona Lake, IN: Eisenbrauns, 2003), 285–98.

Lemche, N. P., *The Canaanites and Their Land: The Tradition of the Canaanites* (JSOTS, 110; Sheffield: JSOT Press, 1991).

Leuchter, M., *Josiah's Reform and Jeremiah's Scroll: Historical Calamity and Prophetic Response* (Sheffield: Sheffield Phoenix Press, 2006).

Leveen, A. B., *Memory and Tradition in the Book of Numbers* (Cambridge: Cambridge University Press, 2008).

Levenson, J. D., 'The Universal Horizon of Biblical Particularism', in M. G. Brett (ed.), *Ethnicity and the Bible* (Leiden: Brill, 2002), 143–69.

——*Resurrection and the Restoration of Israel: The Ultimate Victory of the God of Life* (New Haven: Yale University Press, 2006).

Levine, B. A., *Numbers 1–20: A New Translation with Introduction and Commentary* (AB, 4; New York: Doubleday, 1993).

——'The Biblical "Town" as Reality and Typology: Evaluating Biblical References to Towns and Their Functions', in M. Hudson and B. A. Levine (eds), *Urbanization and Land Ownership in the Ancient Near East* (Peabody Museum Bulletin, 7; Cambridge, MA: Peabody Museum of Archaeology and Ethnology, Harvard University, 1999), 421–53.

——*Numbers 21–36: A New Translation with Introduction and Commentary* (AB, 4A; New York: Doubleday, 2000).

——'The Clan-Based Economy of Biblical Israel', in W. G. Dever and S. Gitin (eds), *Symbiosis, Symbolism, and the Power of the Past: Canaan, Ancient Israel and Their Neighbors from the Late Bronze Age through Roman Palestine* (Winona Lake, IN: Eisenbrauns, 2003), 445–53.

Levine, B. A. and J. -M. de Tarragon, 'Dead Kings and Rephaim: The Patrons of the Ugaritic Dynasty', *JAOS* 104 (1984), 649–59.

Levinson, B. M., *Deuteronomy and the Hermeneutics of Legal Innovation* (Oxford: Oxford University Press, 1998).

Lewis, T. J., *Cults of the Dead in Ancient Israel and Ugarit* (HSM, 39; Atlanta, GA: Scholars Press, 1989).
——'The Ancestral Estate (*naḥălat ʾĕlōhîm*) in 2 Samuel 14:16', *JBL* 110 (1991), 597–612.
——'Toward a Literary Translation of the Rapiuma Texts', in N. Wyatt, W. G. E. Watson and J. B. Lloyd (eds), *Ugarit, Religion and Culture: Proceedings of the International Colloquium on Ugarit, Religion and Culture Edinburgh July 1994* (UBL, 12; Münster: Ugarit-Verlag, 1996), 115–49.
——'How Far Can Texts Take Us? Evaluating Textual Sources for Reconstructing Ancient Israelite Beliefs about the Dead', in B. M. Gittlen (ed.), *Sacred Time, Sacred Place: Archaeology and the Religion of Israel* (Winona Lake, IN: Eisenbrauns, 2002), 169–217.
——'Family, Household, and Local Religion at Late Bronze Age Ugarit', in J. Bodel and S. M. Olyan (eds), *Household and Family Religion in Antiquity* (Oxford: Blackwell, 2008), 60–88.
L'Heureux, C., 'The Ugaritic and Biblical Rephaim', *HTR* 67 (1974), 265–74.
Lightstone, J. N., *The Commerce of the Sacred: Mediation of the Divine among Jews in the Greco-Roman World* (2nd edn; New York: Columbia University Press, 2006).
Lipiński, E., 'ʿAnaq – Kiryat ʾArbaʿ – Hébron et ses sanctuaires tribaux', *VT* 24 (1974), 41–55.
Lipschits, O., 'Demographic Changes in Judah between the Seventh and the Fifth Centuries BCE', in O. Lipschits and J. Blenkinsopp (eds), *Judah and the Judeans in the Neo-Babylonian Period* (Winona Lake, IN: Eisenbrauns, 2003), 323–77.
——'Achaemenid Imperial Policy, Settlement Processes in Palestine, and the Status of Jerusalem in the Middle of the Fifth Century BCE', in O. Lipschits and M. Oeming (eds), *Judah and the Judeans in the Persian Period* (Winona Lake, IN: Eisenbrauns, 2006), 19–52.
Liverani, M., 'Land Tenure and Inheritance in the Ancient Near East: The Interaction between "Palace" and "Family"', in T. Khalidi (ed.), *Social Transformation in the Middle East* (Beirut: American University of Beirut, 1984), 33–44.
——*Israel's History and the History of Israel* (trans. C. Peri and P. R. Davies; London: Equinox, 2005).
Loewenstamm, S., 'The Death of Moses', in G. W. E. Nickelsburg (ed.), *Studies on the Testament of Abraham* (Missoula: Scholars Press, 1972), 185–217.
——'The Death of the Patriarchs in the Book of Genesis', in *From Babylon to Canaan: Studies in the Bible and Its Oriental Background* (Jerusalem: Magnes, 1992), 78–108.
Long, B. O., *1 Kings with an Introduction to Historical Literature* (FOTL, 9; Grand Rapids, MI: Eerdmans, 1984).
Loretz, O., 'Vom kanaanäischen Totenkult zur jüdischen Patriarchen – und Elternehung', *Jahrbuch des Anthropologie und Religionsgeschichte* 3 (1978), 149–201.
——'Stelen und Sohnespflicht im Totenkult Kanaans und Israels: *skn* (*KTU* 1.17 I 26) und *jd* (Jes 56,5)', *UF* 21 (1989), 241–46.
——*Götter – Ahnen – Könige als gerechte Richter: Der 'Rechtsfall' des Menschen vor Gott nach altorientalischen und biblischen Texten* (AOAT, 290; Münster: Ugarit-Verlag, 2003).
Low, S. M. and D. Lawrence-Zúñiga, 'Locating Culture', in S. M. Low and D. Lawrence-Zúñiga, *The Anthropology of Space and Place: Locating Culture* (Oxford: Blackwell, 2003), 1–47.
Loza Vera, J.,'La *bᵉrît* entre Laban et Jacob (Gn. 31.43–54)', in P. Daviau, P. M. Michèle, J. W. Wevers and M. Weigl (eds), *The World of the Aramaeans, I: Biblical Studies in Honour of Paul-Eugène Dion* (JSOTS, 324; Sheffield: Sheffield Academic Press, 2001), 57–69.
Luther, B., 'Die israelitischen Stämme', *ZAW* 21 (1901), 1–76.
Lux, R., 'Der Tod des Moses, als "besprochene und erzählte Welt"', *ZTK* 84 (1987), 395–425.
MacDonald, N., 'Driving a Hard Bargain? Genesis 23 and Models of Economic Exchange', in L. J. Lawrence and M. I. Aguilar (eds), *Anthropology and Biblical Studies: Avenues of Approach* (Leiden: Deo, 2004), 79–96.
Malkin, I., 'Land Ownership, Territorial Possession, Hero Cults, and Scholarly Theory', in R.M. Rosen and J. Farrell (eds), *Nomodeiktes: Greek Studies in Honor of Martin Ostwald* (Ann Arbor: University of Michigan Press, 1993), 225–34.

Mann, T. W., 'Holiness and Death in the Redaction of Numbers 16:1–20:13', in J. H. Marks and R. M. Good (eds), *Love and Death in the Ancient Near East: Essays in Honor of Marvin H. Pope* (Guilford: Four Quarters, 1987), 181–90.

Marsman, H. J., *Women in Ugarit and Israel: Their Social and Religious Position in the Context of the Ancient Near East* (OTS, 49; Leiden: Brill, 2003).

Matthews, V. H., 'Back to Bethel: Geographical Reiteration in Biblical Narrative', *JBL* 128 (2009), 149–65.

McAnany, P. A., *Living with the Ancestors: Kinship and Kingship in Ancient Maya Society* (Austin, TX: University of Texas Press, 1995).

McCarter, P. K., *I Samuel: A New Translation with Introduction, Notes and Commentary* (AB, 8; Garden City, NY: Doubleday, 1980).

——'The Royal Steward Inscription', *COS*, 2.180.

McCarthy, D. J., 'Notes on the Love of God in Deuteronomy and the Father-Son Relationship between Yahweh and Israel', *CBQ* 27 (1965), 144–47.

——*Treaty and Covenant: A Study in Form in the Ancient Oriental Documents and in the Old Testament* (2nd edn; Rome: Biblical Institute Press, 1981).

McKane, W., *A Critical and Exegetical Commentary on Jeremiah. Volume 1: Introduction and Commentary on Jeremiah I–XXV* (ICC; Edinburgh: T&T Clark, 1986).

——*A Critical and Exegetical Commentary on Jeremiah, Volume 2: Commentary on Jeremiah XXVI-LII* (ICC; Edinburgh: T&T Clark, 1996).

McMahon, G., 'The Hittites and the Bible', *BA* (1989), 71–77.

Meier, S. A., 'Destroyer', *DDD*, 240–44.

Mendenhall, G. E., 'From Witchcraft to Justice: Death and Afterlife in the Old Testament', in H. Obayashi (ed.), *Death and Afterlife: Perspectives of World Religions* (London: Praeger, 1992), 67–81.

Merwe, B. J. van der, *Pentateuchtradisies in die Prediking van Deuterojesaja* (Groningen: Wolters, 1955).

Metcalf, P. and R. Huntington, *Celebrations of Death: The Anthropology of Mortuary Ritual* (2nd edn.; Cambridge: Cambridge University Press, 1991).

Mettinger, T. N. D., *The Dethronement of Sabaoth: Studies in the Shem and Kabod Theologies* (ConBOT, 18; Lund: Gleerup, 1982).

——*No Graven Image? Israelite Aniconism in Its Ancient Near Eastern Context* (ConBOT, 42; Stockholm: Almqvist & Wiksell, 1995).

——*The Riddle of Resurrection: 'Dying and Rising Gods' in the Ancient Near East* (ConBOT, 50; Stockholm: Almqvist & Wiksell, 2001).

Meyer, E., *Die Israeliten und ihre Nachbarstämme* (Halle: Max Niemeyer, 1906).

Meyers, C., 'Household Religion', in F. Stavrakopoulou and J. Barton (eds), *Religious Diversity in Ancient Israel and Judah* (London: T&T Clark, 2010), 118–34.

Meyers, E. M., 'Secondary Burials in Palestine', *BA* 33 (1970), 2–29.

——*Jewish Ossuaries: Reburial and Rebirth* (BO, 24; Rome: Biblical Institute Press, 1971).

Milgrom, J., 'The Land Redeemer and the Jubilee', in A. B. Beck, A. H. Bartelt, P. R. Raabe and C. A. Franke (eds), *Fortunate the Eyes That See: Essays in Honor of David Noel Freedman in Celebration of His Seventieth Birthday* (Grand Rapids, MI: Eerdmans: 1995), 66–69.

——*Leviticus 17–22: A New Translation with Introduction and Commentary* (AB, 3A; New York: Doubleday, 2000).

Millard, A. R., 'King Og's Iron Bed and Other Ancient Ironmongery', in L. Eslinger and G. Taylor (eds), *Ascribe to the Lord: Biblical and Other Studies in Memory of Peter C. Craigie* (JSOTS, 67; Sheffield: JSOT Press, 1988), 481–92.

Mitchell, C., '"How Lonely Sits the City": Identity and the Creation of History', in J. L. Berquist (ed.), *Approaching Yehud: New Approaches to the Study of the Persian Period* (SBLSS, 50; Atlanta, GA: Society of Biblical Literature, 2007), 71–83.

Moberly, R. W. L., *The Old Testament of the Old Testament: Patriarchal Narratives and Mosaic Yahwism* (Minneapolis: Fortress Press, 1992).

Montgomery, J. A., 'Hebraica. (2) *yam sup* ('the Red Sea') Ultimum Mare?', *JAOS* 58 (1938), 131–32.
——*A Critical and Exegetical Commentary on the Book of Kings* (ICC; Edinburgh: T&T Clark, 1951).
Moor, J. C. de, 'Rāpiʾūma – Rephaim', *ZAW* 88 (1976), 323–45.
——'Standing Stones and Ancestor Worship', *UF* 27 (1995), 1–20.
Morisi, M., 'Il culto siro-palestinese dei morti e il culto greco degli eroi: l'intiquieta(nte) ricerca del sovrumano tra pietà privata e ufficialità', *Henoch* 20 (1998), 3–50.
Morphy, H., 'Landscape and the Reproduction of the Ancestral Past', in E. Hirsch and M. O'Hanlon (eds), *The Anthropology of Landscape: Perspectives on Place and Space* (Oxford: Clarendon Press, 1995), 184–209.
Morris, I., 'Attitudes Toward Death in Archaic Greece', *Classical Antiquity* 8 (1989), 296–320.
——'The Archaeology of the Ancestors: The Saxe/Goldstein Hypothesis Revisited', *Cambridge Archaeological Journal* 1 (1991), 147–69.
——*Death-Ritual and Social Structure in Classical Antiquity* (Cambridge: Cambridge University Press, 1992).
Mosis, R., 'עבר', *TDOT* 11, 67–71.
Moughtin-Mumby, S., *Sexual and Marital Metaphors in Hosea, Jeremiah, Isaiah, and Ezekiel* (OTM; Oxford: Oxford University Press, 2008).
Mullen, E. T., Narrative History and Ethnic Boundaries: The Deuteronomistic Historian and the Creation of Israelite National Identity (SBLSS; Atlanta, GA: Scholars Press, 1993).
——*Ethnic Myths and Pentateuchal Foundations: A New Approach to the Formation of the Pentateuch* (Atlanta, GA: Scholars Press, 1997).
Na'aman, N., 'Death Formulae and the Burial Place of the Kings of the House of David', *Bib* 85 (2004), 245–54.
——'Josiah and the Kingdom of Judah', in L. L. Grabbe (ed.), *Good Kings and Bad Kings: The Kingdom of Judah in the Seventh Century BCE* (LHBOTS, 393, London: T&T Clark, 2005), 189–247.
Na'aman, N. and N. Lissovsky, 'A New Outlook on the Boundary System of the Twelve Tribes', *UF* 35 (2003), 291–332.
Neiman, D., '*PGR*: A Canaanite Cult Object in the Old Testament', *JBL* 67 (1948), 55–60.
Nelson, R. D., *Deuteronomy: A Commentary* (OTL; Louisville, KY: Westminster John Knox Press, 2002).
Niditch, S., *'My Brother Esau is a Hairy Man': Hair and Identity in Ancient Israel* (Oxford: Oxford University Press, 2008).
——'Experiencing the Divine: Heavenly Visits, Earthly Encounters and the Land of the Dead', in F. Stavrakopoulou and J. Barton (eds), *Religious Diversity in Ancient Israel and Judah* (London: T&T Clark, 2010), 11–22.
Niehr, H., 'Ein unerkannter Text zur Nekromantie in Israel: Bemerkungen zum religionsgeschichtlichen Hintergrund von 2 Sam 12,16a', *UF* 23 (1991), 301–6.
——'Die reform des Joschija: Methodische, historische und religionsgeschichtliche Aspekte', in W. Gross (ed.), *Jeremia und die 'deuteronomistische Bewegung'* (Weinheim: Beltz Athenäum, 1995), 33–54.
——'Zur Semantik von nordwestsemitischen *ʿlm* als "Unterwelt" und "Grab"', in B. Pongratz-Leisten, H. Kühne and P. Xella (eds), *Ana Šadî Labnāni lū Allik: Festschrift für W. Röllig* (AOAT, 247; Neukirchen-Vluyn: Neukirchen Verlag, 1997), 295–305.
——'Aspekte des Totengedenkeis im Juda der Königszeit' *ThQ* 178 (1998), 1–13.
——'The Changed Status of the Dead in Yehud', in R. Albertz and B. Becking (eds), *Yahwism After the Exile: Perspectives on Israelite Religion in the Persian Era* (Assen: Van Gorcum, 2003), 136–55.
——'The Royal Funeral in Ancient Syria', *JNSL* 32 (2006), 1–24.
Nielsen, E., *Shechem: A Traditio-Historical Investigation* (Copenhagen: Gad, 1955).
Nocquet, D., 'La mort des patriarches, d'Aaron et de Moïse. L'apport de l'écriture sacerdotale à la constitution du Pentateuque à l'époque perse', *Transeuphratène* 29 (2005), 133–53.

Noegel, S., 'The Aegean Ogygos of Boeotia and the Biblical Og of Bashan: Reflections of the Same Myth', *ZAW* 110 (1998), 411–26.
North, C. R., *Isaiah 40–55* (London: SCM Press, 1952).
Noth, M., 'Studien zu den historisch-geographischen Dokumenten des Josua-Buches', *ZDPV* 58 (1935), 185–255.
——*The History of Israel* (2nd edn; London: Black, 1960).
——*Numbers: A Commentary* (trans. J. D. Martin; OTL; London: SCM Press, 1968).
Nutkowicz, H., *L'homme face à la mort au royaume de Juda: Rites, pratiques et représentations* (Paris: Cerf, 2006).
Oakdale, S., 'Forgetting the Dead, Remembering Enemies', in G. F. M. Rakita, J. E. Buikstra, L. A. Beck and S. R. Williams (eds), *Interacting with the Dead: Perspectives on Mortuary Archaeology for the New Millennium* (Gainesville, FL: University of Florida Press, 2005), 107–23.
Ockinga, B. G., 'A Note on 2 Samuel 18.18', *BN* 31 (1986), 31–34.
Odell, M. S., 'The City of Hamonah in Ezekiel 39:11–16: The Tumultuous City of Jerusalem', *CBQ* 56 (1994), 479–89.
——'What was the Image of Jealousy in Ezekiel 8?', in L. L. Grabbe and A. O. Bellis (eds), *The Priests in the Prophets: The Portrayal of Priests, Prophets, and Other Religious Specialists in the Latter Prophets* (JSOTS, 408; London and New York: T&T Clark, 2004), 131–48.
Oeming, M. and K. Schmid (eds), *Der eine Gott und die Götter. Polytheismus und Monotheismus im antiken Israel* (AThANT 82; Zürich: Theologischer Verlag, 2003).
Oesterley, W. O. E., *Immortality and the Unseen World – A Study in Old Testament Religion* (London: SPCK, 1921).
Olmo Lete, G. del, 'GN, el cementerio regio de Ugarit', *SEL* 3 (1986), 62–64.
——'Bašan o el "infierno" cananeo', *SEL* 5 (1988), 51–60.
——'Bashan', *DDD*, 161–63.
——*Canaanite Religion according to the Liturgical Texts of Ugarit* (trans. W. G. E. Watson; Bethesda, MD: CDL Press, 1999).
Olyan, S. M., 'The Cultic Confessions of Jer 2,27a', *ZAW* 99 (1987), 254–59.
——'"We Are Utterly Cut Off": Some Possible Nuances of נגזרנו לנו in Ezek 37:11', *CBQ* 65 (2003), 43–51.
——'Some Neglected Aspects of Israelite Interment Ideology', *JBL* 124 (2005), 601–16.
——'Was the "King of Babylon" Buried Before His Corpse was Exposed? Some Thoughts on Isa 14,19', *ZAW* 118 (2006), 423–26.
——*Disability in the Hebrew Bible: Interpreting Mental and Physical Differences* (Cambridge: Cambridge University Press, 2008).
——'Family Religion in Israel and the Wider Levant of the First Millennium BCE', in J. Bodel and S. M. Olyan (eds), *Household and Family Religion in Antiquity* (Oxford: Blackwell, 2008), 113–26.
——'Unnoticed Resonances of Tomb Opening and the Transportation of the Remains of the Dead in Ezekiel 37:12–14', *JBL* 128 (2009), 491–501.
Orta, A., 'Burying the Past: Locality, Lived History and Death in an Aymara Ritual of Remembrance', *Cultural Anthropology* 17.4 (2002), 471–511.
Oswalt, J. N., *The Book of Isaiah, Chapters 40–66* (NICOT; Grand Rapids, MI: Eerdmans, 1998).
Ottosson, M., 'ארץ', *TDOT* 1, 388–405.
Pardee, D., *Les textes paramythologiques* (RSO 4; Paris: Éditions Recherche sur la Civilisations, 1988).
Pardes, I., *The Biography of Ancient Israel: National Narratives in the Bible* (Berkeley, CA: University of California Press, 2000).
Parker, R., *Polytheism and Society at Athens* (Oxford: Oxford University Press, 2005).
Parker Pearson, M., 'The Powerful Dead: Archaeological Relationships between the Living and the Dead', *Cambridge Archaeological Journal* 3.2 (1993), 203–99.
——*The Archaeology of Death and Burial* (Stroud: Sutton, 2003).

Pastor, J., *Land and Economy in Ancient Palestine* (London: Routledge, 1997).
Paton, L. B., 'The Hebrew Idea of the Future Life: II. The Primitive Cult of the Dead', *The Biblical World* 35 (1910), 80–92.
——'The Hebrew Idea of the Future Life: IV. Yahweh's Relation to the Dead in the Earliest Hebrew Religion', *The Biblical World* 35 (1910), 246–58.
——*Spiritism and the Cult of the Dead in Antiquity* (London: Hodder & Stoughton, 1921).
Patton, K. C., *Religion of the Gods: Ritual, Paradox, and Reflexivity* (Oxford: Oxford University Press, 2009).
Peri, C., *Il regno del nemico* (Studi Biblici, 140; Brescia: Paideia Editrice, 2003).
Perrin, B., *Trois textes bibliques sur les techniques d'acquisition immobilière (Genèse XXIII; Ruth IV; Jérémie XXXII, 8–15)* (Revue Historique de Droit Français et Étranger; Paris: Librairie Sirey, 1963).
Petschow, H., 'Zwiegesprächsurkunde und Genesis 23', *JCS* 19 (1965), 103–20.
Pitard, W. T., 'Tombs and Offerings: Archaeological Data and Comparative Methodology in the Study of Death in Israel', in B. M. Gittlen (ed.), *Sacred Time, Sacred Place: Archaeology and the Religion of Israel* (Winona Lake, IN: Eisenbrauns, 2002), 145–67.
Podella, T., 'Nekromantie', *ThQ* 177 (1997), 121–33.
Polaski, D. C.,'What Mean These Stones? Inscriptions, Textuality and Power in Persia and Yehud', in J. L. Berquist (ed.), *Approaching Yehud: New Approaches to the Study of the Persian Period* (Atlanta, GA: Society of Biblical Literature, 2007), 37–48.
Polzin, R., *Moses and the Deuteronomist: A Literary Study of the Deuteronomistic History* (New York: Seabury, 1980).
Pope, M. H., 'Notes on the Rephaim Texts from Ugarit', in M. de Jong Ellis (ed.), *Ancient Near Eastern Studies in Memory of J. J. Finkelstein* (Hamden, CT: Archon, 1977), 163–82.
——'The Cult of the Dead at Ugarit', in G. D. Young (ed.), *Ugarit in Retrospect: Fifty Years of Ugarit and Ugaritic* (Winona Lake, IN: Eisenbrauns, 1981), 159–79.
Porter, A., 'The Dynamics of Death: Ancestors, Pastoralism, and the Origins of a Third-Millennium City in Syria', *BASOR* 325 (2002), 1–36.
Postgate, J. N., 'The Ownership and Exploitation of Land in Assyria in the First Millennium BC', in M. Lebeau and P. Talon (eds), *Reflets des deux fleuves: volume de mélanges offerts à André Flint* (Akkadica, 6; Leuven: Peeters, 1989), 141–52.
Prag, K., 'The Dead Sea Dolmens: Death and the Landscape', in S. Campbell and A. Green (eds), *The Archaeology of Death in the Ancient Near East* (Oxbow Monograph 51; Oxford: Oxbow, 1995), 75–84.
Prendergast, D., *From Elder to Ancestor: Old Age, Death and Inheritance in Modern Korea* (Folkstone: Global Oriental, 2005).
Propp, W. H., 'On Hebrew *śāde*(h), "Highland"', *VT* 37 (1987), 230–36.
Puech, É., 'Palestinian Funerary Inscriptions', *ABD*, 5.126–35.
Pury, A. de, 'Abraham: The Priestly Writer's "Ecumenical" Ancestor', in S. L. McKenzie and T. Römer (eds), *Rethinking the Foundations: Historiography in the Ancient World and in the Bible: Essays in Honour of John Van Seters* (BZAW, 294; Berlin: de Gruyter, 2000), 163–81.
——'Le choix de l'ancêtre', *TZ* 57 (2001), 105–14.
——'Le tombeau de Abrahamides d'Hébron et sa fonction au début de l'époque perse', *Transeuphratène* 30 (2005), 183–84.
——'The Jacob Story and the Beginnings of the Formation of the Pentateuch', in T. B. Dozeman and K. Schmid (eds), *A Farewell to the Yahwist? The Composition of the Pentateuch in Recent European Interpretation* (SBLSS, 34; Atlanta, GA: Society of Biblical Literature, 2006), 51–65.
Raabe, R., (ed. and trans.), *Petrus der Iberer: Ein Charakterbild zur Kirchen- und Sittengeschichte des 5. Jahrhunderts: Syrische Übersetzung einer um das Jahr 500 verfassten griechischen Biographie* (Leipzig: Hinrichs, 1895).
Rad, G. von, *Genesis: A Commentary* (trans. J. H. Marks; 2nd edn. London: SCM Press, 1963).
——*Deuteronomy: A Commentary* (trans. D. Barton; OTM; London: SCM Press, 1966).

Rahmani, L. Y., 'Ancient Jerusalem's Funerary Customs and Tombs: Part One', *BA* 44 (1981), 171–77.
——'Ancient Jerusalem's Funerary Customs and Tombs: Part Two', *BA* 44 (1981), 229–35.
——'Ancient Jerusalem's Funerary Customs and Tombs: Part Three', *BA* 45 (1981), 43–53, 109–18.
Rainey, A. F., 'Looking for Bethel: An Exercise in Historical Geography', in S. Gitin, J. E. Wright and J. P. Dessel (eds), *Confronting the Past: Archaeological and Historical Essays on Ancient Israel in Honor of William G. Dever* (Winona Lake, IN: Eisenbrauns, 2006), 269–73.
Rakita, G. F. M. and J. E. Buikstra, 'Corrupting Flesh: Reexamining Hertz's Perspective on Mummification and Cremation', in G. F. M. Rakita, J. E. Buikstra, L. A. Beck and S. R. Williams (eds), *Interacting with the Dead: Perspectives on Mortuary Archaeology for the New Millennium* (Gainesville, FL: University Press of Florida, 2005), 97–106.
Rakita, G. F. M., J. E. Buikstra, L. A. Beck and S. R. Williams (eds), *Interacting with the Dead: Perspectives on Mortuary Archaeology for the New Millennium* (Gainesville, FL: University of Florida Press, 2005).
Renz, T., *Die althebräischen Inschriften, I* (Darmstadt: Wissenschaftliche Buchgesellschaft, 1995), 447–48.
Ribichini, S. and P. Xella, 'La Valle dei Pasanti (Ezechiel 39.11)', *UF* 12 (1980), 434–37.
Richardson, S., 'An Assyrian Garden of Ancestors: Room I, Northwest Palace, Kalḫu', *SAAB* 13 (1999–2001), 145–216.
Richter, S. L., *The Deuteronomistic History and the Name Theology: lešakken šemô šam in the Bible and the Ancient Near East* (BZAW, 318; Berlin: de Gruyter, 2001).
Robben, A. C. G. M., 'Death and Anthropology: An Introduction', in A. C. G. M. Robben (ed.), *Death, Mourning and Burial: A Cross-Cultural Reader* (Oxford: Blackwell, 2004), 1–16.
Robinson, G., 'The Meaning of יד in Isaiah 56:5', *ZAW* 88 (1976), 282–84.
Rodman, M. C., 'Empowering Place: Multilocality and Multivocality', *American Ethnologist* 94 (1992), 640–56.
Rogerson, J., 'Frontiers and Borders in the Old Testament', in E. Ball (ed.), *In Search of True Wisdom: Essays in Old Testament Interpretation in Honour of Ronald E. Clements* (Sheffield: Sheffield Academic Press, 1999), 116–26.
Römer, T. C., *Israels Väter. Untersuchungen zur Väterthematik imDeuteronomium und in der deuteronomistischen Tradition* (OBO, 99; Göttingen: Vandenhoeck & Ruprecht, 1990).
——'Les récits patriarcaux contre la vénération des ancêtres: Une hypothèse concernant les "origines" d' "Israël"', in O. Abel and F. Smyth (eds), *Le Livre de Traverse: de l'exégèse biblique à l'anthropologie* (Paris: Cerf, 1992), 213–25.
——'Recherches actuelles sur le cycle d'Abraham', in A. Wénin (ed.), *Studies in the Book of Genesis: Literature, Redaction and History* (Leuven: Peeters, 2001), 179–211.
——'Mose in Äthiopien: Zur Herkunft der Num 12,1 zugrunde liegenden Tradition', in M. Beck and U. Schorn (eds), *Auf dem Weg zur Endgestalt von Genesis bis II Regum: Festschrift Hans-Christophe Schmitt zum 65. Geburstag* (Berlin: de Gruyter, 2006), 203–15.
——(ed.), *La construction de la figure de Moïse* (Paris: Gabalda, 2007).
——'Moses Outside the Torah and the Construction of a Diaspora Identity', *JHS* 8 (2008), article 15.
Römer, T. and J. D. Macchi, 'Luke, Disciple of the Deuteronomistic School', in C. M. Tuckett (ed.), *Luke's Literary Achievement* (JSNTS, 116; Sheffield: Sheffield Academic Press, 1995), 178–87.
Rom-Shiloni, D.,'Ezekiel as the Voice of the Exiles and Constructor of Exilic Ideology', *HUCA* 76 (2005), 1–45.
Rouillard, H., 'Rephaim', *DDD*, 692–700.
Rouillard, H. and J. Tropper, 'Vom kanaanäischen Ahnenkult zur Zauberei. Eine Auslegungsgeschichte zu den hebräischen Begriffen ʾwb und ydʿny', *UF* 19 (1987), 235–54.

Rouillard-Bonraisin, H. 'L'énigme des refā'îm bibliques résolue grace aux rapa'ūma d'Ougarit?', in J. M. Michaud (ed.), *La Bible et l'héritage d'Ougarit* (Sherbrooke, QC: Éditions GGC, 2005), 145–82.

Sarna, N. M., *Genesis* (JPS Torah Commentary; Philadelphia: Jewish Publication Society, 1989).

Saxe, A. A., 'Social Dimensions of Mortuary Practices in a Mesolithic Population from Wadi Halfa, Sudan', in J. Brown (ed.), *Approaches to the Social Dimensions of Mortuary Practices* (Washington, DC: Memoir of the Society for American Archaeology 25, 1971), 39–57.

Schaper, J. 'The Theology of Writing: The Oral and the Written, God as Scribe, and the Book of Deuteronomy', in L. J. Lawrence and M. I. Aguilar (eds), *Anthropology and Biblical Studies: Avenues of Approach* (Leiden: Deo, 2004), 97–119.

——'The Living Word Engraved in Stone: The Interrelationship of the Oral and the Written and the Culture of Memory in the Books of Deuteronomy and Joshua', in L. T. Stuckenbruck, S. C. Barton and B. G. Wold (eds), *Memory in the Bible and Antiquity: The Fifth Durham-Tübingen Research Symposium* (WUNT, 212; Tübingen: Mohr Siebeck, 2007), 9–23.

Schiffman, L. H., 'Descriptions of the Jerusalem Temple in Josephus and the *Temple Scroll*', in D. Goodblatt, A. Pinnick and D. R. Schwartz (eds), *Historical Perspectives: From the Hasmoneans to bar Kokhba in Light of the Dead Sea Scrolls* (Leiden: Brill, 2001), 69–82.

Schloen, J. D., *The House of the Father as Fact and Symbol: Patrimonialism in Ugarit and the Ancient Near East* (SAHL, 2; Winona Lake, IN: Eisenbrauns, 2001).

Schmid, K., 'The So-Called Yahwist and the Literary Gap between Genesis and Exodus', in T. B. Dozeman and K. Schmid (eds), *A Farewell to the Yahwist? The Composition of the Pentateuch in Recent European Interpretation* (SBLSS, 34; Atlanta, GA: Society of Biblical Literature, 2006), 29–50.

——'The Persian Imperial Authorization as a Historical Problem and as a Biblical Construct: A Plea for Distinctions in the Current Debate', in G. N. Knoppers and B. M. Levinson (eds), *The Pentateuch as Torah: New Models for Understanding its Promulgation and Acceptance* (Winona Lake, IN: Eisenbrauns, 2007), 23–38.

——'Gibt es eine "abrahamitische Ökumene" im Alten Testament? Überlegungen zur religionspolitischen Theologie der Priesterschrift in Genesis 17', in A. C. Hagedorn and H. Pfeiffer (eds), *Die Erzväter in der biblischen Tradition* (BZAW, 400; Berlin: de Gruyter, 2009), 67–92.

Schmidt, B. B., *Israel's Beneficent Dead: Ancestor Cult and Necromancy in Ancient Israelite Religion and Tradition* (reprinted edn; Winona Lake, IN: Eisenbrauns, 1996; originally published as FAT, 11; Tübingen: J. C. B. Mohr, 1994).

——'Memory as Immortality: Countering the Dreaded "Death After Death" in Ancient Israelite Society', in A. J. Peck and J. Neusner (eds), *Judaism in Late Antiquity* (Leiden: Brill, 2000), 87–100.

Schmitt, R., 'Cultural Memory and Family Religion'. Paper presented at the annual meeting of the European Association of Biblical Studies in Lisbon, Portugal, in August 2008.

——'The Problem of Magic and Monotheism in the Book of Leviticus', *JHS* 8/11 (2008), 2–12. Available online at www.arts.ualberta.ca/JHS/Articles/article_88.pdf (accessed 22 March 2009).

Schramm, B., *The Opponents of Third Isaiah: Reconstructing the Cultic History of the Restoration* (JSOTS, 193; Sheffield: Sheffield Academic Press, 1995).

Schwartz, S., *Were the Jews a Mediterranean Society? Reciprocity and Solidarity in Ancient Judaism* (Princeton: Princeton University Press, 2009).

Schwertuer, S., 'Erwägungen zu Moses Tod und Grab in Dtn 34 5.6', *ZAW* 84 (1972), 25–46.

Scurlock, J. A., 'Death and the Afterlife in Ancient Mesopotamian Thought', *CANE*, 1883–93.

——*Magico-Medical Means of Treating Ghost-Induced Illnesses in Mesopotamia* (Leiden: Brill/Styx, 2006).

Segal, J. B., 'Popular Religion in Ancient Israel', *JJS* 27 (1976), 1–22.

Sered, S. S., 'Rachel's Tomb and the Milk Grotto of the Virgin Mary: Two Women's Shrines in Bethlehem', *Journal of Feminist Studies in Religion* 2 (1986), 7–22.
——'Rachel's Tomb: Societal Liminality and the Revitalization of a Shrine', *Religion* 19 (1989), 27–40.
——'Rachel's Tomb: The Development of a Cult', *JSQ* 2 (1995), 103–48.
Shanks, M. and C. Tilley, 'Ideology, Symbolic Power and Ritual Communication: A Reinterpretation of Neolithic Mortuary Practices', in I. Hodder (ed.), *Symbolic and Structural Archaeology* (Cambridge: Cambridge University Press, 1982), 129–54.
Shemesh, J., 'The Elisha Stories as Saint's Legends', *JHS* 8 (2008), article 5.
Sherwood, Y., 'And Sarah Died', in Y. Sherwood (ed.), *Derrida's Bible (Reading a Page of Scripture with a Little Help from Derrida)* (New York: Palgrave Macmillan, 2004), 261–92.
Shimoff, S. R., 'Gardens: From Eden to Jerusalem', *JSJ* 26 (1995), 145–55.
Shipp, R. M., *Of Dead Kings and Dirges: Myth and Meaning in Isaiah 14:4b-21* (Leiden: Brill, 2002).
Silverman, H. and D. Small (eds), *The Space and Place of Death* (Archaeological Papers of the American Anthropological Association 11; Arlington, VA: American Anthropological Association, 2002).
Singer, I., 'The Hittites and the Bible Revisited', in A. M. Maeir and P. de Miroschedji (eds), *'I Will Speak the Riddle of Ancient Times': Archaeological and Historical Studies in Honor of Amihai Mazar on the occasion of his Sixtieth Birthday* (Vol. 2; Winona Lake, IN: Eisenbrauns, 2006), 723–56.
Ska, J. L., 'Essai sur la nature et la signification du cycle d'Abraham (Gn. 11,27–25,11)', in A. Wénin (ed.), *Studies in the Book of Genesis: Literature, Redaction and History* (Leuven: Peeters, 2001), 153–77.
Slanski, K., *The Babylonian Entitlement narûs (kudurrus): A Study in their Form and Function* (Boston: ASOR, 2003).
Smelik, K. A. D., 'The Territory of Eretz Israel in the Hebrew Bible: The Case of the Transjordan Tribes', in M. Prudky (ed.), *Landgabe: Festschrift für Jan Heller zum 70. Geburtstag* (Kampen: Kok Pharos, 1995), 76–85.
Smith, A. T., 'The Politics of Loss: Comments on a Powerful Death', in N. Laneri (ed.), *Performing Death: Social Analyses of Funerary Traditions in the Ancient Near East and Mediterranean* (University of Chicago Oriental Institute Seminars, 3; Chicago: Oriental Institute of the University of Chicago, 2007), 163–66.
Smith, J. Z., *To Take Place: Toward Theory in Ritual* (Chicago: University of Chicago Press, 1987).
Smith, M. S., 'The Invocation of Deceased Ancestors in Psalm 49:12c', *JBL* 112 (1993), 105–7.
——*The Origins of Biblical Monotheism: Israel's Polytheistic Background and the Ugaritic Texts* (Oxford: Oxford University Press, 2001).
——*The Early History of God: Yahweh and the Other Deities in Ancient Israel* (2nd edn; Grand Rapids, MI: Eerdmans, 2002).
——'When the Heavens Darkened: Yahweh, El, and the Divine Astral Family in Iron Age II Judah', in W. G. Dever and S. Gitin (eds), *Symbiosis, Symbolism, and the Power of the Past: Canaan, Ancient Israel, and Their Neighbors from the Late Bronze Age through Roman Palestinia* (Winona Lake, IN: Eisenbrauns, 2003), 265–77.
Smith-Christopher, D. L., 'Between Ezra and Isaiah: Exclusion, Transformation, and Inclusion of the "Foreigner" in Post-Exilic Biblical Theology', in M. G. Brett (ed.), *Ethnicity and the Bible* (Leiden: Brill, 2002), 117–42.
Snead, J. E. and R. W. Preucel, 'The Ideology of Settlement: Ancestral Keres Landscapes in the Northern Rio Grande', in W. Ashmore and A. B. Knapp (eds), *Archaeologies of Landscape: Contemporary Perspectives* (Oxford: Blackwell, 1999), 169–97.
Sofaer, J. R., *The Body as Material Culture: A Theoretical Osteoarchaeology* (Cambridge: Cambridge University Press, 2006).
Sonnet, J.-P., *The Book within the Book: Writing in Deuteronomy* (Biblical Interpretation Series, 14; Leiden: Brill, 1997).

Spronk, K., *Beatific Afterlife in Ancient Israel and in the Ancient Near East* (AOAT, 219; Neukirchen-Vluyn: Neukirchener Verlag, 1986).
——'Baal of Peor', *DDD*, 147–48.
——'Dadan', *DDD*, 232–33.
——'Travellers', *DDD*, 876–77.
——'A Story to Weep About: Some Remarks on Judges 2:1–5 and its Context', in J. W. Dyk (ed.), *Unless Someone Guide Me: Festschrift for Karel A. Deurloo* (Maastricht: Shaker, 2000), 87–94.
——'Deborah, a Prophetess: The Meaning and Background of Judges 4:4–5', in J. C. de Moor (ed.), *The Elusive Prophet: The Prophet as a Historical Person, Literary Character and Anonymous Artist* (OTS, 45; Leiden: Brill, 2001), 232–42.
Stager, L. E., 'The Archaeology of the Family in Ancient Israel', *BASOR* 260 (1985), 1–35.
——'Jerusalem and the Garden of Eden', *EI* 26 (1999), 183–94.
Stavrakopoulou, F., *King Manasseh and Child Sacrifice: Biblical Distortions of Historical Realities* (BZAW, 338; Berlin: de Gruyter, 2004).
——'Ancestral advocacy and dynastic dynamics in the Books of Kings', in P. J. McCosker (ed.), *What is it that the Scripture Says? Essays in Biblical Interpretation, Translation and Reception* (London: T&T Clark, 2006), 10–24.
——'Exploring the Garden of Uzza: Death, Burial and Ideologies of Kingship', *Biblica* 87 (2006), 1–21.
——'Gog's Grave and the Use and Abuse of Corpses in Ezekiel 39:11–20', *JBL* 129 (2010), 67–84.
——'"Popular" Religion and "Official" Religion: Practice, Perception, Portrayal', in F. Stavrakopoulou and J. Barton (eds), *Religious Diversity in Ancient Israel and Judah* (London: T&T Clark, 2010), 37–58.
Steiner, M. L., 'The Notion of Jerusalem as a Holy City', in R. Rezetko, T. H. Lim and W. B. Aucker (eds), *Reflection and Refraction: Studies in Biblical Historiography in Honour of A. Graeme Auld* (VTS, 113; Leiden: Brill, 2007), 447–58.
Stendebach, F. J., 'Das Schweineopfer im Alten Orient', *BZ* 18 (1974), 263–71.
Sternberg, M., 'Double Cave, Double Talk: The Indirections of Biblical Dialogue', in J. P. Rosenblatt and J. C. Sitterson (eds), *'Not In Heaven': Coherence and Complexity in Biblical Narrative* (Bloomington, IN: Indiana University Press, 1991), 28–57.
Stol, M., *Birth in Babylonia and the Bible: Its Mediterranean Setting* (Groningen: Styx, 2000).
Stordalen, T., *Echoes of Eden: Genesis 2–3 and the Symbolism of the Eden Garden in Biblical Hebrew Literature* (CBET, 25; Leuven: Peeters, 2000).
Stowers, S. K., 'Theorizing the Religion of Ancient Households and Families', in J. Bodel and S. M. Olyan (eds), *Household and Family Religion in Antiquity* (Oxford: Blackwell, 2008), 5–19.
Strecker, G. (ed.), *Das Land Israel in biblischer Zeit* (Göttinger Theologische Arbeiten, 25; Göttingen: Vandenhoeck & Ruprecht, 1983).
Strong, J. T., 'God's *Kābôd*: The Presence of Yahweh in the Book of Ezekiel', in M. S. Odell and J. T. Strong (eds), *The Book of Ezekiel: Theological and Anthropological Perspectives* (SBLSS, 9; Atlanta, GA: Society of Biblical Literature, 2000), 69–95.
Stucken, E., *Astralmythen der Hebraeer, babylonier und Aegypter* (Leipzig: Pfeiffer, 1896–1907).
Sukenik, E. L., 'The Funerary Tablet of Uzziah', *PEQ* 2 (1931), 217–21.
Tadmor, H., 'Was the Biblical *sarîs* a Eunuch?', in Z. Zevit, S. Gitin and M. Sokoloff (eds), *Solving Riddles and Untying Knots: Biblical, Epigraphic, and Semitic Studies in Honor of Jonas C. Greenfield* (Winona Lake, IN: Eisenbrauns, 1995), 317–25.
Talmon, S., '*Yād wāšēm*: An Idiomatic Phrase in Biblical Literature and Its Variations', *HS* 25 (1984), 8–17.
Tappy, R., 'Did the Dead Ever Die in Biblical Judah?' *BASOR* 298 (1995), 59–68.
Thomas, R., *Literacy and Orality in Ancient Greece* (Cambridge: Cambridge University Press, 1992).
Thompson, J. A., *The Book of Jeremiah* (NICOT; Grand Rapids, MI: Eerdmans, 1980).

Thompson, T. L., *The Historicity of the Patriarchal Narratives: The Quest for the Historical Abraham* (BZAW, 133; Berlin: de Gruyter, 1974).
Tiemeyer, L. -S., 'Abraham – A Judahite Prerogative', *ZAW* 120 (2008), 49–66.
Tilley, C., *A Phenomenology of Landscape: Places, Paths and Monuments* (Oxford: Berg, 1994).
——'Identity, Place, Landscape and Heritage', *Journal of Material Culture* 11 (2006), 7–32.
Toorn, K. van der, 'Echoes of Judaean Necromancy in Isaiah 28,7–22', *ZAW* 100 (1988), 199–217.
——'The Nature of the Biblical Teraphim in the Light of Cuneiform Evidence', *CBQ* 52 (1990), 203–22.
——'Funerary Rituals and Beatific Afterlife in Ugaritic Texts and in the Bible', *BibOr* 48 (1991), 40–66.
——'Ilib and the God of the Father', *UF* 25 (1993), 379–87.
——'Ancestors and Anthroponyms: Kinship Terms as Theophoric Elements in Hebrew Names', *ZAW* 108 (1996), 1–11.
——*Family Religion in Babylonia, Syria and Israel: Continuity and Change in the Forms of Religious Life* (SHCANE, 7; Leiden: Brill, 1996).
——(ed.), *The Image and the Book: Iconic Cults, Aniconism, and the Rise of Book Religion in Israel and the Ancient Near East* (CBET, 21; Leuven: Peeters, 1997).
——'Worshipping Stones: On the Deification of Cult Symbols', *JNSL* 23 (1997), 1–14.
——'Cybele', *DDD*, 214–15.
——*Scribal Culture and the Making of the Hebrew Bible* (Cambridge, MA: Harvard University Press, 2007).
——'Family Religion in Second Millennium West Asia (Mesopotamia, Emar, Nuzi)', in J. Bodel and S. M. Olyan (eds), *Household and Family Religion in Antiquity* (Oxford: Blackwell, 2008), 20–36.
Toorn, K. van der and T. J. Lewis, 'תרפים', *TDOT*, 8.765–78.
Toren, C., 'Seeing the Sites: Transformations in Fijian Notions of the Land', in E. Hirsch and M. O'Hanlon (eds), *The Anthropology of Landscape: Perspectives on Place and Space* (Oxford: Clarendon Press, 1995), 163–83.
Tromp, N. J., *Primitive Conceptions of Death and the Nether World in the Old Testament* (BO 21; Rome: Pontifical Biblical Institute, 1969).
Tropper, J., *Nekromantie: Totenbefragung im Alten Orient und im Alten Testament* (AOAT, 223; Neukirchen-Vluyn: Neukirchener Verlag, 1989).
Tsevat, M., 'Studies in the Books of Samuel, II: Interpretation of I Sam 10:2, Saul at Rachel's Tomb', *HUCA* 33 (1962), 107–18.
Tucker, G. M., 'The Legal Background of Genesis 23', *JBL* 85 (1966), 77–84.
Tuell, S. S., *The Law of the Temple in Ezekiel 40–48* (HSM, 49; Atlanta, GA: Scholars Press, 1992).
Turner, L. A., *Genesis* (Readings: A New Biblical Commentary; Sheffield: Sheffield Academic Press, 2000).
Uchelen, N. A. van, 'Abraham als Felsen (Jes 51,1)', *ZAW* 80 (1968), 183–91.
Ussishkin, D., *The Village of Silwan: The Necropolis from the Period of the Judean Kingdom* (trans. I. Pommerantz; Jerusalem: Israel Exploration Fund, 1993).
Valentine, C., 'Academic Constructions of Bereavement', *Mortality* 11.1 (2006), 57–78.
Van Gennep, A., *The Rites of Passage* (trans. M. B. Vizedom and G. L. Caffee; Chicago: Chicago University Press, 1960 [1908]).
Van Seters, J., 'Confessional Reformulation in the Exilic Period', *VT* 22 (1972), 448–59.
——'The terms "Amorite" and "Hittite"', *VT* 22 (1972), 64–81.
——*Abraham in History and Tradition* (New Haven: Yale University Press, 1975).
——*Prologue to History* (Louisville, KY: Westminster John Knox Press, 1992).
——'Divine Encounter at Bethel (Gen 28,10–22) in Recent Literary-Critical Study of Genesis', *ZAW* 110 (1998), 503–13.
——'The Patriarchs and the Exodus: Bridging the Gap between Two Origin Traditions', in

R. Roukema (ed.), *The Interpretation of Exodus: Studies in Honour of Cornelis Houtman* (CBET, 44; Leuven: Peeters, 2006), 1–15.

Vaux, R. de, 'Le sacrifice des porcs', in J. Hempel and L. Rost (eds.), *Von Ugarit nach Qumrân* (BZAW, 77; Berlin: Topelmann, 1958), 250–65.

——*Ancient Israel: Its Life and Institutions* (2nd edn; London: Darton, Longman & Todd, 1965).

Veijola, T., '"Fluch des Totengeistes ist der Aufgehängte" (Deut 21,23)', *UF* 32 (2000), 543–53.

——'King Og's Iron Bed (Deut 3:11) – Once Again', in P. W. Flint, E. Tov and J. C. VanderKam (eds), *Studies in the Hebrew Bible, Qumran, and the Septuagint Presented to Eugene Ulrich* (VTS, 101; Leiden: Brill, 2006), 60–76.

Verdery, K., 'Dead Bodies Animate the Study of Politics', in *The Political Lives of Dead Bodies: Reburial and Postsocialist Change* (New York: Columbia University Press, 1999); reprinted in A. C. G. M. Robben (ed.), *Death, Mourning, and Burial: A Cross-Cultural Reader* (Oxford: Blackwell, 2004), 303–10.

Vernant, J. -P., 'La belle mort et le cadaver outragé', in G. Gnoli and J. -P. Vernant (eds), *La mort, les morts dans les sociétés anciennes* (Paris: Maison des Sciences de l'Homme, 1982), 45–76.

Vincent, L. H. and J. E. Mackay, *Hebron, le Haram el-Khalîl: Sépulture des Patriarches* (Paris: Leroux, 1923).

Volz, P., *Jesaja II* (HAT, 9; Leipzig: Scholl, 1932).

Wallis, G., 'שׂדה', *TDOT*, 14.37–45.

Watts, J. W. (ed.), *Persia and Torah: The Theory of Imperial Authorization of the Pentateuch* (Atlanta, GA: Scholars Press, 2001).

Weidmann, H., *Die Patriarchen und ihre Religion im Licht der Forschung seit Julius Wellhausen* (Göttingen: Vandenhoeck & Ruprecht, 1968).

Weill, R., *La cité de David: Compte rendu des fouilles executées à Jérusalem, sur le site de la ville primitive. Campagne de 1913–1914* (Paris: P. Geuthner, 1920).

Weinberg, J., *The Citizen-Temple Community* (trans. D. L. Smith-Christopher; JSOTS, 151; Sheffield: JSOT Press, 1992).

Weinfeld, M., *Deuteronomy and the Deuteronomic School* (Oxford: Clarendon Press, 1972).

——*The Promise of the Land: The Inheritance of the Land of Canaan by the Israelites* (Berkeley, CA: University of California Press, 1993).

Wenham, G., *Genesis 16–50* (Word; Dallas, TX: Word, 1994).

Wenning, R., 'Bestattungen im königszeitlichen Juda', *ThQ* 177 (1997), 82–93.

——'"Medien" in der Bestattüngskultur im eisenzeitlichen Juda?', in C. Frevel (ed.), *Medien im antiken Palästina* (Tübingen: Mohr Siebeck, 2005), 109–50.

Westbrook, R., *Property and the Family in Biblical Law* (JSOTS, 113; Sheffield: JSOT Press, 1991).

Westermann, C., *Isaiah 40–66* (trans. D. M. G. Stalker; OTL; London: SCM Press, 1969).

——*Genesis 12–36* (trans. J. J. Scullion; Minneapolis: Ausburg, 1985).

Wevers, J. W., *Ezekiel* (NCB; London: Thomas Nelson, 1969).

Whitelam, K. W., 'Israel's Traditions of Origin: Reclaiming the Land', *JSOT* 44 (1989), 19–42.

——'Lines of Power: Mapping Ancient Israel', in R. B. Coote and N. K. Gottwald (eds), *To Break Every Yoke: Essays in Honor of Marvin L. Chaney* (Sheffield: Sheffield Phoenix, 2007), 40–79.

Whitmarsh, T., 'The Writes of Passage: Cultural Initiation in Heliodorus' *Aethiopica*', in R. Miles (ed.), *Constructing Identities in Late Antiquity* (London: Routledge, 1999), 16–40.

Whybray, R. N., *Isaiah 40–66* (NCB; London: Oliphants, 1975).

Williams, H., 'Death Warmed Up: The Agency of Bodies and Bones in Early Anglo-Saxon Cremation Rites', *Journal of Material Culture* 9 (2004), 263–91.

Williamson, H. G. M., *Ezra, Nehemiah* (WBC, 16; Waco, TX: Word, 1985).

——'Isaiah 63,7–64,11: Exilic Lament or Post-Exilic Critique?', *ZAW* 102 (1990), 48–58.

Wilson, I., *Out of the Midst of the Fire: Divine Presence in Deuteronomy* (SBLDS, 151; Atlanta, GA: Scholars Press, 1995).
Winkle, D. W. van,'The Meaning of *yād wāšēm* in Isaiah LVI 5', *VT* 47 (1997), 378–85.
Winter, I. J., 'Idols of the King: Royal Images as Recipients of Ritual Action in Mesopotamia', *JRS* 6 (1992), 14–42.
Wiseman, D. J., *The Vassal Treaties of Esarhaddon* (London: British School of Archaeology, 1958).
Wolff, S. R., 'Mortuary Practices in the Persian Period', *NEA* 65 (2002), 131–37.
Wright, C. J. H., *God's People in God's Land: Family, Land and Property in the Old Testament* (Grand Rapids, MI: Eerdmans, 1990).
Wright, D. P., *The Disposal of Impurity: Elimination Rites in the Bible and in Hittite and Mesopotamian Literature* (SBLDS, 101; Atlanta, GA: Scholars Press, 1987).
Wright, G. R. H., 'Joseph's Grave under the Tree by the Omphalos at Shechem', *VT* 22 (1972), 476–86.
Wright, J. L., *Rebuilding Identity: The Nehemiah-Memoir and Its Earliest Readers* (BZAW, 348; Berlin: de Gruyter, 2004).
Wright, J. W., 'Remapping Yehud: The Borders of Yehud and the Genealogies of Chronicles', in O. Lipschits and M. Oeming (eds), *Judah and the Judeans in the Persian Period* (Winona Lake, IN: Eisenbrauns, 2006), 67–89.
Wyatt, N., 'The Hollow Crown: Ambivalent Elements in West Semitic Royal Ideology', *UF* 18 (1986), 421–36.
——'When Adam Delved: The Meaning of Genesis III 23', *VT* 38 (1988), 117–22.
——'"Supposing Him to be the Gardener" (John 20,15): A Study of the Paradise Motif in John', *ZNW* 81 (1990), 21–38.
——*Myths of Power: A Study of Royal Ideology in Ugaritic and Biblical Tradition* (UBL 13; Münster: Ugarit-Verlag, 1996).
——*Space and Time in the Religious Life of the 'Ancient' Near East* (BS, 85; Sheffield: Sheffield Academic Press, 2001).
——*'There's Such Divinity Doth Hedge a King': Selected Essays of Nicolas Wyatt on Royal Ideology in Ugaritic and Old Testament Literature* (SOTS; Aldershot: Ashgate, 2005).
——'A la Recherche dea Rephaïm Perdus', in J. -M. Michaud (ed.), *Actes du Congrès International Sherbrooke 2005 « Le royaume d'Ougarit de la Crète à l'Euphrate. Nouveaux axes de recherche », Université de Sherbrooke du 5 au 8 juillet 2005* (POLO II; Sherbrooke, QC: Éditions GGC, 2007), 579–613.
——'Word of Tree and Whisper of Stone: El's Oracle to King Keret (Kirta), and the Problem of the Mechanics of Its Utterance', *VT* 57 (2007), 483–510.
——'Royal Religion in Ancient Judah', in F. Stavrakopoulou and J. Barton (eds), *Religious Diversity in Ancient Israel and Judah* (London: T&T Clark, 2010), 61–81.
——'A Garden for the Living – Cultic and Ideological Aspects of Paradise' (forthcoming).
Xella, P., 'Il "culto dei morti" nell' Antico Testamento', in V. Lanternari, M. Massenzio and D. Sabbatucci (eds), *Scritti in memoria di Angelo Brelich* (Rome: Dedalo, 1982), 645–66.
——'Death and the Afterlife in Canaanite and Hebrew Thought', *CANE*, 4.2059–70.
Yeivin, S., 'The Sepulchers of the Kings of the House of David', *JNES* 7 (1948), 30–45.
Yerushalmi, Y. H., *Zakhor: Jewish History and Jewish Memory* (Seattle and London: University of Washington Press, 1996 [1982]).
Young, J., *Writing and Rewriting the Holocaust* (Bloomington, IN: Indiana University Press, 1988).
Zerubavel, E., *Time Maps: Collective Memory and the Social Shape of the Past* (Chicago: University of Chicago Press, 2003).
Zevit, Z., *The Religions of Ancient Israel: A Synthesis of Parallactic Approaches* (London: Continuum, 2001).
Zimmerli, W., *Ezekiel 2 – A Commentary on the Book of the Prophet Ezekiel Chapters 25–48* (trans. J. D. Martin; Hermeneia; Philadelphia: Fortress Press, 1983).
Zorn, J. R., 'The Burials of the Judean Kings: Sociohistorical Considerations and Suggestions', in A. M. Maeir and P. de Miroschedji (eds), *'I Will Speak the Riddle of*

Ancient Times': Archaeological and Historical Studies in Honor of Amihai Mazar on the Occasion of his Sixtieth Birthday, Vol. 2 (Winona Lake, IN: Eisenbrauns, 2006), 810–20.

Zwickel, W., 'Über das angebliche Verbrennen von Räucherwerk bei der Bestattung des Königs', *ZAW* 101 (1989), 266–77.

INDEX OF ANCIENT SOURCES

Hebrew Bible
Genesis
2:4-25 12
2:8–3:24 129
10:15 32
11:30 41
12:1-2 29
12:1-9 17
12:6 46, 99
12:6-7 29
12:7 26
12:8 83, 91
13:3-4 83, 91
13:10 129
13:14-17 26
13:18 46, 51, 52
14:5-6 67
14:13 46
15:2 19
15:5 111, 145
15:7 26
15:17-21 147
15:19-21 67
16:10 145
17:8 34
17:16-17 41
18:1 46
18:10-12 41
18:18 33
18:22-33 43
19:30-38 26
21:33 124
22:17 111, 145
23 32, 33, 34, 36, 37, 38, 50, 53, 60, 99
23:2 51, 52, 98
23:4 34, 36
23:6 35, 37
23:8 36
23:8-9 34
23:9 35, 37, 42, 51
23:10 36
23:10-13 34
23:11 42
23:13 35, 51
23:15 35
23:16 36
23:17 42, 51, 52
23:17-20 36
23:18 36
23:19 33, 42, 49, 51, 52
25:8 9
25:9 42, 48, 51, 52
25:9-10 33, 49
25:12-15 49
25:17 49
26:3-5 26
26:4 111
26:34 32
26:34-35 34, 50
27:46 34
28:5-22 98
28:10-22 17
28:11-12 83
28:11-22 91, 92, 94, 102
28:18 16, 93
28:22 16, 93
29:11 98
31 98
31:1–32:3 17
31:3 99
31:13 16, 83, 91, 93
31:19 99
31:30 99
31:34 99
31:42 101
31:44 100
31:44-54 16, 75, 99, 101
31:45 93
31:45-46 100, 101
31:46 101
31:47 100
31:48 101
31:49 93
31:51 93, 100
31:52 93, 100
31:52-53 100
31:53 100, 101
31:54 101
32:12 145
33:1-17 98
33:4 98
33:18-20 17, 32, 50, 51
33:20 50, 51
35 99
35:1 99
35:1-4 92, 96, 99
35:1-15 91
35:1-16 83
35:1-20 17, 92, 93, 101
35:2-4 99
35:3 99
35:4 46, 96, 99
35:5-8 92, 96, 97
35:8 81, 97, 98, 99, 115, 136
35:9-15 92, 93, 94, 102
35:11-12 92
35:14 16, 93
35:15 93
35:16-18 93
35:16-20 15, 49, 81, 92, 93, 96
35:19 96
35:19-20 16, 93, 136
35:20 13, 16, 93
35:27 51, 52
35:29 9, 33, 48, 49
36:2 32
36:6-8 49
37:34-35 98
47:4-6 32
47:11 32
47:11-12 32
47:13-26 32
47:18-20 32
47:29-30 33, 49, 60, 61, 102
47:30 27
48:4 34
48:7 49, 93, 96
48:21 60
49:24-26 115
49:29 42, 93
49:29-31 9
49:29-32 33, 49, 102
49:29-33 60
49:30 42, 51, 52
49:32 42
50:2-14 27
50:4 98
50:4-6 104
50:5 50, 60, 136
50:5-14 49
50:7-11 50, 60, 136
50:7-14 93
50:13 9, 42, 49, 51, 52
50:25-26 27, 49, 60

Exodus
2:24 45
3:15 124
4:22 43, 144
6:3 45
6:8 45
12:23 63
13:19 27, 50, 60, 122
14:11 27
15:17 145
18:19 62
20:3-5 145
20:12 11
23:24 16
24:1-11 17
24:4 16, 71, 73
26:9 62
28:25 62
28:37 62
31:18 76
32:2-4 99
32:10 80
32:13 45, 111, 142
32–34 43
33:1 45
33:11 57
34:3 62
34:13 16
34:14 145
34:30-35 57
39:18 62

Leviticus
7:18 114
8:6-13 119
8:9 62
14:34 34
19:7 114
19:27-28 144

19:28 19
19:31 19, 145, 146
20:3-6 124
20:5-6 116
20:6 145, 146
20:26-27 146
20:27 145
21:1-11 121
21:1-15 18, 146
21:5 144
21:20 126
22:4 18, 146
22:4-8 121
25:13 34
25–27 31, 35, 119
26:1 16
26:30 118
26:42 45, 142
27:16 34
27:22 34
27:28 34

Numbers
5:2 18, 121, 146
6 121
6:1-12 18, 146
8:2 62
8:3 62
9:6-10 18, 146
9:6-12 121
12:8 57
13:22 52, 64
13:33 67
16 64
16:12-34 63
16:27 64
16:27-34 64
16:30 64
16:32 64
16:33 64
17:7-15 63
18:20-24 140
19 18, 146
20:1 61
20:2-13 59
20:12 59
20:22 61
20:23 59
20:23-26 59
20:24 9
20:28 61, 65
21 121
21:10-11 64, 69
21:11 64
21:20 57
21:35 68
23:14 57
23:28 62
25 62
25:1-16 62

25:2 19, 103
25:8 62
25:9 62
25:18 62
26:9 64
26:9-10 63
26:53-62 125
27:3-4 125
27:7 35
27:12-13 64
27:12-14 56
27:13-14 59
31:16 62
31:19 121
31:19-24 18, 146
31:50 99
32:11 45
32:35 35
32:42 52
33:43-44 64, 69
33:44-48 64
33:47 57, 65
33:51-53 26
34:6 95
35:2 35

Deuteronomy
1:4 68
1:8 45
1:10 111
1:28 67
1:37-39 65
2:10-11 67
2:20 67
3:1-11 26
3:3 68
3:6 69
3:8-13 147
3:10-11 67
3:11 68, 69, 70
3:13 69
3:15 52
3:17 57
3:27 57, 65
3:29 62
4:3 62
4:9 142
4:32-38 45
4:46 62
4:49 57
5:3 143
5:9 145
5:16 11
5:26 103
6:8 78
6:9 78
6:10 45
7:1 34
7:1-6 26
7:5 16, 73

7:12 58
7:17-26 26
9:1-2 67
9:5 45
9:27 45
10:6 61
10:14-22 45
10:22 45, 111
11:6 63, 64
11:10 58
11:18 78
11:18-21 78
11:20 78
12:3 16, 73
14:1 19, 43, 145
14:1-2 144
16:22 16, 73
18:9-12 19, 116
18:9-14 145
18:11 146
19:14 11, 95
20:17 34
20:19-20 115
21:22-23 121
21:23 18, 122, 146
23:2 126
25:5-6 124
26:13-14 145
26:13-15 18, 146
26:14 19
27 17
27:1-3 73
27:1-8 71, 72, 73, 74, 75, 76, 77, 142
27:2 76
27:2-3 71, 74
27:3 78
27:4 76
27:4-8 72
27:8 74, 78
27:16-17 77
27:17 11, 71, 95
27:26 76
28:26 110
28:62 111
29:13 45
30:4 126
30:20 45
31:2 65
31:2-3 59
31:3 59
31:12-13 55, 71, 142
31:14 59
31:14-16 56
31:16 59
31:24-26 76
31–32 75, 78
32:6 43
32:7-16 45

32:8-9 145
32:12-13 142
32:14 69
32:18 42, 44, 115
32:19 145
32:46 76
32:46-47 55, 71, 76, 141
32:48 56
32:48-52 59
32:49 57, 65
32:49-50 57, 64, 65
33:1 57
34:1 57, 65
34:1-6 61, 66
34:1-8 56
34:1-12 59
34:4 45, 59, 65
34:4-5 65
34:4-6 61
34:5-6 56
34:6 62, 71, 140
34:8 98
34:10-12 57

Joshua
1:3 60
1:3-4 55
1:13 142
1:13-15 55
3:13-17 72
3:23 72
4 76, 77
4:1-24 72, 74, 76
4:3-9 71, 73
4:6-7 76, 78, 142
4:7 72
4:9 76
4:19–5:1 72
4:20 76
4:20-24 71, 73, 76, 78, 142
4:23-24 77
7:26 13, 14, 101
8:29 13, 14, 77, 101
8:30-35 71, 74, 76, 77, 78, 142
8:31 77
8:32 75, 77, 78
8:33 62
8:34-35 75, 78
9:10 68
9:24 55, 60
10:27 14
12:3 57
12:4 67, 68
13:8 60
13:12 67, 68
13:15 26, 60
13:20 57, 62

Index of Ancient Sources

13:24 26, 60
13:29 26, 60
13:31 68
13:32 60
13:33 140
14:4-5 140
14:6 57
14:12 67
14:13-15 52
14:15 51
15:1 26
15:6 13
15:7 13
15:13 51, 52
15:20 26
15:54 51
16:1-2 88
18:13 88
18:17 13
18:18 62
18:22 89
19:46 62
19:47 52
19:51 141
20:7 51
21:11 51, 52
22:11 62
22:17 62
22:24-25 125
23:6 77
24 17, 75
24:1-27 78, 142
24:1-33 71, 74
24:2-3 44
24:11-13 26
24:23-27 99
24:25-27 75, 76
24:26 76
24:26-27 99
24:27 75
24:28 77
24:29-33 77
24:30 13, 61
24:32 27, 32, 49, 50, 51, 60, 99, 122, 136
24:33 61

Judges
1:10 51
1:20 52
1:22 89
2:1-5 98
2:9 13, 61
2:10 9
4:5 97
5:7 97
8:24-26 99
8:32 9
9:6 99, 115
9:37 99
16:31 9
20:26 98
21:2-4 98
21:17 124

1 Samuel
7:12 13
10:1-2 94
10:2 13, 15, 49, 95, 96
10:3 97
12:8 55
12:23 43
14:5 62
15:11-13 76
15:12 116, 124, 131
17:4-7 67
20:19 13
28:3 146
28:3-25 19, 145
28:9 146
28:13 19, 13
28:15 19
28:15-19 95
31:13 97, 115

2 Samuel
1:24 98
2:11 52
2:32 9
3:31 70
3:31-36 9
5:1-5 52
5:7-9 52
7:14 44
8:3 13, 131
14:16 19, 103
15:7-10 52
18:17 14, 101
18:18 16, 19, 94, 116, 124, 131
19:2 98
20:1 128
21:9-14 122
21:10 110
21:12-14 9
21:15-22 67
24:18-25 132
24:22 33

1 Kings
1:9 13
2:1 52
2:3 77
2:10 9, 105
2:37 86
3:8 145
6:12 76
7:15-22 16, 118
8:20 76
8:53 45
9:3 124
11:28 91
11:43 9, 105
12:16 128
12:28-29 102
12:28-33 83
12:26–13:10 85
12–13 83, 85
13 90
13:1-2 83
13:1-3 83, 85
13:1-10 83
13:8 90
13:11 90
13:11-32 83
13:14 97
13:16 90
13:21-22 90
13:28-30 9
13:30 90, 91
13:31 91
13:32 90
14:6 77
14:20 9
14:23 16
14:31 9
15:8 9, 105
15:24 9
16:34 64
17:18 57
17:24 57
18:31 91
18:36 44, 91
21:1-4 11
21:3-4 37
21:23-24 110

2 Kings
1:9-13 57
2:1-3 83
2:11 57
2:23-24 83
3:2 16
4:16 57
4:21-22 57
4:25 57
4:27 57
4:40 57
5:8 57
5:14-15 57
5:20 57
6:6 57
6:9-15 57
7:2 57
7:17-19 57
8:2-4 57
8:7-8 57
8:11 57
9:28 9
9:33-37 110
9:37 88
10:26-27 16
13:21 57, 91, 109, 122
13:23 44, 91
14:6 77
17:10 16
17:24-41 90
17:27-28 83, 90
17:34 91
18:4 16
18:12 98
18:31 12
18:31-32 6
19:4 103
19:16 103
20:2 107
20:21 106
21:6 116
21:7 124
21:18 106, 114
21:23-24 106
21:26 106, 114
23 83, 85, 90, 91
23:3 76
23:4 84, 86, 87
23:4-14 83, 86, 121
23:6 84, 86
23:11 84, 86
23:12 86
23:12-13 87
23:14 16, 84
23:15 84
23:15-18 16, 82
23:15-20 81, 83, 89, 90, 102, 109
23:16 84, 87
23:17 96, 131
23:17-18 90
23:18 90, 91
23:19 85
23:19-20 85, 90
23:20 85
23:24 76, 146
23:25 77
23:29-30 106
23:30 9, 106
23:33-34 106
23:34 106
24:6 106
24:12-17 106
25:6-7 106
25:25 106

Isaiah
1:2 43
1:29-30 114

Index of Ancient Sources

4:2 115
5:8 12
5:14 63
6:13 115
8:16 146
8:18-20 146
8:19 19, 103
8:19-20 19, 95, 146
11:1 115
11:10 115
14:1-10 95
14:4-21 111, 113
14:9 118
14:9-11 66
14:12-13 111
14:12-15 111
14:15-20 66
14:18-20 111
14:18-22 109, 124
14:19 110, 112
15:2 98
18:6 110
19:3 19, 146
19:19 13
19:19-20 73
19:20 76
22:12 98
22:15-18 112
22:15-19 105
22:16-18 17
22:17-18 110
24:21 112, 118
24:21-23 111
25:8 63
26:14 24
26:14-15 68
26:14-19 66
28:14-22 112, 119
28:16 119
28:18 119
28:20 119
29:1-4 110
29:4 19, 95
29:22 44
30:19 98
34:17 120
37:4 103
37:17 103
41:8 44
41:8-10 26
44:24-28 25
45:1-4 25
45:10-12 43
48:19 124
51:1-2 40, 42, 44, 45
51:1-3 40, 41
51:2 41, 42, 115
51:3 41, 129
53:8-9 124
55:13 124

56:1-8 123, 126, 127, 128, 129, 130, 142
56:3 124
56:3-5 123, 124
56:5 16, 124, 125, 126, 128
56:5-6 94
56:7-8 126
56:8 126, 127
57:1-13 126
57:3 116
57:3-5 114, 125, 126
57:3-13 19, 112, 115, 120, 125
57:5 115, 116
57:6 19, 115, 116, 125, 128
57:6-7 115
57:7 115
57:7-8 116
57:8 16, 116, 126, 128
57:9 115
57:10 115, 116
57:13 115, 116, 126, 127, 145
60:13 129
63:15 43
63:16 42, 44, 45
63:17 43, 124
64:7 43
65:1-2 114
65:1-4 19
65:1-5 19, 112, 113, 115
65:3 114
65:3-4 113
65:4 114
65:5 113
66:3 114
66:6-13 129
66:17 114

Jeremiah
2:26-27 115
2:27 42, 43, 44
3:4 43
3:6 114
3:19 43, 145
7:32 110
7:32-33 105, 109
7:32-34 109, 121
7:32–8:3 108, 110
7:33 110, 112
7:34 110
8:1-2 82, 109, 112
8:1-3 111, 120, 122
8:2 111, 112
8:3 111, 112

9:21 124
9:22 88
10:10 103
11:19 124
12:9 110
14:7-9 43
14:13 43
15:1 43
15:3 110
16:1-13 110
16:4 88, 110
16:5-8 9
16:13 110
16:14-15 26
16:18 145
20:6 61
22:10 98
22:18-19 112
22:19 107, 110
22:24-30 112
22:26 112
22:28 112
22:29 112
25:3 115
25:33 88
30:10 26
31:8-9 120
31:9 43, 144
31:15 49
31:15-16 98
31:15-17 15, 94, 96
31:17 95
31:21 91, 95
31:38-40 108, 120, 121, 122, 128
31:40 86, 121
32 38
32:2 38
32:6-14 38
32:15-25 38
32:17-23 45
32:20-23 38
32:42-44 38
33:15 115
33:26 44
34:5 9, 118
34:18 76
34:20 110
36:30 107, 112
43:13 16
46:27 26
48:1 57
51:25 118
51:50 143

Ezekiel
4:14 114
8:14 98
11:15 40
11:15-17 40

11:16-17 39
13:10-15 72
16:12 99
16:60 76
16:62 76
17:3-10 115
17:22-24 115
20:5 45
23–24 45
24:16 98
24:23 98
24:26 98
27:31 98
28:12-29 129
29:5 126
31:2-18 115
31:14-18 115
32:4 112
32:27 67
33:23 40
33:23-24 39
33:24 26, 41, 44
33:27 41
33:27-28 40
36:35 129
37:1-14 120
37:11 124
37:11-14 127
37:12-13 122
37:12-14 61
39:11 65
39:11-15 18, 65, 120, 146
39:15 91, 96
39:18 69
40–48 119
43:7 117, 118, 119
43:7-9 107, 112, 117, 119, 120
43:9 117, 119
43:12 119
43–46 120
44:25-27 121
45:7-8 119
45:8-9 119
47:1-12 129
47:13-23 141
47:22 119
48:29 119

Hosea
2:1 43, 103, 145
3:4 16
5:10 12
9:10 45, 62
9:10-12 62
9:13-14 62
10:1 98
11:1 43, 144
12:3-5 83, 91

Index of Ancient Sources

12:5 98
14:8 115

Joel
2:3 129
2:12 98

Amos
4:1 69
4:4 83
5:5-6 83
6:4 70
7:1-9 43
7:17 61

Micah
1:10 98
2:2 12
4:2-4 12
4:6 126
5:1 15, 96
5:13 16
7:14 69
7:20 44

Nahum
1:14 124

Habakkuk
2:5 63

Zephaniah
3:19-20 126

Haggai
2:12-14 18, 146
2:13 121

Zechariah
3:8 115
3:10 12
4:3 115
6:11-12 119
6:12 115
6:13 119
11:4 110
11:7 110
14:8 129
14:10 120

Malachi
1:6 43
2:10 43

Psalms
2:7 42, 44
6:3-10 129
6:7 70
16:2-6 141
16:3-4 19, 141

16:4 141
16:5-6 141
16:6 141
22:13 69
36:9-10 129
47:9 44
48:3 115
49:12 19
68:13 69
68:15 69
68:16 69
72:17 124
78:5 76
79:2-3 110
83:11 88
88:6 124
88:11 24, 66
89:27-28 44
91 129
92:13-15 129
95:3-11 45
104:9 95
105:6 44
105:9-10 44
105:42 44
106:6-33 45
106:17 63, 64
106:28 19, 62, 103
106:29 62
106:30 62
109:13 124
110:7 129
135:13 124
136:5-22 45
137:1-6 143
141:7 63

Job
17:13-14 9
18:16-19 124
21:32-33 9
24:2 12
26:5 66
26:5-7 115
30:23 9
30:31 98
33:14-30 129
33:18 65

Proverbs
1:12 63
2:18 66
3:3 78
6:21 78
9:18 66
10:7 19
15:25 95
21:16 66
22:27-28 11, 71
22:28 77, 95

23:10 11, 95
27:20 63
30:15-16 63

Ruth
4 38
4:10 19, 124, 125
4:11 15, 96

Lamentations
1:2 98
3:4 124

Daniel
4:10-33 115
9:11 77
9:13 77
12:2-3 123
12:3 111

Ezra
1:1-4 25
1:10 98
2:1-70 26
2:59-63 127, 135
2:63 135
3:2 77
4:1-4 31
6:3-5 25
6:21 31
7:6 77
7:11-26 25
7:26 31
9:1-2 31
9:11-12 31
9:14 31
10 31
10:8 31

Nehemiah
1:8-10 143
2:2-5 103, 120
2:7-8 25
2:10 31
2:20 127, 128, 142
3:1-32 127, 128
3:9 98
3:16 14, 108
5:5 31
5:12 31
7:5-73 108
7:6-73 26
7:61-65 135
8:1 77
9:2 31
9:7 44
9:14-15 55
9:23 111
10:29 31
10:31-32 31

11:25-30 48
12:1-26 108
13:1 77
13:23-29 26

1 Chronicles
1:13 32
1:27-28 44
1:32 44
1:34 44
10:12 97, 115
16:16 44
18:3 116
20:4-8 67
27:23 111
28:6 44
29:18 44

2 Chronicles
14:3 16
16:13-14 107
16:14 9, 118
20:7 44
21:18-20 107
21:19 118
23:18 77
24:16 107
25:4 77
26:23 107
28:27 107
30:6 44
30:16 77
31:1 16
32:33 107, 118
33:6 116
33:8 55
34:4-5 86
35:12 77
36:22-23 25

Apocryphal/
Deuterocanonical
Literature
Baruch
1:20 55

Tobit
4:17 19

Sirach
30:18 19
45:18 64
49:15 50

1 Maccabees
5:37 64
5:65 48

2 Maccabees
1:29 55

Index of Ancient Sources

4 Maccabees
2:17 64

Pseudepigrapha
Jubilees
22:1-6 47
22:2-3 47
22:3 47
22:4 47
22:5 47
22:6 47
32:34 15, 96

Life of Adam and Eve
48:6-7 129

Testament of Dan
5:12

New Testament
Matthew
2:18 15

Mark
16:19 57

Acts
1:2 57
1:11 57
1:22 57
7:15-16 50, 60

Ugarit Texts
KTU
1.6 i 15-18 129, 130
1.15 iii 4 116
1.15 iii 15 116
1.22 i 1-5 113
1.22 i 15 65
1.124 113
1.161 113
1.161.2-3 126
1.161.9-10 116
1.100.41 68
1.107.17 68
1.108.1 64
1.108.1-3 68
6.13 15
6.14 15

Classical Authors
Josephus
Antiquities
1.186 46
5.125 70
15.280-81 47

War
31.31-31 46
4.532-33 46
5.18-19 47

Herodotus
Hist.
1.68 70
1.181 70

INDEX OF AUTHORS

Abel, O. 26
Achenbach, R. 122, 147
Ackerman, J. S. 60
Ackerman, S. 18, 93, 95, 98, 114, 116
Ackroyd, P. R. 52
Aguilar, M. I. 33, 79
Albertz, R. 11, 44, 55, 99, 104, 144
Albright, W. F. 118
Allen, L. C. 110, 118
Alster, B. 82
Alt, A. 89
Amit, Y. 98
Anderson, G. A. 98
Anderson Beck, L. 3
Anidjar, G. 38
Antoniaccio, C. M. 4
Ashmore, W. 3, 139
Assmann, A. 79
Assmann, J. 14, 73, 77, 78, 79, 106, 132, 142, 146
Aucker, W. B. 121
Aufrecht, W. E. 10
Aus, R. D. 56, 57

Ball, E. 13
Barkay, G. 9, 118, 121
Barley, N. 20
Barrick, W. B. 85
Barstad, H. M. 34
Bartelt, A. H. 38
Bartlett, J. R. 48, 69
Barton, J. 5, 10, 12, 27, 44, 113, 146
Barton, S. C. 58
Barzel, H. 60
Battersby, C. 23
Bayliss, M. 82
Beaudry, M. C. 7
Beck, A. B. 38
Beck, L. A. 1, 3, 88, 147
Beck, M. 70
Becking, B. 11, 55, 135
Bell, C. 2
Bellis, A. O. 118
Bender, B. 7
Benjamin, A. 23
Bennett, G. 21

Bennett, K. M. 21
Ben Zvi, E. 10, 26, 29, 131
Bergsma, J. S. 38
Berlejung, A. 122
Berman, J. A. 12, 51
Berquist, J. L. 73, 78, 138
Blenkinsopp, J. 6, 11, 19, 30, 31, 34, 42, 43, 48, 89, 104, 116, 119, 125, 127, 128, 132, 135, 141, 144
Bloch, M. 1, 2, 3, 4, 137
Bloch-Smith, E. 8, 9, 10, 14, 15, 18, 19, 22, 82, 117, 132
Block, D. I. 39, 101, 118
Blum, E. 93
Bodel, J. 5, 23
Bodi, D. 40
Borger, R. 82, 88
Bottéro, J. 82
Bray, J. 36
Brett, M. G. 11, 12, 26, 29, 30, 32, 33, 34, 48, 132
Brettler, M. 82
Brichto, H. C. 8, 11, 17, 99, 144
Briant, P. 31
Britt, B. M. 77, 78, 79
Brown, J. 3
Brueggemann, W. 8
Budin, S. L. 62
Buikstra, J. E. 1, 3, 88, 137, 147
Burney, C. F. 98
Burns, D. 108

Campbell, S. 4
Carr, D. M. 79
Carroll, R. P. 31, 112, 121
Carter, C. E. 6
Cathcart, K. J. 110
Chapman, R. W. 3
Charles, D. K. 3, 137
Chesson, M. S. 2, 14-15, 80, 137
Christensen, D. L. 80
Cleary, J. 139
Clements R. E. 73, 138
Coats, G. W. 60
Cogan, M. 82, 85, 111

Cohen, A. C. 113
Cohen, C. 85
Cohn, R. L. 30, 37
Collins, J. J. 127
Connerton, P. 10, 73, 142, 143, 146
Coogan, M. D. 85
Cooper, A. 17, 18, 74, 99, 100
Coote, R. B. 49
Coser, L. A. 14
Cox, B. D. 93, 95
Cox, J. L. 137, 140
Cross, F. M. 89, 140-1
Crossley, J. G. 33
Crüsemann, F. 48

Dahood, M. 114, 116
Daviau, P. 100
Davies, D. J. 2, 4, 25
Davies, E. W. 138
Davies, P. R. 12, 31, 81, 89, 127
Davies, W. D. 8
Day, J. 44, 115, 119
Day, P. L. 95
Dearman, J. A. 12, 38
Deist, F. E. 9
Delamarter, S. 107
Delcor, M. 116
Derrida, J. 38
Dessel, J. P. 89
Dever, W. G. 6, 84, 85, 111
Dieterlin, G. 23
Dietrich, M. 129
Dietrich, W. 143
Dijkstra, M. 47, 55, 57, 58, 79
Douglas, M. 30, 92, 98, 144
Dozeman, T. B. 45, 136
Driver, S. R. 67
Duguia, I. M. 119
Duhm, B. 43
Dutcher-Walls, P. 5
Dyk, J. W. 98

Ebach, J. H. 118
Edelman, D. 27, 31, 87, 99, 108, 131, 143
Ego, B. 129
Eissfeldt, O. 52
Eslinger, L. 70

Evans, C. A. 107
Exum, J. C. 85

Farrell, J. 4
Fayer, J. A. 38
Fensham, F. C. 128
Figueras, P. 122
Finkelstein, I. 89
Fishbane, M. 73, 82, 113
Fleming, D. E. 5, 24
Flint, P. W. 70
Foltyn, J. L. 4
Fortes, M. 23
Francis, D. 4, 21
Franke, C. A. 38
Franklin, N. 106
Frazer, J. G. 21
Frei, P. 31
Frevel, C. 59, 121
Friesen, S. J. 4

Gafni, I. M. 61
Galil, G. 98
Galling, K. 45, 106
Gauley, S. W. 10
Gelb, I. J. 13
Gell, A. 87
Geller, P. L. 3
Gemser, B. 50
Gerleman, G. 34, 35
Gillespie, S. 2
Gitin, S. 6, 84, 89, 111, 126
Gittlen, B. M. 5, 18, 22
Glazier, J. 4
Gluckman, M. 22
Gnoli, G. 2
Goldman, B. 122
Goldstein, B. R. 17, 18, 74, 99, 100
Goldziher, I. 43
Gomes, J. F. 81, 83, 97
Gonen, R. 9
Good, R. M. 44
Goodblatt, D. 47
Goody, J. 4, 73
Goshen-Gottstein, M. 44
Goss, R. 20
Gottlieb, A. 24
Gottwald, N. K. 49
Goulder, M. 40
Grabbe, L. L. 6, 29, 48, 84, 89, 118, 138
Graesser, C. F. 15
Gray, J. 75
Green, A. 4
Greene, S. E. 140
Gros Louis, K. R. R. 60
Gross, W. 89
Grove, D. C. 2
Gruber, M. I. 97

Guillaume, P. 138
Gulde, S. U. 63
Gunkel, H. 43

Habel, N. C. 8, 31, 33, 34, 38, 59, 138
Hachlili, R. 105, 122
Hagedorn, A. C. 31
Halbwachs, M. 14
Hallam, E. 1, 2, 14, 21, 87
Hallo, W. W. 82, 113
Hallote, R. S. 8
Halpern, B. 11, 84, 97, 103, 106, 111, 119, 121, 132, 138, 144
Hamel, G. H. 6
Hamilton, V. P. 33, 35, 37, 52, 99, 138
Handy, L. K. 26
Hanson, P. D. 43
Haran, M. 84
Hardmeier, C. 79, 84
Hare, D. R. A. 91
Harrison, R. P. 3, 24, 65, 66
Havrelock, R. 70
Hayman, A. P. 143
Healey, J. 118
Heard, R. C. 30, 34, 49, 99
Hempel, J. 114
Henke, O. 62
Hertz, R. 2, 9-10
Hicks, D. 7
Hill, A. E. 72
Hillers, D. R. 110
Hinnant, C. 33
Hirsch, E. 3, 7, 136
Hobson, D. W. 11
Hockey, J. 1, 2, 4, 14, 20, 21, 87
Hodder, I. 1
Hoftijzer, J. 72
Hogland, K. G. 25, 31
Holloway, S. W. 26
Holtorf, C. 7
Horst, F. 35
Hostetter, E. C. 67
Houston, W. 114
Houtman, C. 77
Howarth, G. 1, 2, 20, 21
Hübner, U. 67, 70
Hudson, M. 5, 9, 12
Humphreys, S. C. 1
Huntington, R. 1, 2
Hurowitz, V. 131
Hurvitz, A. 85
Hvidberg, F. F. 98

Illman, K.-J. 105
Irwin, B. P. 65
Irwin, W. H. 116

Jacobson, D. M. 46
Jackson, B. S. 73
Jankowski, B. 122
Janowski, B. 129
Japhet, S. 34, 40, 125, 128
Jay, N. 27
Johnston, P. S. 20, 21
Jones, S. 29
Jong Ellis, M. de 65
Jonker, G. 5, 14, 109, 114, 148
Joosten, J. 38
Joyce, P. M. 39
Joyce, R. A. 2
Jupp, P. C. 20

Kallai, Z. 89, 96
Karge, P. 70
Katz, J. 4, 21
Kaufmann, Y. 22
Keane, W. 7
Keel, O. 46, 47, 99
Kellehar, L. 4, 21
Keller, M. 130
Kellermann, U. 108
Keown, G. L. 120
Kessler, J. 25
Khalidi, T. 6
Kieweler, H. V. 96
King, H. 1
King, P. J. 20
Kitchen, K. A. 45
Klass, D. 20, 21
Kletter, R. 89
Kloner, A. 105
Klopfenstein, M. A. 143
Knapp, A. B. 139
Knauf, E. A. 89
Knopf, T. 96
Knoppers, G. N. 30, 31, 104
Knowles, M. D. 138
Köckert, M. 101
Koenen, K. 81
Kooij, G. van der 72
Koole, J. L. 114
Korpel, M. C. A. 135
Krebernik, M. 143
Küchler, M. 46, 47
Kuechler, S. 7
Kühne, H. 68
Kunin, S. D. 140
Kuschke, A. 35

Lachs, S. T. 82
Laneri, N. 2, 3, 15
Lanternari, V. 20
Lawrence, L. J. 33, 79
Lawrence-Zúñiga, D. 7
Lebeau, M. 6
Lehmann, M. R. 36, 120
Lemaire, A. 48

Index of Authors

Lemche, N. P. 26, 56
Leuchter, M. 89
Leveen, A. B. 27, 61
Levenson, J. D. 22, 30, 80, 95, 129
Levin, C. 108
Levine, B. A. 6, 9, 12, 62, 63, 66, 118, 121, 147
Levinson, B. M. 30, 31, 73, 76
Lewis, T. J. 5, 10, 11, 15, 17, 18, 20, 23, 66, 82, 99, 113, 114, 116, 118, 126, 141, 146
L'Heureux, C. E. 67
Lightstone, J. N. 19, 47, 58, 91, 104, 122, 138
Lim, T. H. 121
Lindars, B. 52
Lipiński, E. 52
Lipschits, O. 6, 25, 34, 48, 49, 89, 104
Lissovski, N. 89
Liverani, M. 6, 25, 26, 30, 34, 35, 67, 68, 139
Lloyd, J. B. 66
Loader, J. A. 96
Loewenstamm, S. E. 50, 56
Long, B. O. 105
Loretz, O. 26, 48, 64, 67, 124
Low, S. M. 7
Loza Vera, J. 100
Luther, B. 43
Lux, R. 56

MacDonald, N. 33, 36
Mackay, J. E. 46
Maier, A. M. 32, 106
Malkin, I. 4
Marks, J. H. 44
Marsman, H. J. 97-8
Martin, J. D. 118
Massenzio, M. 20
Matthews, V. H. 81
McAnany, P. A. 14, 24, 27
McCarter, P. K. 96
McCarthy, D. J. 76, 144
McCosker, P. J. 118
McKane, W. 108, 112
McKenzie, S. L. 30
McMahon, G. 32
Meier, S. A. 63
Mendenhall, G. E. 20, 21
Merwe, B. J. van der 41
Metcalf, P. 1, 2
Mettinger, T. N. D. 15, 103, 130
Meyer, E. 43
Meyers, C. 5, 127, 144
Meyers, E. M. 82, 122
Michaud, J. M. 66
Michèle, P. M. 100

Miles, R. 79
Milgrom, J. 20, 21, 34, 38
Millard, A. 70
Mirau, N. A. 10
Miroschedji, P. de 32, 106
Mitchell, C. 138
Moberly, R. W. L. 30
Montgomery, J. A. 72
Moor, J. C. de 15, 67, 97, 100
Morisi, M. 19
Morphy, H. 136
Morris, I. 23
Mosis, R. 14
Moughtin-Mumby, S. 116
Mullen, E. T. 30, 37, 74

Na'aman, N. 89, 106, 117
Neiman, D. 118
Nelson, R. D. 56, 59, 73, 146
Neophytou, G. 4, 21
Neusner, J. 19, 68
Nickelsburg, G. W. E. 56
Nickman, J. 21
Niditch, S. 144, 146
Niehr, H. 11, 19, 68, 89, 91, 113, 118, 119, 121, 147
Nielsen, E. 50
Nocquet, D. 61
Noegel, S. 69
North, C. R. 41
Noth, M. 14, 63, 89
Nutkowicz, H. 19, 106, 114, 121

Oakdale, S. 147
Obayashi, H. 20
Ockinga, B. G. 16
Odell, M. 118, 119
Oeming, M. 6, 25, 49, 143
Oesterley, W. O. E. 22
O'Hanlon, M. 3, 7, 136
Olmo Lete, G. del 69, 113, 115
Olyan, S. M. 5, 9, 14, 23, 93, 98, 109, 110, 115, 124, 126, 127, 144
Oorschot, J. van 143
Orta, A. 137
Osteen, M. 33
Oswalt, J. N. 41
Ottosson, M. 35

Pardee, D. 69
Pardes, I. 27, 135
Parker, R. 5
Parker Pearson, M. 1, 3, 9, 20, 26, 137
Parry, J. 1, 2
Passow, I. D. 82
Pastor, J. 6, 138

Paton, L. B. 21, 44
Patton, K. C. 125
Paul, S. M. 85
Pearce, S. 29
Peck, A. J. 19, 68
Perdue, L. G. 127
Peri, C. 19
Perrin, B. 38
Petschow, H. 36
Pinnick, A. 47
Pitard, W. T. 18
Podella, T. 19
Polak, F. 131
Polaski, D. C. 73, 78
Polzin, R. 79
Pongratz-Leisten, B. 68
Pope, M. H. 65, 69
Porter, A. 4
Postgate, J. N. 6
Prag, K. 4
Prendergast, D. 4
Preucel, R. 139
Propp, W. H. 35
Prudky, M. 70
Puech, É. 121
Pury, A. de 30, 48, 49, 55, 136

Raabe, P. R. 38
Raabe, R. 58
Rad, G. von 33, 97, 144
Rahmani, L. Y. 105
Rainey, A. F. 89
Rakita, G. F. M. 1, 3, 88, 147
Renz, T. 122
Rezetko, R. 121
Ribichini, S. 65
Richardson, S. 115
Richter, S. L. 131
Robben, A. C. G. M. 4, 87
Robinson, G. 125
Rodman, M. C. 7
Rogerson, J. 13, 89, 108
Römer, T. 26, 30, 41, 45, 48, 52, 55, 60, 70
Rom-Shiloni, D. 40
Rosen, R. M. 4
Rosenblatt, J. P. 35
Rost, L. 114
Rouillard, H. 67, 69, 113, 146
Rouillard-Bonraisin, H. 66
Roukema, R. 56, 57
Rowlands, M. 7

Sabbatucci, D. 20
Sanders, J. A. 107
Sarna, N. M. 33, 37, 51
Saxe, A. A. 3
Scalise, P. J. 120
Schaper, J. 58, 74, 77, 79
Schiffman, L. H. 47

Schloen, J. D. 6, 24, 141, 143
Schmid, K. 30, 31, 45, 136, 143
Schmidt, B. B. 19, 20, 21, 22, 23, 67, 68, 106, 113, 114, 116, 117, 132, 144
Schmitt, R. 20, 96
Schorn, U. 70
Schramm, B. 114, 116
Schwartz, D. R. 47
Schwartz, S. 33
Schwertuer, S. 59
Scurlock, J. A. 82, 88, 148
Segal, J. B. 20
Sered, S. S. 96
Shanks, M. 1
Shemesh, J. 57
Sherwood, Y. 38, 77
Shimoff, S. R. 129
Shipp, R. M. 111
Silberman, N. A. 89
Silverman, H. 4, 137
Silverman, P. 21
Singer, I. 9, 32
Sitterson, J. C. 35
Ska, J. L. 29
Slanski, K. 13
Small, D. 4, 137
Small, N. 4, 21
Smelik, K. A. D. 70
Smith, A. T. 3
Smith, J. Z. 139-40
Smith, M. S. 15, 66, 86, 111, 130, 141, 143
Smith-Christopher, D. L. 29
Smothers, T. G. 120
Smyth, F. 26
Snead, J. 139
Sofaer, J. R. 23, 27, 87
Sokoloff, M. 126
Sonnet, J.- P. 58, 61, 72, 73, 76, 79, 146
Spronk, K. 18, 20, 22, 63, 64, 65, 67, 97, 98, 117, 141
Spyer, P. 7
Stager, L. E. 8, 20, 85, 129
Stavrakopoulou, F. 5, 10, 12, 13, 14, 20, 27, 44, 64, 65, 69, 85, 96, 106, 107, 110, 113, 114, 116, 118, 127, 130, 146
Steiner, M. L. 121
Steinkeller, P. 13
Stendebach, F. J. 114
Sternberg, M. 35, 37

Stol, M. 97
Stordalen, T. 12, 129
Stowers, S. K. 23
Strecker, G. 7, 34, 40
Strong, J. T. 119
Stucken, E. 43
Stuckenbruck, L. T. 58
Sukenik, E. L. 107
Sukhitan, L. ix

Tadmor, H. 126
Talmon, S. 124
Talon, P. 6
Tappy, R. 10
Tarragon, J.- M. de 66
Taylor, G. 70
Thackeray, H. St J. 46
Thomas, R. 73
Thompson, J. A. 111
Thompson, T. L. 45
Tiemeyer, L. 40, 53
Tilley, C. 1, 4, 7, 137
Toorn, K. van der 5, 15, 16, 18, 19, 23, 24, 43, 51, 69, 79, 97, 99, 101, 119, 141
Toren, C. 3
Tov, E. 70, 113
Tromp, N. J. 21
Tropper, J. 18, 146
Tsevat, M. 96
Tucker, G. M. 36
Tuell, S. S. 120
Turner, L. A. 33

Uchelen, N. A. van 42
Ussishkin, D. 105

Valentine, C. 20
VanderKam, J. C. 70
Van Gennep, A. 9
Van Seters, J. 32, 45, 55, 93, 131
Vaux, R. de 22, 114
Veijola, T. 19, 70
Verdery, K. 87
Vernant, J.- P. 2
Vincent, L. H. 46
Volz, P. 42

Wallis, G. 35
Warshaw, T. S. 60
Watson, W. G. E. 66, 113
Watts, J. W. 30, 31
Weidmann, H. 43

Weigl, M. 100
Weill, R. 106
Weinberg, J. 6, 31, 127
Weinfeld, M. 8, 58, 98, 135, 145
Wenham, G. J. 33
Wénin, A. 30, 41
Wenning, R. 18, 121
Westbrook, R. 36
Westermann, C. 33, 41, 43, 116
Wevers, J. W. 100, 117
Whitelam, K. W. 26, 49
Whiting, R. M. 13
Whitmarsh, T. 79
Whybray, R. N. 42
Williams, H. 7, 87
Williams, S. R. 1, 3, 88, 147
Williamson, H. G. M. 43, 104
Wilson, I. 130
Winer, M. 7
Winkle, D. W. van 124, 125
Winter, I. J. 118
Wiseman, D. J. 110
Wold, B. G. 58
Wolff, S. R. 18
Wright, C. J. H. 11, 31, 144
Wright, D. P. 10, 18, 86, 99, 106, 147
Wright, G. E. 89
Wright, G. R. H. 50
Wright, J. E. 89
Wright, J. L. 104, 108, 128
Wright, J. W. 49, 52
Wyatt, N. 12, 44, 58, 66, 69, 72, 97, 111, 113, 115, 129, 130

Xella, P. 20, 65, 68, 147

Yeivin, S. 117
Yerushalmi, Y. H. 77, 142, 143
Young, G. D. 69
Young, J. 78-9

Zerubavel, E. 137
Zevit, Z. 15, 20, 57, 94, 99, 109, 112, 115, 121, 126, 147
Zimmerli, W. 118
Zissu, B. 105
Zorn, J. R. 106
Zwickel, W. 118

INDEX OF SUBJECTS

Aaron 59, 61, 65, 140
Abarim 58, 64, 65, 66
Abel-mizraim 50
Abijah 43
Abijam 105
Abimelech 115
Abiram 64
Abner 70
Abraham 28, 29–53, 55, 56, 60, 61, 65, 91, 92, 99, 100, 132, 137, 139, 142
Absalom 14, 16, 94, 124
Achan 13
Achor *see* valley
Adonis *see* deities
adoption 144
agency 3-4, 14, 21, 87, 135, 136, 141, 142, 146
agrarianism 6, 138
agriculture 5, 6, 12, 31, 138, 141
Ahab 11, 37
Ahaz 105, 106, 107
Ai 13
altar 17, 47, 50, 51, 71, 73, 75, 83, 84, 85, 88, 90, 97, 99, 122, 123
Ammonites 70, 127
Amon 106
Anakim 67
ancestors 3, 4, 5, 6, 9, 11, 15, 16, 17, 20, 24, 25, 26, 27, 36, 38, 40, 41, 42, 43, 44, 45, 46, 47, 48, 50, 51, 52, 53, 55, 56, 60, 61, 64, 71, 72, 74, 75, 77, 80, 82, 89, 91, 92, 93, 95, 97, 98, 99, 100, 101, 102, 103, 104, 105, 106, 107, 108, 109, 111, 112, 113, 115, 117, 118, 119, 125, 126, 132, 135, 136, 137, 139, 140, 141, 143, 144, 145, 146, 147, 148
   deified 17, 19, 24, 43, 44, 64, 65, 68, 93, 94, 99, 100, 103, 113, 117, 124
   divine 75, 100, 101, 144

genealogical 49, 55, 61, 135
household 4, 5, 6, 23, 24, 25, 26, 48, 125, 127, 132, 135, 136, 138
local 3, 6, 13, 14, 16, 17, 23, 44, 48, 52, 57, 90, 96, 99, 125, 127, 132, 139, 140
national 30, 48, 51, 80, 96, 138, 139, 144
royal 23, 24, 64, 68, 105, 106, 107, 112, 113, 114, 115, 117, 118, 119, 120, 131, 132
vocational 55, 61
ancestralization 26, 53, 127, 129, 145
ancestry 6, 43, 44, 46, 48, 92, 96
aniconism 130; *see also* iconography
animals 40, 108, 110; *see also* pigs
anthropology 1, 2, 9, 18, 20
Aqhat 15, 16
Arab communities 48, 49, 127
Aramaeans 100
archaeology 9, 10, 18, 47, 86, 88, 118, 122
ark of the covenant 75, 76, 131
Asa 107
ascension (to heaven) 56, 57, 123
asherah (cult object) 83, 84
ashes 84, 86, 87, 88, 90, 120; *see also* cremation
Ashtaroth 68
Ashurbanipal 82
Assyria 82, 88, 115
Atad 50

Baal *see* deities
baby 24
Babylonia 13, 39, 40, 111, 135, 147
Bagohi 128

Bashan 68, 69
Benjamin (person) 93, 98
Benjamin (territory) 13, 88, 95, 96
Bethel 28, 81–102, 103, 105, 107, 136, 143, 146
Bethlehem 92, 93, 96
betulah 95
biblical scholarship 9, 21, 22, 33, 43, 96, 147
bier 70
biological death 23
birth 41, 42, 44, 55, 93, 95, 97, 98, 110, 115
blessing 5, 9, 41, 47, 75, 78, 82, 109, 113, 121, 122, 123, 125
blood 40, 141
Bochim 98
body 23, 78, 80, 87, 109, 112, 144, 147; *see also* corpse
Bohan, stone of 13
bone-burning 81, 83, 84, 85, 86, 87, 88, 89, 90; *see also* cremation
bones 18, 50, 51, 66, 70, 81, 82, 83, 84, 85, 86, 87, 88, 89, 90, 91, 99, 102, 107, 109, 111, 112, 115, 121, 122, 126, 146
book 58, 75, 76
border 13, 48, 49, 50, 52, 59, 61, 65, 68, 70, 73, 96
boundaries 4, 11, 12, 13, 14, 16, 36, 37, 49, 57, 62, 66, 71, 72, 77, 86, 88, 89, 93, 94, 95, 96, 97, 99, 100, 101, 105, 108, 120, 121, 128, 139, 141, 148
   lists of 13, 89, 135
   marker of 11 , 13, 14, 37, 49, 71, 77, 101; *see also* landmark
bride 109, 110
bridegroom 109, 110
built environment 9, 14, 25, 72, 84, 97, 99, 103, 108, 119, 120, 121, 127, 128, 131

Index of Subjects

burial 1, 2, 3, 4, 5, 6, 9, 10, 12, 13, 14, 16, 22, 26, 27, 28, 34, 35, 36, 48, 49, 50, 51, 56, 57, 58, 60, 61, 62, 64, 65, 66, 70, 71, 74, 77, 80, 81, 82, 85, 86, 87, 88, 90, 91, 92, 93, 94, 96, 97, 98, 99, 105, 106, 107, 109, 110, 114, 115, 116, 121, 126, 129, 130, 136, 139, 140, 141, 144, 148; *see also* disinterment; nonburial; reburial
burial ground 32, 33, 34, 37, 39, 48, 49, 50, 51, 52, 60, 121, 129, 136; *see also* cemetery
burial notices 105, 106, 107

cadaver 1, 40, 87, 146; *see also* corpse
cairn 14, 77, 101; *see also* standing stone
Caleb 52
Canaan 16, 29, 36, 37, 60, 122
Canaanites 13, 26, 29, 32, 36, 37, 60, 73, 122
carcass 110
carrion 109, 110
cave 35, 36, 37, 40, 42, 48, 51, 52, 60
cemetery 38, 110
centralization 19, 25, 26, 27, 28, 51, 52, 58, 83, 96, 130, 132, 135, 136, 137, 138, 139, 140, 141, 142, 144
ceremony 72, 77, 99; *see also* ritual
children 43, 63, 64, 94, 95, 110, 115, 118
child sacrifice 64, 110, 115, 118
Christianity 21
circumcision 144
city 5, 12, 13, 25, 26, 31, 35, 36, 46, 52, 69, 77, 83, 86, 90, 103, 104, 105, 106, 107, 108, 110, 112, 115, 117, 119, 120, 121, 122, 125, 127, 128, 129, 130, 131, 141 *see also* urbanism
City of David 105, 106, 107
colonialism 3, 7, 13, 17, 31, 71, 73, 74, 96, 98, 101, 135, 140; *see also* postcolonialism
commemoration 13, 15, 22, 23, 72, 73, 78, 128, 142; *see also* memorialization; remembrance

community 1, 2, 3, 4, 7, 9, 10, 11, 12, 13, 18, 21, 24, 25, 26, 29, 30, 31, 34, 37, 38, 47, 48, 78, 80, 82, 93, 108, 109, 121, 122, 125, 126, 127, 128, 129, 130, 133, 135, 137, 138, 139, 141, 142, 147, 148
conception 44, 110
conquest 26, 27, 31, 32, 45, 60, 68, 70, 131, 135, 139, 140
corpse 1, 9, 13, 14, 18, 22, 23, 36, 38, 40, 49, 57, 61, 80, 81, 87, 88, 93, 96, 101, 108, 109, 110, 111, 112, 117, 118, 120, 121, 146, 147, 148
  abandonment of 17, 39, 40, 109, 124
  abuse of 2, 88, 108, 109, 110, 121; *see also* bone-burning
  exposure of 2, 14, 22, 40, 109, 111, 112; *see also* disinterment
cosmos 12, 46, 58, 69, 72, 95, 114, 115, 129, 132
covenant 44, 45, 60, 72, 75, 76, 119, 123, 142, 143, 145
creation 43, 46
cremation 2, 22, 88; *see also* bone-burning
cult image 15, 24; *see also* iconography; teraphim
cult of the dead *see* dead
cultural memory 7, 14, 15, 73, 77, 78, 80, 123, 137, 143
  see also memorialization; remembrance
curse 5, 11, 60, 75, 77, 78, 82, 110, 111, 122

Dathan 63, 64
David 13, 67, 96, 105, 106, 107, 132
Davidic monarchy 13, 42, 44, 52, 104, 105, 106, 107, 108, 112, 113, 115, 119, 123, 128, 132, 143
dead, the 3, 4, 5, 8, 11, 12, 13, 15, 17, 18, 19, 21, 22, 23, 26, 27, 28, 34, 35, 36, 37, 38, 39, 42, 43, 44, 47, 50, 53, 56, 57, 60, 61, 62, 64, 65, 66, 67, 68, 69, 70, 71, 74, 77, 80, 81, 82, 84, 85, 86, 87, 88, 90, 91, 92, 93, 94, 95, 96, 97, 98, 99, 100, 101, 102, 103, 104, 105, 106, 107, 108, 109, 110, 111, 112, 113, 114, 115, 116, 117, 118, 119, 120, 121, 122, 123, 124, 125, 126, 127, 128, 131, 132, 133, 136, 137, 138, 139, 140, 141, 142, 143, 144, 145, 146, 147, 148
  cult of 11, 22, 62, 101, 103, 107, 112, 113, 114, 115, 116, 118, 119, 128, 132, 138
  deified 17, 19, 24, 43, 44, 65, 68, 69, 94, 10, 113, 117, 124; *see also* ancestor
  territorial 4, 7, 12, 17, 28, 42, 92, 102, 125, 136, 140, 141, 145
Dead Sea 48, 64, 65
death 1, 2, 4, 5, 8, 14, 15, 16, 20, 21, 22, 23, 27, 33, 36, 39, 47, 49, 56, 57, 58, 59, 60, 63, 64, 65, 66, 68, 79, 80, 91, 92, 93, 95, 97, 98, 102, 106, 109, 110, 113, 115, 116, 117, 118, 120, 122, 123, 126, 128, 129, 130
Deborah 92, 96, 97, 98, 99
Decalogue 11, 60
defilement 40, 83, 84, 88, 110, 117, 121, 122; *see also* impurity; pollution
deities 5, 16, 17, 19, 22, 23, 24, 26, 27, 40, 42, 43, 44, 51, 57, 62, 63, 71, 72, 73, 74, 75, 76, 84, 86, 92, 97, 98, 99, 100, 101, 103, 111, 118, 119, 120, 122, 129, 130, 138, 141, 142, 143, 144, 145, 146, 147
  Adonis 130
  Baal 19, 58, 62, 129, 130
  Destroyer 63
  Dread of Isaac 101
  Dumuzi 130
  El 19, 42, 145
  El Shaddai 92
  Elohim of Abraham 100
  Elohim of Nahor 100
  Elyon 145
  God 11, 17, 26, 43, 44, 72, 74, 75, 76, 83, 85, 90, 91, 102, 103, 104, 127, 138, 142, 144, 145, 147
  God of Heaven 103, 104, 127
  Host of Heaven 109, 111
  Living God 103, 145, 147
  Melqart 130
  Molek 69, 115, 119

Index of Subjects

Moon 109, 111
Mot 63, 119, 120
Osiris 130
Rapiu 64, 68, 69
Rephaim 64, 66, 67, 68, 69, 70, 113, 147
shitgods 40
Sun 109, 111
Tammuz 130
teraphim 99
Yhwh 8, 13, 16, 17, 18, 19, 25, 26, 29, 31, 32, 39, 40, 41, 42, 43, 44, 56, 57, 59, 60, 61, 62, 63, 64, 65, 66, 68, 71, 72, 73, 74, 75, 76, 77, 80, 83, 90, 94, 95, 103, 104, 108, 109, 111, 113, 114, 115, 116, 117, 119, 120, 121, 122, 123, 124, 125, 126, 127, 128, 130, 131, 132, 133, 135, 136, 138, 140, 141, 142, 143, 144, 145, 146, 147, 148
Yhwh of Hosts 109, 111
descendant 4, 5, 10, 12, 13, 16, 17, 18, 20, 24, 27, 29, 33, 34, 36, 38, 39, 42, 45, 47, 48, 49, 50, 55, 61, 64, 67, 68, 71, 76, 77, 92, 95, 108, 109, 110, 112, 113, 116, 119, 124, 125, 126, 127, 135, 136, 142, 144, 145, 147
Destroyer *see* deities
diaspora 25, 30, 32, 60, 61, 126, 130, 132, 139, 143; *see also* exile; golah
disinterment 49, 81, 82, 84, 85, 86, 107, 109, 110, 111, 112, 122, 127; *see also* non-burial; reburial
display 14, 46, 70, 72, 73, 80, 90, 131
diversity 27
divination 57, 114, 116, 119
dreams 98, 114
Dumuzi *see* deities
dying-and-rising 130; *see also* resurrection
dynasty 39, 105, 106, 112, 113, 115, 119, 124, 125, 128, 140

Ebal 72, 75
Ebenezer 13
economy 4, 5, 6, 10, 12, 31, 32, 36, 89, 138
Eden 115, 129
Edom 48, 49, 59
Edrei 68
Egypt 13, 15, 27, 32, 38, 46, 55, 60, 73, 106, 122, 139
El *see* deities
El Shaddai *see* deities
Elamites 82
Eleazar 77
Elijah 57, 123
Elisha 57, 91, 122
elites 6, 10, 13, 23, 25, 26, 73, 82, 105, 111, 113, 115, 138
Elyon *see* deities
emigration 28
Emim 67
enemies 13, 88, 94, 95, 101, 147
Enoch 123
Ephraim 88
Ephrath 49, 93, 96
Ephron 35, 36, 37
Esau 48, 49, 50, 92, 98
ethics 12, 34, 144
ethnicity 30, 37, 48, 49, 92, 104
ethnocentrism 29, 34
ethno-territorialism 7, 92, 96, 99, 101
eunuch 16, 123, 125, 126
Euphrates 13
excrement 112; *see also* shitgods
exile 15, 25, 26, 28, 38, 39, 40, 82, 95, 108, 110, 111, 112, 124, 126, 127, 143, 147; *see also* diaspora; golah
exodus 26, 27, 28, 39, 45, 55, 102, 135, 139
exorcism 147

family 4, 5, 6, 8, 9, 10, 11, 13, 24, 32, 42, 47, 60, 61, 77, 86, 90, 92, 101, 109, 111, 112, 126, 127, 132, 135, 144, 145; *see also* household
father 19, 25, 26, 29, 30, 41, 42, 43, 44, 47, 48, 49, 81, 104, 115, 142, 145
favissae 99
fertility 5, 15, 41, 42, 45, 47, 62, 69, 95, 98, 110, 113, 114, 115, 116, 123, 125, 126, 129
field 5, 8, 11, 13, 32, 35, 36, 37, 38, 40, 51, 120, 138, 144
firstborn 64, 144
foreignness 17, 20, 25, 26, 30, 53, 55, 60, 86, 90, 92, 99, 101, 116, 123, 125, 127, 135, 139
forgetting 42, 143

funerary practice 2, 19, 22, 23, 70, 80, 118, 123; *see also* mortuary practice

Gad 66
Galeed 99
garden 12, 106, 114, 115, 129; *see also* Eden; paradise
Garden of Uzza 106
gateway 13, 36, 72, 77, 78, 79, 103, 105, 120, 122
Gedaliah 106
genealogy 14, 26, 27, 42, 44, 49, 53, 55, 61, 108, 127, 135
Geshem 127
ghost 82, 113, 146
giants 66, 67, 68, 70
Gilead 100
god *see* deities
Gog 65
golah 38, 135; *see also* diaspora
grave 1, 2, 4, 9, 11, 12, 13, 17, 18, 21, 27, 33, 34, 35, 39, 50, 55, 56, 57, 58, 60, 61, 62, 69, 70, 77, 79, 80, 82, 84, 86, 88, 90, 92, 93, 94, 95, 97, 98, 103, 104, 105, 108, 111, 114, 116, 122, 123, 126, 129, 132, 133, 136, 138, 139, 146, 148; *see also* burial; tomb
Greek traditions 42, 67
guardian 5, 34, 89, 100, 117, 119, 133

Hamor 32
Haram el-Khalil 46; *see also* Hebron; Machpelah
heavens 47, 56, 57, 86, 103, 104, 109, 111, 115, 122, 123, 127, 129, 142
Hebron 36, 45, 46, 47, 48, 49, 50, 51, 52, 103, 105, 107, 138, 140, 144
Herod 46, 47
Hezekiah 106, 107
Hiel 64
Hittites 32, 33, 34, 35, 36, 37, 50, 139
holiness 86, 117, 119, 121, 129, 144; *see also* sacred
home 8, 23, 27, 28, 60, 95, 113, 139
homeland 27, 29, 55, 60, 104, 124, 135, 137, 139
Hor, mount 61
Horonites 127
Host of Heaven *see* deities

Index of Subjects

household 4, 5, 6, 9, 15, 23, 24, 25, 26, 29, 48, 63, 64, 78, 97, 99, 100, 113, 119, 124, 125, 127, 132, 135, 136, 138, 143, 144, 145; *see also* family

iconography 13, 15, 122, 123, 130; *see also* symbol
identity 2, 6, 11, 15, 24, 25, 26, 41, 55, 61, 81, 87, 132, 137
ideology 1, 3, 4, 5, 6, 7, 8, 10, 11, 12, 14, 17, 25, 26, 27, 28, 31, 32, 33, 35, 37, 49, 51, 52, 53, 55, 56, 60, 61, 67, 74, 80, 81, 88, 90, 91, 92, 103, 106, 113, 115, 120, 124, 125, 128, 129, 130, 131, 132, 135, 136, 138, 139, 140, 141, 143, 146, 147
idolatry 83, 85, 88
Idumaea 48
image *see* cult image
immigration 28, 29, 32, 33, 37; *see also* migration
immortality 79, 129; *see also* mortality
imperialism 5, 6, 8, 13, 25, 26, 30, 31, 32, 89, 117, 131, 141
impurity 18, 122, 138, 146, 147, 148; *see also* defilement; pollution
incense 114
inclusivism 23, 26, 29, 30, 32, 33, 34, 37, 48, 49, 53, 127, 136, 139
incomer 26, 27, 29, 31, 32, 34, 37, 38, 53, 67, 104, 108, 127, 128, 129, 130, 136, 141; *see also* immigration
incubation 98, 114
indigenous 26, 29, 31, 32, 34, 37, 38, 40, 71, 73, 90, 92, 99, 101, 127, 128, 132, 135, 136, 137, 140
infertility 41, 62, 95
inheritance 5, 6, 8, 10, 11, 24, 25
inscriptions 5, 13, 15, 71–79, 82, 84, 107, 116, 121, 128, 130, 131, 146, 148
intercession 43; *see also* mediation
interment *see* burial
invocation 16, 19, 22, 23, 97, 101, 121, 124, 141
Isaac 33, 41, 44, 47, 48, 49, 50, 51, 61, 65, 92, 101, 142
Ishmael 47, 48, 49, 50, 92

Jachin and Boaz 118
Jacob 16, 32, 33, 41, 43, 44, 47, 48, 49, 50, 51, 60, 61, 65, 75, 77, 81, 88, 91, 92, 93, 94, 96, 97, 98, 99, 100, 101, 102, 136, 142, 146
Jehoahaz 106
Jehoiachin 106, 112
Jehoiada 107
Jehoram 107
Jeremiah 38, 124
Jeroboam ben Nebat 83, 85
Jerusalem 14, 25, 26, 27, 28, 30, 43, 47, 60, 81, 83, 84, 85, 86, 87, 88, 89, 90, 102, 103–33, 138, 140, 141, 143, 144, 145
Jeshanah 13
Jesus 57, 123
Jewish communities 29, 30, 46, 48, 49, 53, 60, 121; *see also* Judaism
Joab 43
Jordan, the 50, 55, 59, 61, 70, 71, 72, 76, 77, 79; *see also* river
Joseph 32, 41, 49, 50, 51, 60, 77, 92, 98, 99, 104, 122
Josephus 46, 47, 70
Joshua 12, 59, 60, 70, 75, 77, 78, 79, 139
Josiah 82, 83, 84, 85, 86, 87, 88, 89, 90, 106, 121
Judaism 46, 49, 56, 123, 142

Kadesh 61
Ketef Hinnom 121
Khirbet Beit Lei 121
Khirbet el-Qom 121
Kidron *see* valley
kingship 5, 52, 107, 108, 113, 114, 115, 119
kinship 2, 8, 11, 17, 25, 26, 29, 37, 38, 47, 61, 91, 100, 101, 112, 124, 125, 126, 127, 137, 145
Kiriath-arba 51, 52
Korah 63, 64
kudurru 13, 16

Laban 16, 75, 93, 98, 99, 100, 101
lamentation 94, 95; *see also* mourning; weeping
land *see also* promised land
ancestral 4, 5, 6, 8, 9, 11, 12, 13, 26, 37, 38, 50, 63, 77, 81, 95, 135, 137, 140
cultivated 12, 35, 86, 114, 129; *see also* agriculture
occupation of 4, 17, 25, 26, 27, 29, 34, 35, 38, 39, 40, 41, 50, 53, 66, 67, 69, 70, 71, 74, 89, 92, 93, 96, 99, 101, 103, 104, 105, 106, 107, 108, 125, 130, 131, 133, 139, 140; *see also* colonialism; immigration
purchase of 13, 32, 33, 34, 35, 36, 37, 38, 50, 51, 53, 60, 77, 99, 132
land grant 5, 13, 25, 26, 31, 32, 145
landmark 8, 11, 53, 108, 132; *see also* boundary; monument
landowner 5, 8, 17, 25, 27, 38, 39, 41, 117, 135, 141
landscape 3, 4, 6, 7, 11, 12, 13, 14, 15, 26, 27, 28, 42, 62, 70, 91, 92, 95, 96, 98, 99, 102, 105, 115, 120, 123, 136, 137, 138, 139, 140, 142; *see also* mortuary landscape
law 56, 77, 83, 85, 99, 131, 147; *see also* Torah
Leah 33, 49
Levites 75, 79, 140
libations 23, 82, 109, 113, 115, 141; *see also* offerings
liminality 9, 23, 61, 62, 65, 70, 72, 74, 77, 79, 80, 86, 93, 109, 121
lineage 4, 24, 26, 27, 41, 92, 98, 108, 119, 137, 142, 145
living community 1, 2, 3, 4, 5, 8, 9, 10, 11, 12, 14, 17, 18, 19, 20, 21, 22, 23, 24, 25, 38, 44, 46, 53, 57, 65, 66, 68, 71, 80, 82, 87, 93, 109, 110, 111, 112, 113, 116, 117, 122, 127, 133, 139, 143, 146, 147, 148
localism 3, 5, 6, 13, 14, 15, 16, 17, 23, 24, 25, 26, 44, 48, 49, 51, 52, 57, 81, 90, 96, 99, 108, 123, 124, 125, 126, 127, 132, 137, 139, 140

Machpelah 26, 33, 35, 36, 37, 38, 39, 42, 45, 48, 49, 50, 51, 52, 53, 60, 81, 93, 96, 99, 102, 136, 137, 138, 139
magic 57, 72, 147
Mamre 36, 51, 52
Manasseh (person) 106
Manasseh (place) 66

Index of Subjects

materiality 4, 13, 14, 15, 16, 21, 28, 75, 77, 80, 87, 93, 100, 110, 112, 129, 132, 137, 146
mediation 14, 15, 29, 30, 57, 58, 77, 79, 94, 102, 122, 137, 141, 145
Melqart *see* deities
memorial 14, 16, 17, 55, 56, 71, 72, 76, 77, 78, 79, 80, 90, 91, 95, 100, 101, 107, 116, 118, 123, 124, 125, 127, 128, 131, 132, 140, 146
memorial fires 118
memorialization 1, 13, 14, 22, 26, 50, 58, 71, 72, 77, 78, 79, 80, 90, 96, 98, 99, 100, 101, 102, 113, 123, 124, 125, 126, 128, 130, 131, 132, 133, 140, 141, 142, 143, 146; *see also* cultural memory; remembrance
Memphis 46
Meribah 59
Merodach-Baladan II 82
Mesopotamia 15, 20, 46, 86, 95, 109, 131, 147; see also Assyria; Babylonia
messianism 15
Midian 62
migration 6, 25, 28, 29, 31, 32, 33, 37, 46, 140; *see also* immigration
Miriam 61, 65
Mizpah 13, 99
Moab 56, 57, 59, 61, 62, 65, 79
modernism 3, 15, 20, 49, 53, 96, 127, 147; *see also* Western culture
Molek *see* deities
monotheism 19, 21, 30, 132, 143
monument 13, 14, 15, 16, 46, 77, 78, 80, 83, 93, 95, 100, 115, 116, 118, 124, 125, 128, 131, 140, 146; *see also* memorial; standing stone
moon *see* deities
mortality 56, 57, 69; *see also* immortality
mortuary landscape 4, 12, 14, 15, 27, 28, 70, 96, 99, 102, 136, 137, 139, 140, 148
mortuary practice 1, 2, 9, 10, 14, 15, 16, 17, 18, 20, 22, 23, 25, 27, 92, 94, 97, 100, 101, 104, 107, 108, 109, 110, 113, 114, 115, 116, 118, 119, 121, 123, 124, 125, 126, 128, 129, 130, 131, 137, 138, 139, 140, 147; *see also* funerary practice
Moses 27, 28, 55–80, 122, 123, 138, 139, 140, 142, 146
Mot *see* deities
mountain 57, 58, 59, 61, 64, 65, 69, 71, 71, 95, 105, 115, 119, 127, 129
mourning 36, 95, 98, 109, 144; *see also* lamentation; weeping
myth 7, 12, 27, 31, 32, 42, 43, 45, 46, 55, 57, 62, 64, 66, 67, 68, 69, 70, 72, 77, 86, 91, 93, 97, 102, 105, 108, 111, 112, 115, 119, 120, 129, 130, 131, 132, 135, 136, 137, 138, 139, 140, 145, 147

Naboth 11, 37
Nahor 100
name 16, 19, 113, 123, 123, 124, 125, 128, 130, 131, 141, 143
 name theology 117, 130, 131
 theophoric 19, 43, 64
nationhood 5, 15, 29, 30, 31, 44, 48, 51, 52, 68, 80, 92, 95, 96, 136–48
Nebo (place) 57, 58, 65
necromancy 22, 43
Nehemiah 103, 104, 108, 127, 128
Nephilim 67
night 100, 114
non-burial 109, 110, 112, 122; *see also* corpse exposure; disinterment

oak *see* tree
Oboth 64, 69
offerings 47, 82, 109, 113, 115, 118; *see also* sacrifice
official religion 20
offspring 92, 112; *see also* children; descendants
Og 67, 68, 69, 70
omen 5
oracle 5, 13, 38, 39, 40, 65, 83, 85, 88, 92, 94, 95, 108, 109, 111, 112, 119, 120, 121, 125, 126, 145
orientalism 33
orphan 11
Osiris *see* deities
ossuary 60, 81, 109, 122, 123
Other 20, 21, 26, 66, 70, 100

palace 5, 129
pantheon 24
paradise 129; *see also* garden
Passover 144
paterfamilias 98, 145
patriarchs 26, 27, 30, 31, 32, 34, 37, 39, 43, 45, 46, 48, 49, 50, 51, 60, 61, 91, 92, 93, 98, 102, 135, 136, 138, 139, 140, 145
patrimonialism 6, 141
patronage 31, 141
penis 62, 116, 126
Peor 56, 61, 62, 63, 64, 66
Persians 23, 31, 103, 104
personhood 2, 24, 87
personification 27, 62, 63, 110, 112, 127
petition 15, 22, 35, 37, 42, 43, 95, 98, 103, 104, 117
Philistines 67
Phinehas 77
pigs 114; *see also* animals
pilgrimage 37, 47, 58, 138
Pisgah 57, 58, 65
plague 40, 62, 63
pollution 18, 114, 117, 147; *see also* defilement; impurity
popular religion 20
portion 32, 116, 125, 127, 128, 145
postcolonialism 7, 11, 12, 32; *see also* colonialism
prayer 22, 103
priests 30, 34, 35, 48, 83, 107, 117, 118, 119, 121, 122, 135, 136, 140, 147
primitivism 21
primogeniture 8
progeny 8, 80
promised land 13, 27, 33, 34, 39, 44, 45, 49, 55, 56, 57, 59, 60, 61, 64, 65, 66, 67, 70, 71, 72, 73, 74, 77, 79, 80, 81, 92, 96, 98, 102, 139, 140, 142, 145
property 5, 8, 9, 34, 35, 36, 37, 47, 63, 64
prophets 41, 43, 83, 85, 90, 91, 97, 105, 109, 123, 124, 146
prostitution, cultic 70; *see also* sex; whoring
protection 8, 12, 38, 82, 90, 97, 100, 108, 109, 113, 121, 138, 148
puberty 95

Index of Subjects

punishment 39, 59, 62, 68, 82, 84, 85, 86, 88, 90, 111

Rachel 13, 49, 81, 92, 93, 94, 95, 96, 97, 98, 99
   tomb of 13, 15, 49, 81, 92, 93, 94, 95, 96
Ramah 94, 97
Raphon 64
Rapiu *see* deities
Rebekah 33, 47, 49, 97, 98
reburial 49, 50, 60, 82, 85, 87, 88
regeneration 96, 97, 110, 114, 123, 125, 129
reincarnation 24, 80
relic 20, 109, 111
remembrance 2, 9, 14, 73, 77, 78, 87, 124, 137, 142, 143; see also cultural memory; forgetting; memorialization
repatriation 25, 31, 96
Rephaim *see* deities
restoration 15, 38, 40, 95, 103, 104, 108, 113, 120, 122, 123, 126, 127, 129, 130
resurrection 57, 122, 130
Reuben 13, 66
revelation 57, 71
rite-of-passage 22, 70
ritual 2, 4, 7, 10, 17, 18, 19, 20, 21, 22, 23, 25, 47, 50, 52, 57, 62, 69, 71, 72, 74, 77, 86, 87, 88, 89, 92, 93, 95, 96, 98, 99, 100, 101, 109, 110, 111, 113, 114, 115, 116, 117, 121, 122, 124, 125, 126, 127, 128, 129, 132, 135, 138, 142, 147
ritual exchange 47, 91, 113, 122, 123, 132, 141
river 13, 72; *see also* Euphrates; Jordan
rock 18, 41, 42, 75, 115
ruralism 11, 12, 32, 137

Sabbath 123, 144
sacred 42, 46, 57, 62, 81, 84, 86, 87, 88, 92, 96, 97, 98, 99, 105, 108, 114, 115, 120, 121, 122, 123, 127, 128, 129, 132, 132, 139, 147; *see also* holiness
sacrifice 47, 62, 64, 85, 100, 101, 110, 114, 115, 116, 118, 119; *see also* offering
Samaria 83, 85, 90, 91, 143
Samaritans 49, 85
Sanballat 127

sanctuary 16, 31, 47, 50, 75, 81, 83, 84, 85, 88, 89, 90, 91, 92, 93, 94, 102, 117, 120, 122, 123, 125, 127, 131, 132, 143; *see also* temple
Sarah 33, 35, 36, 38, 40, 41, 42, 49
sarcophagus 70, 80; *see also* tomb
Saul 76, 115
scavenger 110
scribalism 10, 12, 25, 30, 56, 58, 73, 79, 131, 146, 147; *see also* writing
sea 48, 64, 65, 72, 77, 145
secularism 4, 20
serpent 69
sex 62, 114, 116; *see also* prostitution; whoring
Shechem 32, 50, 51, 75, 77, 92, 99, 103, 105, 107, 122
Sheol 63, 111, 115, 119; *see also* underworld
shitgods *see* deities
Sihon 69, 70
skeleton 87, 88; *see also* bones
slaughter 85, 86, 108, 110
Sodom 43
Solomon 105
spirit 3, 14, 82, 95
standing stone 13, 15, 16, 42, 51, 71, 72, 73, 74, 75, 76, 77, 78, 79, 92, 93, 94, 100, 101, 115, 131, 140, 142, 146; *see also* stela
stars 111, 142; *see also* Host of Heaven
state 6, 12, 49, 124
stela 13, 15, 16, 17, 74, 76, 124; *see also* standing stone
succession 8, 106
sun *see* deities
sword 39, 40
symbolism 3, 7, 9, 13, 15, 17, 26, 29, 30, 32, 38, 43, 44, 45, 62, 69, 70, 71, 73, 74, 76, 77, 78, 79, 86, 87, 88, 91, 99, 108, 110, 114, 115, 116, 123, 124, 129, 131, 132, 133, 139
syncretism 83

Tammuz *see* deities
teaching 71, 77, 78, 79, 80, 121, 142, 146
temple 5, 12, 13, 16, 23, 25, 26, 27, 47, 83, 84, 87, 92, 103, 104, 106, 107, 108, 113, 114, 115, 117, 118, 119, 120, 122, 123, 124, 125, 126, 127, 128, 129, 130, 131, 132, 133, 135, 138, 140, 41, 142, 143, 144
teraphim *see* deities
terebinth *see* tree
territoriality 3–18, 24–28, 30–38, 39, 42, 48–53, 55, 56, 57, 60-62, 66, 67, 68–71, 73, 74, 76, 77, 80, 81, 88–89, 90, 91, 92, 94, 95–96, 99–102, 107, 108, 112, 116, 117, 119–120, 124, 125, 127, 128, 130, 131, 132, 133, 135–147
testicles 126
threshing floor 50
Timnath-serah 77
Tobiah 127
tomb 8, 9, 10, 11, 13, 14, 15, 16, 17, 18, 23, 26, 27, 28, 33, 35, 37, 39, 45, 46, 47, 48, 49, 50, 51, 52, 53, 56, 57, 58, 59, 61, 65, 70, 71, 77, 79, 80, 81, 82, 83, 84, 87, 88, 90, 91, 92, 93, 94, 95, 96, 97, 102, 103, 104, 105, 106, 107, 108, 109, 111, 112, 114, 117, 121, 122, 123, 126, 129, 131, 132, 133, 136, 137, 138, 139, 140, 142, 146, 148; *see also* grave
Topheth 108, 110
Torah 44, 55, 58, 60, 71–80, 99, 100, 131, 136, 140, 141, 142, 146
Transjordan 62, 64, 66, 69, 70, 72, 100
tree 36, 42, 46, 75, 81, 92, 96, 97, 9, 99, 114, 115, 123, 124, 129, 139
   Oak of Tabor 97
   Oak of Weeping 97, 98
   Palm of Deborah 97
tribes 30, 48, 52, 60, 66, 70, 92, 95
tumuli 118

Ugarit 15, 16, 24, 63, 64, 65, 68, 69, 113, 116, 118, 126, 141
underworld 9, 35, 62, 63, 64, 65, 66, 67, 68, 69, 70, 72, 74, 77, 82, 85, 87, 91, 95, 105, 109, 110, 111, 114, 115, 123, 126, 129; *see also* Sheol
universalism 46, 127, 132

Index of Subjects

urbanism 5, 10, 12, 31, 137, 138
Uzza *see* garden
Uzziah 107

valley 13, 56, 61, 62, 65, 66, 86, 87, 105, 108, 110, 115, 116, 120, 121, 125, 128
  Achor 13
  Ben Hinnom 108, 110
  Kidron 86, 87, 120, 121
  Slaughter 108, 110
veneration 18–25, 42, 44, 45, 47, 48, 58, 64, 80, 100, 101, 119, 132, 133
virgin *see* betulah

wall 14, 106, 108, 117, 123, 125, 127, 128
warfare 32, 39, 67, 70, 139, 147
wasteland 39, 40, 41, 103, 109, 110; *see also* wilderness
weeping 94, 95, 97, 98; *see also* lamentation; mourning
Western culture 3, 4, 20, 21, 66, 146; *see also* modernism
wet-nurse 92, 97, 98, 99
whoring 62, 114, 117
wilderness 27, 45, 59, 61, 62, 63, 66, 70, 86; *see also* wasteland

wisdom 24, 145
women 40, 62, 75, 95, 97
  matriarch 46, 97
  mother 41, 112
  wife 36, 37, 40, 63, 93
writing 12, 58, 71, 72, 74, 75, 76, 77, 78, 79, 131; *see also* inscriptions; scribalism

Yhwh *see* deities

Zamzummim 67
Zaphon 58, 115, 129
Zedekiah 106
Zion 40, 41, 105, 115, 117, 126, 127, 132

Printed in Great Britain
by Amazon